Hollywood Stardom

Hollywood Stardom

Paul McDonald

A John Wiley & Sons, Ltd., Publication

This edition first published 2013
© 2013 Paul McDonald

Blackwell Publishing was acquired by John Wiley & Sons in February 2007. Blackwell's publishing program has been merged with Wiley's global Scientific, Technical, and Medical business to form Wiley-Blackwell.

Registered Office
John Wiley & Sons Ltd, The Atrium, Southern Gate, Chichester, West Sussex, PO19 8SQ, UK

Editorial Offices
350 Main Street, Malden, MA 02148-5020, USA
9600 Garsington Road, Oxford, OX4 2DQ, UK
The Atrium, Southern Gate, Chichester, West Sussex, PO19 8SQ, UK

For details of our global editorial offices, for customer services, and for information about how to apply for permission to reuse the copyright material in this book please see our website at www.wiley.com/wiley-blackwell.

The right of Paul McDonald to be identified as the author of this work has been asserted in accordance with the UK Copyright, Designs and Patents Act 1988.

Wiley also publishes its books in a variety of electronic formats. Some content that appears in print may not be available in electronic books.

Designations used by companies to distinguish their products are often claimed as trademarks. All brand names and product names used in this book are trade names, service marks, trademarks or registered trademarks of their respective owners. The publisher is not associated with any product or vendor mentioned in this book. This publication is designed to provide accurate and authoritative information in regard to the subject matter covered. It is sold on the understanding that the publisher is not engaged in rendering professional services. If professional advice or other expert assistance is required, the services of a competent professional should be sought.

Library of Congress Cataloging-in-Publication Data

McDonald, Paul, 1963–
  Hollywood stardom / Paul McDonald.
    pages cm
    Includes bibliographical references and index.
    ISBN 978-1-4051-7982-9 (hardback) – ISBN 978-1-4051-7983-6 (paperback)   1. Motion
picture industry–United States.   2. Motion picture actors and actresses–United States.
3. Fame–Social aspects–United States.   I. Title.
    PN1993.5.U6M314 2013
    384'.80973–dc23
                                                            2012036171

A catalogue record for this book is available from the British Library.

Set in 10.5/13 pt Minion by Toppan Best-set Premedia Limited
Printed in Malaysia by Ho Printing (M) Sdn Bhd

1   2013

Contents

Contents

Figures

Tables

Acknowledgments

First and foremost, my love and thanks to Tamar, Jessica and Chloe – the A-plus list! – for sticking with me throughout the whole drama by which a book on stardom was born. Only with the belief and support of my outstanding commissioning editor Jayne Fargnoli was it possible for the book to become a reality, and I'd like to express my gratitude to Ben Thatcher for steering the book through production. It is a key aim of the study which follows is to stake out some new conceptual ground by finding points of connection between two streams of thinking in film scholarship: star studies and industry studies. When making this connection, I was led by the scholarship of Richard Dyer and Janet Wasko. In the past I have had the pleasure of working with both Richard and Janet, and although neither was in anyway involved with the book I thank them for the continuing intellectual inspiration that their own work has given me and which set me on the road to embarking on a study like this in the first place. Research for the book was only possible because of the generous financial assistance I received. A Research Fellowship from the Leverhulme Trust enabled me to take an extended period of research leave and a Small Grant from the British Academy facilitated research trips to Los Angeles. I am greatly indebted to Thomas Austin, Cynthia Baron, Christine Geraghty, Chris Holmlund and Peter Krämer for agreeing to provide references in support of applications for this funding. Resources at key research libraries have been essential to completing this study and for the assistance they provided I would particularly like to thank Sandra Archer at the Margaret Herrick Library, Jonathon Auxier and Sandra Joy Lee at the Warner Bros. Archive, and Sarah Currant and Sean Delaney at the British Film Institute National Library. Along the way Nicola Bertram, Emily Carmen, Eric Hoyt, Steve Neale, John Sedgwick, Deborah Shaw and Yannis Tzioumakis have all helped me considerably by providing information or sources, or otherwise reading sections of the manuscript. Finally, my thanks to Angela Wilson for her great work on preparing the map which appears in Chapter 4.

Introduction

Hollywood film stardom is a cultural and commercial phenomenon. As part of the symbolic content of films, stars have cultural significance because through their on-screen performances they represent meanings about human identity. At the same time, stars are signs of economic value, assets deployed in the film market with the aim of raising production financing, capturing revenues and securing profits. In Hollywood stardom, the symbolic and economic are therefore inextricably bound together.

What follows is a study of stardom as a feature of the contemporary Hollywood film industry. It aims to integrate two seams of enquiry in film scholarship. "Star studies" are concerned with exploring the significance and meaning of popular film actors, while "industry studies" focus on the conditions of production, distribution and exhibition which shape the making, selling and showing of films. Combining insights from both traditions, the book tackles the unique position which the star occupies in Hollywood as person, performer, sign and asset.

Richard Dyer's concept of "star image" has been crucial to legitimizing stars as an object of analysis in Film and Cinema Studies:

> With stars, the "terms" involved are essentially images. By "image" here I do not understand an exclusively visual sign, but rather a complex configuration of visual, verbal and aural signs. This configuration may constitute the general image of stardom or of a particular star. It is manifest not only in films but in all kinds of media text. (1998: 34)

Star image provides a foundational concept for a semiotics of film stardom focused on interrogating the symbolic content and meaning of stars. Unlike

Hollywood Stardom, First Edition. Paul McDonald.
© 2013 Paul McDonald. Published 2013 by John Wiley & Sons, Ltd.

popular literature on film stars, which frequently embarks from the belief that the film roles and other media appearance of a star are merely a set of textual appearances or fabrications behind which lie the true identity of the star, analysis of the star image takes the materiality of texts as the very substance of stardom. Rather than looking for a figure lurking beyond or behind the text, explorations of star images concentrate on the identity produced in or through texts, for "a star image is made out of media texts" (1998: 60).

Emerging in the late 1970s and into the 1980s, Dyer's work on stars was consonant with the broader intellectual agenda shaping Film Studies in the period, where ideology became the overarching problem for studies focused on how the production of representation and meaning was related to questions of cultural, social and political power. What the study of stars contributed to this debate was to offer a tight analytic focus on how well-known figures reproduce and produce beliefs about human identity. As Dyer notes,

> We're fascinated by stars because they enact ways of making sense of the experience of being a person in a particular kind of social production (capitalism), with its particular organization of life into public and private spheres. We love them because they represent how we think that experience is or how it would be lovely to feel that it is. Stars represent typical ways of behaving, feeling and thinking in contemporary society, ways that have been socially, culturally, historically constructed. (1987: 17)

Such has been the importance and persuasiveness of Dyer's theoretical intervention that subsequently the analysis of star images has largely influenced the overall development of star studies as a seam of research in critical and historical film scholarship.

By the late 1980s, theoretically driven forms of film scholarship faced challenges as the "historical turn" (Higashi, 2004) introduced more empirically grounded forms of enquiry. Working in this tradition, Richard deCordova (1990) not only used extensive archival materials to provide an empirically verified account of the emergence of the star system in American cinema but also departed from the tendency of the star image approach to concentrate on individual stars alone. Instead, deCordova traced the origins of the film star system to the emergence of trans-individual categories of knowledge or discourses about the figures performing in early film. Whereas the appearance of a "discourse on acting" from 1907 onwards circulated information about the general occupation of film acting, it was not until the first release of performer names in 1909 that it became possible to identify, individualize and know performers as distinct "picture personalities." While this act of naming provided foundations for stardom, deCordova argues "the star" only truly appeared from 1913 onwards as knowledge about the off-screen private lives of stars became publicly circulated.

> The star emerged out of a marked expansion of the type of knowledge that could be produced about the player. The picture personality was defined . . . by a discourse that restricted knowledge to the professional existence of the actor. With the emergence of the star, the question of the player's existence outside his or her work in film became the primary focus of discourse. (1990: 98)

Although differing in their approaches, with their attention to star texts or discourses, Dyer and deCordova shared a common focus on stars as fundamentally symbolic entities, identities constructed from textual materials. Setting such analytic limits arguably, however, leaves star studies with an incomplete and unsatisfactory account of what a star is. Stars are texts, meaning, images and culture, but they are also more than this. Whether a star agrees to appear in a film or not will frequently influence if the film receives the financing to go into production. Stars are used to sell films through their appearance in marketing media and they are amongst the range of elements which can determine how well a film performs at the box office. In film culture, stars therefore form a point of intersection between meaning and money.

To fully grasp the significance of stars in film culture, it is therefore necessary to place stardom in a particular economic and industrial context. As Janet Wasko argues,

> Motion pictures developed in the USA as an industry and have continued to operate in this mode for over a century. Above all, profit is the primary driving force and guiding principle for the industry. Capital is used in different ways to achieve that goal. . . . The profit motive and the commodity nature of film have implications for the kind of films that are produced (and not produced), who makes them, how they are distributed, and where/when they are viewed. While it is common to call film an art form, at least Hollywood film cannot be understood without the context in which it is actually produced and distributed, that is, within an industrial, capitalist structure. (2003: 3–4)

Studies of star texts and discourses offer valuable insights into the semiotic or textual complexity of stars but without developing any fuller understanding of how stars operate as sources of capital for the film business. In this respect, star studies are representative of the more general limitations of film scholarship. Writing in 1982, Thomas Guback observed:

> Scholarly writing about film displays a curious imbalance that few people seem concerned about redressing. Even a superficial survey reveals that most studies deal with aesthetics, theory of one sort of another, genres, and personalities. Some studies also treat film historically, examine it as a social document, or conceptualize it as a medium that affects its audience. These approaches share, more or less, the assumption that what there is worthwhile to study about film can be grasped with research tools and techniques not unlike those used in literature. Necessarily, differences do exist because of the natures of these media, but film is ultimately seen as text. (p. xi)

In one way or another, Film Studies adopted modes of thinking derived from literary studies, with the consequence that the text was privileged as the beginning and end of analysis. Although with the historical turn, the emergence of the New Film History and New Cinema History productively encouraged attention to the institutionally organized conditions in which films are made, circulated and consumed, these developments by no means represented the whole field. Thirty years after Guback's criticism, textualism in its many different forms still holds considerable persuasive power, and consequently much of film scholarship still appears resistant to engaging with the commodity form of film. Guback exposes the limitations of this approach when he comments:

> Although [this] scholarship has illuminated many aspects of cinema . . . it has not come to grips with the basic character of film in capitalist society. Film is a commodity, and exchange value sets the broad parameters that determine not only how the medium will be used, but also the shape of the industrial structure that makes, distributes and exhibits it. (1982: xi)

Thinking of films principally as texts obscures the commodity status of movies, with the consequence that Film Studies is left with only a partial and limited account of what a film is. Following this mode of analysis, exclusive attention to the star-as-texts or the discursive construction of stardom has left star studies with an incomplete understanding of stars and stardom.

In the book which follows, star studies and industry studies are therefore integrated in order to mount a form of analysis with dual regard for stars as symbolic and economic entities. This is not an altogether new departure. Responding to how star studies developed in the 1980s, Barry King criticized how "writers on stardom are seemingly obsessed with matters of signification" (1987: 145), and instead he proposed the need for attention to how stardom "develops out of and sustains capitalist relations of production and consumption" (p. 149). King therefore positioned stars industrially, focusing on "stardom as a form of working" (1986: 155) and on the star as "a personality with box-office power" (p. 166). Danae Clark (1995) criticized how the focus on matters of meaning, beauty and pleasure alone had resulted in the formation of an aesthetic tradition in star studies which supports capitalist production by denying how stars are one category of labor working in Hollywood. Moreover, Clark argued attention to stars over other actors repeated the auteurist concern of taking an elite (in that case a pantheon of great directors) as its exclusive focus and thereby ignoring how they topped the hierarchy within a particular category of creative producers. Clark therefore considered stars to be "a privileged class within the division of actors' labor" (p. 5) and placed actors as active subjects contesting their position within the hierarchy of "labor power differences" (p. 14). King and Clark therefore provided a clear alternative to the textualist and discursive terrain set out by Dyer and deCordova. With these interventions, *studies of stars* have not therefore been entirely blind to matters of industry, yet *star studies* as a particular tradition of analysis and enquiry has largely concentrated on questions of meaning and the discursive construction of stars.

In critical studies of media culture, the recent development of "celebrity studies" may have expanded attention beyond film stardom to other instances and categories of mediated fame, yet again overriding attention to matters of symbolic and cultural significance have largely reproduced the exact same limits as star studies by failing to adequately grapple with the conditions in which celebrity is produced and circulated. There is discussion of how "celebrity . . . describes a type of value that can be articulated through an individual and celebrated publicly as important and significant . . . [with] connotations that link it to modern power structures (i.e. capitalism)" (Marshall, 1997: 7). Mention is made of the "economy of celebrity," the "celebrity-commodity," the "celebrity industries" and to "manufacturing celebrity" (Turner, 2004), yet with insufficient detailed attention to the economics of celebrity, how those celebrity industries actually work, or to how they make celebrity.

Star studies may have emphasized the symbolic/cultural aspect of stardom over the economic/commercial, yet in Hollywood stardom the two aspects are inseparable. Writing on Hollywood, Richard Maltby observes how "movies are products for consumption," and so "it is through a thoroughgoing acknowledgement of their commercial existence, not a denial of it, that their complexity can be most fully examined" (2003: 553). Maltby describes Hollywood as producing a "commercial aesthetic," for "Hollywood's aesthetic practices serve commercial purposes" (p. 11). "In Hollywood," he argues, "commerce and aesthetics are symbiotic" (p. 11). Stars feature in this commercial aesthetic as elements of symbolic content and signs of value. Redressing the imbalances of star studies, this book is explicitly concerned with the business of Hollywood stardom. It tackles stardom as a component of Hollywood's commercial aesthetic, advancing a form of analysis which can be described as the *symbolic commerce of stardom*, by which stardom is regarded as just one of the devices used in Hollywood film to conduct commerce through symbolic means.

While responding to what have been some of the limitations of star studies, adopting this approach does not necessitate the wholesale rejection of star images. In seeking to situate stars commercially, it is important to not simply enforce a new and ultimately limited critical purview by exclusively emphasizing commerce without attention to the symbolic dynamics of stardom. Stars circulate in public culture through textual forms. Somewhere in the world is the flesh-and-blood Brad Pitt but he is only "present" and known to his audience as an ensemble of textual materials. It is essential to therefore hold onto the idea of star image for this serves as the best means for analyzing the symbolic contents of stardom and to conceptualize the forms in which star identities are circulated in cultural markets. By necessity, star images must feature in this approach for they are the textual forms through which star identities are produced and circulate as symbolic currency in the film market.

Examining stardom across the confluence of symbolic and economic realms, the aims of this book are more conceptual than historical. It is a study which does not set out to make a historical statement by discerning a particular phase in the development of Hollywood stardom. Even so, the study displays a historicist belief that understanding any cultural or economic phenomena necessitates attention to specific conditions of existence. Rather than wander across Hollywood history freely choosing examples to best fit the arguments presented, the book therefore sets particular historical parameters by concentrating on stardom in the two decades from 1990 to 2010. Focusing on these decades places the business of stardom within particular industrial circumstances: the consolidation of conglomerate

Hollywood, the growth in value of the Hollywood's overseas box office, the maturation of the home entertainment market, and the emergence of new distribution technologies for the delivery of films to private and individual-ized contexts of consumption. With event movies based on comic book or fantasy franchises ruling the heights of box office, this is also a period in which many commentators raised questions over whether stars still played a valuable part in the commercial success of Hollywood cinema. Despite these reservations, stardom survived as a feature of Hollywood cinema, with the major studios continuing to make films fronted by a select group-ing of lead actors. When taking this focus, the book is not therefore arguing Hollywood stardom experienced a distinct period of change in the years 1990 to 2009: in fact, a great deal of what follows emphasizes strong con-tinuities between these decades and earlier periods. Instead, the book has a synchronic rather than diachronic objective, concentrating on a small slice of Hollywood history to outline a range of dynamics simultaneously at work in shaping the production and value of stardom. Although set within a particular historical period, the insights provided here should present some ground for examining how the symbolic commerce of stardom operates in other periods.

Part One of the book lays out the conceptual and contextual foundations of this study. Chapter 1 introduces a series of general dynamics underpin-ning the symbolic commerce of stardom and discusses how stars relate to the commodity form of film. It outlines how A-list stars sit at the top of the hierarchy of acting labor in Hollywood and identifies the "cast" of stars who characterized Hollywood stardom in the period covered. To move beyond the purely symbolic realm of the star-as-texts or star-as-image, Chapter 2 explores the star-as-brand as a means of conceptualizing the symbolic and commercial work of stardom. This chapter explores the analogy between stars and brands and looks at the functions of the star name as a branding vehicle. In the first of the book's three case-study chapters, Chapter 3 then draws these ideas together with an exploration of the Tom Hanks brand. With Part Two, chapters deal with the industrial conditions which support the production of stardom and the place of stars in the economics of contemporary Hollywood. Chapter 4 outlines the defining trends of the "post-studio star system" as a feature of conglomerate Hollywood, discussing the functions undertaken by agents, managers and publicists in the production of stardom, the role of star-fronted independ-ent production companies and the place of television in supplying new talent to the system. It is argued that under the operations of this system, the relationship of stars to studios is characterized by conditions of dependent independence. Chapter 5 considers how stars present a financial paradox in Hollywood, for they are both valuable assets and expensive burdens. The chapter analyzes the box-office performance of star films and the inflationary impact of star fees and gross participation agreements on production costs. A case study of Will Smith in Chapter 6 illustrates the post-studio system at work, exploring how Smith's stardom involved the negotiation of racial identity across media, the operations of his independent production company, and his commercial performance at the international box office. Whatever symbolic and economic effects stars have in Hollywood film is achieved through performance. Hollywood stardom is produced across multiple media but foundational to star status is the appearance of stars in films. Part Three explores the symbolic construction of the star performance on-screen through the workings of the film medium but also the voice and body of the actor. Chapter 7 outlines how star performance achieves symbolic and economic effects by positioning the actor between spectacle and narrative in the enactment of the star brand. While the box office is a crucial measure star status, in Hollywood awards form an alternative index of value based on artistic legitimacy. Focusing on the acting categories in the Academy Awards, Chapter 8 therefore looks at the role of awards as forms of "symbolic capital" and for how these define the "prestige star" as an alternative configuration of stardom to the commercially defined A-list. With a case study of Julia Roberts, Chapter 9 then explores the enactment of a particular star brand, the effects produced by that brand in the film market, how the brand was translated into award-winning success, but also the factors at work in the decline of star value.

It was just noted that film stardom is a multiple-media system. The visibility of film stars extends way beyond the films they appear in to various forms of broadcast, print and online media, involving coverage not only the star's on-screen existence but also his or her off-screen life. However, the primary concern here is with whatever symbolic and commercial value stardom has for Hollywood film. Inevitably that value is contingent on meanings and effects created beyond film but the primary focus here will be on the symbolic and commercial workings of star brands specifically in the film market with some occasional references to the deployment of stars in television advertising or the wrangles over star names in the online universe.

PART ONE
Star Business

1

The Symbolic Commerce of Hollywood Stardom

Hollywood stardom is founded on the marketability of human identities. As one comment in a 1959 issue of the trade paper *Variety* noted, "Always the same obvious truism – show business is a business of names, personalities, values generated by the traits and skills and charms of potent (at the box office) individuals" (Green, 1959: 1). In the economics of Hollywood film, stars are valued as a guard against risk. Regardless of whether the budget is a few million or in the hundreds of millions, feature film production is an expensive enterprise. At the same time, the film industry is constantly confronted by the fact that it is pouring money into making things that people don't actually need, and so unlike other goods such as basic foodstuffs, consumer demand for films is uncertain and capricious. With this mixture of high-cost investment and uncertain demand, the industry treasures concrete, material signs of content which consistently draw audiences. Popular cycles or genres can offer some certainties through the repetition of thematic and stylistic tropes, whereas the value of stars is tied up with how they represent versions of human identity. In the figure of the star, the symbolic/cultural and economic/commercial are inextricably linked. Film stars have cultural significance because they represent people and as those representations circulate in media markets, so they become figures for exchange. Since stars only portray certain categories or types of identity and not others, then stardom has symbolic and cultural power. Equally, as assets deployed in the market with the aim of securing commercial advantage, stars are a source of economic power. Examining the symbolic commerce of Hollywood stardom therefore requires understanding and critically evaluating the practices and processes which support the production, dissemination and presentation of popular identities in the film market. Initially this chapter sets out some basic dynamics at work in the symbolic commerce of stardom before considering how stardom is configured in Hollywood.

Commercial and Symbolic Dynamics of Film Stardom

Hollywood film is a form of mass communication. As John Thompson notes, mass communication is characterized by *"the institutionalized production and generalized diffusion of symbolic goods via the fixation and transmission of information and symbolic content"* (original emphasis, 1995: 26). Thompson poses five features defining mass communication, each of which can be applied to Hollywood film generally but can also be applied specifically to identify the foundational dynamics at work in the symbolic commerce of stardom.

1. Industrially produced fame

In common with other industries for mass communication, Hollywood operates by "technical and institutional means of production and diffusion" (Thompson, 1995: 27). Feature films are "complex cultural goods" (Caves, 2000: 10) or "joint products" (Becker, 1982: 35) for they require multiple inputs for their production. Films stars feature in these collaborative efforts as individuals working within the specialized division of labor that facilitates the making, circulation and presentation of film products. At the same time, Hollywood stardom itself is a work of collective creation, involving the co-ordination of numerous contributions and resources.

Film stars are not born, they are made. This may seem an excessively obvious point, yet it is worth emphasizing as popular documentaries and biographies so frequently tell quite a contrary story by reproducing the belief that the fame which a star enjoys arises only from the magnetic, compelling qualities which s/he conveys on screen. Although not philosophically systemized, this popular view is nevertheless a theory of stardom for it makes certain conceptual presumptions which can be summarized as the three I's. The *individual* is presumed to be the source and origin of stardom. Secondly, the qualities which mark out star status are *innate*, something natural which the individual is born with. Usually those qualities can't easily be defined: the star just has a certain "something," the "it" factor which distinguishes him or her from others. Finally, because the person was born this way, there is the sense that stardom is *inevitable*, a view summarized in popular literature on stardom with observations along the lines of "from the moment of the first appearance in film, s/he was destined for stardom." This manner of thinking can be described as the charismatic theory of stardom, for it attributes fame to the natural enigmatic attractions of the individual. It is a theory which is popular because it would appear to have some proof to support it and so holds a certain persuasive appeal. Stars are indeed individual people. On screen, they do seem to radiate qualities which make their presence far more compelling than that of other performers around them. As all they bring to the screen is their bodies and voices, why not believe star presence is an entirely natural creation, and when faced with that magnetic presence, with the gift of hindsight it can seem the coming of fame was only a matter of time.

While romantically attractive, however, the charismatic theory gives an entirely misleading account of the material conditions in which film stardom is produced. Although this view celebrates the exceptionalness of certain individuals, film production, distribution and exhibition always involves multiple personnel and resources. Now the charismatic theory is not blind to the workings of industry but simply sees such arrangements as mere secondary considerations, a transparent infrastructure enabling the greatness of the star to shine through. When seriously considered, however, these inputs become so central to the making of stars that it is impossible to imagine stardom happening without them. In Hollywood, stars depend on agents to procure work for them. Managers steer their careers, while lawyers draw up the deals which will secure remuneration for the star's services. Casting directors make decisions about which performers are suitable for which scripts. Without producers, there would be no films for stars to appear in. Close analysis of the aesthetics and form of film reveal that whatever compelling quality a performer brings to the screen is largely the result of how cinematographers, grips (i.e. lighting technicians), sound mixers and editors manipulate the elements of film to give the star an auratic presence on screen. Marketing teams aim to cultivate public interest in films featuring stars, and in due course critics and reviewers will judge the merits of those films. Media exposure of film stars is not confined to films alone, and journalists and photographers in the gossip industry continually report and capture the off-screen lives of stars. Consequently, publicists work at managing the star's media exposure. Star films only become available to the public because theater programmers book them, stores buy the necessary video units to rent or sell, or buyers acquire television rights. After all these efforts, the popularity and commercial success of stars is contingent on ticket sales or units rented and bought, and so the movie consuming public are always participants in the making of stardom.

Film stardom is therefore never an individual, innate or inevitable effect. It requires the organized collective actions of multiple participants. Whatever aura of presence the star brings to the screen is largely due to the artful manipulation of film form. Once these factors are taken into consideration, it becomes impossible to accept stardom is natural or predestined. Instead, fundamental to the symbolic commerce of stardom is the recognition that **stardom is a product of industrialized cultural production, the outcome of multiple, highly organized, inputs and actions.** In common with other arenas of artistic production, Hollywood stardom is an outcome of "collective activity" (Becker, 1982: 1). Hollywood stardom is industrially produced fame, generated at numerous points across film development, principal photography, post-production, marketing, physical distribution, exhibition, reviewing and consumption. Rather than the source, the individual is the outcome in the production of stardom.

2. Mediated fame

Like other forms of mass communication, the film medium produces "a structured break between the production of symbolic forms and their reception" (Thompson, 1995: 29). Film places the actor in the context of mediated performance: the actor is on show but not physically present to an audience. This process of mediation is not limited to films alone but is an inter-textual effect achieved across multiple media channels, including the press, television, internet and book publishing. It is this insight which is at the core Richard Dyer's (1998) concept of "star image": by forcing a division between the star-as-person and the star-as-texts, the idea of star image directly challenges the charismatic theory, for whatever meaning or significance a star has cannot be attributed to the internal innate qualities of individuals but rather to the external material signifying substance of films and other media texts. If stars appear significant, it is because star texts connect with wider systems of belief about human identity. Star images may represent individuals but they are not the product of the individual. A second dynamic at work in the symbolic commerce of stardom is then how **stars appear and circulate in public culture as mediated identities.**

While the break between person and texts is essential to grasping the commercial work of film stardom, by avoiding discussion of the industrial conditions in which star texts are produced, the star image concept still preserves a kind of charismatic mythology, for it leaves unanswered certain pressing questions: where do stars come from?; in what conditions and through what processes are star images created? By ignoring the markets in which those images circulate, star studies have avoided interrogating in any depth the question why does Hollywood produce stars? It is precisely the aim of studying the symbolic commerce of stardom to therefore situate the production and value of star images within these conditions and markets.

3. Dispersed fame

By separating the contexts of production and consumption, mass communication "extends the availability of symbolic forms in space and time" (Thompson, 1995: 30). This is crucial to stars entering the market. Stars are mediated figures: images of the star body and the recording of the star voice can be separated and circulated independently of the star's physical presence. By this separation, **stars are temporally and spatially dispersed identities scattered across local, regional, national and global markets**.

4. Reproduced fame

Tied to the last point, with "the public circulation of symbolic forms," media products take on "mass" characteristics as they become "available in principle to a plurality of recipients" (p. 30). While the costs of making the original film negative are high, the unit cost is relatively low for replicating the film on celluloid prints or digital copies for showing in cinemas, duplicating discs to feed the home entertainment market, or creating downloadable files. Therefore **stars are mass-reproduced identities**.

5. Commodified fame

Finally, mass communication results in the "commodification of symbolic forms" (p. 27). It is worth considering this dynamic at some length for it is fundamental to the symbolic commerce of stardom. Thompson argues symbolic forms become commodities when they are subject to two types of "valorization." "Symbolic valorization" defines how cultural works gain "symbolic value" by "the ways in which, and the extent to which, they are esteemed by individuals – that is, praised or denounced, cherished or despised by them" (p. 27). Symbolic forms become commodities when their symbolic value is accompanied by "economic valorization," the "value for which they can be exchanged in a market . . . becom[ing] objects which can be bought and sold . . . for a price" (pp. 27–8). By the combination of these two types of value, symbolic works become "symbolic goods" (p. 28).

Once this basic fact is established it is necessary to ask, however, what type of symbolic good is a film? John Sedgwick and Michael Pokorny note the film commodity has two aspects: a material aspect, "strips of photographic representations on celluloid . . . which are the object of transactions between producers, distributors and exhibitors" (2005: 10), and an immaterial aspect, "the form in which the film is consumed in the mind of each member of the cinema audience" (p. 11). On the latter note, it is useful to think of any film as an "experience good" (Caves, 2000: 3) or "experience product" (Bakker 2001: 466). A film is both a tangible good – the material film object – and an entertainment service – the delivery and exchange of emotional, humorous, or enlightening experiences.

Stars are not directly symbolic commodities because in the business of the box office or the home video market, consumers cannot actually buy stars. Walk into any multiplex and try buying, say, Sandra Bullock. It's impossible. Across posters in the lobby, electronic noticeboards, the box-office counter, or automated ticket dispensers, all information and systems are focused on buying the film. Likewise in bricks-and-mortar video retail and rental stores, or with platforms for online retail, distribution and downloading, the point of transaction is always orientated toward purchasing the film. So while it possible to buy a ticket to see *The Proposal* (2009) or otherwise to rent or download *The Blind Side* (2009), it is just not possible to buy the star of these films, Bullock. Now the star may very well be the only reason the consumer chooses to pay to see a film, however even in such cases, the star cannot be directly purchased. It is in this sense then that Sedgwick and Pokorny describe stars as a "derivative commodity-type" (2005: 7), for buying the star is secondary to, and so derived from, buying the film. Furthermore, in keeping with the whole experiential exchange of film consumption, the act of transaction only provides an *experience* of the star.

Stars can't be bought by consumers yet the presence of a star may lead the consumer to "buy into" the idea of a film. Stardom is used as a strategy to induce consumers to pay for a ticket or buy or rent a video unit. Any performer who has gained a track record of positive audience response has acquired symbolic valorization, which the industry may then choose to deploy as a means of securing economic value from the film. In the film market, audiences are never guaranteed and so therefore the industry must work to stimulate and regularize demand. To do this, it is necessary to find a delicate balance between novelty and assurance. As Sedgwick and Pokorny note, uniqueness is a key characteristic of the film commodity (p. 13): although similarities may exist, and genres feed on such resemblances, no two films, even remakes, are exactly identical. Indeed differences between films are crucial to stimulating consumer desires to watch a film. Promoting uniqueness permeates the whole of film advertising: "each film is marketed competitively against all others currently in distribution. In this way, although film advertising differentiates its product, the industry differs from general practices in individuating each item it makes" (Staiger, 1990: 6)

While necessary to the commerce of film, uniqueness equally presents a problem for both the consumers and producers of film. Until a film is actually seen, consumers are left uncertain about just exactly what it is they are paying for. As Sedgwick observes, "If novelty is an irreducible characteristic of film as a commodity, it follows that, *ex ante*, consumers do not know fully what they want" (2005: 197). Repeat viewings of films do happen yet the majority of transactions around films depend on consumers paying for the first time to see something which remains (at least in part) unknown. Stimulating the "want-to-see" aspect of film consumption depends precisely on preserving the unknowability of the film, yet this presents the film consumer with a question: why pay – particularly when the same expenditure could be made on more certain rewards – for an experience where it is impossible to be sure what to expect or whether it will be satisfying? Paying for a ticket, or purchasing or hiring a film, entails a certain amount of risk, for until the film has been watched, a moviegoer can never be certain what s/he will get and whether it will deliver pleasure or disappointment. Now the producers of the film do know of its content but they don't know for certain what the film-consuming public will actually think of it or whether they will even pay to see it. Acknowledging the vagaries of success in the film business, screenwriter William Goldman famously opined that "the single most important fact, perhaps, of the entire movie industry" is that "NOBODY KNOWS ANYTHING" (1984: 39). This is only partly true. Film producers do know what mixtures of content have succeeded in the past, and so with the aim of securing future success, they may choose to repeat those formulas while still preserving some uniqueness. Yet as the history of the film market demonstrates, simply repeating the particular combination of aesthetic and textual inputs which worked on one occasion doesn't guarantee capturing the popular imagination another time round. This should not be taken as meaning film popularity is open to sheer randomness: consumption choices do demonstrate regular patterns but yet they are never entirely assured. Rather, it is more appropriate to regard the sellers and consumers of film as meeting in a state of what Richard Caves (2000: 3) describes as "symmetrical ignorance": consumers don't know for certain what they will get and producers have no absolute certainty what consumers will like.

This play of certainty and uncertainty is therefore endemic to the commerce of film. To stimulate the want-to-see factor, uniqueness is required, and so the main substance of the movie must be kept tantalizingly unknown by creating differences between films. At the same time, pure uniqueness can only bring risks for film consumers and producers, and so both constituencies depend on similarities or continuities between films for assurance. Stars have their place in the commerce of cinema precisely because they provide a means for managing this balance between uncertainty and certainty, difference and continuity, or uniqueness and familiarity. Sedgwick explains:

> Each film is unique in that it comprises a set of characteristics which differentiate it from other films. Such a set typically includes genre, plot, screenplay, star billing, direction, cinematography, art direction, supporting actors, sets, locations, wardrobe and make-up, music and length. However, this complexity creates a major problem for film production companies because of the uncertainty it poses for audiences. Since box-office revenues are based upon the reception of each film by consumers who make choices between rival unique products, studio heads and producers will be concerned to reduce the degree of uncertainty that uniqueness entails. They will seek to influence consumer choice and hence film earnings by incorporating certain deliberate design features into the product, the most important of which, historically, have been narrative storytelling conventions, stars, genre, production studio and director. (2000: 13)

For this to work, stars themselves must be both unique and familiar entities. No two stars are identical and yet casting a star immediately imports a known set of meanings familiar from other films. In this respect it is worthwhile recalling Janet Staiger's description of stars as "a monopoly on a personality" (1985: 101). Star monopolies achieve a delicate balance between uniqueness and standardization: there is only one Brad Pitt but he is always Brad Pitt. Foregrounding the distinctive individuality of stars provides the industry with a means of product differentiation and product assurance: casting Sandra Bullock differentiates a film from a Julia Roberts movie while at the same time setting off a chain of associations with previous films featuring the star. In the symbolic commerce of Hollywood stardom, therefore, **stars have symbolic and economic value as signs of difference and similarity.**

This symbolic and commercial significance will be picked up and explored in more detail with the next chapter. Before progressing much further, however, it is necessary to attend to two key questions: what is a star, and who were the stars in the period covered by this study?

Bankability, A-list Status and the Talent Hierarchy

"Star" is a slippery term. For example, search films on Internet Movie Database (www.imdb.com) and anyone who takes the lead in a film is listed under "Stars." And so, according to IMDb, the environmental documentary *An Inconvenient Truth* (2006) "stars" ex-Vice President Al Gore and British comedy *Looking for Eric* (2009) "stars" relatively unknown TV actor Steve Evets (who?). Renowned avant-garde short *Window Water Baby Moving* (1962) "stars" the director Stan Brakhage along with his wife Jane, who is seen giving birth to their daughter Myrrena, who also joins IMDb's star roster. Rejecting the seductive appeal of the charismatic theory of stardom and putting aside the common phase "a star is born," can anyone actually be a star at the very moment they are born? With this casual overuse of the term, nearly anyone who appears on a screen gets to be labeled a star. By potentially accommodating everyone in film as a star, this open definition does not provide ground for understanding Hollywood stardom. Consequently, it is necessary to adopt a more restrictive definition.

In the parlance of Hollywood, stars are "talent." Used in this way the term has no evaluative purpose – i.e., it is not employed to suggest stars are talented – but is rather a classificatory label, a term applied to describe "any person or animal working as an on-camera performer," although its use may be extended "to include all those involved in the artistic aspects of filmmaking (i.e., writers, actors, directors, etc.) as opposed to the people involved on the business end of film" (Cones, 1992: 508). Hiring star talent is itemized in production accounting under "above-the-line" expenses, "costs relating to acquiring the story rights, property rights associated with the screenplay, script development and signing the producer, director and principal members of the cast" (p. 1). In this way, stars are differentiated from the "below-the-line" costs of "mechanical charges, crew labor, overhead, extras, art and set costs, camera, electrical, wardrobe, transportation, raw-film stock and post-production" (p. 48).

Star talent is part of the creative labor-force involved with the collective work of feature film production. More specifically, film stars are film actors. Frequently professional critics and reviewers, but also the general movie consuming public, reject the quality of star acting – "s/he can't act" – yet this should not distract from the fact that Hollywood stars do act in films. Judgments of good or bad cannot dismiss the practical evidence that film stars serve a particular symbolic function in movie production, for they use their voices and bodies to represent characters on screen. All films stars are therefore film actors, yet not all film actors are stars. Hollywood stardom depends on a talent hierarchy which forms material distinctions between actors. On screen, stardom is produced and differentiated as script and elements of film form differentiate between actors, with stars granted greater narrative time and space as the film medium stages stardom. This audio-visual presentation of the actor is not enough, however, to make the star. Crucial to the workings of stardom is the circulation of the name. For Richard deCordova (1990), public circulation of names from 1909 onward played a key part in developing the discursive system of film stardom by inaugurating the "picture personality" as a knowable figure. Each year thousands of actors work in film but the consuming public never remember their names and those names are not used as vehicles to sell films. As an industrially orchestrated mechanism, naming therefore distinguishes stars from the large professional acting community.

Even so, there are still many actors whose names are known to audience members but yet who do not enjoy star status. Viewers of *Boogie Nights* (1997), *Out of Sight* (1998), *The Limey* (1999), *Magnolia* (1999), *Traffic* (2000), *Punch-Drunk Love* (2002), *Welcome to Collinwood* (2002), *Anger Management* (2003) or the remake of *The Taking of Pelham 1 2 3* (2009) may be able to place the name against the distinctive features of one of Hollywood's favorite Latinos for hire, Luis Guzmán, and possibly to even recognize his voicing of the Chucho character in the dog comedy *Beverly Hills Chihuahua* (2008). Hollywood film employs a multitude of recognizable and familiar character actors, supporting names distinguished from the vast population of anonymous actors. Yet although their names are known, these are not stars. Naming is therefore a necessary but not a sufficient condition of stardom. Rather, star status depends on how the name is deployed. Screen credits, posters, trailers and websites all assert that *The Taking of Pelham 1 2 3* is not Guzmán's film but rather belongs to Denzel Washington and John Travolta, or as some posters for the film paraphrased, "Washington" and "Travolta." Hollywood's hierarchy of actors is physically materialized in time and space as the names of stars appear before or above a film's title. Foregrounding certain actors in this way is the most obvious symbolic evidence that stars are names which sell. Dissemination of the name makes the star a known and recognizable sign of value, a form of currency which can be deployed in circuits of exchange across the film market in anticipation of profits.

Casting directors Janet Hirshenson and Jane Jenkins have a long and distinguished career in Hollywood. After working at Francis Ford Coppola's Zoetrope Studios, the pair established The Casting Company, casting films featuring many of conglomerate Hollywood's biggest star names, including *Ghost* (1990), *A Few Good Men* (1992), *The Last Action Hero* (1993), *In the Line of Fire* (1993), *Mrs Doubtfire* (1993), *Ransom* (1996), *Air Force One* (1997), *The Perfect Storm* (2000), *How the Grinch Stole Christmas* (2000), *Something's Gotta Give* (2003) and *The Da Vinci Code* (2006). As industry insiders, Hirshenson and Jenkins's take on Hollywood's hierarchy of actors is very revealing for how it nuances between different tiers of film actor. "Wannabes" are "the bottom of the ladder . . . people just out of acting school or fresh off the bus from Kansas or New Jersey," while "Unknowns" are "actors no one has heard of (yet!)" but who are members of the Screen Actors Guild with representation by an agent, and who may have a couple of screen credits (Hirshenson and Jenkins, 2006: 16). "Working actors" are "familiar to industry insiders and film buffs . . . but you've probably never heard of them, though you may well recognize their faces"; they are actors who play "the best friends, the doctors, the gangsters, the cops – the bedrock of day-to-day moviemaking" (p. 16). Guzmán could very well be placed in this category.

These actors may be fortunate enough to graduate to become "Names," actors who "might lack the youth, looks, or charisma to be considered Stars, but . . . make a solid, essential contribution to any film they are in" (p. 19). Hirshenson and Jenkins place William H. Macy in this category, for "his presence can green-light an independent film or a TV movie" (p. 19).

Hirshenson and Jenkins acknowledge there are differences of status even within this category, with actors such as Paul Giamatti, Philip Seymour Hoffman, Laura Linney and Frances McDormand sitting towards the top as "actors who are Stars in some contexts and top Names in others. In the bigger movies, these performers play the tasty supporting roles, but they may well get the leads in small, independent, or otherwise offbeat films" (p. 21). Hoffman demonstrates this trend well. On *Capote* (2005) he took the lead role in a film produced by a number of independent companies for an estimated $7m but released in most leading territories through Sony's distribution division. His next appearance, however, was in *Mission: Impossible III* (2006), a high-budget production from Paramount, one of the Hollywood major studios. Hoffman may have played the lead in *Capote* but on *Mission: Impossible III* he was on supporting duties, playing villain Owen Davian opposite the film's actual star, Tom Cruise. *Mission: Impossible III* was made for an estimated $150m by Cruise/Wagner Productions, Cruise's production company, with the studio handling international distribution. *Capote* grossed $49 million internationally, while *Mission: Impossible III* went on to sell $398 million in tickets. Afterwards, Hoffman eased back into the indie zone, sharing top billing with fellow indie player Linney in *The Savages* (2007) and leading the cast of *Before the Devil Knows Your Dead* (2007), before dipping his toes once more into a major studio movie with the Universal/Paramount co-production *Charlie Wilson's War* (2007), where he was squarely ranked behind the star names of Tom Hanks and Julia Roberts.

Further divisions in the Names category are determined by gender. As Hirshenson and Jenkins note, "the Hollywood hierarchy favors men – conventional wisdom has it that movies with strong men in the lead do better than films anchored by women" and so a distinction can be drawn between "the woman who takes second place *only* to a man and the woman who'll take supporting roles under a female lead" (emphasis in original, p. 21). Based on her supporting roles opposite Liam Neeson in *Kinsey* (2004) and Jeff Daniels in *The Squid and the Whale* (2005), Linney is placed in the former category by Hirshenson and Jenkins, while McDormand belongs to the latter for her supporting performances opposite female leads in *Something's Gotta Give* and *North Country* (2005).

Finally, the hierarchy is topped by the "Stars." Again, there are gradations of status within this category. Hirshenson and Jenkins place Halle Berry, Cate Blanchett, Robert De Niro, Cameron Diaz, Will Ferrell, Jake Gyllenhaal, Samuel L. Jackson, Kevin Kline, Heath Ledger, Al Pacino, Meryl Streep,

Owen Wilson, Kate Winslet and Reese Witherspoon in this category as "actors who become the selling point for the movie, one of the main reasons people will come to see it" (p. 22). However, these are topped by the "A-list," "Stars who can get a picture made: their mere presence in the cast is enough to guarantee funding" (p. 22). For Hirshenson and Jenkins, George Clooney, Russell Crowe, Johnny Depp, Eddie Murphy, Vince Vaughn, Mark Wahlberg, Denzel Washington, Robin Williams and Bruce Willis populate this tier, and they note the gendered bias underpinning Hollywood stardom with Julia Roberts "pretty much the only A-list actress in town" (p. 22). Finally, topping the hierarchy is the "A-plus list" – Tom Cruise, Matt Damon, Harrison Ford, Mel Gibson, Tom Hanks, Jack Nicholson, Brad Pitt and Will Smith – "guys who can not only get a picture made but who can practically guarantee it will turn a profit" (p. 23).

As these tiers indicate, the talent hierarchy is defined by commercial considerations. "Bankability" becomes the distinguishing criterion of star status. As John W. Cones explains, bankable "describe[s] someone or something (e.g. actors, directors, producers, projects, distributors, etc.) whose commitments can be taken to a bank and on which the bank will lend money for film production purposes, partly because of the prior successful performances of such individuals, entities or projects" (1992: 43). For several years in the 1990s, Hollywood reporter James Ulmer used estimates of bankability to rank actors in *The Hollywood Reporter*'s regular "Star Power" index. For Ulmer, bankability "is defined as the degree to which an actor's or director's name alone can raise 100% financing up front for a feature film, regardless of any other elements attached to the project" (2006: iii). To measure bankability, Ulmer devised his own proprietary rating system based on polling and interviewing industry professionals. Film buyers, sellers, sales agents, company directors and financiers in North America and some of the leading international territories for Hollywood film scored actors on a 100-point scale in three different levels of production budget, banded as up to $8 million, mid-range films of $8–30 million, and then over $30 million (pp. iii–iv).

With this research, the Ulmer Scale has posed a similar hierarchy to that offered by Hirshenson and Jenkins. The *A-plus list* are "'Fireproof' stars . . . guarantee[ing] an upfront sale, regardless of script, cast, producer of director brought to the package. Their names alone assure studios of a strong opening weekend" (p. 1). Meanwhile, the *A list* do "not trigger an automatic upfront sale, but they're a sure bet if the directors and budgets are right, and the material is consistent with the actor's past work. Like their

A+ peers, they can virtually guarantee a wide studio release for their films" (p. 3). Ulmer further differentiates between the *B+ list* ("actors boast[ing] nearly the same clout as the A stars, but elements in the film package, such as budget and co-stars, may weigh heavier. They can usually guarantee studio distribution" (p. 8)), the *B list* ("sometimes trigger[ing] an upfront sale. But other factors – such as the script genre, director, co-stars and budget – become all the more important. Their name value sometimes guarantees territorial sales for free and pay TV, cable, video and DVD" (p. 20)), and the *C list* ("actors [who] have little, if any, ability to trigger a presale based on their names alone. With the right co-stars, directors and budgets, however, they can occasionally enhance territorial sales in the ancillary markets" (p. 37)). Economic value is therefore central to defining stardom in Hollywood, where stars represent an exclusive elite of bankable actors.

Hollywood Stars, 1990–2009

"Star" is a relational rather than substantive term: certain actors can only be regarded as stars because others aren't. Star status is contingent on the commercial performance of films, and as the market is a dynamic arena of transactions, stardom is never fixed. Saying any actor *is* a star is therefore always conditional on his or her standing in the market. Hirshenson and Jenkins published their account of the actor hierarchy in 2006 but writing five years later it is difficult to imagine Mel Gibson holding his position amongst the A-plus listers or that Johnny Depp would not have progressed to the top tier and Angelina Jolie joined and probably surpassed Julia Roberts as the only female A-lister. As the bankability of actors rises and falls, star status constantly fluctuates. Although the names may change over time, the structure which supports stardom remains. As Hirshenson and Jenkins note, "what never seems to change is the hierarchy itself. Some parts need to be filled with Stars, others with Names, still others belong to Working Actors. Keeping track of who goes where is a big part of our job" (2006: 23). There is then a paradox at the core of the star system, for although Hollywood stardom praises the exceptionalness of the individual, the individual is always the product of collective action and the distinction of star status is dependent on occupying a position relative to others. Star status is therefore forever conditional, a product of the hierarchical system rather than the individual.

Since star status rests on shifting ground, when considering who is a star in any period, it is necessary to therefore find evidence of which actors were perceived to hold bankable status. Ulmer's index provides one manifestation of such perceptions. Similarly, since 1932, the Quigley Publishing Company has annually polled film exhibitors in the US to gauge their views on whom they regard as the top money-making stars in any year. As Bill Quigley (2010) explains, the poll is conducted as

> an annual survey of motion picture theatre owners and film buyers, which asks them to vote for the ten stars that they believe generated the most box-office revenue for their theatres during the year. It has been long regarded as one of the most reliable indicators of a Star's real box-office draw because the selections are done by people whose livelihood depends on choosing the films that will bring audiences to their theatres.

Although not based on any precise calculation of value, the poll offers an interesting if impressionistic account of the commercial status of actors, and as such provides an index of star status (Table 1.1). In the decades covered here, certain actors made one time appearances in the poll based on single films: e.g. Tim Allen, Sasha Baron Cohen, Jackie Chan, Billy Crystal, Robert De Niro, Vin Diesel, Dakota Fanning, Will Ferrell, Tommy Lee Jones, Demi Moore, Michelle Pfeiffer, Steven Seagal, Vince Vaughn, and Catherine Zeta-Jones. As others made repeat appearances in the annual rankings, however, they came to represent the era's elite strata of bankable actors: Sandra Bullock, Nicolas Cage, Jim Carrey, George Clooney, Sean Connery, Kevin Costner, Russell Crowe, Tom Cruise, Macaulay Culkin, Matt Damon, Johnny Depp, Leonardo DiCaprio, Michael Douglas, Robert Downey Jr., Clint Eastwood, Jodie Foster, Whoopi Goldberg, Harrison Ford, Mel Gibson, Tom Hanks, Angelina Jolie, Nicole Kidman, Eddie Murphy, Mike Myers, Jack Nicholson, Brad Pitt, Julia Roberts, Meg Ryan, Adam Sandler, Arnold Schwarzenegger, Will Smith, John Travolta, Denzel Washington, Robin Williams, Bruce Willis, and Reese Witherspoon. These names defined stardom in the decades 1990 to 2009 and so provide the main "cast" of names who will feature in this study.

Stardom depends on exclusion, for the specialness of film stars can only be affirmed if the overwhelming majority of other working actors lack star status. Although the movement of performers up and down the hierarchy may suggest fluidity and openness, it is necessary to recognize Hollywood stardom as a culturally prescribed system. Reviewing the rankings reported

Table 1.1 Quigley poll of the top ten money-making stars, 1990–2009.[1]

	1990	1991	1992	1993	1994	1995	1996	1997	1998	1999	2000	2001	2002	2003	2004	2005	2006	2007	2008	2009
Arnold Schwarzenegger	1	2																		
Julia Roberts	2	4		6	3		4	2	10	1	2	3		5	7					
Bruce Willis	3									4										
Tom Cruise	4	1	1	2	4		1*	5	6	6	1	1	2	4	2	1	8	7		
Mel Gibson	5	10	2	8	7	7	1*		6	8	6		9							
Kevin Costner	6	1	3	4		10*	9													
Sean Connery	8						7													
Harrison Ford	9			5	5	4	8	1			10									
Robin Williams		3	10	3		5	6	9	4										5	
Macaulay Culkin		5	5																	
Jodie Foster		6			8															
Jack Nicholson			4					6												
Whoopi Goldberg			6	9																
Michael Douglas			7		9	10*														
Clint Eastwood			8	1																
Tom Hanks				7	1	1			1	2	8	8	1	8	1	10	5	10		6
Jim Carrey					2	2		7	2	9	9			1	5					
Tommy Lee Jones					10			10												
Brad Pitt						3									9	4				8
Sandra Bullock						6	5			10										1
John Travolta						9	3	8												

Star	2000	2001	2002	2003	2004	2005	2006	2007	2008	2009
Leonardo DiCaprio	3	3	5	3	2					
Will Smith	4	7	7	8	7	3	2	1		
Meg Ryan	5	9								
Adam Sandler	7	3			10	9		6		
Eddie Murphy	8	4								
Mike Myers		5		3						
George Clooney		3	2	3		6	5	3	8	
Russell Crowe		5	4	7			6	6		
Nicole Kidman			5	6	2					
Denzel Washington			6	8	6	8	6	4	5	10
Reese Witherspoon				4		8	7			
Johnny Depp				6	9	2	1	1	2	
Will Ferrell					9		7	9		
Nicolas Cage					4			8		
Angelina Jolie						3			9	
Matt Damon							4	3		
Robert Downey Jr.								2		5
Shia LaBeouf								4		9

* indicates a tie

Source: compiled and adapted from Quigley (2010). Reproduced by permission of the Quigley Publishing Company

[1] Does not include the 23 names who appeared only once in these years, e.g. Patrick Swayze (1990), Billy Crystal (1991), Sylvester Stallone (1993), Demi Moore (1995), Cameron Diaz (1998) and Dakota Fanning (2006). Names are organized according to the year and ranking when they first appeared on the poll in the period. Reading downwards provides an account of the new star names that appeared in the decade, while reading across offers an indication of the longevity of star status.

from responses to the Quigley poll supports Hirshenson and Jenkins's contention that Hollywood stardom is a gendered system. In 1995, when *The Hollywood Reporter* took a small poll amongst seven top agents, studio heads and a major film critic, five of whom were female, most agreed Roberts and Bullock had enough box-office attraction to guarantee a good opening weekend for a film. A smaller proportion had confidence in Jodie Foster, Demi Moore, Meg Ryan, Michelle Pfeiffer, Sharon Stone and Barbra Streisand to open a film, and there was some belief Kim Basinger, Geena Davis, Whoopi Goldberg, Whitney Houston, Nicole Kidman, Winona Ryder, Alicia Silverstone and Meryl Streep could open the right film (Waldman, 1995). On the Quigley rankings, between 1990 and 2009, Bullock, Kidman and Witherspoon made repeat appearances but Roberts emerged as the only female star with any longevity over the two decades (see Chapter 9). Additionally, Hollywood stardom remains a racially circumscribed system. Since the Quigley poll began in the 1930s, only a few African-American actors have featured in the rankings. What the A-plus status of Will Smith possibly obscures is how, with the exception of Denzel Washington, he is the only black actor to consolidate a position amongst the star elite since Eddie Murphy in the 1980s (see further commentary in Chapter 6). When considered in this context, the appearance on the poll over two consecutive years of Whoopi Goldberg – a star both female *and* black – was truly remarkable.

In the decades which this study focuses upon, Jennifer Aniston, Cate Blanchett, Kirsten Dunst, Megan Fox, Maggie Gyllenhaal, Anne Hathaway, Katherine Heigl, Helen Hunt, Alicia Silverstone, Kristen Stewart and Naomi Watts were just some of the white female actors to gain recognition. Likewise, the African-American, Asian or Latina actors Don Cheadle, Selma Hayek, Queen Latifah, Martin Lawrence, Lucy Liu, Jennifer Lopez, Bernie Mac, Eva Mendes, Chris Rock, Zoë Saldana, Jada Pinkett Smith also became well-known figures. Frequently these actors achieved lead billings in films: for example Dunst in *Elizabethtown* (2005), Heigl in *27 Dresses* (2008), Silverstone in *Excess Baggage* (1997), Cheadle in *Traitor* (2008), Latifah in *Beauty Shop* (2005), Lawrence in *Big Momma's House* (2000) or Mendes in *Live!* (2007). Yet at best, these were actors who achieved – in Hirshenson and Jenkins's terms – the status of "Names." Even if a claim could be made for these performers as stars, they never joined the pantheon of A or A-plus listers for the films they appeared did not achieve the box-office returns to grant them any bankable eminence.

Reflecting on the status of the female star at the start of the 1990s, Mark Johnson, producer of *Rain Man* (1988), suggested the industry was witnessing a historical transition.

> Actresses have a much tougher time now . . . There aren't nearly as many good roles. In the '40s, you had the great romantic comedies with strong women characters. Carole Lombard, Barbara Stanwyck, Bette Davis outdrew the men. In the '50s, Doris Day was as much of a draw as Rock Hudson. Elizabeth Taylor was enormous in the '60s, Streisand in the '70s. But, for at least five years now, we haven't had a real strong female box office draw. (quoted in Dutka, 1990)

Johnson is mistaken, however, in suggesting the secondary status of female stars is merely a modern trend in Hollywood's history. Even though Lombard and Stanwyck played strong roles they were never regarded as major commercial draws, and in the decades when their box-office power was at its highest, Day, Taylor and Streisand were always exceptions in a male-populated star market. Since the Quigley poll first ran, few female performers have enjoyed consistent runs of three or more consecutive years in the top ten rankings. More women appeared on the poll during the 1930s than in any other decade, but most enjoyed fleeting glimpses of fame. Only Marie Dressler (1932–4), Janet Gaynor (1932–4), Joan Crawford (1932–6), Norma Shearer (1932–4), Shirley Temple (1934–9), Ginger Rogers (1935–7), and Sonja Henie (1937–9) maintained consistent runs, with Bette Davis (1939–41), Betty Grable (1942–51), Greer Garson (1944–6) and Ingrid Bergman (1946–8) the most reliable female names of the 1940s. These decades were the high point of Hollywood female stardom, for after the Second World War the polls overwhelmingly indicated industry opinion regarded male stars as the most reliable money-makers. In a market historically dominated by the box-office power of male stars, those periods of success enjoyed by Doris Day (1959–66), Elizabeth Taylor (1960–3 and 1965–8), Julie Andrews (1965–8), Barbra Streisand (1972–5 and 1977–80), Jane Fonda (1978–82) and Julia Roberts (1997–2001) were uncharacteristic. In Hollywood, the secondary status of female stars is therefore a long-standing trend.

Age is another demographic definer of stardom. Those names who defined Hollywood stardom in the 1990s achieved their status while still in their 20s. Roberts was 22 when her star-making role in *Pretty Woman*

(1990) went on release and Tom Cruise was 23 when *Top Gun* (1986) hit screens. Tom Hanks was 27 when *Splash* (1984) gave him the break from which to build his movie career and Mel Gibson was in his late 20s by the time he transported the fame he'd achieved in Australian cinema to Hollywood. Aged 32, Jim Carrey came relatively late to stardom as his three films of 1994 made him a big screen sensation, while Harrison Ford was already 38 before *Raiders of the Lost Ark* (1981) provided him with a hit built around his central presence. Child performers have achieved prominence in Hollywood but only occasionally: after Shirley Temple and Mickey Rooney in the 1930s, it was over five decades later before Macaulay Culkin's fame briefly glimmered in the early 1990s. As the example of Culkin shows, child actors may achieve fame and may even become "a name" but without attaining the same bankable status as their elders.

Age intersects with the gendered economy of Hollywood stardom to differentially affect the decline of male and female stars. No ceiling is formally instituted of course, yet there is widespread acknowledgment in Hollywood that female stardom does not survive into the late 1930s: "It's a Hollywood truism that male stars hit their stride at just the same time (mid-30s) that things start to go south for their female colleagues" (O'Sullivan, 2001: 9). An *L.A. Weekly* reporter noted "Today's actresses must be lucky enough to catch a hit in their 20s and hope their agents give them good advice through their 30s – otherwise they play girlfriends as long as their looks last and then fade from view" (Thompson, 1990). Acceptance of this gendered age disparity is most acutely thrown into relief with the multiple instances across the history of Hollywood films when aging male stars have been cast in romantic ties with a far younger supporting female actor. In the late 1990s, as he advanced to middle-age and beyond, Harrison Ford was paired with Wendy Crewson on *Air Force One* (by the time of release he was 55, she 41), Anne Heche (she 28, he 55) for *Six Days, Seven Nights* (1998), Kristen Scott Thomas (she 39, he 57) in *Random Hearts* (1999), and Michelle Pfeiffer (she 42, he 58) on *What Lies Beneath* (2000). The middle-aged female star is maybe a contradiction in terms but even in the rare cases when a leading older woman is cast in a role which sees her form a relationship with a younger man, such films "are almost always about the oddity of the situation" notes screenwriter Janet Roach (1994: 19). Working through its narrative of age appropriate romance, *Something's Gotta Give* manages to stage both trends. When the central couple of Erica and Harry – played by 57-year-old Diane Keaton and (nine years her senior) Jack Nicholson – split up, she has a relationship with 39-year-old

Keanu Reeves, but this ultimately amounts to nothing more than a fling, for Erica finally finds contentment by reuniting with the older and the far more suitable Harry.

What these patterns reveal is how star status is socially and culturally demarcated. Symbolically and economically, Hollywood stardom only valorizes certain forms of identity. The population of the A-list elite is restricted by not only economic status but also social distinctions of gender, race and age. Historically, Hollywood stardom has worked through a system in which commercial value is produced almost exclusively through a small cohort of white male actors roughly aged from their mid 20s to their mid 50s. This is reflected in the study which follows. Case-study chapters on Will Smith and Julia Roberts are included because both belong to the modern star elite and their examples helpfully illustrate general dynamics at work in the symbolic commerce of stardom, and yet they are equally untypical of the general workings of Hollywood stardom.

Genre, Actorly, Prestige and Posthumous Stardoms

Bankability offers a measurable if imprecise gauge of star status. It defines stardom in economic terms and is the organizing principle behind the talent hierarchy in Hollywood. To understand stars as a feature of Hollywood's commercial aesthetic it is vital to recognize how economic value defines star status. Even so, there are other configurations of stardom which are not strictly defined by the highest strata of the film market alone.

There are certain actors who do not belong to the A-list, yet through repeated and commercially successful associations with particular types of film they become *genre stars*. As already suggested, genres perform a similar commercial function to that of stars, creating continuities in the market to guard against uncertainty. Generic conventions contribute to the formation of strongly identifiable and saleable star identities, and the importance of genre has therefore been in evidence amongst the highest echelons of the talent hierarchy. In the mid 1990s, Ulmer's index was dominated by stars strongly associated with action. In 1994, for example, Tom Cruise (ranked 2nd), Harrison Ford (3rd), Mel Gibson (4th) and Arnold Schwarzenegger (5th) populated the A-plus list. Continuing the action theme, Ulmer's (1994: 29) A-list also included Sylvester Stallone (15th), Bruce Willis (20th), Steven Seagal (26th) and Jean-Claude Van Damme (29th). Seagal and Van Damme were never included amongst Quigley's top rated stars and never appeared in any of the top grossing movies during the decade, yet the direct bond between actor and genre made both box-office attractions. Comedy is the other domain of the genre star. Robin Williams (10th) was the only comic actor to appear on Ulmer's version of the A-plus list in 1994 but other performers identified with comedy such, as Eddie Murphy (28th), Whoopi Goldberg (30th) and Meg Ryan (33rd) were positioned amongst the A-list and Billy Crystal (47th), Bill Murray (49th), Woody Allen (51st), Goldie Hawn (53rd), Michael J. Fox (57th) and Steve Martin (63rd) appeared on the B-plus list (p. 29). Although performers like Seagal, Van Damme, Allen or Martin did not belong to the highest strata of Hollywood, they could still deliver films of a certain type which made some impact at the box office, and so while they did not rank amongst the *most* bankable stars, they still had commercial value.

In other cases, film fame is based precisely on how some actors have acquired high-profile reputations by breaking continuities between films roles and genres and/or by appearing in films which do not belong to the popular market. In 1994, Ulmer ranked Meryl Streep low down on his A-list in 42nd position but this was only after she'd flirted with the popular mainstream in *Death Becomes Her* (1992) and *The River Wild* (1994), which respectively ranked 21st ($30 million rentals) and 33rd ($45 million gross) in terms of their box-office performance at the end of the years they were released in North America (Klady, 1995b; *Variety*, 1993). Otherwise Streep was more strongly associated with resolutely un-commercial fare such as *Defending Your Life* (1991) or *The House of Spirits* (1993), which ranked 76th ($8 million rentals) and 143rd ($6 million gross) in the relevant years (Klady, 1995b; *Variety*, 1992).[1] Dustin Hoffman once referred to her as the "Eleanor Roosevelt of acting" (quoted in Plaskin, 1990: J1) and she has been described as "The Grande Dame of the Cutting Edge" (Goodridge, 2003) and the "First Lady of American Film" (Feeney, 2004: N11). Tom Rothman, co-chairman of Fox Filmed Entertainment and a long-time friend of Streep's called her "the Tiger Woods of actresses . . . a virtuoso talent that somehow exists on a higher plane than even the very best" (quoted in Galloway, 2008). As noted above, for Hirshenson and Jenkins, Meryl Streep was classed as a "Star" but didn't belong to the A or A-plus lists. Writing in *Time*, however, Belinda Luscombe argued "Meryl Streep is not a star. A legend, but not a star. At least not in the business sense. Everyone acknowledges her talent, but very few can be relied on to turn out for a movie just because she's in it" (2006: 55). Following Luscombe's line, it may therefore be incorrect to attempt to regard a performer like

Streep as in any way a star. Yet by her reputation Streep has enjoyed a status which has lifted her far above the rank and file of the general acting profession. What Streep represents is the *actor star*, a performer of renown whose fame is based on artistic over commercial credentials.

Furthermore, a significant part of Streep's renown has come from her outstanding record of winning multiple awards for her performances, most significantly her history of Academy Award nominations and wins. By the end of 2009, Streep had accumulated 16 nominations in the acting categories of the Oscars, including two wins. Awards attach distinction to film actors and in Streep's case she has become the quintessential *prestige star*, a category which, based on their own distinguished records of multiple Academy Award honors, has over time included Ingrid Bergman, Marlon Brando, Bette Davis, Robert De Niro, Katharine Hepburn, Dustin Hoffman, Jack Lemmon, Jessica Lange, Jack Nicholson and Spencer Tracy. A-list status is dependent on the capacity for an actor to accumulate economic capital through the box office and other revenue streams whereas prestige stars gain artistic distinction by accumulating the symbolic capital of awards and other forms of acclaim. Prestige stars are actually a sub-set to actor stars: they are the "A-list" of actorly stardom. A fuller discussion of the role of awards in producing prestige stardom follows in Chapter 8 but for now it must be noted that while actorly and prestige stardom are both configured around privileging the artistic over the economic, it is important to recognize neither category exists independent of commercial forces. Streep may not sit at the forefront of the box office but distributors have used her name to market films which have sold more tickets than many other films released in the same years, even though, as Luscombe points out, the audience explicitly drawn by Streep's name may be relatively few. In which case, actorly and prestige stardom do not oppose art and commerce but rather achieve commerce through art.

Stardom is time-bound as bankability confers value according to the current state of the market. Consequently film fame can therefore be quite fleeting. However, there are other configurations of stardom which are shaped by the enduring longevity of film fame. Articulations of the *star legend* are based on assertions of durability and permanence that exceed the high spots of a performer's marketable value. Through box-office sales, A-list status is linked to public acceptance, but the public have no say in conferring legendary status. Individual film fans may establish websites such as www.hollywoodlegends.net and hollywood-legends.webs.com but legendary stardom is largely mediated through the authority of cultural businesses and institutions. Publishing houses and broadcasters have their say in making Hollywood legends the subjects of books and documentaries. When the American Film Institute set out in 1999 to identify 25 men and 25 women to be hailed as legends of American cinema, it imposed a definition of "American screen legend" as "an actor or a team of actors with a significant screen presence in American feature-length films whose screen debut occurred in or before 1950, or whose screen debut occurred after 1950 but whose death has marked a completed body of work." Pre-selected lists of 250 nominees was prepared for female and male performers from which members of the "film community," comprising "artists, historians, critics and other cultural leaders," were invited to select (AFI, n.d.). When announcing the project, the AFI's Chairman Tom Pollock admitted the pivotal date of 1950 was arbitrary but that the main consideration was that an actor "had to have lasted a long period of time before leaving a legacy," and the Institute's Director and CEO Jean Picker Firstenberg encouraged jurors to "consider not only the body of work but the context in which it was achieved . . . Wars and social mores had their effect on their careers. This is not a popularity contest" (both quoted in Honeycutt, 1999: 4 and 64). The results produced a list of the great and good of American film stardom (Table 1.2). Some of the selected names had been leading box-office attractions, although commercial value did not define legendary status. Amongst the women in particular, it is notable how enduring renown was not measured by the market. Katharine Hepburn topped a list which also included Greta Garbo, Marlene Dietrich, Mae West and Joan Crawford amongst the top ten, all names once described in a 1938 advertisement sponsored by the Independent Theater Owners of America appearing in *The Hollywood Reporter* as "players, whose dramatic ability is unquestioned but whose box office draw is nil." According to the ad "Dietrich . . . is poison at the box office."[2] What the AFI list therefore represents is a canon of star greatness, a cultural historical index of star status independent of the economic measure that defines the Quigley poll.

Although the cultural historical measure of legendary status is defined without recourse to the market, through the mini-industry of popular biographies on stars from the past, legends are still commercial selling points. Furthermore, legendary permanence ensures that despite death, the legend can still be a revenue source. Elizabeth Taylor, seventh of the AFI's female legends, died on 23 March 2011, and within two days of the star's passing, British tabloid newspaper the *Daily Mirror* had published its *Elizabeth Taylor: Hollywood Legend* (Mirror Group, 2011). A week later

Table 1.2   The American Film Institute's greatest American screen legends.

	Male	Female
1	Humphrey Bogart	Katharine Hepburn
2	Cary Grant	Bette Davis
3	James Stewart	Audrey Hepburn
4	Marlon Brando	Ingrid Bergman
5	Fred Astaire	Greta Garbo
6	Henry Fonda	Marilyn Monroe
7	Clark Gable	Elizabeth Taylor
8	James Cagney	Judy Garland
9	Spencer Tracy	Marlene Dietrich
10	Charlie Chaplin	Joan Crawford
11	Gary Cooper	Barbara Stanwyck
12	Gregory Peck	Claudette Colbert
13	John Wayne	Grace Kelly
14	Laurence Olivier	Ginger Rogers
15	Gene Kelly	Mae West
16	Orson Welles	Vivien Leigh
17	Kirk Douglas	Lillian Gish
18	James Dean	Shirley Temple
19	Burt Lancaster	Rita Hayworth
20	The Marx Brothers	Lauren Bacall
21	Buster Keaton	Sophia Loren
22	Sidney Poitier	Jean Harlow
23	Robert Mitchum	Carole Lombard
24	Edward G. Robinson	Mary Pickford
25	William Holden	Ava Gardner

Reproduced by permission of the American Film Institute.
Source: AFI (1999)

Elizabeth Taylor: The Lady, the Lover, the Legend, 1932–2011 (Bret, 2011) was out and a week after that *Elizabeth Taylor: The Life of a Hollywood Legend: 1932–2011* (Sprinkel, 2011) and *Elizabeth Taylor: A Passion For Life – The Wit and Wisdom of a Legend* (Papa, 2011) were in print, followed a few months later by *Elizabeth Taylor: Last of the Hollywood Legends* (Lloyd, 2011). Legendary stardom therefore feeds *posthumous stardom*. With posthumous stars, the cultural historical value of legendary status finds an

Figure 1.1 Legendary stardom and the tourism business. Ingrid Bergman, Arlanda Airport, Stockholm, 17 November 2011. Photo by the author.

"after-life," or more appropriately an "after-market," as the dead star becomes the subject, or correctly the object, of enduring merchandising lines and other commercial opportunities (Figure 1.1).

Several characteristics are shared by posthumous stars. During her screen career, Taylor was fully endorsed as a box-office attraction, appearing nine times on the Quigley poll between 1958 and 1968 inclusive. Generally, however, posthumous stars attain greater cultural and commercial significance than when they were alive. James Dean (18th on the AFI list of male legends) was a regular television actor with a single film lead in *East of Eden* (1955) at the time he died. *Rebel Without a Cause* (1955) was released a month after the fatal accident and *Giant* (1956) just over a year later. The first two films were modest successes, ending in 13th and 12th positions respectively amongst *Variety*'s annual rankings of "Top Grossers" for 1955 and 1956, while *Giant* was a clear-cut hit, ranking 3rd for 1957 and immediately occupying 9th spot on the trade paper's list of "All-time B.O. Champs" at that stage in Hollywood history (*Variety*, 1956: 1; 1957: 1; and 1958a: 60 and 1958b).[3] With the pre-sold security of a best-selling book behind it and established film names Elizabeth Taylor and Rock Hudson in the leading roles, *Giant*'s success cannot be attributed solely, if at all, to any after-effect of Dean's death. Dean was never a major box-office draw, yet since his death, his film reputation has been magnified and his name and likeness have stimulated multiple product lines for over half a century.

By the time she died in 1962, Marilyn Monroe (the AFI's sixth-ranking female legend) had appeared in enough successes to confirm her star status, although her box-office value was significantly surpassed by several other female stars in the 1940s, '50s and '60s. Monroe appeared on Quigley's top 10s in 1953, 1954 and 1956, but her record fell far short of equaling Betty Grable run of appearances every year between 1942 and 1951, or Doris Day's 10 appearances from 1951 to 1966 (Quigley, 2010). According to *Variety*'s annual round-ups of the highest-grossing films, by the time she died Monroe had taken leading roles in just three films featured amongst the top ten films, while by 1965 Taylor had appeared in 10, Day in five and several other female, performers including Ingrid Bergman, Dorothy McGuire, Lana Turner, Grace Kelly and Deborah Kerr, could claim more successful records (Sedgwick, 2002: 210). Bergman and Kelly remain legends (the AFI say so) but Monroe's posthumous value has overwhelmingly outstripped that of her more commercially successful peers.

Despite limited box-office value, in the decades since their deaths, Dean and Monroe have remained highly visible figures in consumer product markets. From Hollywood's past, possibly the only other dead stars to enjoy similar levels of visibility are Audrey Hepburn and Elvis Presley, although Presley's fame does not result from his film work. All remain not only famous but commercially exploitable after their deaths. Excluding Presley, each made her or his name in films, yet their continuing value has nothing to do with movie sales and everything to do with other products. All have commercial after-lives on calendars, books, posters, t-shirts, greetings cards, mugs, socks, and ironing-board covers. During their lifetimes, each was subject to widespread media coverage, but of the hundreds if not thousands of images generated during the period of their lives, their visibility is largely limited to the reproduction of a small repertoire of key iconic images. Apart from a few shots from *Roman Holiday* (1953), in Hepburn's case her continuing visibility is almost entirely sustained through reproductions of a few posed shots taken by photographer Howell Conant during the production of *Breakfast at Tiffany's* (1961) (Figure 1.2). Dean, Monroe, Presley and Hepburn may be dead but the value of the posthumous star lives on.

These versions of stardoms therefore offer different accounts of star significance and value. With the bankable hierarchy of the A and A-plus

Figure 1.2   The Audrey Hepburn industry. Star merchandise at the Deutsche Kinemathek Museum für Film und Frensehen, Berlin, 5 September 2010. Photo by the author.

lists, stardom is delineated by the index of economic valorization. In contrast, alternative versions of stardom are configured outside reference to the market. Actorly and prestige stardoms are measured by artistic valorization, while legendary and posthumous stardoms are the products of cultural historical valorization. While not contingent on the market, these alternative versions of stardom nevertheless remain highly marketable and as such still feature in the symbolic commerce of Hollywood stardom.

The Star Market

Film stardom can be configured in multiple ways, yet in the symbolic commerce of Hollywood, it is bankability and box-office performance which ultimately defines star status. As Ulmer notes

> Some people have asked why the film industry has become so obsessed with measuring and quantifying its actors, poking around into their "bankability" and "financial viability" and "global saleability". Aren't there other "abilities" that those philistine bean counters out in Hollywood care about – such as,

say, *acting* ability? Can't they just loosen up and realize that *this* is what an artist's true "power" is really about?

No, they can't. The town doesn't work that way. (original emphasis 2000: 18)

In Hollywood's commercial aesthetic, it is the bankable elite of the A and A-plus lists who define stardom. In the study which follows, a restricted definition of Hollywood stardom is therefore adopted because Hollywood stars are a restricted category of actors. The focus will mainly be upon the most bankable actors working in Hollywood over the period 1990 to 2009. Taking commercial status as a measure of star status inevitably leads to an economic definition of stardom and it could be argued that this results in a form of analysis which instates an economic determinist account which neglects the cultural dynamics of stardom. Yet Hollywood defines stardom in economic terms and so any study of film stars must confront that fact. It is either by ignoring or only superficially tackling the commerce of stardom that star studies has forced an unsatisfactory and ultimately false division between the cultural and commercial aspects of stardom. As noted in the Introduction, in Hollywood stardom the symbolic/cultural and economic/commercial are inextricably bound together, for money is made through meaning and whatever meanings enter the marketplace are always conditional upon their bankability. Bankability is never, therefore, simply the effect of economic forces. Acting, script, *mise-en-scène* and the circulation of the name are all necessary components of the symbolic production of stardom. A certain elite of actors top the talent hierarchy because of their bankability, yet that status depends on the signs and meanings they bring to the film market.

Hollywood stardom produces and circulates only certain versions of human identity for the film market, regulated by the parameters of gender, race and age. While this system undoubtedly has ideological consequences, whatever cultural limitations exist, Hollywood stardom cannot simply be regarded as the major studios foisting representations on a compliant public; audiences always play their part in forming this market of identities through the tickets and units they buy. "Hollywood," says producer David Brown, "has no principles except profit. If casting midgets and octoroons would get people into theaters, they'd cast nothing but midgets and octoroons. If 90-year-old women opened a picture, Hollywood would be awash in 90-year-old women" (quoted in Roach, 1994: 20). Whatever range of representations and identities are available and circulate in the film market through stardom therefore emerge from the dialectical exchange between what the industry offers and what the audience chooses to pay for.

Examining and critically evaluating the symbolic commerce of Hollywood stardom then raises certain foundational questions. What arrangements are in place to support the production, reproduction, circulation and presentation of star identities? What versions of identity are generated through those arrangements, and how are they disseminated across media markets? And within those markets, how do stars function as signs of difference and similarity with symbolic and economic value? It is these questions which now motivate the study which follows.

Notes

1 Figures are derived from *Variety*'s annual rankings (Klady, 1995b; *Variety*, 1992 and 1993). Due to changes in the trade paper's reporting, differences appear between "rentals," i.e. the share of revenues returned to the distributor after exhibitor expenses have been deducted, and "gross" representing the total receipts from tickets before deductions.
2 Titled "Wake Up! Hollywood Producers," the advert appeared in *The Hollywood Reporter*, 3 May 1938, p. 3.
3 *Variety*'s rankings did not include films which had opened in the latter months of these years. Hence, *Rebel Without a Cause* and *Giant* were ranked under 1956 and 1957 although both opened in the previous years.

2

Star-as-Brand

In the previous chapter it was argued that stars have symbolic and economic value as signs of difference and similarity. This chapter examines this idea further. By combining signification with commerce to create distinctions and continuities between products, stars can be likened to brands. A brand is not a product but a way of perceiving a product. To conceptualize the workings of brands, marketing theory has adopted various human metaphors, applying terms such as "brand identity," "brand personality" or "brand-as-person" (Davies and Chun, 2003). According to this thinking, branding is understood as a process of attributing human characteristics or traits *as if* a product/service were a person. Similarly, stars have value in the media marketplace for how they provide ways of seeing the film product, but in the symbolic commerce of stardom, the branding metaphor is reversed: instead of the brand-as-person, the star is a person-as-brand, a symbolic vehicle used to create a set of impressions deployed in selling a particular film experience.

Thinking of the star-as-brand moves analysis beyond the symbolic realm of star image to consider how the mediated identities of stars operate in the film market. With the star image, analysis is confined to questions of meaning. Those questions remain important for studying the symbolic commerce of stardom but now take on a more explicitly commercial focus as they are used to interrogate the star brand. New questions are introduced onto the critical and analytical agenda:

- how do stars create perceptions of film products?
- how do those perceptions position films in media markets?

Hollywood Stardom, First Edition. Paul McDonald.
© 2013 Paul McDonald. Published 2013 by John Wiley & Sons, Ltd.

- how do the images of stars "perform," in the commercial sense of revenue capture, in the market?
- and how commercially valuable are stars?

Addressing these questions, the purpose of analysis is not just to ask what a star means but to also understand what a star does. These concerns will be picked up throughout this study but as a starting point this chapter explores the analogy between stardom and branding, considering the branding functions of the star name, and considering how stars feature in different categories of brand extension.

Branding and Stardom

Historically, the practice of branding emerged in the mid nineteenth century with the rise of modernity in capitalist societies: "The thinking that lay behind branding was very simple, but highly original. It was to take a household product, a commodity, no different fundamentally from any other made by another manufacturer, and to endow it with special characteristics through imaginative use of name, packaging and advertising" (Olins, 1989: 115). Branding strategies spread into many sectors of the consumer market so that by the time cinema emerged at the end of the century, branding was already a well established business practice. Early films were branded according to the names of production companies (Bowser, 1990: 103), while tying-in consumer products to film content or placing branded products on show in the on-screen diegetic world became common practice as some films were turned into shop windows (Lehu, 2007; Segrave, 2004). From the very earliest decades of the medium, film was therefore firmly embedded in a branded universe.

Definitions of branding share a common belief in how commercial competition can be conducted through using symbolic means to identify and differentiate products in the market. For example, in the 1980s the Ad Hoc Task Force for Marketing Definitions of the American Marketing Association (AMA) agreed a description of a brand as "a name, term, design, symbol, or any other feature that identifies one seller's good or service as distinct from those of other sellers" (Bennett, 1988: 18). With the brand, symbolic and economic value are conjoined in the marking of difference. Brands are not just signs (the interaction between signifier and signified) but signs for products or services. Jean-Noël Kapferer (2008: 12)

poses a tripartite "branding system" linking brand names or symbols
with a brand concept and a product or service. Through the circulation
between name/symbol, concept and product/service, branding forms a
semiotics of commerce as signs mark differences in meaning between
goods. The branding system brings together the "brand signifier" (the
name/material symbol) with the "brand signified" (the associated intangi-
ble concept or concepts) and their "referent" (the corresponding product
or service). Where branding enhances consumer knowledge, recognition,
awareness, or perceptions of a product, the brand becomes an asset, and if
the deployment of such assets can be shown to improve economic returns
to such an extent that these would be lesser without the application of the
brand, then "brand equity" is created. Brands have a symbolic component,
but as Kapferer argues, "to have value, brands must produce economic
value added" (p. 15).

"Classical" definitions have regarded the brand as an inert physical object
manipulated by sellers to secure advantage. Developments in marketing
theory have, however, moved increasingly towards conceptualizing the
brand as a living entity (Hanby, 1999: 12). Instead of simply identifying a
product, marketing embraces the belief that "to stand out and be successful,
brands must be imbued with human characteristics and traits" (Csaba and
Bengtsson, 2006: 118). This work is conceptualized through human metaphors, speaking in the language of "brand identity," "brand personality"
and "brand-as-person." "A brand is not the name of a product," Kapferer
stresses, but "is the vision that drives the creation of products and services
under that name. That vision, the key belief of the brands [sic] and its core
values is called identity" (2008: 171). Describing the facets of brand identity, Kapferer adopts explicitly organic metaphors when he states "A
brand . . . has physical specificities and qualities – its 'physique' . . . a combination of either salient objective features (which immediately come to
mind when the brand is quoted in a survey) or emerging ones" (p. 182).
Brand identity rests on a set of core values, the brand's "personality," what
Jennifer L. Aaker (1997: 347) describes as "the set of human characteristics
associated with a brand." Kapferer argues "A brand has a personality. By
communicating, it gradually builds up character. The way in which it
speaks of its products or services shows what kind of person it would be if
it were human" (2008: 183). David A. Aaker (2002: 142) suggests "The same
vocabulary used to describe a person can be used to describe a brand personality. In particular, a brand can be described by demographics (age,
gender, social class, and race), lifestyle (activities, interests, and opinions)

or human personality traits (such as extroversion, agreeableness, and dependability)." In his Brand Personality Scale (BPS), David Aaker suggests brands may convey qualities of being "down-to-earth," "honest," "wholesome," "cheerful," "daring," "spirited," "imaginative," "up-to-date," "reliable," "intelligent," "successful," "Upper class," "charming," "outdoorsy" or "tough" (pp. 143–5). Behind this thinking is a belief in "relational marketing," motivated by "worrying less about the imminent sale than about establishing an enduring relationship between the customers and the brand. We form relationships with people, not products – hence the notion of brand personality, as if we were describing the profile of a friend" (Kapferer, 2008: 151).

Hollywood stardom reverses this anthropomorphization of the brand: instead of the brand-as-person, stardom is founded on the person-as-brand. Adapting Kapferer's branding system provides a basic framework for understanding the star-as-brand (Figure 2.1). Fundamental to the production of meaning in film stardom is the relationship between star-signifiers, the material markings of the body and the voice, and collections of connotations or star-signifieds with which they are associated. Analyzing the ideological implications of this relationship has been central to the study of star images. In the symbolic commerce of stardom, however, questions of meaning must be extended to consider how a star sells films or rather the film experience. As with brands, it must be remembered that it is not the star sign – the combination of signifier and signified – which is sold; rather the star sign functions as a means for perceiving the product on sale, i.e. the film. Viewing the circulation between star sign and film as

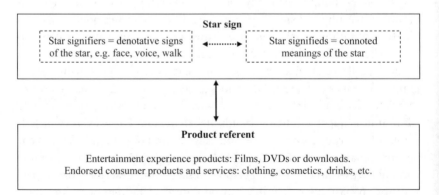

Figure 2.1   The star brand system.

a form of branding illuminates how this exchange is not just a semiotic but also a commercial relationship. It is in this interpenetration of the symbolic and economic, and of meaning with market value, that concepts of branding contribute to understanding the symbolic commerce of film stardom.

As the brand is not the product but a way of conceptualizing the product, then Kapferer describes brands as "conditional assets": "There are no brands without products or services to carry them . . . brands cannot exist without a support (product or service)" (p. 10). In the commerce of cinema, stars similarly function as conditional assets, for they only have commercial value because they appear in films, magazines or other products. As the market sells films and not film stars (see previous chapter), the branding function of stardom arises in how a star imports a set values and meanings, the star's "personality," as a way of seeing and selling a film. As producer Larry Marks once remarked "Stars separate you from the pack . . . They should tell the audience a lot about what to expect . . . Meryl Streep means a movie is classy. Arnold Schwarzenegger means that there will be bodies flying" (quoted in Harmetz, 1988). Where the inclusion of a star can be shown to influence performance at the box office or home entertainment market, then it is possible to speak of star equity or value, the effect of deploying the star personality for actual economic gain.

This analogy between star and brand is not lost on Hollywood itself. Rogers & Cowan is one of the leading public relations firms in Hollywood. Starting his career managing media exposure for Rita Hayworth, Claudette Colbert and Joan Crawford, Henry C. Rogers became a veteran of the Hollywood PR business (Rogers, 1980). Subsequently, the company he formed in 1950 with fellow publicist Warren Cowan has continued managing publicity for many of the leading names in Hollywood into the contemporary era (see Chapter 4). Rogers & Cowan openly acknowledge the status of stars as brands, proclaiming on their website

> Celebrities AREN'T JUST LIKE brands. They are brands . . . At Rogers & Cowan, we have a simple mantra: celebrities are brands. In the media-dominated world we live in, celebrities inhabit a special kind of marketplace, built on emotional appeal, personal cache, and how much they're seen, emulated, and talked about. (original emphasis, Rogers & Cowan, n.d.)

Michael Levine, publicity expert and founder of Los Angeles entertainment PR firm LCO-Levine Communications Office, regards the celebrity brand as the quintessence of branding.[1]

Helping an entertainment personality create and maintain an image is the precise definition of Branding in perhaps its purest form. We all know what a human being is like, because we're all human beings. Assigning specific traits to a person to create a brand identity that resonates with the public in unprecedented ways and helps to elevate that particular human being into someone who is admired (in some cases, revered) is what Branding is all about. (2003: 125)

While thinking of stardom in terms of branding can productively draw attention to the symbolic and commercial workings of Hollywood, it is necessary to appreciate differences between the product brand and the star brand. As Levine outlines,

Branding a human being's personality is not the same as branding a consumer product. For one thing, the person will have some characteristics, emotions, and feelings before the Branding process begins, unlike a can of soda or a wireless telephone service. Also, even though there is a considerable amount of crafting done on a celebrity's brand before the public ever gets to see that person in an interview, a personal appearance, or a film or TV role, there is no way to totally control the brand. The human being will have a life outside the context of the brand . . . That is the difficulty of personal Branding. A consumer product, an inanimate object, will behave that same way repeatedly unless something has gone very wrong. But a person – particularly one with money and power – will often behave in one way when the cameras are rolling and another when they are not. (pp. 126–7)

It is important then to recognize stars as organic or living brands. They are brands which work and live. Unlike branded foodstuffs or clothing, stars have a hand in their own production (and potentially also their destruction). Products have a metaphoric "life-cycle" but stars have a literal life-cycle.

Stars and brands serve the same commercial function – to distinguish between products while also preserving assurance by continuity. Product differentiation is not an effect of creating actual differences between products but rather the outcome of communicating dissimilarities to encourage *varying perceptions of products* which result in actual changes to purchasing behavior. Differentiation works across two axes. Vertical differentiation is achieved when objective features hierarchically order products according to differences in quality, thereby providing a mechanism for setting different prices. So, for example, when compared to travelling steerage, first-class flight has tangible and objective features that signal higher quality available at a higher price. Horizontal differentiation, on the other hand, is a "response to different consumer tastes," so the same product may come, for example, in a variety of colors or flavors (Pepall, Richards and Norman, 2008: 130). These axes of quality and preference can be applied to films and stars. Due to the money sunk into production, some films objectively have higher production values than others, with the presence or absence of stars just one of the features signaling quality. Films-featuring-stars therefore form a particular tier on the vertical axis, with individual stars creating differences across the horizontal: Sandra Bullock, Cameron Diaz, Nicole Kidman, or Julia Roberts are just different "shades" of contemporary female stardom.

While it is possible to position stars within these axes, it should be noted stars can only provide an uncertain and ambiguous mechanism for vertical differentiation. Vertical differentiation depends on selling differences in quality: "consumers agree on what is the preferred or best product, the next to best product, and so on . . . while all consumers agree in their ranking of products from highest to lowest quality, they differ in their willingness to pay for quality" (p. 145). Tiering prices for distinct classes of air travel is possible because objective differences in service meet with a consensus of consumer opinion. With films, however, a star may be used alongside other production values to create a display of quality, yet this does not guarantee audience agreement. Casting Brad Pitt in a film is an objective marker of difference: his presence becomes an indicator that more time and money has probably been spent on development and production than on many other films. While the content of the film product therefore conveys quality, movie consumers may not agree the promise of Pitt's presence will deliver quality. In such a situation, there would be a dislocation between an objective qualitative feature – Pitt's presence – and the judgments of quality formed by consumers.

A second problem with assuming stardom is a mechanism for vertical differentiation is that the presence or absence of stars is not tied to any distinction in price. At a single cinema, tickets are uniformly priced, so it costs the movie consumer just as much to see the spectacular made for $250 million as it does to see the low-budget $5 million production. Consumers are not free to "differ in their willingness to pay for quality," and so while stars may be used as markers of distinction, no price premium is imposed for the inclusion of "star quality." Likewise, the presence or absence of stars makes no difference to the prices charged for home video sales or digital downloads. At the theatrical box office, it costs just as much to see a film featuring Pitt as it does one without him. Instead, price differences only apply between venues or outlets, or otherwise across the temporal sequencing of release and retail windows, with discounted pricing staggered down the chain of pay-per-view and subscription television windows, or between new releases and older titles for sales and rentals on home video formats. This does not mean stars cannot function as markers of vertical differentiation but their impact is never certain. If the purpose of brands is to generate perceptions about products, then stars have a horizontal function based on how the meanings they bring to films service differences in taste, while vertically their use is found in creating at best merely the *appearances* of superior quality.

In the commerce of popular film, stars achieve horizontal distinctions by creating differentiating similarities. Here the star brand intersects with the dynamics of uniqueness and uncertainty of the whole film commodity as discussed in the previous chapter. Horizontal distinctions are formed at two levels. A star brings to a film a certain branded identity or personality which is distinguishable from that of other stars. For Brad Pitt to have any differentiating effect, to distinguish him from say Tom Cruise or Johnny Depp, he must always be Brad Pitt. Horizontal distinctions are therefore achieved at the level of differences between stars, and so stars must present and preserve standard identities: paradoxically, they must always appear the same if they are to signal differences. However, the commerce of film demands uniqueness to stimulate audience interest. At a secondary level, therefore, the string of performance by a single star creates differences while preserving continuity. A common criticism often leveled at stars is that their acting ability is limited because they always appear the same in every film. Yet this is precisely the purpose of star performance: star brands can only have value if the star is to some extent continually present. Between 1994 to 1999, Pitt consecutively played a suave vampire for *Interview with the Vampire: The Vampire Chronicles* (1994), a headstrong son in *Legends of the Fall* (1994), a dogged police detective in *Se7en* (1995), the inmate of an asylum in *Twelve Monkeys* (1995), an assistant district attorney in *Sleepers* (1996), an IRA fighter in *The Devil's Own* (1997), an Austrian mountain climber in *Seven Years in Tibet* (1997), death in human form with *Meet Joe Black* (1998), and a fantasy alter-ego in *Fight Club* (1999). Each performance was distinct from the others and yet on each occasion Pitt was still Pitt. How star acting balances the competing forces of difference and similarity is a matter to be examined in more detail in Chapter 7 but for the moment it is enough to say star acting achieves differentiation through continuity by enacting limited variability.

The Functions of Star Names

In Hollywood stardom, two key sign vehicles are employed to mark the difference and continuity of the star: the body and the name. Chapter 7 is reserved for a full discussion of the branded body of the star in performance but here the functions of the star name will be dealt with.

"In essence," Kapferer argues, "*a brand is name that influences buyers*" (original emphasis, 2008: 11). Equally, in the symbolic commerce of stardom, names are deployed in the hope of encouraging certain consumption decisions. As Jeanette Delamoir and Tanya Nittins note, names are "fundamental organizing principles both of stardom and brands" (2006: 29). It was only with the public circulation of actor names from 1909 onwards that a star system became possible in American cinema (deCordova, 1990). Naming identifies, individualizes and differentiates performers on screen and so remains foundational to Hollywood stardom, for stardom simply could not work if audiences were continually left asking "who is that?" Star names serve symbolic/cultural and economic/commercial functions, not only designating a particular identity but also a proposition in the market. Placing "Brad Pitt" on a poster identifies both a particular actor and a commercial offering. This dual function integrates star names into the wider currency of names in consumer capitalism. For both stars and brands, designations become part of a "name economy" that "involve[s] a long-term accumulation of social and cultural capital that is then converted into economic capital and back again" (Moeran, 2003: 300).

Rather in the manner Michel Foucault asked of the author's name – "How does it function?" (1969: 121) – a similar question can be directed at stardom: in the symbolic commerce of film stardom, what do star names do? Star names serve several symbolic functions. First, the name is a marker of uniqueness. Stars may be visually and possibly aurally recognizable but it is the name of the star which is the great differentiator, distinguishing one actor from another. To preserve distinctions and avoid confusion, the actors Stewart Granger and Michael Keaton adopted assumed names as their originals – James Stewart and Michael Douglas – were already taken by other actors (Granger, 1981: 46; Douglas, 2007: 2). Such is the value of the name as a marker of difference that protecting its uniqueness extends beyond stardom to permeate the whole acting profession. According to the Screen Actors Guild's (SAG) membership rules and regulations, no two members can have identical working names: "It is the Guild's objective that no member use a professional name which is the same as, or resembles so closely as to tend to be confused with, the name of any other member" (SAG, n.d.: 3). In the case of any disputes over names, the Guild's Name Duplication Committee is on hand to arbitrate towards reaching an equitable resolution. As a system for regulating differences, SAG's rules therefore recognize how the name is a key resource and sign of value in markets for media labor.

Secondly, names are not empty labels but sources of meaning: they not only differentiate but also signify. "Obviously not a pure and simple refer-ence," Foucault noted of the author's name, "the proper name . . . has other indicative functions. It is more than a gesture, a finger pointed at someone; it is, to a certain extent, the equivalent of a description" (1969: 121). Similarly, star names don't just designate, they describe a collection of meanings. Stars are well known actors and the star name functions to compress what is known of the person. In Hollywood stardom, names alone are enough to bring to the screen rich collections of pre-conceived ideas about a performer. The difference maybe small but placing "Tom Hanks" rather than "Tom Cruise" on a poster promises profound differ-ences in meaning. In a sphere of intensive symbolic production such as film, participants become acutely aware of the meanings which a name can convey, and so it is unsurprising to find the management, invention and modification of names has been common practice throughout Hollywood history. Frances Gumm was still performing in vaudeville with her siblings as one-third of singing act The Gumm Sisters when actor and singer George Jessel recommended they adopt a more attractive name and introduced the act as The Garland Sisters (Shipman, 1994: 39). Shortly afterwards, and reportedly influenced by a line in a Hoagy Carmichael song, Frances modi-fied her forename, so that by the time she signed to MGM in 1935, she was already Judy Garland (pp. 48–9). Stories vary over how Marion Morrison, who started out as a prop man under the name "Duke," became John Wayne, but an oft-repeated account has it that the change was made after Winfield Sheehan and Sol Wurtzel, production executives at the Fox Film Corporation, complained the original was unsuitable for a leading man and didn't sound American enough (Roberts and Olson, 1995: 84; Zolotow, 1974: 84–5). In the early 1930s Paramount were eager to sign another leading man to rival their own contract star Gary Cooper and looked toward Broadway actor Archibald Leach to fulfill that role. Leach was a British émigré but Paramount's general manager B. P. Schulberg wanted a more American sounding name. Fay Wray recommended Leach adopt Cary Lockwood, the name of a character he'd recently played on stage. While the forename chimed with Schulberg (it rhymed with Gary) the studio already had a Lockwood under contract. Leach was therefore presented with a list of potential surnames from which he arbitrarily chose Grant (Eliot, 2004: 57). Roy Fitzgerald (his stepfather's surname) was a perfectly fine appellation for a future truck driver but after he met agent and talent scout Henry Willson at the Selznick studio, by mixing the Rock of Gibraltar with the Hudson River, Willson found a name which more appropriately encapsulated Rock Hudson's towering build (Oppenheimer and Vitek, 1986: 21).

Normally only studio executives or other industry participants held the authority to rename actors but on occasions the opinions of the movie-going public were also consulted. MGM executive Harry Rapf famously organized for the periodical *Movie Weekly* to run a competition inviting readers to nominate a name for his new "discovery" Lucille Le Sueur. Running over six weeks between March and May 1925, the competition was a publicity stunt, raising the profile of Le Sueur and announcing her forthcoming appearance in *The Circle* (1925). At the same time, the competition was also a branding exercise for it functioned to define the meaning of the actor in the market. Potential entrants were provided with what amounted to a branding brief: when considering names, entrants were instructed

It must be short or of only moderate length.
It must be suitable to the individual, who will use it during her entire picture
   career.
It must be euphonious, pleasing and yet have strength.
It must be a name easy to remember and quick to impress.
It must not infringe upon nor imitate the name or any other artiste.
(*Movie Weekly*, 1925a: 33)

Parameters were therefore set to define the actor name as signifier – its length and uniqueness – and a signified set of connoted values – "euphonious," "pleasing," "strength" and "quick to impress." From what were reported to be "hundreds of thousands" of entries, Rapf and his fellow judges from the *Los Angeles Examiner*, *Los Angeles Times* and *Movie Weekly* favored "June Carter," "Betty Bowen," "Margery Ames" and "Alma Dale" but finally awarded the $500 first prize to Mrs. Louis M. Antisdale of Rochester, NY for suggesting "Joan Crawford" (*Movie Weekly*, 1925b: 47).

One effect of re-naming was to obscure the national and ethnic origins of performers. Margarita Carmen Cansino's Spanish lineage was erased as she became Rita Hayworth. While working on her earliest films at Fox, the studio shortened her forename to Rita but retained the surname as they were keen to cultivate her as the next Dolores Del Rio. After signing to Columbia in 1937, Harry Cohn quickly requested she find a more anglicized name and so she continued her career under her mother's maiden name (Leaming, 1989: 36). The European Jewish ancestry of Frederick Austerlitz Jr., Bernard Herschel Schwartz and Issur Danielovitch was concealed when they became, respectively, Fred Astaire, Tony Curtis and Kirk Douglas.[2] Teamed with his sister Adele, "Freddie" Austerlitz was part of a dance act and still a young child when his mother and his dance teacher decided the duo should perform under the name Astaire (Levinson, 2009: 10–11). According to Curtis, early in his movie career he decided to change his name and so anglicized the Kertész surname of his Hungarian ancestors, initially considering Jimmy or Johnny Curtis before settling on Anthony (Curtis and Paris, 1993: 95). Douglas was searching for a professional name when he made the change whilst performing in summer stock (Douglas, 1988: 77).

By the 1990s and 2000s, incidents of re-naming had become less common amongst stars. When she joined the Screen Actors Guild, Margaret Hyra adopted her maternal grandmother's maiden name to register as Meg Ryan (Morton, 2000: 31). Caryn Elaine Johnson combined the surname of a distant Jewish relative with a gimmicky first name to become Whoopi Goldberg (Parrish, 1997: 53–4). To avoid suspicions of nepotism favoring his career, Nicholas Coppola, nephew of renowned director Francis Ford Coppola, adopted the name Nicolas Cage (Markham-Smith and Hodgson, 2001: 25). Meanwhile, Sandra Bullock, George Clooney, Kevin Costner, Russell Crowe, Cameron Diaz, Leonardo DiCaprio, Mel Gibson, Nicole Kidman, Julia Roberts, Adam Sandler, Denzel Washington and Renée Zellweger all worked under their birth names.

Although not a major modification, a noticeable trend amongst some modern male stars has been the tendency to abbreviate forenames. John Joseph Nicholson became "Jack" and Clinton Eastwood Jr. became "Clint." Thomas Cruise Mapother IV dropped the Mapother at the same time he became plain "Tom." Similarly, John Christopher Depp II changed to "Johnny," Edward Reagan Murphy preferred "Eddie," James Eugene Carrey chose "Jim," William Bradley Pitt became "Brad," Matthew Paige Damon shortened his forename to "Matt," Michael Myers became "Mike," and Willard Christopher Smith Jr. was just plain "Will." Small those these changes are they point to how the star name is more than just a title. Brad, Eddie, Jack, Jim, Johnny, Matt, Mike, Tom and Will strike a more familiar and friendly ring than the originals, carrying connotations of informality which brings the star closer to the audience as if he were a personal buddy. As these examples suggest, star names are precise and complex micro-messages forming compressed identities in which one or two words compact together an intricate array of meanings and values.

Star names are also significant in the international market for star labor. Linguistic differences create an obstacle, a "cultural discount" (Hoskins and Mirus, 1988), impeding cross-border flows of media products. Similarly, as carriers of culturally inscribed meanings, the linguistic badge of the star name can also enable or restrict the entry of performers to cultural markets. In the transnational migration of talent into Hollywood, even with his martial arts skills, arguably Chan Kong-sang may never have broken into Hollywood if he were not already known as Jackie Chan through his Hong Kong career. In this case, adopting the "Jackie" moniker was more than just another case of the informalization of male star names; the change bridged geo-cultural difference to achieve a semblance of cultural proximity that could aid Chan's access to English-speaking markets.

A third function of the name is to anchor the dispersal and repetition of the star's presence. Star names are scattered across media, appearing in trailers and on posters, amongst the opening and closing credits of films, on DVD boxes, in magazines, book jackets, and on blogs. As noted in the previous chapter, it is through this multiplicity of texts that star identities are mediated, while channels of mass communication ensure not only the spatial and temporal dispersal of star fame but also the reproducibility of stars. Richard deCordova sees the name as carrying the performer's identity outside the photographic image, "refer[ring] to an identity that extends beyond the single film – into other films, into advertising preceding the film, and into other extrafilmic practices" (1990: 21). Although the star name is scattered and dispersed, it symbolically anchors the image or identity of a star by forming an intertextual link unifying the ensemble of star texts. Equally, the name provides a commercial anchor, serving to link a multiplicity of products as star traverse media and appear across temporally and spatially extended markets. Names alone are enough to give stars presence in cultural markets.

Finally, because of their symbolic and commercial utility, star names are prized possessions. As symbolic markers signifying commercial entities, star names serve a similar function to that of trademarks. As Jacqueline C. Lipton (2008: 1455) observes, famous figures from the fields of music, television, film and sports "have the most commercially valuable personal names in the sense that they trade to a large extent on their names and likenesses for their livelihood." Lipton notes, however, that under US federal law "this kind of trading on a personal name does not automatically mean that the name functions as a trademark" (p. 1455). According to title 15, chapter 22 of the United States Code, or the "Lanham Act" as it is known, a trademark is "any word, name, symbol, or device, or any combination thereof . . . used by a person . . . to identify and distinguish his or her goods, including a unique product, from those manufactured or sold by others and to indicate the source of the goods" (Office of the Law Revision Council, 2010: 1012). A mark is given full protection when placed on the US Patent and Trademark Office's principal register of trademarks and to receive that protection there must be a distinctive relationship between the mark and the product it signifies. Here arises the difficulty of assuming a straightforward comparison between star names and trademarks. Either individually or in combination, "Brad" and "Pitt" are not unique or distinctive marks: indeed, as the previous discussion has illustrated, the regular informalizing of male names suggests how certain stars have assumed titles precisely because they convey commonality. As they are widely shared, personal names are therefore not granted trademark protection (15 USC §1052(e)). Even so, under the doctrine of "secondary meaning," names of persons may be accepted as distinctive and achieve protection if evidence is provided that through regular use over a period of at least five years, the name has become synonymous with a particular product.

With the popularization of the internet, secondary meaning has become particularly significant in resolving claims for protecting the use of star names in disputes over the registration of domain names. It is worth considering some of these cases for what they reveal more generally about the symbolic and commercial functions of star names. In the online economy, sites and their addresses can become valuable pieces of virtual "real estate" and anyone can register a name which is not already taken. Incidents of "cyber-squatting" occur in situations where registrants who do not hold rights to trademarks nevertheless register domain names that directly reproduce or suggest registered marks with the aim of opportunistically selling these on for a profit. Cyber-squatting has therefore resulted in disputes over domain name ownership. To find a mechanism for resolving such disputes, the Internet Corporation for Assigned Names and Numbers (ICANN), the organization responsible for managing the domain name system, collaborated with the World Intellectual Property Organization (WIPO) on devising the Uniform Domain Name Dispute Resolution Policy (UDRP), approved in 1999 (WIPO, n.d.). In situations where a trademark holder considers a domain name registrant to have infringed a registered mark, before entering full litigation the dispute can be mediated through the URDP as an expeditious and relatively low-cost route to resolution.

When considering cases under the URDP, arbitration panels apply three criteria to judge if there are grounds for complaint: the complainant must demonstrate the relevant domain name is "identical or confusingly similar to a trademark or service mark in which the complainant has rights," that the registrant has "no rights or legitimate interests in respect of the domain name," and the "domain name has been registered and is being used in bad faith." Evidence of "bad faith" includes acquiring the domain for the sole purpose of selling it on to the complainant at a profit, or intentionally using the domain name for commercial gain by attracting internet users to the site or other online locations in a way that is likely to cause confusion with the complainant's mark (ICANN, 1999). Decisions in these proceedings see the domain name cancelled, transferred to the complainant, or otherwise the complaint is denied.

Creating a clash of unique identifiers, cyber-squatting presents challenges to the protection of star names in the online universe: domain names exactly locate sites on the World Wide Web and star names are prized for uniquely identifying individuals. To signify the star in the market requires maintaining exclusive use over the star name, yet the domain name registration process is open. Within six months of the URDP being adopted, in March 2000 lawyers acting on behalf of Julia Roberts submitted a complaint against Russell Boyd, who in November 1998 had registered the domain name www.juliaroberts.com. Discussing the case, the panel convened by the WIPO Arbitration and Mediation Center applied the three URDP criteria. Boyd claimed he'd registered the domain name from a sincere interest in Roberts, but as the original site at juliaroberts.com carried no content about the star until the time of the complaint, the panel was satisfied he had no rights or legitimate interest in the domain name. He was also found to have acted in bad faith for not only had Boyd demonstrated a pattern of opportunistic conduct by registering multiple domains in the names of famous actors or sports stars but had also tried to sell juliaroberts.com through the online auction site eBay. Central to deliberations over whether Boyd's registration of the domain name was likely to cause confusion was the question of whether secondary meaning could be attributed to a star's name. In the complaint submitted on Roberts's behalf, it was alleged "The Respondent's use of www.juliaroberts.com infringes upon the name and trademark of Complainant and clearly causes a likelihood of confusion" (cited in WIPO, 2000). Boyd conceded the domain name was identical or confusing similar with that of the star but challenged her claim to hold common-law trademark rights in her name. On this issue, the panel acknowledged the star's name was not a registered trademark but resolved the matter by determining "the name 'Julia Roberts' has sufficient secondary association with Complainant that common law trademark rights do exist" (WIPO, 2000). A decision was therefore reached in favor of Roberts and the panel was able to order that the domain name be transferred to the star.

Over the next few years, stars Nicole Kidman, Kevin Spacey and Tom Cruise all used the URDP as a mechanism to win the transfer of domain names. A point of interest is how, during their discussions, the panels in the cases had to define stardom. Roberts was identified as "a famous motion picture actress" who "is widely featured in celebrity publications, movie reviews, and entertainment publications and television shows, and she has earned two Academy Award nominations" (WIPO, 2000). In *Nicole Kidman vs. John Zuccarini, d/b/a Cupcake Party*, the panel regarded Kidman as "a well-known actress" who "has starred in numerous motion pictures" and "received various awards for her acting" (WIPO, 2001). As the panels considered the cases under trademark law, it was necessary to contemplate the commercial significance of star names, and so what is particularly interesting with these cases is how the findings of the panels described the commercial definition of stardom. In the Roberts case, the panel noted she "is currently ranked #1 at the box office" (WIPO, 2000) while the Kidman panel were satisfied that "There is little question but that Kidman has established common law trademark rights in her name. By virtue of her successful films, she has achieved renown" (WIPO, 2001). In *Kevin Spacey vs. Alberta Hot Rods*, the panel decided in favor of the complainant because in their view "a celebrity's name can serve as a trademark when used to identify the celebrity's performance services" and so agreed with Spacey's claim that "the public associated his name with his acting services" (National Arbitration Forum, 2002). In *Tom Cruise vs. Network Operations Center /*

Alberta Hot Rods, the star asserted ownership of common law trademark and service mark rights in "Tom Cruise" because

> the public has come to recognize and associate the name "Tom Cruise" as a symbol that identifies and distinguishes the entertainment services provided exclusively by him, and that through long and continuous use, international recognition and extensive advertising and promotion, TOM CRUISE has acquired distinctiveness and secondary meaning as a trademark and service mark. (WIPO, 2006)

In these cases, star names were considered to have common law trademark rights because over time they had acquired secondary meanings as distinctive marks for particular performance services. This conclusion is, however, disputed by Anthony M. Verna:

> actors' and actresses' names are not distinctive of a movie . . . Kevin Spacey starred in . . . *K-Pax* . . . a science fiction movie about a person who claimed to be an alien . . . [but also starred in] *Midnight in the Garden of Good and Evil* . . . a movie about a murder in Savannah, GA and the eccentric people who live in the town.
>
> Does Kevin Spacey make one type of movie? Absolutely not . . . How can the name "Kevin Spacey" be distinctive of anything except that he is an actor? It is not distinctive of the source of the commercial product – the movie. (2004: 168–9)

Verna correctly points out that star names are never tied to any single type of film but this does not necessarily mean star names should not be likened to trademarks. The Nike swoosh (which under trademark law should be considered as an "arbitrary or fanciful mark") is never singularly attached to just one type of sports shoe but rather to a whole array of footwear and sports attire. What it is not used for, though, is as a mark for cleaning products. Likewise, the names of Hollywood film stars are not attached to just one type of film or a single studio but rather to a restricted diversity of films. Verna is mistaken to presume the measure of whether star names are trademarks or not lies with whether they are distinctive of a particular type of film or company. Star names always primarily signify the star and only secondarily certain expectations about films. The star name always signifies the star. "Kevin Spacey" is always a distinctive mark for Kevin Spacey. If the purpose of trademarks is to uniquely "indicate the source of the goods," what the star name indicates is the source of the star performance not the source of the film. Regardless of what type of film Spacey appears in, his name always functions to mark the actor as a creative source. Whether recognized under trademark law or not, it seems reasonable to therefore consider star names as (to appropriate the terms of Cruise's complaint) symbols that function to identify and distinguish entertainment services provided exclusively by a particular performer.

Extending the Star Brand

Brands are built through repetition, as continuity is spread across a particular class of product or service. "Brand extension" occurs, however, whenever an established brand is then applied to other product categories. Similarly, extensions of the star brand take place when stars make departures from the type of role or functional activities for which they have become well known. These take several forms which can broadly be divided these between creative and business extensions, under which nestle various sub-categories.

Creative extensions define all instances where a star's familiar image is stretched to new areas of creative work. Here, *artistic extensions* occur where a star takes roles aimed at moving beyond a familiar on-screen image to extend his or her "range." In film culture, genres operate as product categories, and one of the most obvious demonstrations of artistic extension comes when stars jump between genres to perform in a different category of film product. After a series of high comedy roles in *Ace Ventura: Pet Detective* (1994), *The Mask* (1994) and *Dumb & Dumber* (1994) rapidly established Jim Carrey as a physical comedian, the star began to branch out with straighter dramatic roles in *The Truman Show* (1998) and *The Majestic* (2001). Although still tinged with comedy, the dramas shifted Carrey towards a different "product category." Secondly, some stars broadened their creative scope by engaging in *functional extensions*, whereby they go beyond acting to undertake other tasks in the division of labor. Star-producers (e.g. Sandra Bullock *All About Steve* (2009) and Reese Witherspoon *Legally Blonde 2: Red, White and Blonde* (2003)) are just one category of "Hollywood hyphenate" alongside star-directors (e.g. Jodie Foster *Little Man Tate* (1991)), star-director-writers (e.g. George Clooney *Good Night, and Good Luck* (2005)) and star-director-producers (e.g. Clint Eastwood *Gran Torino* (2008)). *Media extensions* occur where a film star aims to parlay his or her brand equity from one media sphere to another.

In most cases Hollywood film stardom has been the recipient of big name talent migrating from successful music or television careers (see Chapter 4) but in other cases actors who have made their name in film try their hand in other performance contexts, usually theatre (see discussion of Roberts on Broadway in Chapter 9).

Business extensions take two forms. *Executive extensions* are a corporate variation on the functional extensions just described, involving stars moving beyond acting and into management by forming their own independent production companies, a trend discussed in more detail with Chapter 4. Secondly, film stardom is deeply commercial but *commercial extensions* arise where film star equity is deployed to sell categories of product other than films. Signing Hollywood film stars to product endorsement deals has a nakedly commercial purpose: i.e. selling a product or service through association with a star's name and identity. Among stars of the 1990s, Brad Pitt was probably the most active endorser. Even before reaching stardom, Pitt was appearing in ads for Pringles crisps and Levi jeans. Later he became an endorser for Heineken, Honda, Toyota, and watches from both Rolex and Tag Heuer. When considering female performers, a gendered pattern emerges in the product ranges endorsed by leading names. Scarlett Johansson (L'Oreal), Nicole Kidman (Chanel No.5), Gwyneth Paltrow (Estée Lauder), Julia Roberts (Lancôme), Charlize Theron (Dior) and Reese Witherspoon (Avon) all lent their names and faces to cosmetics and scents. While many Hollywood stars have fully indulged in this practice, they have also aimed to distance themselves from any taint of commerciality by undertaking endorsement campaigns overseas. Japan, the second largest market for Hollywood films after North America, particularly became a favored ground for stars to appear in product advertising: Cameron Diaz appeared in campaigns for mobile phone provider SoftBank, Harrison Ford drank Kirin beer, and Bruce Willis was associated with cars from Subaru. Pitt inevitably didn't want to miss out on the Japanese bounty, and so he also worked for SoftBank and appeared in campaigns for the tinned coffee Roots.

Hollywood stars join music and sports figures amongst the ensemble of celebrity endorsers. Grant McCracken describes celebrity endorsements as working through the process of "meaning-transfer," by which "properties . . . reside in the celebrity and . . . move from celebrity to consumer good and from good to consumer" (1989: 310). Many anonymous actors can and indeed are used in product advertising, and they can be hired at lower fees than well known names, but McCracken argues the benefit of using a star or celebrity is that they bring a precise set of pre-constituted meanings to a campaign: "Celebrities have particular configurations of meanings that cannot be found elsewhere" (p. 315). Stars not only bring exposure to a product but in the process of meaning-transfer they provide a shortcut for the complex work of creating a "personality" or "identity," for using the well-known-person-brand makes concrete the brand-as-person. Star endorsements "give commodities culturally acceptable personalities" (Moeran, 2003: 308). To describe the exchange which occurs in the relationship between stars and the characters they play, Richard Dyer talks in terms of "fit" (1998: 129). Similarly, endorsements fit stars to products. Endorsements are communication transactions which aim for effectiveness through fitting attributes of the star brand with an idea of the product. In this way, the star endorser becomes a cultural mediator, "used to explain and support the meanings of commodities that manufacturers wish to convey to consumers" (Moeran, 2003: 308). For those involved with producing the endorsement campaign, the aim is to achieve star-product congruence (Seno and Lukas, 2007: 126). In the case of products which have already acquired some form of brand identity, there is a reciprocal transfer of meaning between the endorser image and the brand image, so that star and product becomes locked together as "co-brand partners": "Framed in a co-brand context, the endorsing party is no longer simply an agent receiving a financial reward for product support or backing. Rather, the endorsing party emerges co-brand-like as an exchange partner with another brand. Thus, as a unit of analysis, the celebrity is elevated to the same level as the endorsed brand" (p. 123).

When Swiss company Nestlé, the world's largest food manufacturer, wanted to push its Nespresso home coffee system onto the consumer market in Europe, it hired the services of Hollywood star George Clooney. Nestlé had a reputation for quality, priding itself on maintaining a number of "billionaire brands," and the company already had a long history of selling varieties of instant coffee through its Nescafé brand. A composite of Nestlé and "espresso," Nespresso aimed to replicate the quality of barista brewed coffee in the home by using a system combining a specially designed machine with the "software" of different coffee flavors contained in "portioned" pods. Between Nescafé instant and the Nespresso system, Nestlé was therefore engaged in vertically differentiating its coffee brands. Although Nespresso had been around since 1986, it had never been a success until Nestlé made a major push to promote the product in 2006.

Several factors contributed in building an image of quality for the Nespresso system. By omitting any reference to Nestlé, advertising created a distance from the "vulgarities" of instant coffee. When the product was rolled out in the UK, a sense of distinction and exclusivity was cultivated by setting up a few specialized "boutiques" in the high-class department stores Harrods and Selfridges, while online orders could be made by subscribing to the Nespresso "club." In addition, the product was also priced higher than standard instant coffees.

Nestlé therefore sought to imbue Nespresso with a sense of distinction and hiring Clooney was part of this strategy. Through a series of print ads in magazines and newspapers, together with television spots, Clooney became not only the face but the personality of Nespresso. The campaign aimed to create a transfer of meaning between star and product by orchestrating congruence between a coffee-making system and the sophistication, style and cool which had become central elements of Clooney's image. For the first of the television spots, titled "The Boutique," artful French music video-maker, feature film director and Oscar winning screenwriter Michel Gondry was hired. The spot self-consciously makes comic play on Clooney's reputation as "gorgeous George." When Clooney enters one of the boutique stores, he overhears two women talk about "dark," "very intense," "balance," "unique," "mysterious," "an intense body," "delicate and smooth," "strong character," "rich, very rich," "deep and sensual," "and a delicious after taste." They are of course talking about the coffee but the intentional confusions of the script make explicit the meaning-transfer process: both Clooney *and* Nespresso are dark, intense, deep, sensual, etc. As the managing director of Nespresso UK observed at the start of the campaign, "The brand represents a number of qualities including sophistication, style and charm, and George Clooney embodies all of these qualities. . . . We are delighted that he agreed to star in our first movie" (WENN, 2006). Clooney reciprocated, saying his properties in Italy and the US were already home to Nespresso machines.

In the ad Clooney did not play any named character but rather appeared to just be himself. However, as McCracken points out, "the celebrity endorser represents not himself but his stage persona . . . a composite of his fictional roles" (p. 312). McCracken takes his point from Michael Schudson's analysis of James Garner in Polaroid ads from the late 1970s and early '80s, where Schudson observes the film and television actor "does not play himself, the person, nor does he play a particular fictive character.

Instead, he plays what I would call the generalized James Garner role ... handsome, gentle, bumbling, endearing, a combination of Bret Maverick from *Maverick* (1957–62) and Jim Rockford from *The Rockford Files*" (1993: 212). Likewise, the Clooney of the Nespresso campaign was not a natural, transparent statement of self but rather the generalized George Clooney role, a composite of the suave, urbane, debonair charm tinged with light humour which he'd carried across his roles as Jack Taylor in *One Fine Day* (1996), Jack Foley in *Out of Sight* (1998), Danny Ocean in the first two installments of the *Ocean's* series, and Miles in *Intolerable Cruelty* (2003). "When the celebrity brings ... meanings into an ad, they are," McCracken argues, "merely passing along meanings with which they have been charged by another meaning transfer process" (p. 315). This repetition of meaning follows a commercial logic, for as McCracken notes, typecasting is essential for the endorser/product relationship to work: "Without typecasting, actors are unable to bring clear and unambiguous meanings to the products they endorse" (p. 316). In star endorsements, the process of meaning transfer need not be purely unidirectional, flowing from star to product alone: as McCracken suggests "an advertising campaign can sometimes have the effect of a new dramatic role" (1989: 316). Clooney gave Nespresso a personality based on his existing screen roles but in turn, for consumers exposed to the campaign, the Nespresso appearances also added to Clooney's mediated identity.

Achieving the co-branding "fit" of star and product does not inevitably increase sales. In Nestlé's case, however, after running the Clooney campaign, by the end of 2008 the company could proudly announce revenues from sales of Nespresso products had reached the target of $1.7 billion two years ahead of schedule. Although only 5 percent of Nestlé's total sales, Nespresso had become the company's fastest-growing brand (Saltmarsh, 2009). Responding to the competition, in November 2010 Italian coffee maker Lavazza hired Julia Roberts for a single 45-second television spot to advertise their own pod system, A Modo Mio. In the ad an actor plays Sandro Bottecelli painting Roberts as Venus. When he complains she will not smile, his problems are answered by Italian entertainers Paolo Bonolis and Luca Laurenti providing the model with a cup of Lavazza and she smiles. Roberts was reportedly paid $1.5 million for the ad (Wood, 2010). Potentially, thousands of other actors could have been paid a lot less to do the same thing, but what the makers of the commercial bought was the briefest glimpse of Roberts's distinctive wide smile (see Chapter 9). Unlike Clooney and Nespresso, here the co-branding association was not produced by importing a whole composite of meanings from the star's image but just a single physical feature.

Stardom as Endorsement

Clooney agreed to work for Nespresso on condition the campaign only ran in Europe (Mulier, 2007) and Roberts's Lavazza spot was specifically for the Italian home audience. Working on coffee campaigns in Europe, both stars physically distanced their commercial's work from the North American market. Certainly stars need to be protective for in Hollywood there is a very real stigma attached to endorsements. In a 2005 interview, Russell Crowe blasted fellow Hollywood names for their advertising work:

> I don't use my "celebrity" to make a living. I don't do ads for suits in Spain like George Clooney, or cigarettes in Japan like Harrison Ford . . . to me it's kind of sacrilegious – it's a complete contradiction of the fucking social contract you have with your audience. I mean, Robert De Niro's advertising American Express . . . Gee whiz, it's not the first time he's disappointed me.[3]
> (Heath, 2005: 241)

Crowe's criticism appeared to suggest there can be a realm of stardom which exists outside of commerce, a social contract without an economic contract. Endorsements are not, however, an add-on to stardom. Rather, the product endorsements which stars engage in are significant precisely because they make directly visible and obvious how commerce is endemic to stardom. In films, the branding function of the star is hidden or obscured behind the dramatic role, buried in the narrative circumstances, lost in the immersive pleasures of the fictional world. With endorsements, however, the commercial functionality of the star is laid bare, as stars lend their highly mediated identities to the promotion of certain goods and services. Likewise, when deployed in films, stars play roles but through their presence they also effectively "endorse" the film product. "Star endorser" is something of a tautology because really all film stardom is endorsement. Brands create visions of products and Hollywood star brands produce perceptions of film products. Through the star branding system, star and film exist in a co-branding relationship, a mutual exchange of meanings in which the casting of the star imparts meaning to the film while reciprocally the particular role adds to the generalized image of the star.

Notes

1 Maybe unsurprisingly, Levine has done an effective job of branding himself. Through the eponymous online presence, www.michaellevinewebsite.com, Levine promotes his own activities as business executive, author and services as a "motivational speaker."
2 Possibly responding to anti-Semitism in their home country of Austria, Astaire's grandparents converted to Catholicism in 1867 (Levinson, 2009: 1).
3 Ford actually advertised Kirin beer, not cigarettes.

3

The Extraordinary Ordinariness
of Tom Hanks

Tom Hanks is ordinary. From his early comedies to the later heroic roles, over a string of performances on screen, Hanks has played a succession of honorable and likeable everyman roles. Hanks's star status, however, has been founded on how his performance of ordinariness has been used to secure extraordinary box-office value. By the time *Toy Story 3* (2010) finished its theatrical run, Hanks had starred in, added his voice talents to, or directed and written films which have accumulated over $8 billion at the global box office. Hanks's stardom therefore rests on a paradox, for he is the multi-billion dollar everyman.

Bringing together the concerns of the previous two chapters, this chapter offers a case study exploring the Hanks brand. What the Hanks brand represents is just one example of the interpenetration of the symbolic and the economic in Hollywood stardom. Branding depends on the deployment of a specific and durable set of meanings in the market, and so the chapter starts by considering the meaning of the Hanks brand and how this has received widespread public acceptance. It then considers the production of that brand across a series of phases in Hanks's career. Taking the example of *Saving Private Ryan* (1998), analysis of character construction and marketing media examines the relationship between the Hanks brand and a single film. Reflecting on the example of Hanks, the chapter concludes with some general observations on the temporal dimension of the star brand.

Hollywood Stardom, First Edition. Paul McDonald.
© 2013 Paul McDonald. Published 2013 by John Wiley & Sons, Ltd.

"Mr Popularity"

Hanks's popularity has been built on a particular form of branded identity, combining gender and nationhood as a modern American everyman. Writing of Hanks in *The New Yorker*, Kurt Andersen described him as "our cinematic saint next door, the perfect baby boomer, Hollywood's shining exemplar of unpretentious goodness and decency in an industry where nice guys finish closer to last than first" (1998: 104). For Betsy Sharkey (2009), film critic for the *Los Angeles Times*, Hanks is "our Jimmy Stewart, a heartland guy, good people . . . Hanks is the boy next door grown into an ordinary Joe of a man that we could imagine talking T-ball, crab grass and the trouble with the Dodgers over the backyard fence." Steven Spielberg, who directed Hanks in *Saving Private Ryan*, *Catch Me If You Can* (2002) and *The Terminal* (2004), but also shared executive producer credit with the star for the HBO television miniseries *Band of Brothers* (2001) and *The Pacific* (2010), has described Hanks as "quintessentially America's favorite son" (quoted in Schickel 2009: 30).

It is a peculiar habit in commentary on Hollywood stardom for observers to frequently view modern performers through how they evoke stars of the past, and in Hanks case this has seen him frequently identified with James Stewart. Of Hanks, film writer, producer and director Nora Ephron once said "There are two kinds of romantic leading men in American movies; there's the godlike person you never met, like Cary Grant, and then there's the boy next door you've known all your life, like Jimmy Stewart. Tom falls into the second category" (quoted in Fox, 2009). Ephron substantiated this comparison on-screen by casting Hanks in *You've Got Mail* (1998), a virtual remake of the Stewart 1940 comedy *The Shop around the Corner*. Similarly, in *The Huffington Post*, writing on male stars, reporter John Farr (2008) distinguished romantic leads from everyman leads who "may or may not win their female co-stars, but regardless of outcome, they usually have to work much harder at it. They reflect us more as we actually are- wary, uncertain, awkward, caught in the maelstrom of life and not always winning without a fight." In this category, Farr placed Hanks amongst a lineage that included Dustin Hoffman, Jack Lemmon and Stewart. With such comparisons, one star brand is read through the meaning and significance of other branded identities.

This ordinary everyman image has won Hanks a popular public following. In February 2006, Los Angeles-based agency Davie-Brown Talent, part of The Marketing Arm, the entertainment marketing network of the Omnicom Group, launched the Davie-Brown Index (DBI). Davie-Brown functioned as an agency for the booking of celebrities by corporate advertisers and the DBI was designed as

> an independent index for brand marketers and agencies that determines a celebrity's ability to influence brand affinity and consumer purchase intent. The DBI provides brand marketers with a systematic approach for quantifying and qualifying the use of celebrities in marketing campaigns by evaluating a celebrity's awareness, appeal and relevance to a brand's image and their influence on consumer buying behavior. (The Marketing Arm, 2011a)

The Marketing Arm presented the service as aiding "star alignment": "because our business is a mix of art and science, we created the Celebrity DBI . . . that determines a celebrity's ability to influence consumers when representing or endorsing a given brand" (The Marketing Arm, 2011b). By 2011 the DBI was measuring perceptions of over 2,800 celebrities using online surveys, amongst a panel 4.5 million members. For a subscription fee of $20,000 per year, the service provided advertising and marketing professionals with data to assess the potential value and thereby the cost of hiring a celebrity for a campaign. During the development of the service, advertising agencies and marketers were consulted to identify which characteristics they considered of greatest importance for effective celebrity endorsements. Data on eight attributes was therefore captured: "'appeal,' 'notice' (their pop ubiquity), 'trendsetter' (their position as such), 'influence' (do they have any?), 'trust,' 'endorsement' (spokespersonability), 'aspiration' (do we want his or her life?), and 'awareness' (expressed as a percentage)" (McDonald, 2006). Scores were then averaged to produce the index (Bialik, 2010). In the first year the index ran, Hanks took top spot, an achievement he could only secure by scoring high on key attributes such as trust and appeal. Hanks headed the index until 2009 when he was knocked into second place by Barack Obama (Brodesser-Akner, 2009). Despite his strong showing on the DBI, ironically Hanks has steered clear of product endorsement campaigns. Instead, Hanks's commercial value has been confined to those films he has effectively "endorsed" by appearing in.

Other polling has further confirmed the public esteem in which Hanks is held. Starting in 1993, market research company Louis Harris & Associates began annually polling a representative sample of the US population to

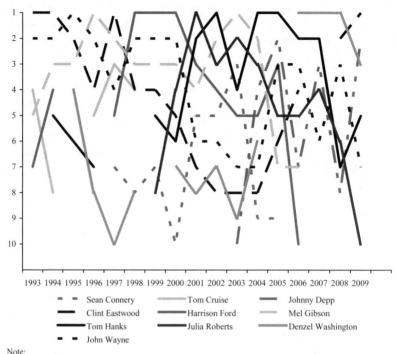

1993 1994 1995 1996 1997 1998 1999 2000 2001 2002 2003 2004 2005 2006 2007 2008 2009

▪ ▪ Sean Connery	Tom Cruise	Johnny Depp
Clint Eastwood	Harrison Ford	Mel Gibson
Tom Hanks	Julia Roberts	Denzel Washington
▪ ▪ John Wayne		

Note:
Selected names are limited to stars who appeared in the top ten of the poll for six or more years over the period. In some years stars tied for the same rank.

Figure 3.1   Harris poll of "America's favorite movie star": rankings of selected names in the top ten, 1993–2009. Sources: compiled from Harris Interactive (1999, 2000, 2001, 2002, 2007, 2008, 2009 and 2010) and Louis Harris & Associates (1993, 1994, 1996, 1997 and 1999).

determine "America's Favorite Film Star." Respondents reply to a standard question – "who is your favorite movie star?" As the enduring presence of John Wayne and Clint Eastwood indicates, the popularity of legendary stars amongst the public is not tied to the current state of popular cinema. Hanks appeared amongst the top ten on the Harris poll for the first time in 1994, and barring a couple of years, he enjoyed a near continuous run over the next 16 years, occupying first place in 2002, 2004 and 2005 (Figure 3.1). According to demographic groupings in the United States, in various years Hanks has moved in and out of being the most popular star amongst men and women, white Americans, Gen Xers and "Matures" (62+), people in the East and the Midwest, and political conservatives (Harris Interactive, 2001: 1–2; 2002 1–2; 2007: 1 and 2008: 2).

Aside from his popularity, Hanks has been viewed as a figure of considerable power and influence in Hollywood. For several years, the monthly film magazine *Premiere* compiled its "Power List," a hierarchy of the "100 Most Powerful People in Hollywood." Not exclusively an index of star status, actors appeared on the list alongside directors, producers, studio executives and media moguls. Although an entirely impressionistic exercise, the list provided an interesting insight into who was considered by industry commentators to be the most influential figures in the business. After winning the Best Actor Oscar for his performance in *Philadelphia* (1993), Hanks appeared on the list for the first time in 1994, ranked 29th, but after the massive global box office ($677 million) of *Forrest Gump*, the following year he jumped to sixth place. Until the magazine ceased publication in 2006, Hanks appeared year after year on the list, never dropping below 16th place. It was a convention with the list that each figure who featured received a mini-profile headed by a short descriptive label. In Hanks's case, *Premiere* repeatedly affirmed his amiability with labels like "new Jimmy Stewart" and "Mr Smith Goes to Hollywood," "Mr Popularity," "Mr Nice Guy," "Saint Woody" (a nod to his animated character in the *Toy Story* (1995/1999/2010) series of features), "American Idol," "The Gold Standard," "Gentleman Tom" and "Global Warmer" (*Premiere*, 1995: 119; 1996: 79; 1997: 89; 1998: 69; 2000: 79; 2003: 57; 2004: 60; 2005: 82; and 2006: 71). Perceptions of Hanks's power and influence in the industry were therefore bound in with these compact descriptions of his symbolic and cultural meaning.

Although these indexes of popularity and influence are not tied directly into the box office, in the eyes of the industry Hanks is a star with box-office power. He first appeared on Quigley Publishing's poll of film exhibitors in 1993 and took the top spot in 1994, 1995 and 1998, the years in which he scored high-grossing box-office hits with *Forrest Gump, Apollo 13* (1995) and *Saving Private Ryan* (see Chapter 1, Table 1.1). That feat was repeated in 2002, the year *Road to Perdition* and *Catch Me If You Can* were released, and although *The Ladykillers* and *The Terminal* fell a long way short of being hits in 2004, the $184 million grossed by *The Polar Express*, his third film of that year, was enough to convince exhibitors that Hanks deserved top spot for a fifth time.[1] With Hanks, popularity is therefore intertwined with profit potential.

Ordinary Guy, Extraordinary Situation

A series of phases have marked the emergence and consolidation of the Hanks brand. With the first of these, Hanks was established as a comedy actor as several series of the ABC sitcom *Bosom Buddies* (1980–2) paired Hanks with Peter Scolari as advertising creatives who, through circumstance, must cross-dress in order to remain residents of a women-only hotel. Although he never fronted a major television hit series, *Bosom Buddies* gave Hanks network exposure and established him as a comedy actor. This was enough for him to be considered for the lead in the film comedy *Splash* (1984), the first feature from Disney's new live action production arm Touchstone Pictures. Before Hanks was cast in the film as Allen Bauer, it is rumored Dudley Moore, Burt Reynolds and Chevy Chase were all offered the part (Andersen, 1998: 118). Earning $34 million in rentals for Disney's distribution arm Buena Vista, *Splash* concluded 1984 in 12th position amongst the high-earning rental films in North America for that year (*Variety*, 1984: 16). With this hit behind him, Hanks was able to land further comedy leads in *The Man with One Red Shoe* (1985), *Volunteers* (1985), *The Money Pit* (1986), *Nothing in Common* (1986), *Dragnet* (1987), *Big* (1988), *The 'burbs* (1989), *Turner and Hooch* (1989) and *Joe Versus the Volcano* (1990). These comedies marked the second phase in Hanks's career. Commercially, the films had mixed fortunes, but Hanks acquired enough of a successful track record at the box office to show he was capable of delivering hits. *Dragnet* accumulated over $40 million in North American rentals for the distributor Universal, while *Big* delivered rentals of nearly $51 million to Twentieth Century Fox and *Turner and Hooch* brought in over $34 million for Buena Vista (*Variety*, 1988: 19; 1989: 16; and 1990: 24). To assess levels of commercial success, these figures need to be seen in the context, and in the years they were released, amongst *Variety*'s annual rankings of the biggest rental films, these three titles were respectively positioned 8th, 5th and 14th. By the end of the 1980s, *Big* in particular had become the defining statement in the symbolic and commercial production of Hanks's stardom.

What the early film comedies established was the fundamentals of the Hanks brand. In the opening of *The Money Pit*, Hanks's character Walter Fielding, Jr. appears to self-reflexively summarize the Hanks's on-screen identity at this phase in his career, referring to himself as "a conventional kinda guy. That's all I ever wanted to be, just conventional. A little home in the suburbs, a white picket fence, maybe a dog, 2.4 kids, and just to round it out . . . a wife." It is a description that could be applied to many of the characters Hanks played in this period. With the possible exception of *Bachelor Party* (1984), where the character of Rick Gassko is the zany centre of the comedy capers, Hanks played regular, middle-of-the-road guys who happen to find themselves surrounded by a whole ensemble of crazy characters. As one interviewer observed, Hanks tended to play "the 'wacky but safe' guy" (Mosby, 1994: 17). With his early career, Hanks therefore acquired an on-screen image which could be summed up by the tagline for the poster advertisement for *Joe Versus the Volcano*: "An average Joe" who finds himself in "An adventurous comedy."

Hanks's everyman brand is a product of the roles he is cast in and the narratives they occupy. But it is also an effect of the way he looks. Maybe what seems so grounded and authentic about Hanks's everyguy brand is that he appears to *embody* ordinariness. For Sharkey (2009), Hanks has "got, as my mom would say, a nice face, open and honest. Eyes that look at you straight on; a smile that doesn't miss life's ironies but doesn't relish them either; a wiry build that's become more substantial over the years." If Hanks conveys a sense of everyman ordinariness, it is only in relative terms. Comparing Hanks to the pantheon of contemporary Hollywood male stars, Sharkey (2009) observed "he doesn't have is the swooning looks of a Brad Pitt or George Clooney; the chiseled hardness of Tom Cruise; the defiant aloneness of Denzel Washington; the crazed passion of Mel Gibson; or the eclectic dramatic moves of Johnny Depp or Robert Downey Jr." All meaning is produced through differences, and in the world of Hollywood stardom, Hanks's ordinariness is contingent on those other male stars who make a show of being astonishing, amazing, strange or bizarre. Hanks is therefore ordinary in relative terms. In the previous chapter it was suggested the symbolic and commercial status of the star brand is positioned in the film market by horizontal and vertical axes of differentiation. On the horizontal axis, Hanks's ordinariness marks difference as he performatively and physically signals a "shade" or "flavor" of contemporary American masculinity other than that of his peers – Pitt, Clooney, Cruise, Washington, Gibson, Depp or Downey Jr. Yet as a member of the A-list aristocracy, the casting of Hanks vertically differentiates by bringing to a film the appearances of distinction and quality. Whatever sense of ordinariness Hanks conveys is therefore always firmly and powerfully situated within the extraordinary hierarchy of Hollywood stardom.

Re-working the Hanks Brand

Already during this phase Hanks was making bids to break away from comedy and to re-work his on-screen identity. With *Every Time We Say Goodbye* (1986) he starred in a Second World War romance and although he played a comedian in *Punchline* (1988), comedy played little part in this serious drama. He had also begun to win some critical kudos through the awards system. Although the Academy of Motion Picture Arts and Sciences rarely grant nominations or awards to comedy performances, for his role in *Big* Hanks was nominated in the Best Actor in a Leading Role Oscar category. Even though he did not take away the award, for the same performance the Hollywood Foreign Press Association gave Hanks the Golden Globe for Best Performance by an Actor in a Motion Picture: Comedy/Musical and the Los Angeles Film Critics Association voted him Best Actor.

This re-working of the brand began in earnest from the early 1990s as Hanks's career entered a third phase when he diversified from straightforwardly comedic roles and towards dramatic roles tinged with humor. The phase started when Hanks took the role of Wall Street bond trader Sherman McCoy in *The Bonfire of the Vanities* (1990), the film adaptation of Tom Wolfe's 1987 novel on the greed and ambition of the Reaganite 1980s. As the millionaire McCoy is used to represent the moral corruption of the age, for an actor known because of his fundamental amiability, the character marked a distinct extension of the brand. Despite the difficulties of fitting that brand to the substance of the film, Hanks was the first choice of the film's producer Peter Guber, while director Brian de Palma was considering Steve Martin for the role and the studio, Warner Bros., preferred Tom Cruise. Guber, however, defended his choice for how the casting of Hanks could make McCoy a redeemable figure: "You look at this arrogant rich guy and you know that somewhere in his past he was a likeable kid. Tom Hanks brings that to it. You're waiting for him to fulfill your best expectations, not your worst expectations. So as he loses everything, he loses the arrogance, and you begin to think, See, I was right!" (original emphasis, quoted in Salamon, 2002: 10). Commercially and critically, *The Bonfire of the Vanities* was a failure. With an estimated production budget of $47 million, Warner Bros. was left with approximately $8 million in rentals from the North American release.[2] This poor reception presented no major obstacle to the re-working of the Hanks brand, however, and the third phase continued as

Hanks played an irascible baseball coach in *A League of Their Own* (1992) and a widower who finds new love in *Sleepless in Seattle* (1993).

Transformation of the brand did not occur by accident nor was it outside the control of the star. As noted in the previous chapter, stars are living, breathing brands. While studios and other contributors all play their part in the production of the star brand, stars themselves are equally active agents in the making and managing of their symbolic and commercial identities. In Hanks's case, he openly acknowledged the re-working of his brand was a deliberate strategy on his own part with a clear creative purpose. In interview, he admitted he'd taken the decision "I'm not going to play pussies any more . . . What are pussies? Those kind of guys who don't have a girlfriend, who can't commit, who run around trying to make sense of their lives and have some kind of Peter Pan syndrome." He instructed his agent "If it's a story about a lawyer who loses his job and breaks up with his girlfriend, just throw it out. I'm looking to play men who are my age and are going through something bigger." Hanks said the change offered "a pretty big moment of clarity for me . . . I decided that I was not going to take on a job unless it was test of my range, and my abilities and my emotional horizon" (quotes cited in Gardner, 2007: 148–9). This phase therefore represented the star's own self-conscious creative extension of his branded identity. He reflected on this period, saying

> I realized that it was much more important to say no to stuff than it was to say yes. I had fuck-you money . . . My agent said, "What do you want to do?" I said, "Well, it's not like I know what I want to do, but I sure know what I don't want to do. And I don't want to play guys anymore going 'Oh, I'm not in love and I wish I was' . . . 'and I'm just trying to get to work today but my car keeps breaking down in funny ways.'" They're boring, they've got nothing to do with my life, and I don't want to have to waste time even considering them. (cited in Andersen, 1998: 122)

For the Hanks brand, this period was a transitional phase in which the star intentionally re-worked his brand to shift from light comedian to serious actor. Two roles marked the culmination of this transition. In *Philadelphia* (1993), Hanks legitimized himself as a dramatic actor by winning the Best Actor Oscar for his portrayal of a lawyer dying of AIDS. Richard Schickel described Hanks portrayal of the lawyer Andrew Beckett as "his truly heroic and, of course, tragic role" (2009: 32). Starring as the eponymous *Forrest Gump* (1994), for which he won his second Oscar, Hanks continued the comedic average Joe type he was so well known for but also took his every-guy image in a new direction as the role became the first in a short run of characters who bear witness to the making of late twentieth century American history. In *Apollo 13*, Hanks played Jim Lovell, commander of the ill-fated space mission, and in *Saving Private Ryan* he played Captain John H. Miller who leads a unit of US Rangers as they storm Omaha beach during the D-Day invasion.

Between *Apollo 13* and *Saving Private Ryan*, Hanks voiced the Woody character in the animated feature *Toy Story* (1995). Woody is an interesting creation for he compacts together a rich array of meanings which play off and contribute to the Hanks brand. Visually, the character shares the same ordinary looks and lanky physicality as Hanks. Woody is a cowboy toy and when his ring pull is yanked, it triggers the voice box to utter a stream of Western clichés: "Reach for the sky," "Yee-haw! Giddyap, pardner! We got a get this wagon train a movin'," "This town ain't big enough for the two of us," "Somebody's poisoned the water hole" and "There's a snake in my boots." In the pre-title sequence, Sheriff Woody heroically foils a make-believe bank robbery staged by Mr. Potato Head. Woody is therefore immersed in American mythology, evoking the cinematically mediated folklore of the Wild West. At the same time, he does not display the "stalwart and rugged qualities" which for Frederick Jackson Turner (1893: 15) defined the frontiersman and which have also characterized many cinematic Western heroes. Instead, Woody is a sensitive soul: the whole narrative of *Toy Story* is driven by the emotional drama of Woody getting over the jealous feelings he has as the interloper Buzz Lightyear displaces him in the affections of their owner, Andy. Woody does not occupy "the outer edge of the wave – the meeting point between savagery and civilization . . . the hither edge of free land" (p. 3) which marked Jackson Turner's vision of frontier but rather a commonplace residential suburban landscape. Instead of striking out for unchartered lands, Woody is always trying to get home. For Jackson Turner, "the frontier is productive of individualism" (p. 30) but Woody is all about bonding and sharing. He is the one continuous figure running through the film's opening title sequence, which is accompanied by the Randy Newman song "You've Got a Friend in Me," and as the lyrics are sung in the first person, so the song belongs to Woody. An ethos of friendliness and companionability is articulated, in which "Some other folks may be a little bit smarter than I am, Big and stronger too, maybe, But none of them will ever love you the way I do, It's me and you, boy." Despite his outward westerner trappings, Woody is therefore a kind of anti-frontiersman, a sensitive suburban stay-at-home who simply wants to get on with folk. Sid, the evil kid who lives next door, refers to Woody as "that wimpy cowboy doll." Amongst the toys he enjoys a certain amount of influence and authority, but he is always a benign leader of his "people" and periodically shows himself to be susceptible to moments of self-doubt. Like Gump and Lovell, Woody is a hero by accident rather than design or destiny. Woody did represent another comedic figure for Hanks but with Lovell and Miller he completed the shift which Schickel describes from "relatively ordinary demi-juveniles" to "some straightforwardly romantic leads" before entering this phase of "conventionally heroic figures, all of whom are pretty mainstream American" (2009: 30).

As an actor with international fame, paradoxically Hanks's ordinariness is a creation of the extraordinary world of Hollywood stardom. Regarding Hanks as "ordinary" may suggest there is something natural and transparent about the meanings he brings to the screen, but as ever with Hollywood stardom, his significance depends on the construction of meaning: ordinariness is a contrivance, the effect of selected roles, scripts and narrative situations. Hanks's ordinariness is not some fundamental neutral state of just being. Schickel description of Hanks as "our great anti-show off" (p. 34) is deceptive, for in a profession entirely based on showing off, Hanks's stardom has been built on making a show of ordinariness.

It should be noted that while Hanks's film career progressed through these phases, the Hanks brand was also dispersed across various creative and business extensions. The move from comedy to drama already represented an instance of artistic brand extension and Hanks expanded his creative functions and business activities by setting up the independent production company Clavius Base with producer Gary Goetzman. Clavius Base produced the feature film *That Thing You Do!* (1996) which Hanks directed, wrote and took a supporting role in. Hanks also extended his work across media, as the company produced the television mini-series *From the Earth to the Moon* (1998), a dramatic recreation of the Apollo space program. Hanks not only hosted the series but also took credits as an executive producer and for some episodes a writer too. Goetzman and Hanks went on to form a second production company, Playtone, named after the fictitious music recording company in *That Thing You Do!* Rather than an effect of branding, these extensions could be regarded as Hanks simply diversifying his creative and business roles, but as *From the Earth to the Moon* had a clear thematic link with *Apollo 13*, so the material fed on pre-existing knowledge of Hanks's on-screen identity.

Banking Captain Miller

From the comedies to the historical dramas, from the cross dressing Kip or "Buffy" in *Bosum Buddies* to the daring leadership of Cpt. Miller, Hanks appears to have achieved a remarkable change in his on-screen identity. Departing from comedy to take serious dramatic roles or moving from sitcom player to become a serious Oscar winning actor, Hanks has shown a self-conscious intent to re-work his stardom by calculated artistic brand extensions. Yet the shifts achieved have not fundamentally changed the Hanks brand. Those transitions have created difference in the midst of continuity with the movement from comedic-safe everyman to heroic-safe everyman. Preserving this continuity within difference can be understood through close attention to Hanks's role in *Saving Private Ryan*.

Across his performances, Hanks has enacted a collection of meanings about America and masculinity, and Miller encapsulates the confluence of nation and gender central to the star's symbolic and commercial signifi-cance. After landing on Omaha beach, Miller is given orders to form a unit and embark on a mission in search for a single paratrooper, James Francis Ryan (Matt Damon), whose brothers have all been killed in action. Although the landing and subsequent combat demand acts of immense courage, the film does not regard this as an isolated or individual condition. Miller's unit is schematically organized around its social representativeness. In the press book for the film, Tom Sizemore's character Sergeant Horvath was described as "the veteran solider" (Anon., 1998: 10), opposite Edward Burns as Private Reiben, "a wisecracking New Yorker" (p. 11). The remain-der of the ensemble comprised Vin Diesel as Private Caparzo, "a tough New York Italian with a gentle side," Giovanni Ribisi playing Wade, "the squad's dedicated medic," Barry Pepper as Private Jackson, "a Bible-quoting Tennessee sharpshooter whose dead aim proves to be a godsend," and Adam Goldberg taking the role of Private Mellish, "a Jewish kid from Yonkers, who knows he has more at stake in fighting the Nazis" (p. 12). As filtered through this social "melting pot," the ensemble represents the fight-ing of the war as the shared objective and effort of a national collective.

This schematic representativeness extended to Hanks as Miller. To his men, the captain is an enigma: nobody knows anything about his life before military service, not even Horvath, who has accompanied Miller on a series of campaigns. Consequently, the men run bets on where Miller originates from. To diffuse a tense situation amongst his unit, Miller finally divulges,

"I'm a schoolteacher . . . I teach English composition . . . in this little town called Adley, Pennsylvania. Last 11 years . . . I've been at Thomas Alva Edison High School . . . I was the coach of the baseball team in springtime." He confesses fears that the horrors of war may have changed him beyond all recognition:

> Back home, when I'd tell people what I do for a living, they think "Well, now that figures." But over here, it's a . . . a big . . . a big mystery. So I guess I've changed, some . . . Sometimes I wonder if I've changed so much, my wife is even gonna recognize me whenever it is I get back to her . . . And how I'll ever be able to . . . to tell her about days like today.

Earlier Miller questioned the wisdom of endangering eight men to save the life of one but nevertheless dutifully committed to his mission. In his heart, however, the operation is motivated by private objectives.

> Ah, Ryan, I don't know anything about Ryan. I don't care. The man means nothing to me, he's just a name. But if . . . huh, you know, going to Ramelle and finding him so he can go home, if that earns me the right to get back to my wife, well then . . . then, that's my mission.

After locating Ryan in the devastated French town of Ramelle, Miller encourages the young paratrooper to remember his dead brothers by recalling them in a particular context. He tells Ryan, "Well when I think of home, I . . . I think of something specific. I think of my, my hammock in the backyard or my wife pruning the rosebushes in a pair of my old work gloves."

On a superficial level, Miller appears miles away from Walter Fielding, Jr. in *The Money Pit*, yet on further consideration Miller is just another run out for Hanks's characterization of the conventional guy who wants nothing more than a home and a wife. Miller articulates exactly the same ambitions and sense of self as Fielding. Surviving the bloodbath of the Omaha landing may have been nothing short of miraculous but Miller's speech reveals Hanks once again playing the ordinary guy in extraordinary circumstances. As Hanks has remarked about his heroic roles as Lovell and Miller, "[t]hey are ordinary guys who have accomplished some quite substantial things" (quoted in Freer, 2009: 184). Miller's ordinariness makes his heroic actions and eventual death while defending the bridge at Ramelle all the more poignant, for he is not fighting the war over any great principle but just doing a job and the only thing which motivates him – what he holds dear

– is returning to his wife. Hanks reportedly intervened directly in the scripting of Miller. When he first received the script, Hanks claims "Captain Miller was a stock, one-dimensional war hero who'd won the Medal of Honor and chomped on a cigar and said 'Come on, you sons of bitches'," but after he talked with Spielberg, Hanks claims "they changed every word of it" (cited in Andersen, 1998: 120). If this is correct, it would suggest the star's status granted him the creative agency to re-work Miller in ways that directly fed off the ordinariness of the Hanks brand. Miller, in his rewritten form, provided the right form of dramatic material to fit with the Hanks brand but at the same time the character was given substance and "fleshed out" by the pre-existing meaning of the Hanks everyguy identity.

With stars as with all brands, their function is to create certain perceptions about products. Hanks was therefore hired for *Saving Private Ryan* to not only play a particular dramatic role but to also provide a prism through which the film could be viewed. Hanks "endorsed" the film by lending his branded identity to the film. When thinking about the deployment of star brands, it is therefore essential to examine how stars are integrated into film marketing strategies. For DreamWorks, the studio responsible for financing and distributing the film, the Hanks brand provided a reference point to position *Saving Private Ryan* in the film market. By the time the film was released, Hanks was already a recognized box-office asset: he'd starred in or otherwise contributed to 21 feature films, accumulating a combined gross theatrical box office of nearly $1.6 billion in North America alone. Over $1 billion of that sum came from the last six films he'd taken starring roles in. Aware of their considerable box-office power, during the development of *Saving Private Ryan* Hanks and Spielberg were reported to have accepted lower upfront salaries in exchange for deals giving both 20 percent of the film's gross box office (Busch, 1996b: 1). In return, DreamWorks got a very saleable asset. Not only did Hanks take the lead role in the film but when it came to promoting the film, his name and likeness were foregrounded in marketing media. Key art for certain designs in the poster campaign was composed so that a head and shoulders portrait shot of Hanks was placed centrally and in front of similar portraits of Damon, Sizemore and Burns. His name was billed above the film title. In the theatrical trailer, Hanks is featured as a central presence: not only does his voice form a bridge to cohere the flow of images, but visually he is the first actor to be isolated in close-up. A montage of actor faces runs with their respective name credits on-screen, and Hanks is first in line before Burns, Sizemore and Damon. Just before the closing title frame of the trailer, the final shot is a short zoom-in to a big close-up of Hanks's eyes, giving the impression that everything we've seen – or rather will see, because of course trailers always function to offer promises of coming attractions – arise from Hanks's/Miller's perspective (something not borne out by the film itself). Across the posters and trailers, Hanks therefore became the most prominent and consistent element to anchor the campaign and these micro-texts give concrete form to the talent hierarchy of Hollywood stardom.

Posters and trailers are used as means of paid advertising but movie marketing also works to raise exposure and awareness through the publicity generated by press coverage. In this context, press books are not simply an information resource but a means of packaging and addressing a film to media outlets. Analysis of these materials reveals the terms in which films have been presented to media outlets with a view towards encouraging certain perceptions about a film. For *Saving Private Ryan*, the press book followed a standard format, with a plot synopsis, cast and crew lists, and profiles of the main creative talent involved in the production. Interestingly, the published profile of Hanks framed his career in particular terms.

TOM HANKS (Captain Miller) became the first actor in over 50 years to win back-to-back Best Actor Academy Awards® when he took home his second Oscar® for his unforgettable performance in the title role in Robert Zemeckis' "Forrest Gump." In addition, his work in the film brought him a Golden Globe Award and a Screen Actors Guild Award. The year before, he had been honored with his first Academy Award®, as well as a Golden Globe Award for Best Actor, for his moving portrayal of AIDS-stricken lawyer Andrew Beckett in Jonathan Demme's "Philadelphia."

The profile continued by noting Hanks's Golden Globe Award and Oscar nomination for *Big*, and Golden Globe nomination for *Sleepless in Seattle*. By way of a conclusion, the profile made perfunctory reference to "[h]is other film credits includ[ing] 'Bachelor Party', 'Splash', 'A League of Their Own', 'Punchline', 'Nothing in Common', and 'Volunteers'" (p. 31). In this selective account of Hanks's career, certain credits were included, with others excluded or marginalized. Downplaying the comedies and focusing on Hanks's awards and nominations, the profile framed and packaged Hanks's career through cataloging various markers of prestige, presenting him as a sign of artistic quality. As a vehicle for producing certain perceptions of the film, Hanks's stardom was thereby used to legitimize the artistic standing of the film. Between the star brand and the endorsed film, a chain of associations is set in play: Hanks's career is documented in a selective manner so that the artistic standing of the lead actor is imported to give gravitas to the film. In their advertising and publicity efforts, the marketing team at DreamWorks therefore not only deployed Hanks as a saleable attraction but also as a sign of artistic quality.

Released in late July 1998, the high point of the summer season when all the major Hollywood studios line-up their main event titles for the year, *Saving Private Ryan* was rolled out in North America across 2,463 theaters for an opening three-day weekend of $31 million. Eventually concluding its run in mid-November, the film grossed over $191 million at the North American box office. On 9 February the following year, the nominees for the 71st Academy Awards were announced. *Saving Private Ryan* was nominated for ten awards, including Hanks in the Best Actor category. Anticipating the film's likely success, on the weekend before the nominations were announced, DreamWorks gave the film a second run out, returning it to 1,027 theaters. With the ceremony for the 71st Academy Awards nearing, DreamWorks issued posters, hailing the "11 Academy Award Nominations" which the film had picked up, and drawing special attention to Hanks's Best Actor nomination. When the winners were announced on 21 March, *Saving Private Ryan* won in five categories, and although Hanks did not take home an award that night, in the five weeks between the announcement of the nominations and the awards ceremony, Hanks's nomination helped the film gross a further $20 million. With the Oscars over, the awards became the motor to support a theatrical re-release over another two months, so that by late May 1999, in total the film had accumulated $217 million at the domestic box office and a further $265 million internationally.

As noted in Chapter 1, stars are derivative commodities: Hollywood stars are not directly sold to the public but are used as means for selling films. Hanks's performance as Miller was therefore not sold to the public but it was deployed as one element contributing to the commercial and critical success of *Saving Private Ryan*. As discussed, anecdotal evidence suggests that during production the role was modified in ways that led to the finished performance reproducing meanings already firmly embedded in the Hanks brand. Marketing media focused on and foregrounded Hanks's presence. Hanks as Miller was just one selling point for the film and equally the star-director status of Spielberg was promoted on posters and in trailers as one of the draws for the film. Although the innovative and spectacular opening 20-minute sequence of the landing on Omaha became one of the key talking points amongst critics and audience members, it did not feature as a prominent element in the promotional campaign for the film. Alongside stardom, genre provides another mechanism for prefiguring the appeals of films. While the combat film has enjoyed a long history in American cinema, by the time *Saving Private Ryan* entered development and production it was not regarded as a popular genre, and Spielberg and Hanks were advised a new Second World War saga was unlikely to do well at the box office. The fact that the film did therefore go on to become a hit, ending 1998 ranked third on *Variety*'s top-grossing films in North America that year (Klady, 1999: 33), suggests the film's central actor and director were maybe more important factors than genre in the making of the film's commercial success.

Saving Private Ryan drew on the Hanks brand but also provided a further platform for the extension of that brand. As noted earlier, the Hanks brand has undergone various artistic, functional, executive and media extensions. This pattern continued after the completion of *Saving Private Ryan*, for Hanks and Spielberg became executive producers on *Band of Brothers*, a 10-episode television mini-series for HBO which follows Easy Company of the US Army 101st Airborne division as it fights across mainland Europe during the closing months of the Second World War. In the same manner as *From the Earth to the Moon* fed off *Apollo 13*, so *Band of Brothers* preserved thematic continuity with *Saving Private Ryan*. Again, series and feature were separate products but star brand power was invoked as the series was promoted under the banner "Tom Hanks and Steven Spielberg Present."

Continuity and Change in the Star Brand

Star brands work as vehicles for creating perceptions about films. Through the prism of the star's branded identity, films are positioned in the market across lines of similarity and difference. To have any symbolic or commercial value, the star brand must therefore present a strong and stable set of meanings. Yet star brands are never static and continually they are subject to transformation. When looking at the star brand, it is therefore necessary to not only think of how the brand functions to produce similarity and difference but also how that brand undergoes continuity and change.

As this chapter has outlined, Hanks's career progressed through a series of phases, each of which marked different stages in the making of the Hanks brand. Television work did nothing more than establish Hanks as a comedy actor, but with the film comedies of the 1980s, Hanks took a series of roles that not only affirmed his place as a leading comedy performer but also saw him acquire a distinct on-screen identity as a modern everyman. This set of meanings was firmly attached to genre but from the start of the 1990s the Hanks brand moved into a third phase as the star purposefully set about re-working his branded identity by displacing comedy with serious dramas. In many respects, this intention involved rejecting the Hanks brand and the stable set of meanings on which Hanks's stardom had been built upon. Despite these changes, however, the everyguy image remained, transcending and traversing the comedy and serious roles. After *Philadelphia* and *Forrest Gump*, by the time of *Saving Private Ryan* the Hanks brand stood not only for everyman representativeness but also award-winning acting.

Looking at Hanks therefore offers some ground for abstracting a general temporal logic in the symbolic and commercial production of the star brand. In the earliest years of their careers actors, including those who will at a later stage in their careers become stars, are initially brand-less. This is simply because, in the terms suggested by casting directors Janet Hirshenson and Jane Jenkins (2006) and outlined in Chapter 1, within the talent hierarchy they remain "wannabees," "unknowns" or "working actors." Through their acting, these categories of performer bring meaning to a film but do not fulfill the basic branding function of creating perceptions for selling the film in the market. With the "name" or a star, however, meaning is linked to commerce as the actor is deployed in the service of making a distinctive offering in the film market. By necessity, the star brand is an effect of time, as both a distinctive set of meanings and a successful commercial track record must be accumulated. The star brand is formed when by a series of commercial successes, which do not need to be consecutive, the actor is not only identified with a distinct set of meanings but also gains economic status. Those meanings form a core set of durable attributes to be deployed in most, if not necessarily all, of the star's future performances. It is the stability of these core characteristics which enables the star to continue functioning as a sign of horizontal differentiation. These meanings will persist but in due course the star brand may also acquire other attributes which then supplement and embellish the core. With star brands, it can therefore be productive to look for those meanings which define the core of the brand on top of which there is the accretion of supplementary or secondary meanings which expand the brand and possibly over time take it in new directions.

Notes

1 In North America, by the end of 2002 *Road to Perdition* had grossed $104 million and *Catch Me If You Can* had only started its run over the Christmas holiday that year but had already grossed nearly $72 million of the $165 million it would eventually amass. Two years later, *The Terminal* grossed $78 million but *The Ladykillers* was considered a resounding failure, grossing just $40 million.

2 As the film was released in North America over the last week of 1990 and continued its run into the next year, it is not possible to place it amongst *Variety*'s annual rankings. But considering the rankings for 1991 (*Variety*, 1992: 82), the amount of rentals would have ranked the film in equal 76th position.

PART TWO
Star System

4

Post-Studio Stardom

Stardom requires systematic arrangements for the collaborative production of the individual. During the 1930s and '40s the star system was largely internalized within the major studios. From the 1950s onwards a post-studio star system emerged as stars joined a growing freelance market for creative labor and relationships between those freelance stars and the studio they worked for were conducted through various intermediaries. In this context, "post-" does not mean the studios ceased to play an active part in the making of stars but rather the new system materialized as many of the main functions involved with the production of stardom moved outside the studios, Even so, the majors remained the leading financiers and distributors of films featuring stars.

Rather than a system in its own right, the production of Hollywood stardom is a sub-system within larger arrangements for the making, selling and showing of movies. A small grouping of free-standing studios dominated Hollywood in the 1930s and '40s but from the early 1960s onwards the industry experienced structural transformation as changes of ownership resulted in the studios becoming subsidiary units of larger corporations. Simultaneously, the movement of the studios into television production, together with the arrival of new technologies for the privatized exhibition and consumption of films, transformed the conduct of the studios and the film market. Consequently, the post-studio star system became a component of conglomerate Hollywood and stars circulated in a film market transformed by media diversification.

Hollywood Stardom, First Edition. Paul McDonald.
© 2013 Paul McDonald. Published 2013 by John Wiley & Sons, Ltd.

Initially this chapter outlines the system of "vertically integrated stardom" which characterized Hollywood in the 1930s and early-1940s before moving on to consider the main trends and conditions which have shaped the post-studio star system, charting the rise of conglomerate Hollywood, the functions performed by specialized intermediaries in the production of stardom, the involvement of stars in independent production, and the role of television in supplying new talent to the system.

Vertically Integrated Stardom

In the 1930s and '40s, the dominance of the American film business by five major studios – Twentieth Century Fox, Metro-Goldwyn-Mayer (MGM, a subsidiary of Loew's Inc.), Paramount, Radio-Keith Orpheum (RKO) and Warner Bros. – was achieved by their vertical integration of operations across the whole commodity chain, from film production to distribution and exhibition. Although the "Big Five" only operated a minority share of theaters in the US, their ownership of key first-run theaters gave them control over the primary window for movie consumption. Forming a second tier of firms, Columbia and Universal operated as producers and distributors, while United Artists which released films from independent producers. Collectively, the Big Five and Little Three were the largest producers and suppliers of films, with total output from these studios peaking in 1937 when they released 408 features (Weinstein, 1998: 72).[1] Independent exhibitors owned the majority of theaters in the US but were dependent on the Hollywood majors for a regular supply of films to fill their screens and meet the demand of a mass regular cinema-going public.

Making films in volume required keeping a fixed and permanent range of human, technological and physical resources on hand, and so the major studios internalized the full range of production functions. This included a regular supply of key creative personnel, with actors, directors and writers retained under long-term contracts. In this context, the majors became both the producers and owners of star talent. Certain basic practices were followed to groom and train performers to progress from novice apprentice to star (Basinger, 2009: 36–72). Exclusive service contracts not only ensured studios could make good the time and money invested in building the careers of actors but also ensured a ready supply of talent was on tap to feed the regularized production of films. As Michael Pokorny and John Sedgwick comment,

Under the circumstance that the vertically integrated majors during the classical period required upward of fifty films per season during the 1930s, it is
not unsurprising that the studios adopted a corporate approach to the
resource-coordinating problem: they chose to internalize the process through
a set of term contracts, rather than acquire human resources for the express
purpose at hand through the market . . . The internal authority structure
enabled studio executives to systematically plan for and direct the activities
of those idiosyncratic assets under contract. (2005: 173 and 78)

Contracts could be signed for a maximum of seven years, and these papers
defined the relationship of star to studio, stipulating the terms of the star's
service and compensation. By long-term contracting, studios built up and
retained impressive "stables" of stars. Paramount's star roster included
Claudette Colbert, Gary Cooper, Marlene Dietrich, Paulette Goddard, Cary
Grant and Carole Lombard. MGM, the second most powerful of the majors,
boasted it had "More stars than there are in heaven," with a stable that
included Joan Crawford, Clark Gable, Judy Garland, and Norma Shearer
all under contract. Fox's stable included Shirley Temple, Betty Grable and
Gene Tierney, while Warner Bros. could count Humphrey Bogart, James
Cagney, Bette Davis and Errol Flynn amongst its contract players. Formed
in 1930, RKO was the last of the majors to emerge and while never assembling a line-up of stars to rival the other majors, the studio's series of
musicals featuring Fred Astaire and Ginger Rogers became a highlight for
the studio in the period, with other contracted players including Irene
Dunne, Katharine Hepburn, and Robert Mitchum. As Pokorny and
Sedgwick observe, for the studios, retaining actors in this way had the
benefit of "reduc[ing] the risks associated with not securing the contracts
of desired artistes, where substitution was problematic, since studios maintained what were in effect stock companies of players" (p. 178).

Studio term-contracts specified the duration of the star's employment,
the compensation paid, and periods of work and vacation (or "lay off" as
they were known). Exclusivity was vital to monopolizing the services of an
actor. James Cagney first signed to Warner Bros. on 30 June 1930 and his
contract was headed with clauses requiring the following obligations.[2] On
the part of the studio "The Producer hereby employs and engages the Artist
to render his exclusive services as a motion picture and/or legitimate star
actor, as well as for the purpose of making records and to perform such
other duties as hereinafter provided, for and during the period of this
agreement" (p. 1). In Cagney's case "The Artist hereby accepts such employment and agrees that he will, throughout the term hereof and during any

extension thereof as hereinafter provided, act, pose, sing, speak or otherwise appear and perform solely and exclusively for and as requested by the Producer in and about its said business" (pp. 1–2). In a period when the whole industry was facing criticisms that the movies had become a morally corrupting force in society, the studios were acutely sensitive to ensuring the actors they presented on-screen could equally be beacons of acceptable behavior off-screen. Cagney's contract therefore included a standard "morality clause."

> The Artist agrees to conduct himself with due regard to public convention and morals, and agrees that he will not do or commit any act or thing that will tend to degrade him in society or bring him in public hatred, contempt, scorn, or ridicule, or that will tend to shock, insult or offend the community or ridicule public morals or decency or prejudice the Producer or the motion picture industry in general, and that he will not do or commit any act or thing that will tend to injure his capacity to at all times fully comply with and perform all of the terms and conditions of this agreement, or which will tend to injure his physical or mental qualities. (p. 11)

Although the studios were competitors, inter-firm co-operation and collusion saw stars traded between studios: "Loan of Services" clauses granted that a studio the option to "lend, rent or lease the services of the Artist or any Producer of recognized standing" (p. 11). Contractual obligations therefore gave the studios exclusive ownership of the actor's voice and body.

Contracts ran for a specified duration, usually measured in years, setting out a schedule according to which a studio held options to choose whether or not to annually extend an actor's employment for a limited run of future years, and with each extension accompanied by pay increments. These renewal points granted the space for agents and lawyers acting on behalf of stars to negotiate more favorable terms for their clients. Cagney joined Warner after a career on the stage, and with his value on the big screen untested, he initially accepted relatively modest terms of compensation and casting in supporting roles. With the lead role of Tom Powers in *The Public Enemy* (1931) (a role originally offered to his co-actor Edward Woods), however, Cagney made an impact. With nearly four years still left to run on the original contract, a new five year agreement was signed in October 1931, and when the first option extension was due for renewal, a third contract was signed. In both cases, Cagney obtained better terms of compensation (Table 4.1).

Table 4.1 James Cagney and Warner Bros.: main contract terms, 1930–49.

	1930	1931	1932	1938	1938	1939	1949
Commence	23 June	16 Sept.	9 Nov.	13 Jan.	14 March[1]	23 Oct.	6 May
Period	5 years	5 years	5 years	14 weeks	78 weeks		156 weeks
Commitments				1 film	5 films	11 films	3 films. Entitled to make three outside pictures, two for Cagney Productions and one for United Artists, although these could come from Warner Bros. if necessary.
Compensation	$400pw	$1,400pw	$3,000pw[2]	$150,000	$4,500pw first 52 weeks; $5,000pw remaining 26 weeks	$1.65m–$150,000 per film. Plus 10% of gross receipts per film after rentals exceeded $1.5 million.	$250,000 per film
Extensions	1yr $550pw 2yr $750pw 3yr $1,000pw 4yr $1,250pw	1yr $1,750pw 2yr $2,250pw 3yr $2,750pw 4yr $3,500pw	1yr $3,500pw 2yr $4,000pw 3yr $4,500pw 4yr $5,000pw				

[1] Moved to 25 April.
[2] $1,750pw paid with the remainder impounded in a trust fund at the Bank of America for Warner Bros. to file claim for damages due to any breach of contract. The studio reserved similar amounts for the four extension years.

Despite these salary inflations, Cagney continued a running battle with the studio over his pay and conditions, and disrupted production by failing to report for work. When his 1932 contract was agreed therefore, to discipline the star the terms allowed Warner Bros. to withhold a proportion of Cagney's weekly salary to be impounded in a trust fund held at the Bank of America, against which the studio could file for damages in the event of any breach of contract. When this agreement expired, Cagney broke with Warner to make a couple of films for the independent Grand National Films. This departure was short lived, however, and Cagney returned to Warner Bros. in January 1938, at which point he signed two consecutive short-term contracts binding him to making set numbers of films for the studio. A similar multi-picture agreement followed the next year, but still frustrated by his work for the studio, in 1942 Cagney teamed with his brother William to form their own independent production company, making films for distribution through United Artists. When Cagney returned to Warner Bros. for a final time in 1949, he was an independent star-producer, and agreed a deal committing him to only three films for the studio between which he could alternate two films for Cagney Productions and one for United Artists (although with the option that these be made at Warner if Cagney and the studio were willing).

Long-term contracts tied stars to studios and defined the terms by which star labor could be managed and deployed. Yet as the example of Cagney illustrates, the system was not monolithic: although the restrictive conditions laid out in contracts severely limited the autonomy of stars, there was still room for leading actors and stars to negotiate advantageous agreements. Claudette Colbert, for example, joined Paramount in the late 1920s after a successful career on the stage, and her initial five-year contract with Paramount paid a lucrative salary plus the option to continue appearing on Broadway (Parish, 1972: 97). At the time her contract was renewed in June 1936, she was able to negotiate a pact committing her to making only five films over three years with a fee of $116,666 per movie, followed by an option for a further year to make three films for $150,000 each (p. 1).[3] Alongside this fixed compensation, Colbert was also granted participation in a percentage of any gross receipts exceeding twice the production costs (see next chapter). This deal allowed Colbert to make a certain number of films for other studios, including *Tovarich* (1937) for Warner, *Drums across the Mohawk* (1939) at Fox, and *It's a Wonderful World* (1939) and *Boom Town* (Jack Conway 1940) both at MGM. By the late 1930s, Colbert had become the highest-paid star in Hollywood, earning $350,833 in 1937 and

$301,944 the following year (pp. 108–9). But after signing in 1940 for two further films, Colbert refused to renew with Paramount, preferring instead to go freelance (p. 113).

Also under contract at Paramount, Cary Grant became frustrated by what he saw as his second-tier status to the studio's main male lead, Gary Cooper. When it came time to renew his contract in 1936, Grant refused and hired theatrical agent Frank W. Vincent to negotiate his exit from Paramount. Vincent made an offer to Paramount, requesting a new deal paying Grant $75,000 per film and giving him story approval. Paramount head Adolph Zukor rejected this proposal, insisting instead that Grant make a payment of $11,800 to buy out the remaining months on his contract and commit to a last loan-out with Paramount collecting the fee. Grant agreed and was loaned to Columbia for *When You're in Love* (1937). Going freelance was a considerable risk, for although studio contracts were restrictive, they did offer actors a certain degree of career stability. Grant however benefited from the negotiating skill of Vincent who managed to persuade Harry Cohn, Columbia's president and head of production, to offer Grant a non-exclusive four film deal, paying $50,000 for the first two films and $75,000 on each of the remainders. Cohn's only stipulation was that Grant should make one movie a year for his studio, a modest request considering the five per year he'd averaged at Paramount. Vincent pushed the advantage even further when he obtained an identical contract with RKO to run simultaneously with Grant's Columbia's arrangement (Eliot, 2004: 141–5). Vincent therefore secured for his client what Marc Eliot describes as "an avant-garde deal," working on non-exclusive terms for two studios simultaneously (p. 145). Grant retained strong relationships with both studios, making films for Columbia up to 1944 and his last RKO picture came in 1948, but as a freelancer he was also at liberty to make occasional films for MGM, Warner and Grand National.

With the stars aligned with the studios, and the majors operating across the whole commodity chain, so the Hollywood of the 1930s and '40s created a system of "vertically integrated stardom": stars were made and then owned by the studios, which then deployed their creations as assets across all stages in the production, distribution and exhibition of films. While such arrangements predominated, the period also saw some performers contracting their services on a non-exclusive or freelance basis. Cagney, Colbert and Grant worked as vertically integrated stars, with their services tied to Warner and Paramount, but their careers also demonstrated how the system in this period allowed the space for actors to find opportunities for freelancing, non-exclusive pacts and independent production.

Conglomerate Hollywood

Following investigations into the economic dominance of the Hollywood studio oligopoly, in 1938 the US Department of Justice filed suit against the majors claiming unfair trade practices. Amongst the key issues here was block-booking, the practice by which distributors forced exhibitors to accept films in pre-constituted bundles. Initially the matter was settled when the studios signed consent orders in 1940 agreeing to a range of terms, including limiting to five the number of features sold in blocks. This had an immediate effect on production output: in 1940, the eight majors collectively released 363 titles but by 1950 the number had dropped to 263 (Weinstein, 1998: 72). When the studios fell short of fulfilling the obligations of the decree, further action was taken however, and in May 1948 the US Supreme Court ordered the Big Five to sell off their theater chains in a move to force a wedge between production/distribution and exhibition.[4] Industrial reorganization was not the only challenge facing Hollywood in the decades following the Second World War. In the years immediately after the war ended, affordable housing in new suburban conurbations expanded home ownership and drew populations away from the urban centers where the main first-run cinemas were located. Suburban migration combined with greater investment in family living as marriage rates increased, couples wed younger, and from the mid 1940s to the mid 1960s the "baby boom" enlarged the size of families. Furthermore, by the mid 1950s television ownership was reaching levels to capture and retain a sizable audience in the home (Gomery, 1992: 83–8). Suburbanization, new financial and familial commitments, and the distractions of cheap in-home entertainment, therefore all contributed towards a dramatic decline in cinema-going in the US which continued until the early 1970s.

Hollywood's response to these circumstances brought about large-scale changes in the organization of the film business. In the wake of the Supreme Court's decision, RKO, always the junior member of the Big Five, was split up in 1957, while MGM, once the second most powerful of the studios, commenced a decades-long decline until the studio ended up towards the periphery of Hollywood. Struggling in a shrinking film market, the remaining studios were ripe for takeover, and all the Hollywood majors gradually found new owners. Starting in the 1960s, Hollywood witnessed a first wave of conglomeration as Universal, Paramount and then Warner Bros. were all acquired by new owners. In the case of Paramount and Warner, the studios came under the ownership of corporations operating diverse business interests outside entertainment. Warner is a particularly interesting case in this context. By the end of the decade, the studio had changed hands twice, ending up the property of Kinney National Services, a company involved with the businesses of car-parking, funeral homes and cleaning services. Kinney eventually sold off its non-entertainment assets to concentrate on its film, television and music businesses, and in 1972 was renamed Warner Communications. WCI was the precursor for the second stage of conglomeration which gained momentum in the following decade as the majors became part of diversified media conglomerates, a phase characterized by News Corporation's acquisition of Fox in 1985 and Sony's takeover of Columbia in 1989. Disney had never joined the majors and by the mid 1980s its film business was in dire straits, but following a change in management, by the 1990s the studio had risen to the forefront of Hollywood.

Several of the studios passed through the hands of successive owners but these developments were just details in a larger pattern of historical change. With the rise and consolidation of conglomerate Hollywood, the studio system did not disappear but was transformed as the film pro-duction and distribution operations of the leading studios became integrated into widely diversified media corporations. By the end of the first decade of the 21st century, six major companies, all divisions of larger media and communication conglomerates, were at the center of Hollywood cinema: Twentieth Century Fox (part of News Corporation), Paramount (owned by Viacom), Sony Pictures Entertainment (a division of the Sony Corporation), Universal (part of NBC Universal), the Walt Disney Company, and Warner Bros. (a division of Time Warner). Whereas the studios of the 1930s and '40s operated as free-standing enterprises specializing in film, conglomeration resulted in the Hollywood studios becoming components of diversified media empires, with operations spread across television pro-duction and distribution, branded news and entertainment channels, video games, recorded music, consumer products, newspapers, book publishing, advertising, consumer electronics, retail chains, theme parks and resorts, and internet businesses.

Production output from the majors had begun to decline in the 1940s, but responding to the fall in admissions, the studios cut back further: by

1960, output from the majors totaled 191 titles and a decade later was down to 158 (Weinstein, 1998: 72). This had several effects. Instead of keeping in-house all the resources necessary for making films, the studios external- ized production inputs, downsizing their operations by selling off physical assets and reducing overheads by releasing costly talent from their con- tracts. Instead of aiming to produce a large slate of films, the majors adopted a project based model of production, in which personnel and resources were only brought together to make a single film. On some projects, the studios continued to self-produce but in other instances limited their role to that of financier, providing funding to independent producers to make films for the studio to distribute. With this model, it was no longer necessary for the studios to maintain all production services, and so consequently the studios either sold off their physical facilities or otherwise leased these to independents. Furthermore, with the reduction in production output, the overhead costs of retaining employees on long-term contracts could no longer be sustained and so costly stars, direc- tors and other talent were released from their contracts. As the result of these changes, conglomerate Hollywood emerged as a paradoxical con- struction. On the one hand, Hollywood became bigger as the studios were integrated into larger corporate structures, while on the other, the studios got smaller as they downsized with the externalization of production inputs drawn from outside service providers and the freelance pool of creative and craft labor.

Restructuring the industry provided a context for various other changes. Throughout its history, American cinema has seen the production of large- scale high-budget productions (Hall and Neale, 2010). By the 1990s, the industry was applying the term "event movies" to describe its most lavish high-cost productions. As the majors aimed to bring ever more elaborate scenes of spectacle to the screen, the costs of production rose (see next chapter). Inflated production expenditure exposed the studios to greater risk, which had to be balanced by building ever-larger audiences. Consequently, marketing and distribution costs increased to secure blanket advertising exposure and the reproduction of prints in the numbers neces- sary for films to open wide and create nationwide or global impact. Between 1990 and 2007, amongst the six Hollywood majors, the average cost of producing a movie swelled from $26.8 million to $70.8 million, while over the same period, average expenditure on prints and advertising for a release in North America rose from $12 million to $35.9 million (MPAA, 1999: 16 and 18, and 2008: 7).

Although the fortunes of the majors largely rested on the few event movies they released, the high costs of production and distribution encouraged the search for other lucrative market opportunities. At the start of the 1990s, independent companies were almost entirely responsible for the distribution and production of "specialty films," a catch-all phrase for any types of film falling outside the popular mainstream. Although the specialty market would remain a small niche, as the decade progressed, the majors – drawn by the healthy cost-to-profit ratios which some independent productions had achieved – began to move into the specialty market by either acquiring successful independent companies with a record of distributing and producing speciality titles, or otherwise launching their own subsidiaries for the same purpose. Unlike the mammoth costs associated with event movie production, specialty films could frequently be made on low or medium budgets, and whereas the event movie made its mark by staging conventional narrative patterns of cause and effect together with the presentation of astonishing aural and visual spectacle, certain forms of specialty film were more character than story driven, employing an aesthetic that emphasized understated actions, "quirky" characters, inconsequential scenes, and open-ended or non-linear narrative structures. With this move, the Hollywood studios muddied the distinction between the independents and the majors. Although subsidiaries of the majors, specialty producer-distributors such as Sony Pictures Classics (1992–) or Fox Searchlight (1994–) occupied the same market segment as independent producers or distributors. Consequently, these divisions formed what became known as "Indiewood," creating a three-tier structure in the American film business divided between the Hollywood majors, their Indie subsidiaries, and the genuine independent sector (King, 2009; Perren, 2012).

The increased costs of making and releasing films was offset by the emergence of new moving image media which multiplied outlets and revenue streams for film exhibition. In the battle over the economy of consumer attention, although the addition of any new media platform potentially presents film with further competition for the eyeballs of viewers, historically Hollywood has repeatedly demonstrated its eagerness to opportunistically co-opt new technologies and turn these to its own ends. With the popularization of television ownership in the 1950s, the studios not only moved into program production but also sold and licensed films for broadcast, opening a new exhibition window onto audiences outside the theater. Following the market launch of consumer price video-recorders in the late 1970s, over the next decade the majors began to form their own divisions for the distribution of films on cassette. Home entertainment divisions became standard features of the labyrinthine structures of conglomerate Hollywood, and in many cases, the same parent companies who owned the studios also ran specialized pay-TV services. Subsequently, with widespread consumer adoption of high-speed broadband, the studios made moves towards online models of film distribution. While the theatrical box office continued to provide the most visible and high-profile window for the entry of films into the marketplace, with these changes the majority of film viewing overwhelmingly shifted from the collective mode of consumption in theaters and towards more privatized contexts of consumption, either by in-home viewing or through mobile personal media platforms (e.g. laptops or phones).

The conglomeration of Hollywood was therefore accompanied by a range of concomitant trends: reductions in the number of films made and a move towards a project-based model of production; the externalization of production inputs and growth of a large freelance labor market; the risks and rewards of event movie production; muddying of the distinction between the majors and independent sectors of production and distribution; dispersal of the film market across multiple media platforms and revenue streams; and the prevalence of domestic or private methods for viewing. Amidst these changes, vertical integration did not disappear, for while the studios sold off their theaters they still maintained their distribution and production functions, and Hollywood's opportunistic cooption of new media outlets resulted in conglomerates controlling the distribution of movie to variegated exhibition windows for the dissemination of film entertainment across diverse outlets.

Representation to the Stars

Conglomeration did not represent the end of the studio system but rather its re-versioning for a new media age and marketplace. Concurrently, substantial changes reorganized the star sub-system. As already noted, freelancing was evident during the decades of the vertically integrated system, but as the studios cut their overheads and released talent, the independent status of stars was standardized. This had several effects. Freelance stars became bargaining chips, for producers needed to obtain commitments upfront from bankable stars to secure production finance. Whereas the long-term contract fixed levels of star compensation for numerous films across an extended period of time, single-picture deals gave space for the most bankable stars and their representatives to argue for ever more lucrative terms between projects, with the consequence that star fees became dramatically inflated (see next chapter). As the studios produced fewer films so stars appeared less frequently: in the 1930s, a vertically integrated star may have made three to five films every year for his or her employer, but by the 1990s it was common for stars to average maybe a single film in any year or none in some years. For the stars, this situation brought benefits and hazards. One hit could be enough for an actor to demand highly inflated remuneration for his or her next film. At the same time, because they made fewer films, expectations were raised that stars should constantly deliver at the box office. The status of the star as both possible asset and potential liability therefore intensified.

Agents, attorneys, personal managers, accountants and independent publicists were all part of the Hollywood community of the 1930s and '40s, but with the growth of the freelance labor market, these roles assumed greater importance in the production of stardom. Under the project model of production, freelance talent is signed for each separate film, intensifying the level of negotiating activity and the importance of various intermediaries to liaise between stars and studios. Talent agents obtain work for their clients but once the basic terms are in place, it is left to the lawyers to negotiate and finesse the details of "the deal." Freelance stars not only work in films but may be involved a whole array of other businesses, and so stars hire personal managers to provide overall career guidance and accountants to manage their books. Publicists meanwhile manage the media exposure of stars.

Agents and managers share certain functional similarities but there are clear grounds for demarcation between the roles. Under section 1700.4 of the California Labor Code, a talent agent or agency is classed as "a person or corporation who engages in the occupation of procuring, offering, promising, or attempting to procure employment or engagements for an artist or artists" (State of California, n.d.). License to operate is made by application to the Labor Commissioner. No similar regulation applies to managers, although as they do not have an agent license, they are forbidden from procuring work for clients. Agents will represent stars in dealings around individual professional commitments but managers pride themselves on taking a more holistic view of a star's career by providing advice across all professional and business matters. In return for the service they provide, agents receive a commission fee on client earnings: guild arrangements limit the agent's cut to 10 percent commission (hence why agents as often called "ten percenters"), although some agencies have been prepared to lower their terms in order to attract big names. Managers, on the other hand, can typically charge around 15 percent commission (Biederman, 1999: 13).

Publicists cultivate and control the public visibility of Hollywood stars: they are "gatekeepers" between stars and the media. In the 1930s and '40s, the studios managed publicity through their own in-house departments, possibly working at renaming a performer, creating a fake biography for him or her, producing a gallery of portrait and glamour photos for circulation to the press, and raising media and public awareness by "planting" stories about the performer in newspapers or film magazines. As the studios were the leading advertisers in those publications, it was not difficult to leverage the cooperation of the magazines in this process, and budding stars were introduced to influential magazine staff for interviews (Basinger, 2009: 45–56). When the studios downsized, however, the publicity function moved outside the studios. External PR companies are now involved with the production of Hollywood stardom from two directions. Studio distributors may hire external firms to handle publicity for a particular film, either during the production itself or when the film is shown at festivals, released theatrically and launched on the home entertainment market. Freelance stars also hire publicists to work for them on a personal, individual basis. In the latter capacity, the publicist's role is both proactive and reactive, pushing to create opportunities to increase a star's visibility but also possibly handling any media fallout which may occur as a consequence of a star's private off-screen indiscretions.

Acknowledging the importance of the roles played by these intermediaries and advisors invites attention to the overall structural conditions in which stardom is now produced. While business histories of Hollywood frequently concentrate on the majors, even at the height of the vertically integrated era, the leading studios always drew on services and labor from outside sources (Scott, 2005: 30). In the modern Hollywood film business, the small cluster of major studios are nodal points, owned by their conglomerate parents, supplied by the large freelance labor pool and a multitude of specialist service providers. With the rise of the post-studio star system, industrial structuring did not suddenly invent the need for agents, attorneys, managers or publicists, but rather intensified their functions. Looking at the agency business in the 1930s, Tom Kemper described agents as an "invisible subsystem . . . serving the studio system" (2010:

116–17). He suggests that acknowledging the role of agents "demonstrate[s] how the studio system actually functioned through a diffused operational network . . . show[ing] how this industry functioned through relationships and networks as much as through internal management within the major studios" (pp. 25–6). The post-studio star sub-system did not invent these networks but rather expanded their role and importance for the production of stardom. In conglomerate Hollywood, the major studios employ star clients represented by a network of intermediaries and advisors with responsibility for key tasks relating to the cultivation and management of stardom.

Although existing outside the conglomerate core of Hollywood, this network has equally been subject to the same processes of concentration and consolidation as witnessed amongst the major studios. It is useful to see this process as working in three ways. *Corporate concentration* occurred as the rise of conglomerate Hollywood was accompanied by the emergence of large corporate agencies and PR firms. During the 1940s, the William Morris Agency (WMA) and Music Corporation of America (MCA) both bought their way into Hollywood by acquiring established agencies (pp. 242–5). Under the direction of Lew Wasserman, MCA demonstrated wider ambitions, commencing television program production in 1950 through its Revue Productions division and purchasing Universal's studio facilities in 1958 (McDougal, 1998: 158 and 244). Entering television production created a conflict of interest as MCA became both employer and representative of talent. Although Guild regulations explicitly forbid such practice, in 1952 MCA obtained waivers from the Screen Actors Guild and Writers Guild of America clearing the way for MCA to continue as an agent-producer (pp. 185–7). The agency's power and influence attracted the attention of the Justice Department, however, which began investigating MCA on grounds of violating anti-trust law. Consequently, in 1962, to clear the ways for buying Decca Records – which owned a majority share in Universal – MCA voluntarily spun off the agency business, acquired Decca, and took over whole ownership of Universal in what became the earliest stage in the formation of conglomerate Hollywood (pp. 296–301). Other corporate agencies filled the gap left by MCA but a new power block emerged as WMA was joined in the mid 1970s by International Creative Management (ICM) and Creative Artists Agency (CAA) to form a triumvirate representing the majority of star talent in conglomerate Hollywood.[5] A few other names were handled by other smaller agencies: in 1991, Bauer-Benedek merged with the Leading Artists Agency as the United Talent

Agency (UTA), and in 1995 four former ICM agents established Endeavor (Mcdonald, 2008). By 2009, however, Endeavor had merged with WMA as William Morris Endeavor, so that CAA, ICM, UTA and WME formed a concentrated core of firms controlling the supply of star talent.

Similar developments occurred amongst the main PR firms representing Hollywood stars. In the mid 1990s, Baker, Winoker, Ryder (B|W|R), Bragman, Nyman and Cafarelli (BNC), Huvane Baum Halls (HBH), PMK, and Rogers & Cowan (R&C) were at the forefront of entertainment PR in Hollywood. In the space of just two years, between 1998 to 2000, advertising and marketing conglomerate Interpublic acquired R&C, PMK, BNC and HBH, with the latter three eventually merged to become PMK*BNC. B|W|R was also acquired in 1999 by Ogilvy PR, a division of the British marketing group WWP. These companies therefore integrated Hollywood stardom into the larger media economy. For these companies, film stars are just one category of client. B|W|R, for example, handled PR for Adam Sandler, Reese Witherspoon and Renée Zellweger, alongside individual clients included music stars (e.g. Christina Aguilera, Meatloaf, Britney Spears and Snoop Dogg), film and television composers (e.g. Jerry Goldsmith), film directors and producers (e.g. Judd Apatow and Jay Roach), and sports personalities (e.g. Shaquille O'Neal, Tiger Woods and Magic Johnson). Talent was only a branch of B|W|R's activities, and the company also handled publicity for numerous corporate clients (e.g. Amazon.com, Apple, Coca-Cola, eBay, Estee Lauder, General Motors, Kodak, Microsoft, Nike, Xerox, PepsiCo and Yahoo), along with fashion designers and lines, events, beverages and consumables, travel destinations, and non-profit organizations. B|W|R's Los Angeles office was a small component of WWP, an empire which in 2011 owned over 300 companies with 2,400 offices in 107 countries across Europe, North America, Latin America, the Middle East, Africa and the Asia-Pacific (WPP, n.d.). B|W|R's (n.d.) website was proud to announce the intrusive aim "Get 'em where they live . . . work . . . commute . . . shop . . . talk . . . think . . . sit . . . party . . . read . . . write . . . chill . . . fly . . . eat . . . drink . . . dance . . . play," and the company certainly had enough outlets and the right corporate organization to make that claim entirely possible. Other stars preferred to have their publicity handled by independent firms including 42West, I/D Public Relations, Slate, and WKT PR. Together, these firms represented a tight clustering of companies filtering the media exposure of Hollywood stars.

In the vertically integrated star system, the studios concentrated talent through their stables of contract players. Freelancing marked the end to that system but in the post-studio era the large corporate agencies have built similar concentrations of star assets. Corporate concentration has therefore resulted in *talent concentration* as the leading agencies stockpile star clients. MCA grew by absorbing other agencies and CAA quickly acquired a reputation for aggressively stealing leading film actors from competitors. ICM, UTA and WME represent star names in Hollywood but CAA has retained the largest and most impressive star roster of conglomerate Hollywood (Table 4.2). PR firms and entertainment attorneys keep several stars on their books, although without the same levels of talent concentration seen amongst the agency oligopoly. For stars, one of the main benefits often associated with hiring a manager is the personal one-to-one attention believed to be missing from the large agencies. However, the contrast is not so clear cut. Unlike agents, managers are not legally permitted to procure work for clients (although industry rumors suggest some have) and at the biggest agencies the most prized A-list names receive dedicated attention from teams of representatives anyway.

In the project system of film production, talent concentration provides agencies with the resources to combine actors, directors, producers and writers into temporary ensembles of creative labor. When MCA started out in the 1920s as a booking agency for music artists and bands, "packaging" talent for radio was already well practiced. Bundling talent together, an agency not only accrued the standard 10 percent commission from each individual client but also a packaging fee paid by the network. Packaging went on to become commonplace in television although how far the practice extended to film is questionable. MCA combined clients on films including *Who Was That Lady?* (1960), *Let's Make Love* (1960) and *The Misfits* (1961) (McDougal, 1998: 228 and 302–5). At WMA, agents Bill Haber, Ron Meyer, Michael Ovitz, Rowland Perkins and Mike Rosenheld became well acquainted with packaging for television, and so when they left *en masse* to form CAA, the new agency acquired a reputation for bundling together star talent for film production. Led by Ovitz, in the 1980s CAA was widely perceived to be packaging the stars, directors and writers it represented. *Stripes* (1981), *Tootsie* (1982) and *Rain Man* (1988) were just some of the films in the decade which brought together CAA stars and directors. Concerns were expressed that with packaging, the leading agencies were usurping the traditional role of the producer by directly creating projects. Yet even in the 1980s, considered the high period of film packaging, perceptions of widespread packaging far outweighed the actual prevalence of the practice. Few films involved leading talent from the same

Table 4.2 Stars, leading actors and agents, 2010.

CAA	ICM	UTA	WME
Drew Barrymore	Halle Berry	Johnny Depp	Jack Black
Cate Blanchett	Jodie Foster	Kirsten Dunst	Russell Crowe
Sandra Bullock	Samuel L. Jackson	Harrison Ford	Matt Damon
Gerard Butler	Al Pacino	Jennifer Lopez	Robert De Niro
Nicolas Cage	Mickey Rourke	Gwyneth Paltrow	Kate Hudson
Jim Carrey			Hugh Jackman
George Clooney			Keira Knightley
Jackie Chan			Edward Norton
Marion Cotillard			Adam Sandler
Daniel Craig			Ben Stiller
Tom Cruise			John Travolta
Penélope Cruz			Denzel Washington
Cameron Diaz			
Robert Downey Jr.			
Colin Farrell			
Will Ferrell			
Jamie Foxx			
Jake Gyllenhaal			
Maggie Gyllenhaal			
Tom Hanks			
Anne Hathaway			
Scarlett Johansson			
Angelina Jolie			
Nicole Kidman			
Demi Moore			
Mike Myers			
Liam Neeson			
Brad Pitt			
Keanu Reeves			
Julia Roberts			
Meg Ryan			
Will Smith			
Kevin Spacey			
Meryl Streep			
Naomi Watts			
Robin Williams			
Bruce Willis			
Kate Winslet			

Note: Correct at 21 January, 2010
Sources: compiled using data from ATA (2010) and pro.imdb.com.

agency, and even amongst those which did, the combinations were frequently made for reasons of expediency rather than calculated exploitation.
Legal Eagles (1986), for example, had all the characteristics of a package,
with CAA representing not only Robert Redford and Debra Winger but
also director Ivan Reitman and the team of writers. For their services,
Redford received $5 million, Winger and Reitman obtained $2.5 million
each, and the writers were hired for $750,000. Of the $32 million production budget, nearly one-third was therefore paid for CAA clients, and
despite the film's poor box office, CAA reaped its commissions (Davis,
1989). Rather than a hermetically formed bundle of talent conceived in the
calculating mind of an opportunistic agent, however, it was Reitman who
requested the hiring of Redford and Winger after the script was rewritten
to accommodate a romantic element (Natale and Fleming, 1991: 217). How
far packaging therefore became common practice or merely a new mythology in Hollywood is debatable. Rather than orchestrating packages, agents
more commonly simply combined talent on films.

Applying the term "Hollywood" to film creates a unity between industry
and place. Los Angeles is not only home to the major studios but is also
the locational site for the *geographic concentration* of leading talent agents,
managers, attorneys, and PR firms representing stars (Figure 4.1). Many of
these businesses are not located in the district of Hollywood itself but
situated in Beverly Hills, Burbank, Culver City and Santa Monica. As
Allen J. Scott (2005: 14) notes, industrial agglomeration is characterized by
"the dense gathering together of many individual units of production in
one place, and . . . by the existence of strong functional inter-dependencies
and overspill effects . . . linking these units together." This pattern of locational concentration benefits the operational efficiency of industries by
"increasing-returns effects that bolster the competitive advantages of every
individual unit of production out of which it is composed" (p. 14). In the
star sub-system, all interested parties – stars, agents, attorneys, managers,
publicists and studio executives – benefit from how proximity enables them
to directly participate in exchanges of knowledge. On the agents of the
1930s, Kemper comments

> A routine rendezvous involving an agent and client or studio executive
> facilitated important swaps of information. An exchange performed, for
> example, in the informal setting of a restaurant, within the speculative
> and contingent manner of gossip (the latest information about artists and
> projects or hypothetical explorations of combinations of clients on particu-
> lar projects) could subsequently translate into serious deals. Serious deal

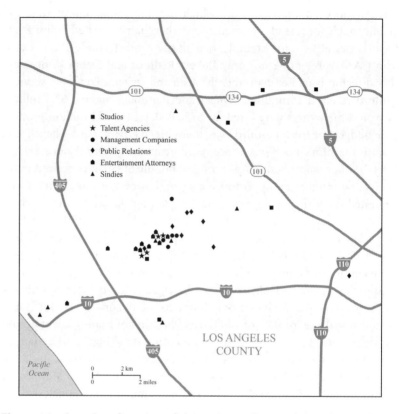

Figure 4.1   Star city: clustering of the major studios, sindies and providers of services to stars.

making relied on free-form explorations; on casual, uncommitted conversations; and accurate, up-to-date reports. (2010: 6–7)

These same benefits and ways of working have continued and extend to the whole network of suppliers and buyers of star talent in conglomerate Hollywood: to be in the movie town is fundamental to being in the know. Amongst this situated community, the close clustering of businesses creates a definite place for the production of Hollywood stardom, a locus which may be termed "Village Hollywood." As the products and output of this locale are dispersed across geographically extended space and time, so Village Hollywood feeds Global Hollywood. As Scott notes,

In one sense, Hollywood is a very specific place in Southern California, and, more to the point, a particular locale-bound nexus of production relationships and local labor market activities. In another sense, Hollywood is everywhere, and in its realization as a disembodied assortment of images and narratives, its presence is felt broadly across the entire globe. (2005: 138)

In the post-studio star system Village Hollywood represents the geographic concentration of firms in Los Angeles which works as an engine for making and disseminating film-star fame to the world's leading film markets.

Reflecting on the demise of vertically integrated stardom, Jeanine Basinger argues "there's no longer one simple system creating and defining stars for the public's endorsement. In short, there is no star machine. It's gone with the wind" (2009: 525–26). This would not seem to be the case, however, for a "machine" has very much survived, only in different form. Corporate, talent and geographic concentration have ensured the production of stardom still operates through a tightly circumscribed network of "players." The post-studio star sub-system is a network of leading agents, PR firms, personal managers and attorneys who conduct the various functions involved with the production of stardom. Star publicity is further integrated into the larger media economy as many of the leading PR firms representing Hollywood A-listers are also owned by larger advertising or marketing corporations.

Star-Producers

With the vertical disintegration of the majors in the decades following the Second World War, opportunities arose for independent producers to fill the gap in the market left by the reduction in output from the studios. Many of the newly freelance stars therefore took the opportunity to establish their own production companies. This was not an altogether new trend. Constance Bennett had partnered in the short-lived Bennett Pictures (1935) and her sister Joan collaborated with director Fritz Lang and her husband, the producer Walter Wanger, in Diana Productions (1947). After Warner contract players James Cagney and Bette Davis warred with the studio's management, the formation of Cagney Productions (1942–53) and B. D. Productions (1942) were declarations of independence. These were early steps in a trend which was to snowball from the late 1940s onwards. Humphrey Bogart's Santana Pictures/Productions (1949–53), Alan Ladd's

Jaguar Productions (1954–60), Kirk Douglas's Bryna Productions (1955–), Marilyn Monroe Productions (1956–7), and Marlon Brando's Pennebaker Productions (1957–65) marked a wave of star-led independent production companies. Husband and wife Tony Curtis and Janet Leigh carried their relationship over to a business marriage with Curtleigh (1957–60), and in the latter years of his career, Cary Grant was appearing in films made through his independent companies Grandon (1958–60), Granart (1959), Granley (1962–6) and Granox (1964).

Many of the star-led independents were short-lived, in some cases making maybe no more than one or two films, but others became well established features in the newly restructured industry. This was especially apparent in the cases of those companies which expanded into television production. After the film *A Man Called Sullivan* (1945), Bing Crosby Productions (1945–79) completed a number of further features but made its biggest mark as a prolific producer of television series including hospital drama *Ben Casey* (1961–6) and prisoner of war comedy *Hogan's Heroes* (1965–71). Before entering film, Crosby had already moved between media working as a recording artist and appearing on radio, but his company further expanded the star's presence when it commenced production of the television showcase *The Bing Crosby Show* (1964–5). In a similar fashion, after making a number of films, producer Marty Melcher used his company Arwin (1954–73) to create a further outlet for his wife's talents through *The Doris Day Show* (1968–73). John Wayne partnered with producer Robert Fellows to form Wayne-Fellows Productions in 1952 and starting with *Big Jim McLain* (1952) made a number of films featuring the company's star principal, including *Hondo* (1953). After Wayne bought out Fellows, the company was renamed Batjac (1953–74) and continued making films fronted by the star for another two decades, along with a television series of *Hondo* (1967) (not featuring Wayne) aired on the ABC network.

Burt Lancaster was a key exemplar of the emergent star-producer. Agent Harold Hecht was instrumental in launching the film career of Lancaster and the two went on to partner in the formation of Hecht-Norma Productions in 1948 and Hecht-Lancaster (1954–5), before producer James Hill joined in 1957 to form Hecht-Hill-Lancaster. The movement of stars like Lancaster into production management is part of what Denise Mann (2008) describes as the "postwar talent takeover" of Hollywood. Stars not only gained a greater say in creative decision making but also actively participated in the development of film projects as they combined the roles of actor and producer. As Mann notes, this change saw "the ascension of a new generation of professional-managerial cultural workers" (p. 243). Although free of direct studio control, stars and their companies relied on production financing and distribution from the studios: in the case of Hecht and Lancaster, their ventures were bankrolled by United Artists and the films released by the studio.[6]

In conglomerate Hollywood, the star-led independent production company, or what will be referred to here as the "sindie," has now become an established feature of the industry landscape (Table 4.3). Star-producers combine the creative and business extensions discussed in Chapter 2: the star not only participates in the creative functions of developing and steering productions but may also be involved to some extent in the business responsibilities of managerial decision-making and raising finance. However, the real business acumen is usually provided by teaming with a partner who has experience and expertise in other aspects of the business. Tom Cruise linked up with his former agent Paula Wagner to form Cruise/Wagner, while Adam Sandler partnered with producer Jack Giarraputo to form Happy Madison. George Clooney and director Steven Soderbergh established Section Eight, and after that company closed, Clooney launched Smoke House Productions with producer Grant Heslov. Although independent, in many cases sindies are tied to major studios with first-look deals, by which a studio pays the company's overheads and provides development financing in return for right to first refusal on the production or distribution of films developed by the sindie (Cones, 1992: 197). With the studio bankrolling the creative independence of stars, such arrangements often lead to the charge that the studio-sindie relationship is nothing more than a "vanity deal." First-look arrangements do not exclusively bind sindies to studios and so both star and company remain at liberty to make films for other studios. While the star is the figurehead, he or she will not appear in all productions from the independent outfit and may still make films without any involvement from the sindie. Working through their own companies provides stars with not only creative but also financial benefits. A star can lower his or her tax burden by channeling income through the company, so that taxation is paid under capital gains instead of the higher rate applied to personal income.

Sindies condense many of the dynamics at work in the post-studio star system. Not only do they represent the creative and business extensions of stars but also show how, despite their independent status, freelance stars still retain close affiliations with the major studios. For example, in June

Table 4.3 Stars and sindies: selected names and companies.

Star sindie (years of operation)	Partners	Studio affiliations	Selected productions featuring the star	Selected productions with the star as producer or executive producer
George Clooney				
Section Eight Productions (1999–2006)	Steven Soderbergh	Warner Bros. (1999–2006)	Ocean's Eleven (2001), Syriana (2005), The Good German (2006)	Insomnia (2002), Far from Heaven (2002), A Scanner Darkly (2006)
Smoke House Productions (2006–)	Grant Heslov	Warner Bros. (2006–9) Sony (2009–)	Leatherheads (2008), The Men Who Stare at Goats (2009), The American (2010)	
Tom Cruise				
Cruise/Wagner Productions (1992–)	Paula Wagner	Paramount (1992–2006) & United Artists (2006–)	Mission: Impossible (1996), War of the Worlds (2005), Lions for Lambs (2007)	Without Limits (1998), The Others (2001), Elizabethtown (2005)
Mel Gibson				
Icon Entertainment (1989–)	Bruce Davey	Warner Bros. (1991–9), Paramount (1996–2002) & Fox (2002–4)	Hamlet (1990), Braveheart (1995), Payback (1999), We Were Soldiers (2002)	The Passion of the Christ (2004), Paparazzi (2004), Apocalypto (2006)
Tom Hanks				
Playtone (1998–)	Gary Goetzman		Cast Away (2000), The Polar Express (2004), Charlie Wilson's War (2007)	My Big Fat Greek Wedding (2002), The Ant Bully (2006), Mamma Mia! (2008)
Brad Pitt				
Plan B (2002–)	Brad Grey & Jennifer Aniston (2002–5)	Warner Bros. (2002–5) & Paramount (2005–)	The Assassination of Jesse James by the Coward Robert Ford (2007)	Charlie and the Chocolate Factory (2005), The Departed (2006), A Mighty Heart (2007)

Adam Sandler				
Happy Madison (1999–)	Jack Giarraputo	Sony/Columbia (1999–)	Little Nicky (2000), I Now Pronounce You Chuck & Larry (2007), You Don't Mess with the Zohan (2008)	Deuce Bigalow: Male Gigolo (1999), Anger Management (2003), The House Bunny (2008)
Ben Stiller				
Red Hour Productions (2001–)	Stuart Cornfeld & Jeremy Kramer	DreamWorks (2001–9) Fox (2009–)	Zoolander (2001), Dodgeball (2004), Tropic Thunder (2008)	Tenacious D in The Pick of Destiny (2006), Blades of Glory (2007), The Ruins (2008)
Will Smith				
Overbrook Entertainment (1997–)	James Lassiter & Ken Stovitz	Universal (1997–2001) & Sony/Columbia (2002–)	Ali (2001), I, Robot (2004), Hitch (2005), I Am Legend (2007)	Saving Face (2004), The Secret Life of Bees (2008), Lakeview Terrace (2008)
Reese Witherspoon				
Type A Films (2000–)	Debra Siegal	Intermedia Film (2000–2) & Universal (2002–)	Legally Blonde 2: Red, White & Blonde (2003), Penelope (2006), Four Christmases (2008)	

2002 Brad Pitt partnered with Brad Grey to form the sindie Plan B. Jennifer Aniston, a leading actor in her own right and at the time married to Pitt, became an equity partner in the venture. Grey owned the leading management firm Brillstein-Grey, which alongside Pitt and Aniston represented over 150 clients, including Adam Sandler and Nicolas Cage, and the television production division Brad Grey Television produced many series for network and cable, including *The Sopranos* (1999–2007) (Fleming and Adalian, 2005). Plan B secured a three-year first-look deal with Warner Bros., who supported the venture by supplying development funding and granting the two Brads first-dollar gross participation in any films they produced (Fleming and Harris, 2002). Many projects were in development but Plan B had still to produce a film when in January 2005 Grey departed to take the post of chairman and CEO of Paramount. Shortly afterwards, with their marriage in trouble, Aniston and Pitt announced they would be separating, and Pitt took over Plan B. Although Grey had limited know-how of film production and no experience of running a studio, when Paramount appointed him it was recognized the studio was primarily buying his expertise in fostering talent relations (McNary, 2005: 27). Grey was able to quickly deliver on that reputation. Within hours of the new head joining the studio, Paramount announced the signing of Pitt to do *Babel* (2006), and when Plan B's Warner deal was due to expire, in June 2005 the sindie moved to Paramount for a new three-year first-look deal (Foreman, 2005; McNary and McClintock, 2005). Plan B projects *Charlie and the Chocolate Factory* (2005) and *The Departed* (2006) had been in development at Warner and were distributed by that studio but with the release of *Year of the Dog* (2007) and *A Mighty Heart* (2007) through the specialty subsidiary Paramount Vantage, the transition was completed. Although Pitt's star power undoubtedly obtained Plan B advantages unlikely to be granted to many other independent production outfits, the company did not become a promotional outlet for the star. With the exception of *The Assassination of Jesse James by the Coward Robert Ford* (2007), Pitt did not appear in Plan B productions, preferring instead to remain a producer. "We made an edict at the beginning that we would focus on stories and storytellers," he claims: "I get to be part of stories that I may not be right for as an actor; but as a film lover I think they're amazing stories to tell" (quoted in Hayes, 2006: 14).

Most sindies remain relatively small-scale outfits, producing a few occasional films and relying on the distribution operations of major studios for releasing in domestic and international markets. Mel Gibson's Icon

Productions, however, became a mini-studio, producing dozens of films, establishing operations in international territories, diversifying from film into television, and vertically integrating production and distribution functions. By the late 1980s, Gibson was already a major box-office draw but even his bankability was not enough for any major studio to green-light a new feature version of *Hamlet* with himself in the lead. Icon was therefore founded in August 1989 with the purpose of making *Hamlet* (1990), teaming Gibson's star value with the business know-how of his former accountant Bruce Davey. Gibson became chairman and steered creative matters while Davey handled business affairs for the company and its productions (Moore, 1996: N18). Icon financed *Hamlet* and distribution was handled by Warner Bros., the studio which Gibson had already formed a strong relationship with after starring in the first two installments of the *Lethal Weapon* (1987/1989) series.

In January 1991, the relationship between star, sindie and studio was further consolidated with a first-look deal and Icon established its office on the Warner lot. There followed a run of Icon productions for Warner Bros. starring Gibson, with *Forever Young* (1992), Gibson's directorial debut *The Man Without a Face* (1993), and *Maverick* (1994). As the 1990s progressed, however, Icon expanded beyond its star asset, producing a generically eclectic range of films, including teenpic *Airborne* (1993) and thriller *187* (1997) for Warner, and making the period drama *Immortal Beloved* (1994) for Columbia. While the Warner deal gave Icon the security of studio backing, it also limited the company's negotiating power: "I think the traditional first-look producing deal is handcuffs," Davey commented (quoted in Shackleton, 1996). To expand its options, Icon therefore formed an unusual arrangement in February 1996 when Ed Limato and Jeff Berg, Gibson's agents at ICM, together with attorney Nigel Sinclair, secured concurrent deals with Warner and Paramount committing Icon to making four films for each studio over three years (Galloway, 1996b). Paramount had courted Gibson after paying Icon $17.5m for the US rights to *Braveheart* (1995), on which Gibson starred and directed (Johnson, 1996b). These commitments remained largely unfulfilled, as Icon made *187* and *Leo Tolstoy's Anna Karenina* (1997) for Warner, while Gibson starred in *Payback* (1999) for which Paramount took care of domestic distribution and Warner handled releasing in certain international territories. When this arrangement expired, Icon ended its relationship with Warner, signing a three-year first-look deal with Paramount and moving offices onto the studio's lot (Hindes, 1999a; Kit, 1999a).

Icon expanded its functions and territorial reach with Icon Entertainment International (IEI), established in September 1995 as a London-based international sales office for Icon productions and third-party films the company took an interest in (Dunkley, 1995). To build a film library, IEI acquired international rights to 20 films from the US producer-distributor Kings Road Entertainment and paid Italian media group RCS £10 million to acquire the London-based sales company Majestic and its 220 film title library, including certain of Icon's own productions which Majestic had co-financed (e.g. *The Man Without a Face*) (Dawtry, 1996; Fleming, 1995b; Galloway, 1996a). From November 1998, Icon increased its presence in the UK market as Icon Film Distribution (IFD) was launched to handle the UK theatrical releasing for Icon productions and films from other producers (Carver, 1998; Honeycutt, 1998). Icon also became involved with UK production on the comedies *Spice World* (1997), *Kevin and Perry Go Large* (2000) and *Blackball* (2003). A second IFD division followed in February 2001 to cover Australia and New Zealand (Murdoch, 2001). IFD became the leading independent distributor in Australia and in 2008 further asserted its presence in the territory after acquiring the distributor Dendy Films and arthouse exhibition chain Dendy Cinemas (Boland, 2008; Bulbeck, 2008). Territorial expansion was accompanied by media diversification, with television becoming part of Icon's production portfolio as the company made feature-length productions *Bravo Two Zero* (1999) for the BBC, *The Three Stooges* (2000) for ABC and cable movie *Invincible* (2001) for TBS Superstation, along with the comedy and drama series *Complete Savages* (2004–5), *Kevin Hill* (2004–5) and *Clubhouse* (2004–5).

In the UK and Australia/New Zealand Icon could self-distribute in leading overseas English-language territories, and so when the Paramount deal was up for renewal in 2002, the sindie was unprepared to concede to the studio's request to retain foreign rights to Icon productions. Icon moved on, signing a two-year first-look deal with Fox, the company responsible for handling the international release of *Braveheart* (Gardner and Kilday, 2002). With *Paparazzi* (2004) the only outcome, the deal delivered very little, and after Fox passed on backing the Icon production *The Passion of the Christ* (2004), Gibson's directorial depiction of the last day of Christ with dialog in Aramaic, Hebrew and Latin, there was a clear parting of interests between the two parties (Snyder and Brodesser, 2004). Instead Icon raised the financing independently, with Fox securing domestic home video rights and theatrical distribution in the Catholic-dense Latin

American markets of Argentina and Brazil. Once the Fox deal expired and
Passion grossed $370.8 million domestically and $241.1 million internationally, Icon resisted signing any further first-look deals with the majors.
On the subject of forming long-term attachments with studios, Gibson
commented,

> There are advantages and disadvantages. If you are affiliated with one of the
> studios, they are the back wall, and they support you. If they are not there,
> there is no net. But if you manage to make it across to the other side, you'll
> be all right. Even though we don't have an overall deal with a studio, there
> is no reason why we can't just partner up with them on a thing or two.
> (quoted in Galloway, 2004).

Without studio ties, Icon self-financed Gibson's next directorial project,
Apocalypto (2006), but opened up competitive bidding for distribution
rights, with Disney winning North American rights for theatrical and video
while a range of independent companies acquired the rights to international territories (Fleming, 2005). There was some scaling back of Icon's
international operations when the IEI and IFD divisions in the UK were
sold in November 2009 to Stadium Entertainment, a venture backed by
New York industrial group Access Industries. Despite the sale, the UK division retained the Icon name and agreed a first-look deal with Icon
Productions while continuing to jointly acquire territorial distribution
rights with Icon Australia (McNary, 2009).

As these examples suggest, in the post-studio system, star agency is dispersed across multiple functions, territories and media. As actor, producer,
director, chairman and businessman, Gibson represents the full range of
creative and business extensions of stars in the post-studio system. Through
Icon, Gibson not only featured as a leading actor but also a commercially
successful producer and director, heading a company with operations
spread across three continents. These extensions do not only represent the
star occupying a wider range of jobs. On *The Man without a Face* and
Braveheart, Gibson both directed and starred, and so posters for the films
naturally featured his name for star billing. With *The Passion of the Christ*
and *Apocalypto* however, Gibson did not act, yet his name was still used to
advertise "A Mel Gibson Film" and "Mel Gibson's *Apocalyto*." Deploying the
name in this way extended the Gibson brand, for although the star made
no appearance in the films, his identity was still used as a promotional
prism through which to create perceptions of the films.

Sources of Stars

Hollywood film stardom has always been a multiple-media system. Film
advertising and publicity employ the full panoply of broadcast, print and
online media to address audiences, while the star sub-system draws on
names from other entertainment media to replenish the supply of film
talent. In the first half of the twentieth century, acting talent was recruited
from the dramatic stage (e.g. Humphrey Bogart, Claudette Colbert, Bette
Davis, Clark Gable, Greer Garson, Katharine Hepburn, Gregory Peck,
James Stewart and Spencer Tracy) while comedians came from vaudeville
(e.g. Bud Abbott and Lou Costello) or nightclubs (e.g. Dean Martin and
Jerry Lewis). Singers transitioned from fronting dance bands to carving out
recording and possibly radio careers (e.g. Gene Autry, Bing Crosby, Doris
Day, Dick Powell, Frank Sinatra) before entering films. Sports occasionally
also supplied the system, with figure skater Sonja Henie and competitive
swimmers Johnny Weissmuller and Esther Williams starting up new careers
in Hollywood.

In the decades after the Second World War, however, it was television
which became the main breeding ground for Hollywood stardom. From
the late 1940s, US television created its own separate star system and during
the 1950s cross-media interactions expanded as Hollywood film actors
made regular or guest appearances on the small screen (Murray, 2005;
Becker, 2008). By poaching existing names, television stole "*pre-sold* stars
for the new medium" (emphasis added, Murray, 2005: xiii). Equally, film
plundered television actors, with some names eventually rising to the
Hollywood A-list. In the 1960s, Clint Eastwood segued from television
cowboy to film cowboy, and during the next decade, Burt Reynolds jumped
from dramatic theater to television and then film. During the 1980s, television series *Bosom Buddies* (1980–2), *Family Ties* (1982–9), *Mork and Mindy*
(1978–82) and *Moonlighting* (1985–9) were respectively the springboards
for the film careers of Tom Hanks, Michael J. Fox, Robin Williams and
Bruce Willis. Likewise, *In Living Color* (1990–4), *Glory Days* (1990) and *St.
Elsewhere* (1982–8) were stepping stones in the career trajectories of Jim
Carrey, Brad Pitt and Denzel Washington as they rose to the A-list in the
1990s. NBC's long-running comedy and variety showcase *Saturday Night
Live* (1975–) has been a magnet for performers from television, film and
music, and appearances on the show featured prominently in the early
careers of many of the key comic actors and stars of conglomerate

Hollywood, including Billy Crystal, Eddie Murphy, Mike Myers, Dan Ackroyd, Ben Stiller, and Will Ferrell.

Shifting from television to film has not always followed a linear path of progression to Hollywood stardom. George Clooney spent many years juxtaposing supporting roles in television series and films until his main stint (1994–9) as Dr Doug Ross on the Warner Bros.-produced television medical drama *ER* (1994–2009) led to film leads. For several years, Clooney was concurrently a well known television actor while emerging as a rising film performer with his roles in *From Dusk Till Dawn* (1996), *One Fine Day* (1996), *Batman and Robin* (1997) and *The Peacemaker* (1997). Television fame is not a precondition of film fame and there are many cases where an inauspicious television career has provided merely a training ground for future film names. Sandra Bullock, Meg Ryan, Ben Stiller and Renée Zellweger all moved from undistinguished television careers to what, at least for an initial number of years, were undistinguished film careers. Television has therefore occupied two roles in the Hollywood film star system: as a platform for building pre-sold fame and as a screen apprenticeship. While noting these connections, it is important to also recognize how television fame has never guaranteed film success. NBC sitcom *Friends* (1994–2004) captured a massive international audience and so understandably when the show ended, Hollywood studios were keen to sign members of the main cast (Jennifer Aniston, Courtney Cox, Lisa Kudrow, Matt LeBlanc, Matthew Perry and David Schwimmer) for films. All landed leading roles but only Aniston maintained any semblance of a notable record of lead film credits, although even she never joining the A-list pantheon.

In the post-studio star sub-system, US television has become the primary source of new talent but other in-roads to stardom have still remained. Tom Cruise, Matt Damon, Johnny Depp, Angelina Jolie and Julia Roberts also rose to film stardom with little or no involvement from television. These are therefore examples of *film-generated film stardom*. Jackie Chan, Russell Crowe, Mel Gibson (American born but starting his acting career in Australia) and Nicole Kidman are just some of the most recent names in the long history of transnational in-flows of actors supplying the Hollywood star system. Each established their names through working in film and/or television overseas before moving to Hollywood and as such represent *imported film stardom*. Following the examples of Bing Crosby, Doris Day and Frank Sinatra, Will Smith achieved *cross-media stardom* as his film career was energized by the fame he achieved in music and television (see

Chapter 6). These transitions built on the pre-sold value of fame between entertainment media but in other cases actors have achieved stardom after careers outside the entertainment field: Cameron Diaz carved out a film career after modeling and former competitive bodybuilder Arnold Schwarzenegger showed how sports still occasionally produce film stars. With these cases, Hollywood has witnessed instances of *cross-sector stardom*.

Returning to television, it is important to situate this breeding ground for film stardom within the same patterns of corporate concentration which have shaped the film industry. The feeder and training functions performed by television further place the production of Hollywood stardom outside the province of the film studio oligopoly. However, television performers gain the widest exposure through the concentrated bottleneck of the main US networks – ABC, CBS, NBC and Fox. But as changes of ownership have brought those networks under the same conglomerate parentage as the major film studios, then it becomes necessary to recognize that it is not the major film studios nor the leading television networks which hold centralized control over the dissemination of Hollywood stars, but rather it the diversified media conglomerates who are the purveyors of stardom.

Dependently Independent Stars

Conglomerate Hollywood has provided the industrial context for the formation of the post-studio star sub-system. With vertically integrated stardom, stables of stars were retained by the studios under long-term contract, but the post-studio system emerged from the 1940s onwards as freelancing became standardized and key functions involved in the production of stardom moved outside the studios to be conducted by various categories of external service provider. With the post-studio system, film stardom is now produced and disseminated across an industrial nexus which includes the major studio financier-producer-distributors and the US television networks (in most cases with the same owners), along with talent agents, PR firms, entertainment attorneys and personal managers.

Freelance employment, negotiating power, inflated salaries, independent companies, and creative autonomy: with all these factors in play, it may be assumed post-studio stardom has floated free of the studio oligopoly. Despite these changes, the studios have remained central to the workings of stardom. Independence may have complicated the relationships between stars and studios but modern Hollywood stardom is still dependent on the majors. In conglomerate Hollywood, the six majors are the main employers of star talent. Only the majors have the resources available to finance the types of film paying the levels of compensation demanded by star names. Ownership of independent companies may give stars greater say in production decisions but frequently these operations are bankrolled by the majors. Actors can only become stars because they appear in films variously distributed, financed or produced by the majors. To gain the widespread exposure which confirms their fame, stars need to appear in films supported by global distribution networks and marketing operations which only the major studios can provide. As the main site of film consumption shifted from the theater to the home, so it is the home entertainment divisions of the majors which have had the reach and influence to saturate retail and rental outlets with multiple video copies. Furthermore, the majors now belong to the same corporate parents who own the national television networks or who operate pay-TV services channeling films into the home. With the majors therefore controlling the main means for the production and circulation of film, paradoxically Hollywood stardom gained independence over the very same period as stars became even more dependent on a small cluster of companies to provide opportunities to make their films and to bring them to the attention of audiences across globally extended media markets. In short, Hollywood stars still need the majors, for post-studio stardom has not removed the central importance of the majors as the key makers and disseminators of star-driven entertainment.

Even so, the transition from the vertically integrated to the post-studio systems has effected real change in the production of stardom and the relationship between the stars and the studios. Schematically mapping oppositions (Table 4.4) between these systems may suggest a wholesale historical transition from one system to another, although strong strands of continuity have persisted between the two. In many respects, post-studio stardom did not *replace* the vertically integrated system but rather *unlocked and regularized* opportunities for creative and managerial independence which had remained irregular and intermittent in the former era. In a system where long-term exclusive contracts were commonplace, vertically integrated stars could only obtain *limited independence* in their creative and business affairs. Post-studio stardom unlocked this independence. And yet,

Table 4.4 Main features of vertically integrated vs. post-studio stardom.

	Vertically integrated stardom	Post-studio stardom
Industry organization		
Studios	Free-standing studios Oligopoly of five major firms vertically integrating film production, distribution and exhibition	Subsidiaries of media and entertainment conglomerates Oligopoly of six major firms vertically integrating production and distribution for film and television. Parent companies diversified across other media, e.g. music, games
Production	Full-service studios Internalize inputs In-house production Central-producer and producer-unit systems Series production	Studios financing independent producers and contracting services from network of specialized firms Externalize inputs Studios engaged in direct production and financing of independent producers Package-unit system Project production
Distribution	Concentrated amongst the majors Dominance of domestic market	Concentrated amongst the majors Dominance of domestic market Increased importance of international market
Exhibition	Mass audience Theatrical	Segmented audience Theatrical, home video, pay-TV, free TV, online
Stars		
Relation to studios	Exclusive long-term contracts Limited freelance opportunities Limited independence	Freelance Dependent independence
Contracts	Term contracts Few single or multi-picture deals	Single or multi-picture deals
Agents	Liaison between stars and studios Small- and mid-scale businesses	Procuring work for star clients Large corporate agencies
Managers	Personal advice and career coaching	Personal advice and career coaching
Publicists	Produced by the publicity departments of the studios	Controlled by external PR firms

in the post-studio star system, the creative and working freedoms enjoyed by freelancing stars have been accompanied by the binding of the major studios into large media and communications corporations with powerful control over the outlets and channels through which films reach the public. Independent of the studios while reliant on the studios, working for the studios but not owned by the studios – these are the very dynamics which define the working contradictions of stardom in conglomerate Hollywood as the relationship of stars to studios has become characterized by conditions of *dependent independence.*

Notes

1   This volume of releases comprised titles directly made by the studios together with films either subcontracted to "Poverty Row" or made by smaller independent production companies, and included some imports, particularly from Britain.

2   The following section draws on the Cagney legal files held in the Warner Bros. Archives, University of Southern California. Quotations are taken from the 1930 contract.

3   Initially the agreement was for seven films but was revised in 1940. From contract summary dated 10 June 1936 with revisions dated between 1937 and 1944 in the Paramount production files at the Margaret Herrick Library.

4   Although the majors were allowed to retain their premiere city center venues.

5   Paralleling the rise of conglomerate Hollywood, the agency business experienced its own complex history of acquisitions and mergers. The Ashley Famous Agency, the business of former WMA agent Ted Ashley, was sold to Kinney National Services in 1967. Two years later Kinney acquired Warner Bros.-Seven Arts, but as the owner of a studio and an agency, Kinney confronted the same conflict of interest as MCA at the time of the Decca deal, and so the agency was sold off to Marvin Josephson Associates where the business was merged with London International to become the International Famous Agency (IFA). Former MCA agents Freddie Fields and David Begelman established Creative Management Associates (CMA) in 1963 and five years later absorbed the General Artists Corporation (GAC). Marvin Josephson Associates in turn bought out CMA in 1975, merging the business with IFA to form International Creative Management (ICM) (Rose, 1995: 306 and 338–9; and Stine, 1985: 373 and 378–9). Creative Artists Agency was formed in January 1975 when five agents left WMA, and to quickly build a client list, in October 1976 CAA merged with the Martin Baum Agency, inheriting the latter's roster of star clients (Slater, 1997: 43–55 and 74).

6 In many respects, United Artists had prefigured the structural model of independence on which the whole post-studio star system would later be founded. Established in 1919 by star actors Charlie Chaplin, Douglas Fairbanks and Mary Pickford, together with star director D. W. Griffith, the motivation behind launching the studio was to form an independent company that provided its founders with creative and financial control over their work. Rather than become a full producing studio, UA subsequently functioned as distributor and financier for films from independent producers.

5

Money and Talent

There is a financial paradox at the heart of Hollywood stardom. On the one hand, the industry treasures stars for their value at the box office, while on the other complaining the astronomical levels of compensation paid to stars inflate production costs, thereby limiting the potential for films to reach profits. Edgar Morin noted "in the composition of the unpredictable alloy that constitutes a film, the star is the most precious and therefore the costliest substance" (1961: 6). Similarly, John Sedgwick observes:

> Stars are human capital . . . the outcome of past investment decisions in the formation of an idiosyncratic persona . . . and function as a means of attenuating the financial risk associated with film projects, while paradoxically adding to it as a consequence of the high fees they are able to charge for their services. (2000: 180)

In the post-studio system, stars are free agents and can be hired by any studio hoping to reap the financial advantages of attaching a star to a film. At the same time, with that freedom the price of talent can always be argued upwards. Stars may, and it is only *may*, bring riches but equally demand riches in return. Stars are both asset and burdens, guarding against risk while increasing risk.

Concentrating on this economic contradiction, this chapter initially looks at the place of stars in the market for Hollywood films over the period 1990 to 2009, exploring industry beliefs in the value of stars and analyzing how stars performed at the box office over the two decades. This is followed

Hollywood Stardom, First Edition. Paul McDonald.

by an examination of the costs of hiring stars. Due to belief in their commercial power, stars receive high levels of fixed compensation paid as a set
fee and contingent compensation in the form of participating in a share of
income from a film. The chapter explores the inflation of star fees from the
1980s onwards and how stars share in revenues through elaborate gross
participation arrangements. The excesses of star compensation have been
widely viewed as signaling how the post-studio system has seen stars wrestle
power away from the studios, but the chapter concludes by looking at how
changes in the film market have provided producers with opportunities to
re-model star compensation in the name of new fiscal constraints.

Analyzing the economics of Hollywood stardom faces certain obstacles.
Studios do not publish the exact details of production budgets or revenues.
While the business openly and proudly declares the performance of films
at the box office, since the mid 1980s revenues from home video have
exceeded ticket sales, and yet video sales data is not freely available. As
conditions of confidentiality keep star contracts out of the public domain,
so any discussion of star compensation must be prefaced by the caveats
"it is reported that" or "it is rumored that." With this limited body of information, rather than precise evaluations of value and cost, analysis is inevitably limited to merely outlining the enigmatic economics of Hollywood
stardom.

Stars and the Box Office, 1990–2009

A series of longer-term trends shaped the market for Hollywood films in
the period 1990 to 2009. Following the rapid decline of cinema admissions
in the first two decades after the end of the Second World War, from the
late 1960s onwards annual attendance in the US plateaued at between four
and five attendances per capita per annum.[1] With the popularization of
television and consumer video, the home became the main site of film
consumption. In North America, between 1997 and 2008, video annually
accounted for between 70 to 73 percent of combined consumer expenditure at the box office and on video retail and rental.[2] After the dip of the
1970s and '80s, Hollywood's revenues from the international box office
increased during the 1990s. According to figures reported by the Motion
Picture Association of America (MPAA), in 2001 international territories
represented over 47 percent of the worldwide box office for Hollywood
movies and by 2009 that proportion had risen to nearly 64 percent (MPA,

2005 and MPAA, 2011: 3).[3] Increases in the average combined costs of producing and distributing movies massively outstripped inflation: in 1980, amongst members of the MPAA, the average cost of making, releasing and marketing movies stood at \$13.7 million but by 2007 that figure had risen to \$106.6 million (MPAA, 1998 and 2008: 7). These increases were most obviously demonstrated by the new benchmarks in financial excess set by the making of *Terminator 2: Judgment Day* (1991) (\$102 million), *Waterworld* (1995) (\$175 million), *Titanic* (1997) (\$200 million), *X-Men: The Last Stand* (2006) (\$210 million), *Spider-man 3* (2007) (\$258 million) and *Pirates of the Caribbean: At World's End* (2007) (\$300 million).

Industry opinion in the 1980s and 1990s held on to beliefs that stars are essential for "opening" films and that they offer a form of "insurance" against the risks and uncertainties of the market. For Greg Rutowski, vice president of West Coast operations for exhibition chain AMC Entertainment Inc., "Exhibitors are attracted to films that have major stars attached, because they can produce . . . box office" (quoted in Frook 1991). With industry eyes focused on the initial three-day weekend as the measure of a film's future box-office performance, stars are considered essential for attracting the media and public attention necessary to open a film. "The bottom line is," remarked one executive at Twentieth Century Fox, "if you've got a \$43 million film and you don't have a star to pull the opening weekend, you better have a great concept" (quoted in Brennan and Cohn, 1993: 29). "The biggest worry for any producer is whether or not a project will 'open' successfully," notes film critic Michael Medved, "and big-name stars can provide crucial reassurance. In today's cut-throat market-place, a film that fails to attract attention and audiences in its very first weekend has little chance to make up for lost ground; it will be judged 'dead in the water' and pulled from distribution" (1993: 25). For producer Scott Rudin "Certain actors buy you that first weekend . . . [they provide] the base of an audience that's big enough to make the movie a success if you've made the right movie" (quoted in Harmetz, 1988). Using the attractions of stars to open a film is considered indispensable, for "By the second weekend a movie is on its own, succeeding or failing on audience word of mouth. Audiences can be wild about a film . . . but the film will fail if the opening-week audience is not large enough to spread the word" (Harmetz, 1988).

Belief in the necessity for stars is therefore widespread in the industry. But do stars actually have the value which the industry places on them? Econometric analyses of the function and value of stars in the film market during the post-studio era have provided inconsistent conclusions. Steven

Albert concluded that although stars may never guarantee hits, they provide audiences with "markers" of film types and so influence consumer behavior: "the value of stars, as a group, is partly due to their marking successful film types in a consistent, predictable way . . . the power bestowed upon stars is a justified action based on an understanding of the characteristic connection between stars and consumer behavior in the motion picture industry" (1998: 251). When combined with the right type of film, stars therefore provide a means of predicting success,

> giv[ing] the film producer one consistent way in which to understand consumption patterns in relation to successful films. Thus, in the film industry, a star is often the key ingredient to getting a film made. Not only because they have box-office appeal, but also because they mark a known part of a consumer choice mechanism. (p. 264)

Other work, however, suggests that while stars may increase revenues, this is true of any high-budget investment in film product, and that sequels, good reviews and ratings can all have greater impact on revenues, leading to the conclusion that "stars play no role in the financial success of a film" (Ravid, 1999: 488). In their analysis, Arthur De Vany and W. David Walls concluded "star movies have more staying power than opening power" (1999: 305), for stars keep films on more screens over the duration of their runs. Industry executives may look to stars as insurance but for De Vany and Walls the business remains profoundly uncertain with success dependent on unpredictable consumer choice.

> There are no formulas for success in Hollywood . . . much conventional Hollywood wisdom is not valid. By making strategic choices in booking screens, budgeting, and hiring producers, directors and actors with marquee value, a studio can position a movie to improve its chances of success. But, after a movie opens, the audience decides its fate. The exchange of information amongst a large number of individuals interacting personally unleashes a dynamic that is complex and unpredictable. Even a carefully managed and expensive marketing program cannot direct the information cascade. (p. 286)

Consequently, they conclude,

> The studio model of risk management lacks a foundation in theory or evidence. Revenue forecasts have zero precision, which is just a formal way of saying that "anything can happen." Movies are complex products and the

cascade of information among film-goers during the course of a film's theatrical exhibition can evolve along so many paths that it is impossible to attribute the success of a movie to individual causal factors. . . . The audience makes a movie a hit and no amount of "star power" or marketing hype can alter that. The real star *is* the movie. (original emphasis, p. 286)

Although there may be no "science" to success, nonetheless historical evidence of continuing industry stability and profitability would suggest that "somebody in the film business must know something" (Pokorny and Sedgwick, 2010: 58).

There is then a question mark over just how important stars are to success but regardless the industry has preserved its belief in star power and so it is necessary to consider stardom as a dynamic at play in the workings of the film market. A starting point is to examine how stars feature in patterns of popularity. Each year many films are released but very, very few are hits. During the 1980s, on average a total of 426 new films were released in North America each year, of which MPAA members accounted for 145 (MPAA, 1998). In the 1990s, annual releases from all producers averaged 426 in total, with the Hollywood majors responsible for 185, and in the following decade those figures stood at 525 total and 186 MPAA.[4] Despite the number of films entering the market, a large share of revenues is concentrated amongst just a few films: from 1990 to 2009, per annum the top five films accounted for 13 to 19 percent of the total gross box office in North America, while the top 20 grossed 35 to over 43 percent of the total.[5] This small portion of releases represented the hits, the vast majority of which were distributed by the Hollywood majors. Focusing on the top 20 films in these years will therefore provide a sample from which to trace shifting patterns of popularity across the whole North American market and the place of stars in those patterns.

During the 1990s, the power of the film series was demonstrated by *Batman Returns* (1992), *Batman Forever* (1995) and *Batman and Robin* (1997), together with *Jurassic Park* (1993) and *The Lost World: Jurassic Park* (1997) and new run-outs for James Bond in *GoldenEye* (1995), *Tomorrow Never Dies* (1997) and *The World Is Not Enough* (1999). Disney scored hits with popular family animated features, including *Beauty and the Beast* (1991), *Aladdin* (1992), *The Lion King* (1994), *Toy Story* (1995) and *Toy Story 2* (1999). Comedies rarely appeared at the forefront of the box office but still featured amongst the top 20s, coming in various forms from the family-friendly (e.g. *Home Alone* (1990), *Sister Act* (1992)) and character-based (e.g. *Mrs Doubtfire* (1993) and *The Nutty Professor* (1996)), to the gross-out (e.g. *There's Something About Mary* (1998)) and parodic (e.g. *Hot Shots!* (1991)). Horrors featured occasionally (e.g. *Scream* (1996) and *The Blair Witch Project* (1999)) but never amongst the stand-out hits. Romantic dramas were rarely hits, but as *Ghost* (1990) and *Titanic* showed, when they hit they really hit.

By repeatedly fronting major hits, a small cohort of actors represented Hollywood stardom in the decade:

Kevin Costner, e.g. *Dances with Wolves* (1990), *Robin Hood: Prince of Thieves* (1991) and *The Bodyguard* (1992);

Arnold Schwarzenegger, e.g. *Total Recall* (1990), *Terminator 2: Judgment Day* and *True Lies* (1994);

Mel Gibson, e.g. *Lethal Weapon 3* (1992), *Ransom* (1996) and *Lethal Weapon 4* (1998);

Tom Cruise, e.g. *A Few Good Men* (1992), *The Firm* (1993), *Jerry Maguire* (1996) and *Mission: Impossible* (1996);

Harrison Ford, e.g. *Presumed Innocent* (1990), *Patriot Games* (1992), *The Fugitive* (1993), *Clear and Present Danger* (1994) and *Air Force One* (1997);

Bruce Willis, e.g. *Die Hard 2: Die Harder* (1990), *Die Hard with a Vengeance* (1995), *Armageddon* (1998) and *The Sixth Sense* (1999);

Julia Roberts, e.g. *Pretty Woman* (1990), *Sleeping with the Enemy* (1991), *My Best Friend's Wedding* (1997), *Notting Hill* (1999) and *Runaway Bride* (1999);

Tom Hanks, e.g. *Sleepless in Seattle* (1993), *Forrest Gump* (1994), *Apollo 13* (1995) and *Saving Private Ryan* (1998);

Jim Carrey, e.g. *The Mask* (1994), *Ace Ventura: When Nature Calls* (1995) and *Liar, Liar* (1997);

Will Smith, e.g. *Independence Day* (1996) and *Men in Black* (1997).

In several of these cases, star success was closely tied to generic popularity. More than any other genre, action cinema defined popularity in the 1990s, and was a common component to many of the hits which Schwarzenegger, Gibson, Cruise, Ford, Willis and Smith landed in the decade. Rather than a single category, action was a dramatic mode intersecting with multiple generic forms, so that Schwarzenegger featured in sci-fi action, Gibson in cop-action and Ford in action-thrillers. Outside the action hegemony, other genres directly determined stardom. Comedy may not have featured strongly amongst the hits, but Carrey's rise to star status was based on his highly idiosyncratic physicalized comedy. Although Roberts endeavored to break the genre mold by consciously diversifying the range of films she appeared in, it was in romantic comedy that she made her biggest mark on the box office (see Chapter 9). Hanks, meanwhile, proved that stardom did not have to be tied to genre. After his comedies of the 1980s, apart from the romcom pairing of *Sleepless in Seattle* and *You've Got Mail* (1998), Hanks incorporated his everyman image into a diverse range of dramatic contexts (see Chapter 3).

Focusing on the hits alone, however, limits understanding of how stars feature in the film market and it is necessary to look beyond the highest revenue earners and consider box-office performance across the entire life-cycle of a star. Taking the examples of Cruise, Hanks, Ford, Roberts and Carrey illustrates a series of dynamics at work that position stars in relation to box-office success. First, in the cases of the hits identified above, their commercial success came after strong initial weekends in Hollywood's domestic market, indicating some support for the industry's belief in the opening power of stars. Secondly, the life-cycles of these performers demonstrate how stars experience peaks and troughs in box office performance. Amongst the stars of the 1990s, Cruise and Hanks were the most consistently successful (Figures 5.1 and 5.2; see also De Vany and Walls, 1999: 309). With Ford, Roberts and Carrey (Figures 5.3, 5.4 and 5.5), highs were promptly followed by lows. Ford starred alongside Michelle Pfeiffer in *What Lies Beneath* (2000) and the film grossed $291 million worldwide, but when Paramount invested $100 million in making *K-19: The Widowmaker* (2002), a quarter of which was spent on Ford's salary (see discussion later), the studio was obviously hoping for more than the $66 million which the film grossed worldwide. With *Hollywood Homicide* (2003) ($75 million budget / $51 million worldwide gross) and *Firewall* (2006) ($83 million worldwide gross) the aging Ford's days as a box-office attraction clearly seemed to be over, that is until *Indiana Jones and the Kingdom of the Crystal Skull* (2008) grossed $787 million worldwide. Made for an estimated $14 million and grossing over $463 million worldwide, *Pretty Woman* made Roberts's name but over the next decade she only scored hits intermittently (this is discussed further in chapter 9). Universal enjoyed a hit with the Carrey vehicle *Liar, Liar* ($45 million budget / $303 million worldwide gross) and so were prepared to invest $82 million in making *Man on the Moon* (1999) but the film was a flop, grossing only $47 million worldwide. This was not enough to dissuade the studio from rehiring the star for *How the Grinch Stole Christmas* (2000) but as the film grossed $345 million worldwide, it showed Carrey could still deliver at the

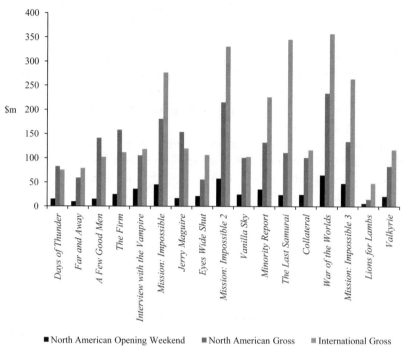

■ North American Opening Weekend   ■ North American Gross   ■ International Gross

Note:
Includes all films where Cruise took a starring role between 1990 to 2009 and so excludes his voice work on *Space Station 3-D* (2002) and films where he played a cameo or supporting role (i.e. *Magnolia* (1999), *Austin Powers in Goldmember* (2002) and *Tropic Thunder* (2008)).

Figure 5.1   Tom Cruise at the box office, 1990–2009. Source: compiled using data from www.boxofficemojo.com.

box office. Star status does not, therefore, depend on consecutive hits, only regular hits. Star status can persevere providing it is "hammocked" between hits. As one studio executive remarked "To get cold takes two or three movies that have contempt for the audience" (quoted in Natale, 1994: 42).

A third feature to note in the life-cycle of stars is that even the dips in box-office performance do not necessarily represent "failures." Analyzing the risk environment of Hollywood film production in the 1990s, Michael Pokorny (2005) finds high-budget features were just one class within any major studio's overall production portfolio, which included various medium- and low-budget movies.[6] Although high-budget productions achieved better rates of return (i.e. the ratio of money gained or lost relative to the original investment) and also featured amongst the highest-grossing titles, they also increased the possibility of substantial losses, and a studio's

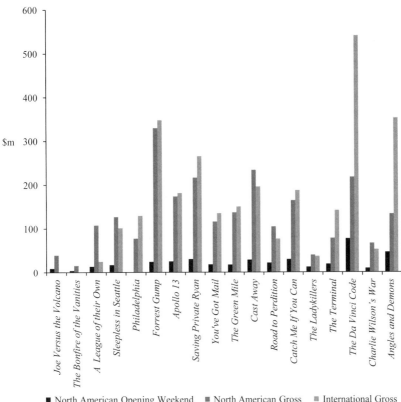

Note:
Includes all films where Hanks took a starring role between 1990 to 2009, excluding films where he voiced animated characters (i.e. *Toy Story* (1996), *Toy Story 2* (1999) and *The Polar Express* (2004)) or took a supporting role (i.e. *Radio Flyer* (1992), *That Thing You Do* (1996) or *The Great Buck Howard* (Scott McGinly, 2008, US)). International data unavailable for *Joe Versus the Volcano* (1990) and *The Bonfire of the Vanities* (1990).

Figure 5.2   Tom Hanks at the box office, 1990–2009. Source: compiled using data from www.boxofficemojo.com.

production slate was constructed "with a view to distributing risk across the portfolio" (p. 292). Between 1990 and 2009, stars delivered high-budget, big-grossing hits but also gave visibility and exposure to the equally necessary mid-range films. After *Mission: Impossible 2* (2000), Cruise went on to work for Paramount again on *Vanilla Sky* (2001). Reported budgets for the two films were respectively $125 million and $68 million, indicating the films were regarded as quite different categories of production by the studio. Compared to the established franchise commerciality of *Mission: Impossible 2*, *Vanilla Sky* was a less marketable proposition. A remake of

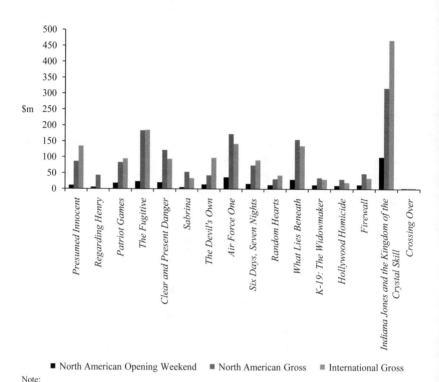

North American Opening Weekend   ■ North American Gross   ■ International Gross
Note:
Chart includes all films where Ford took a starring role between 1990 to 2009 and so excludes his cameo in *Jimmy Hollywood* (1994). International data unavailable for *Regarding Henry* (1991).

Figure 5.3   Harrison Ford at the box office, 1990–2009. Sources: compiled using data from www.boxofficemojo.com and www.the-numbers.com.

Spanish feature *Abre los ojos* (1997), *Vanilla Sky* replayed the original's narrative ambiguity, and was a vanity project for the star. At the worldwide box office, *Mission: Impossible 2* grossed $546 million and *Vanilla Sky* $203 million. Although the revenues of one far out-stripped the other, both should be regarded as commercial successes within the different tiers of the market they belonged to. Similarly, a few years later, when Cruise starred in the $65 million production *Collateral* (2004), the film's $218 million worldwide box office looked rather pale against the $457 million worldwide gross of Cruise's previous film, *The Last Samurai* (2003) (budget $140 million), or the $592 million which his next feature, *War of the Worlds* (2005) (budget $132 million), achieved. *Vanilla Sky* and *Collateral* did not equal the box-office performance of Cruise's outstanding hits but still performed well in a different tier of the market.

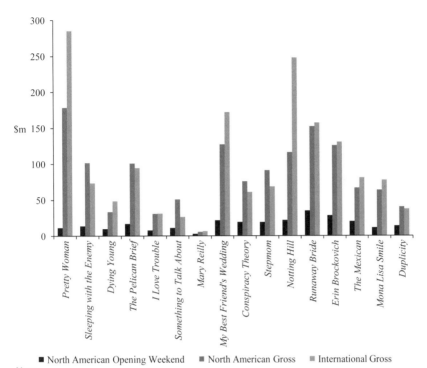

■ North American Opening Weekend   ■ North American Gross   ■ International Gross

Note:
Chart includes all films where Roberts took a starring role between 1990 to 2009 and so excludes her cameos in *The Player* (1992) and *Grand Champion* (2002), supporting-lead performances in *Flatliners* (1990), *Hook* (1991), *Michael Collins* (1996), *America's Sweethearts* (2001) and *Charlie Wilson's War* (2007), voice work on *The Ant Bully* (2006) and *Charlotte's Web* (2006), and films where she played a significant role as part of a larger ensemble cast (i.e. *Prêt-à-Porter* (1994), *Everyone Says I Love You* (1996), *Ocean's Eleven* (2001), *Full Frontal* (2002), *Closer* (2004), *Ocean's Twelve* (2004) and *Fireflies in the Garden* (2008)).

Figure 5.4   Julia Roberts at the box office, 1990–2009. Sources: compiled using data from www.boxofficemojo.com and www.the-numbers.com.

Finally, with the general upturn of the international market witnessed in the 1990s, overseas territories played a significant part in the overall commercial success of star films. In the cases of Ford, Roberts and Carrey, the international box office for their films generally neared or equaled the level of domestic ticket revenues, and with Cruise and Hanks overseas revenues regularly exceeded domestic success. Hollywood maybe a globally dispersed cinema but most international income for the major studios comes from just a small concentration of national markets: Japan, Germany, Britain, Spain, France, Australia and, by the end of the first decade of the twenty-first century, China (Epstein, 2006: 204; McClintock,

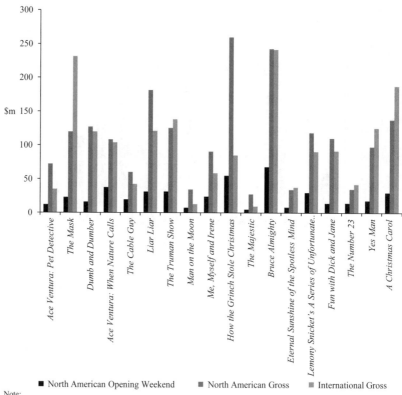

■ North American Opening Weekend   ■ North American Gross   ■ International Gross
Note:
Includes all films from Carrey's first starring role until the end of 2009, excluding his supporting role in *Batman Forever* (1995) and voice work on *Horton Hears a Who!* (2008) and *Under the Sea 3D* (2009).

Figure 5.5   Jim Carrey at the box office, 1994–2009. Source: compiled using data from www.boxofficemojo.com.

Jaafar, Holdsworth et al., 2010; and Waterman, 2005: 155–204). Looking at Roberts, her major hits all performed well in Hollywood's leading overseas territories, with Germany, France, Italy and the UK proving key territories (Figure 5.6).

Stars featured amongst the hits of the 1990s but by the following decade changing patterns of popularity raised significant questions over the importance of stars to box-office success. Franchise series performed well in the 1990s but by the next decade they overwhelmingly ruled the box office. Fox's *Star Wars* prequels (1999/2002/2005) and *X-men* (2000/2003/2006/2009) series, Columbia's *Spider-man* (2002/2004/2007) films, and DreamWorks/Paramount's *Transformers* (2007/2009) movies were at the forefront of the domestic and international box offices. It was

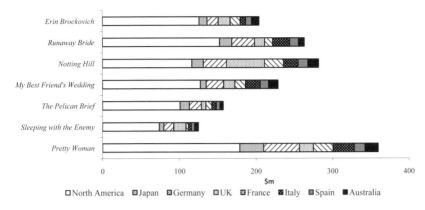

Erin Brockovich
Runaway Bride
Notting Hill
My Best Friend's Wedding
The Pelican Brief
Sleeping with the Enemy
Pretty Woman

0   100   200   300   400
$m
□ North America ■ Japan ▨ Germany ▥ UK ▨ France ■ Italy ■ Spain ■ Australia

Figure 5.6   Julia Roberts international box office for selected hits, 1990–2000.
Source: author's analysis of data from Klady (2010: 47).

Warner Bros., however, who most successfully exploited the trend, producing the *Harry Potter* (2001/2002/2004/2005/2007/2009/2010) series and launching a new run of *Batman* features (2005/2008), while New Line Cinema, a component of Time Warner's Entertainment Group, made *The Lord of the Rings* (2001/2002/2003) trilogy. Beyond the major studios, only Summit Entertainment's *Twilight* (2008/2009/2010) saga managed to muscle its way towards the upper strata of the decade's box office. These franchises made billions without casting any A-list names. Instead their success was founded on milking high-profile pre-sold properties – comic-book heroes, best-selling books and popular toys. In the 1990s, Michael Keaton, Val Kilmer and George Clooney each assayed playing Batman, and when Christian Bale took the role for Warner's re-launch of the franchise, it confirmed actors were endlessly substitutable in the franchise series. Maybe Johnny Depp's inimitable performance as Captain Jack Sparrow in Disney's *Pirates of the Caribbean* (2003/2006/2007) series provided the only evidence that a particular actor was in any way essential to this category of popular film.

Franchise movies were just one factor marking the waning power of stars. Certain low-budget features without stars scored well at the box office while expensive productions featuring stars performed below expectations. Focusing on the North American box office for 2009 illustrates these trends at work. Amongst the *Variety*'s (2010) "domestic top 250" for that year, franchise installments *Transformers: Revenge of the Fallen, Harry Potter and the Half-Blood Prince, New Moon, X-Men Origins: Wolverine, Fast & Furious* and *Star Trek*, together with animated features *Up, Monsters vs. Aliens* and *Ice Age: Dawn of the Dinosaurs*, all featured amongst the top 20. Meanwhile, buddy comedy *The Hangover* – ranked sixth for the year – showed how films on modest budgets without stars could do big box-office business. The same was true of sci-fi political allegory *District 9* (ranked 29th) and camcorder horror *Paranormal Activity* (31st). Reflecting on these outcomes, producer Peter Guber remarked "The (major movie) machine didn't fly last summer, if you look at the movies and the names, they were not star-driven movies, they really weren't" (quoted in Dobuzinskis, 2009). Sandra Bullock scored dual hits with the genre products *The Blind Side* (eighth) and *The Proposal* (13th) and she headed Quigley's (2010) "top ten money-making stars" for the year. But Bullock could not present a persuasive case for upholding belief in the power of stars. Since she first came to prominence in the mid 1990s, Bullock's films had never performed consistently well and until 2009 she hadn't fronted an outright hit. On his "Power List" in 2000, James Ulmer placed Bullock at the top of the B-plus list and said of her "she can't choose a role to save her life, unless it's in romantic comedy . . . She can't open a movie on her name alone" (2000: 77). Indeed, nearly a decade later, with Bullock's third film of 2009, *All About Steve* (ranked 85th), her presence did not guarantee commercial success or even good romantic comedy.

Bullock achieved success in a year when established members of the A-list failed to draw audiences into theatres. As *The Blind Side* was strongly reminiscent of *Erin Brockovich* (2000), maybe unsurprisingly the earlier film's A-list lead Julia Roberts was offered the role before Bullock. Originally Twentieth Century Fox was interested in producing the film, but according to one industry source "Their analysis was that we can only make it with Julia Roberts . . . It was a list of one" (quoted in Masters, 2009b). Likewise, Roberts declined *The Proposal* before it went to Bullock (Abramowitz, 2010). Roberts was considered first choice in both cases from an enduring belief in her box-office attractions, but rather than work on those two films she chose *Duplicity*, which ended 2009 ranked 77th on *Variety*'s (2010) top 250. *Duplicity* was just one of several star-fronted features which performed far below expectations that year, including Adam Sandler in *Funny People* (ranked 62nd), Bruce Willis in *Surrogates* (79th) and Russell Crowe in *State of Play* (82nd). Where star names did appear to have an impact was amongst a second tier of popularity, outside the top 20, with Robert Downey Jr. in *Sherlock Holmes* (21st), Carrey in *A Christmas Carol* (22nd), Hanks in *Angels and Demons* (23rd), Depp in *Public Enemies* (33rd) and Nicolas Cage in *Knowing* (39th). Faced with these changing trends in popularity, by the first decade of the twenty-first century commentators were mourning the "death of the movie star" (Rugaard, 2010). Steve Zeitchik of *The Hollywood Reporter* observed "The average number of top grossing films over the last few years that are driven by stars has fallen by 200–300 per cent" (quoted in Goodwin, 2008). *Variety*'s editor Peter Bart (2007) commented "Here's the new benchmark for predicting box office performance. If a movie star heads the cast, downgrade the forecasts . . . while movie stars today can help open a picture, they sure as hell can't guarantee success"; Bart suggested the industry was now confronting the question "Has the basic concept of a movie star become something of an anachronism?"

When looking at the place of stars in the modern market for Hollywood film, where video accounts for the majority of revenues, then focusing on box-office performance can only give an incomplete picture. The aforementioned limitations of data prevent any thorough consideration of how stars feature in the video market, although while not offering an exact mirror of film success, annual lists of the top retail and rental titles follow the same general patterns of popularity found at the box office. In which case, the provisional conclusion can be drawn that stars have no greater or lesser value in the video market than they do at theatrical box office. Concentrating on the box office measures commercial performance in terms of revenues and as such can be read as an index of the popularity of films featuring stars amongst audiences. But from the industry side, the success of stars depends not on revenues but profitability (Sedgwick and Pokorny, 1999: 321). Again, the absence of key data is an obstacle to meticulous analysis, however anecdotal evidence from industry reporting on star fees and participation deals provides a guide towards understanding what impact the cost of stars has on the making of films and so on their future profitability, and it is to this matter that the chapter now turns.

Talent Inflation

Enduring belief in the ability of stars to create certainties in the uncertain world of the film market has enabled talent agents and entertainment attorneys to demand and get huge levels of compensation paid to their clients. As Medved observed, "Those few performers who can be counted on to 'open' a picture through their mere presence – Cruise, Schwarzenegger, Costner, Gibson, Connery, Harrison Ford, Demi Moore, Clint Eastwood,

Whoopi Goldberg, and a mere handful of others – can seem to be worth whatever they get" (1993: 25).

In the 1980s and into the '90s, industry belief in the power and value of stars led to a dramatic inflation in the cost of star talent. Key to these developments was the emergence of two independent production companies, Carolco and Cannon, with ambitions to rival the majors. Both companies employed a common strategy, pre-selling distribution rights to raise production finance and using those funds to create action films with an eye to the international box office where the genre sold well (Wyatt, 2000). This formula led Carolco to build talent relationships with the decade's two leading action stars. Producing duo Mario Kassar and Andrew Vajna first worked with Sylvester Stallone on *First Blood* (1982) and *Rambo: First Blood Part II* (1985) and with Carolco they went on to make *Rambo III* (1988), *Lock Up* (1989) and *Cliffhanger* (1993) featuring the star. Carolco also made *Red Heat* (1988), *Total Recall* and *Terminator 2: Judgment Day* with Arnold Schwarzenegger. Using the same pre-sell strategy, Cannon hired Stallone for *Cobra* (1986) and *Over the Top* (1987) while also cultivating a new action star in the form of Chuck Norris.

While the international box office in the 1980s was still struggling to recover from the slump of the 1970s, action features were valuable currency, reaping rich fortunes equal to and sometimes surpassing domestic takings. Mike Simpson, vice president and joint head of the motion picture department at the William Morris Agency, was quoted as saying "The pictures that travel best are those in which language isn't central. . . . That usually means action-adventure pictures – almost always with male leads. Third World countries, in general, have a macho attitude toward film" (in Dutka, 1990). These conditions drove up the price of action stars. After *Rambo: First Blood Part II* grossed $150 million in the domestic market and an equivalent amount overseas, Carolco reportedly paid Stallone $16 million to appear in *Rambo III* (Harmetz, 1988), a far less successful episode in the series ($54 million domestic, $135 million international). Still, belief in Stallone's value led Cannon to pay $12 million for the star's services on *Over the Top*, another commercial failure. Schwarzenegger was rumored to be paid $8 million for *Red Heat* and to have picked up $11 million for *Total Recall* (Harmetz, 1988 and 1989). While the former performed poorly, the latter was a hit, grossing $119 million in the domestic market and a further $142 million internationally. On *Terminator 2: Judgment Day*, the star's price increased to $15million (Arnold, 1990). In this case a significant determinant in the pricing of talent was the sequel factor: with the original

1984 feature, Schwarzenegger had made the Terminator role his own, and so could not easily be substituted. Although the star's price was high, and the $102 million budget appeared astronomical, a gross of $205 million domestic and $315 million international confirmed Schwarzenegger was worth it.

Carolco and Cannon played a significant part in the escalation of star salaries but the popularity of action had a more general impact on the cost of talent. After hits with the first two installments in the *Lethal Weapon* (1987/1989) series for Warner Bros., Mel Gibson was commanding $6 million per movie. Fox took a big gamble when the studio paid Bruce Willis $5 million to star in *Die Hard* (1988) (Harmetz, 1988). At that point Willis was best known for his comedy role in the television series *Moonlighting* (1985–9) but when the film went on to gross $83 million in North America and $58 million internationally, the gamble seemed vindicated. When returning to the studio for the sequel, Willis's price was rumored to have risen to somewhere between $7 million and $8 million (Gold, 1990). It was the value of action in the international market which continued to drive up the price to talent in the first half of the 1990s. Independent company Savoy Pictures made news in December 1994 when signing Stallone for $20 million against 20 per cent of the gross for a commitment to star in a future unnamed action film (Eller, 1994). Although that film was never made, Stallone continued to set new benchmarks for star salaries, subsequently signing with Universal in April 1995 for $17.5 million to appear in *Daylight* (1996) (Fleming, 1995c).

Stallone's *Daylight* deal was the first step in a brief flurry of deal-making activity which over a period of just five months pumped up the price of talent. On 9 June 1995, *Variety* reported Columbia TriStar was offering Jim Carrey up to $17 million to appear in *The Cable Guy* (1996). Just four days later it was confirmed that Carrey's representatives, Nick Stevens of the United Talent Agency and attorney Deborah Klein of Bloom, Dekom, Hergott and Cook, had brokered an agreement with the studio rewarding their client with $20 million in a pay-or-play deal, including 15 percent of the gross (Cox, 1995 and Fleming, 1995a). Carrey's price was high but understandable: in the industry vernacular, he was "hot." Carrey stormed onto the Hollywood A-list on the back of a rapid succession of box-office hits, with leads in *Ace Ventura: Pet Detective* (1994), *The Mask* and *Dumb & Dumber* (1994), which collectively accumulated a worldwide box office of $706 million (see Figure 5.5). *The Cable Guy* deal was agreed only days before the opening of *Batman Forever*, in which Carrey took a supporting but nevertheless stand-out role, and that film went on to sell over $336 million in tickets worldwide.

Carrey's price rocketed in a very short time: Morgan Creek paid only $450,000 for him to appear in *Ace Ventura: Pet Detective* but for *Dumb & Dumber* New Line had to cough up $7 million. Aware of his rising box-office value, Carrey had been declining lavish offers, including £18 million from the Motion Picture Corp. of America to appear in *The Thief of Santa Monica*. Carrey's box-office power was only one factor at work in setting his price on *The Cable Guy*. Columbia had originally developed the project for *Saturday Night Live* cast member Chris Farley but an existing commitment tied him up until the end of 1995 and Mark Canton, chairman of Columbia TriStar, urgently wanted a big film for the studio to roll out in summer 1996. Canton's acceptance of Carrey's terms was widely criticized amongst the industry, for the executive had already acquired a reputation for unnecessarily inflating star salaries after paying extravagant fees to attach Schwarzenegger to *The Last Action Hero* (1993), Robin Williams to *Jumanji* (1995) and Woody Harrelson to *The Money Train* (1995).

Carrey's $20 million price tag set a new benchmark for star compensation, leading to expressions of anxiety amongst an industry concerned over its wider impact on production costs. "I'm hoping people will stay cool and not pay all of these prices," commented one studio executive: "Once you pay it the next person will demand it. I'm sure Sly and Arnold will demand it now, but hopefully everyone will remain calm" (quoted in Busch and Fleming, 1995). Michael Medavoy, former chairman of TriStar Pictures, directly blamed escalating production costs on talent, arguing "You have to question whether anyone deserves that kind of money . . . Anyone who doesn't see the apocalyptic future is either blind or downright stupid" (quoted in Hettrick, 1995: 4). Over time, Medavoy's concerns appeared prophetic, for despite Carrey's presence, *The Cable Guy* performed poorly, grossing $60 million at the domestic box office and $43 million internationally, to fall far short of what Columbia most likely hoped for when the studio signed the hottest name of the moment. Even so, a single failure was not enough to stop the general inflation of star salaries. Long before *The Cable Guy* opened domestically in June 1996, Carrey had already consolidated his price when on 7 August 1995 it was announced he'd accepted $20 million to star in Universal's *Liar, Liar* (Busch and Laski, 1995), and on that occasion the star gamble delivered a hit. If *The Cable Guy* proved the insecurities of the economics of talent, *Liar, Liar* signaled the continuing value of stars.

Universal's offer to Carrey came as part of a policy of investing in star talent. With the exception of the costly *Waterworld*, starring Kevin Costner, Universal had shied away from big-budget productions fronted by A-list talent. In June 1995, the studio underwent a change of ownership when the Canadian beverage company Seagram acquired an 80 percent stake in the parent company MCA/Universal, and Ron Meyer, former agent and founding partner in Creative Artists Agency (CAA), was swiftly hired as President of MCA. In his time at CAA, Meyer had built a strong roster of A-list clients, and his appointment was strategically aimed at building talent relationships. This was immediately evident when the day after signing Carrey for *Liar, Liar*, Universal agreed a $60 million three-picture non-exclusive deal with Stallone, a former client of Meyer's (Laski, 1995). Casey Silver, President of the Universal Pictures division, actually negotiated the deal but it was Meyer who had established the $20 million-per-film price tag for Stallone's services when he'd landed the Savoy deal on behalf of his then client. Stallone's Universal deal took a long time to bear fruit, resulting only in *D-Tox* (eventually released in 2002) before the deal was terminated in February 2000 (McNary, 2000: 5).

Within the industry, Carolco, Savoy and Canton were commonly blamed for inflating the cost of star talent (Brodie and Busch, 1996: 22; Johnson, 1996a: 118). Following Carrey and Stallone, the "$20 million club" soon included Tom Cruise, Tom Hanks, Harrison Ford and Arnold Schwarzenegger (Dawes, 1996). As producers attempted to stand firm on resisting demands to push beyond that level, in early March 1996 Jack Valenti, President of the MPAA, addressed a convention of exhibitors to portentously warn how escalating costs were a "huge, hairy beast slouching toward our future" (quoted in Bates, 1996: D4). Even so, it was only a matter of time before a studio broke ranks in order to land an A-list name. On 12 March 1996, Warner Bros. concluded negotiations with Schwarzenegger to appear in *Batman and Robin* for $20m (Busch, 1996a). Alongside his salary, it was rumored Schwarzenegger had been granted a share of merchandising revenues. This may have looked like just another $20 million payday but what made the deal remarkable was that Schwarzenegger had not signed to star but to provide just six weeks' work playing the supporting role of the film's villain, Mr. Freeze (Brennan, 1996: F1). Still, the $20 million threshold stood for a few years until in early February 2000 when it was announced Columbia were paying Mel Gibson $25 million for *The Patriot* (2000) (Hoffman, 2000). By October that year, Gibson's rewards had been matched by Harrison Ford who took $25 million for *K-19: The Widowmaker* (Fleming, 2000a). In due course, Cruise, Hanks and Carrey, together with comic actors Mike Myers and Adam Sandler, all joined the "$25 million club" (MacKenzie, 2004). Schwarzenegger, however, had already raised the bar even higher, landing a deal in December 2001 paying $29.25 million against participation in the gross to take a supporting role in *Terminator 3: Rise of the Machines* (2003) (see discussion later).

Membership of the $20 million or $25 million clubs was inevitably exclusive, notably limited to a few white male stars. Topping a 1990 survey of female star salaries was Barbra Streisand at $5 million per film, followed by Bette Midler ($4 million), Meryl Streep and Goldie Hawn (both at $3.5 million) and Kathleen Turner ($3 million), with a number of others, including Cher, Michelle Pfeiffer, Jane Fonda, Debra Winger and Kim Basinger in the $2–3 million bracket (Thompson, 1990). By 1993, it was estimated Cruise and Schwarzenegger were each commanding $15 million, while the highest-paid female stars – Julia Roberts and Whoopi Goldberg – were receiving $7 million apiece (Medved, 1993: 24). While Carrey and Stallone were setting the $20 million benchmark, in 1995 Sandra Bullock, Jodie Foster, Goldberg, Whitney Houston, Pfeiffer, Roberts, and Alicia Silverstone represented a $10 million club of female stars (Hindes, 1995: 7). In February that year, Demi Moore made news as Castle Rock Entertainment agreed to pay £12.5 million for her to appear in *Striptease* (1996) (Klady, 1995a). Moore's time at the top was short-lived, however, and it was Roberts who went on to set new heights as she received $17 million for *Runaway Bride* and became the only female member of the $20 million club for her work on the Universal and Sony co-production *Erin Brockovich* (Petrikin, 1998a; *The Hollywood Reporter*, 1999). Further rumor speculated she was paid $25 million for *Mona Lisa Smile* (2003) (Neumaier, 2006). This gendered pay disparity reflects general industry skepticism over the ability of female stars to open films (see Chapter 1).

In addition to their extravagant salaries, A-list performers can also demand production companies pick up the bill for certain "perks," additional luxuries befitting the lifestyle of a star. A large comfortable trailer to accommodate the star while filming is standard, with other costs incurred to support an entourage that may include personal assistants, cooks, bodyguards, stand-ins, drivers, trainers, therapists, hair and make-up artists, and nannies. On *The Scarlet Letter* (1995), Demi Moore reportedly billed $877,000 in entourage costs while Julia Roberts charged $841,000 for *I Love Trouble* (1994) and Melanie Griffith accumulated costs of $859,000 while working on *Born Yesterday* (1993) (Cox, 1997b: 50). By the mid 1990s, perks packages were estimated to add between $1 million to $3 million to the production budget for a film. In one of the greatest statements of star excess, when signing to work for Mandalay Entertainment on the Roman Polanski directed feature *The Double* in Paris, John Travolta reportedly demanded the production company not only ship his private trailer over from LA and pay for over a dozen assistants, but also insisted his private plane be retained in Europe on 24-hour standby at a rental cost charged to the production. In return, Travolta agreed to work a maximum of 12 hours per day, with just one or two "heavy dialogue" days per week (p. 1).

Gross Deals

With contingent compensation, creative talent participates in taking a share of income from a film, what in Hollywood vernacular is called the "backend." Any participants are paid from the *gross receipts* accrued from the theatrical box office, non-theatrical (e.g. in-flight entertainment) exhibition, video rental and retail, television licensing, and ancillary markets such as merchandise. In the case of the theatrical box office, gross receipts report the monies received by the distributor after exhibitors have taken their share of ticket sales, while with video a royalty (usually 20 percent) is drawn from the wholesale price of units. Gross receipts are subject to the deduction of various fees and expenses. A *distribution fee* is taken for the service of handling a film and is defined as a proportion of gross receipts (anywhere between 15 and 40 per cent) rather than the actual cost of releasing the film. Multiple *distribution expenses* are then deducted to cover costs directly incurred from releasing the film. These include advertising, publicity, the reproduction and transportation of theatrical release prints, taxes, trade association fees (i.e. membership dues paid to the association to which the distributor belongs, in the case of the Hollywood majors the MPAA), and checking or collections costs (expenses relating to monitoring the accuracy of ticket sales reported by exhibitors). *Production expenses* represent the direct costs of making the film and any interest incurred on those payments. Finally, *overheads* are charged as a contribution towards the general running of the business.

Participations come in two forms, "gross" and "net." There is no absolute definition of the distinction as both are always contractually defined. In the broadest of terms, however, gross participations are measured after certain "off-the-top" expenses (e.g. trade dues, checking costs, currency conversions) are claimed by the distributor, whereas net participations are paid from gross receipts minus the distribution fee, distribution expenses, and the production expenses. Whatever fixed compensation is paid to participants effectively becomes an advance against contingent income, and the proportions awarded to gross or net participants are measured by percentages or "points." More than any other aspect of the industry, participations reveal the notoriously labyrinthine workings of Hollywood's deal-making and accounting practices, and given the number of variables involved, participation agreements can take many forms. As Harold Vogel comments "Participation arrangements are limited only by the imagination and bargaining abilities of the individuals who negotiate them" (2007: 180). Participations mark out status and power relations in the talent hierarchy: "The price of talent is correlated with the quality of its contingent compensation: high priced talent takes gross, lower priced talent takes net, and still lower priced takes naught" (Goldberg, 1997: 538). Only stars and the most powerful directors and producers have the leverage to demand gross participations. Gross points are a badge of talent power. Stars are envied for their capacity to command the most lucrative category of "first-dollar gross" deals, but as these are subject to off-the-top deductions, what they actually share in is the *adjusted gross receipts*. As one Viacom executive observed, "The first truism of Hollywood is: Nobody gets gross – not even a top first-gross player" (cited in Epstein, 2010: 91).

In Hollywood the levels of participation enjoyed by stars have become a persistent area of tension in dealings between studios, stars and other talent. From the studio side, complaints are voiced that as gross participants take their cut regardless of how well a film performs commercially, they share in revenues without sharing the risk. As a high-level studio executive remarked, "God has not created a better way of compensating actors and directors than the first-dollar gross deal . . . You get paid first, no matter if there are budget overruns, lawsuits or any other problems" (quoted in Fleming, 2007b: 67). With stars reaping the benefits without carrying the risks, one studio executive emotively declared "talent eats while studios bleed . . . In what other business would the first money out go to the partner who put up no money?" (cited in Fleming, 2008: 49). Star participations also impact on the rewards paid to other creative talent. Signing bankable stars who demand gross may be necessary for getting a film into production but as gross participations can be included as a production expense, so the involvement of gross players pushes back the threshold at which payment of net points are triggered, so that "often the greater potential for conflict may not be with the participant against the studio but instead with the participant against all *other* participants!" (original emphasis, Vogel, 2007: 182).

Participants in the industry share skepticism over the value of net points. Concerns are expressed, sometimes through lawsuits, that the obfuscatory complexity of Hollywood's "creative" accounting benefits the studios at the expense of "cheating" the net participants. There is widespread cynicism that with clever book-keeping, studio accountants can identify enough costs to show that even the highest-grossing movies record a loss. Consequently, industry players and commentators have readily poured scorn on net participation. As director and writer David Mamet once commented, "the first rule of Hollywood is there is no net" (quoted in Stayton, 1988: 98). During deliberations in the case of *Buchwald vs. Paramount*, in his deposition the film's star Eddie Murphy famously dismissed net participations as "monkey points" (O'Donnell and McDougal, 1992: 200). In the opinion of industry reporter Gabriel Snyder (2009) "Net points are about as valuable, and confer as much status, as collecting beads for taking your top off at mardi gras. Everyone gets them and they're never worth anything." Although the probability of net points actually delivering a payout is slim, such arrangements can still be reasoned as serving to instill incentivizing effects by inducing contracted talent to hold an interest in the future commercial performance of the films they work on (Goldberg, 1997).

As noted in the previous chapter, participation deals were already in place throughout the decades of the vertically integrated star system. During the 1930s, the leading agents were able to secure percentages of the gross for their star clients. Agent Myron Selznick secured contracts for both Katharine Hepburn and Fred Astaire with RKO that paid a share of gross receipts for the films they appeared in. When Charles Feldman, Selznick's biggest competitor in the agency business, renegotiated Irene Dunne's contract with RKO, the terms included awarding the star 25 percent of gross receipts. Such deals were not confined to the leading agents alone. Hawks-Volck, one of the smaller agencies, landed a deal with Fox on the behalf of client Ronald Colman that paid $100,000 per film plus 10 percent of the gross. It was not only the stars under contract with the major studios who commanded participation deals. Freelancer Frederic March, another of Selznick's clients, expected participation in the gross from any producer who hired his services (Kemper, 2010: 71, 88 and 150–51). When James Cagney signed an 11-film deal with Warner Bros. in 1939, the terms included $150,000 per film plus 10 percent of the gross once receipts passed

$1.5 million (see previous chapter, Table 4.1). Claudette Colbert's contract renewal with Paramount in 1936 (see previous chapter) not only included fixed compensation of $166,666 per film but also advances of $33,333 against percentages of gross receipts in excess of twice production costs. These percentages were stepped, so that Colbert received 10 percent of the first $100,000 excess, rising incrementally to 12½, 15 and 17½ percent for each subsequent $100,000 excess before reaching 20 percent for any receipts which exceeded twice production costs by $400,000.[7]

In these cases, straightforward and rudimentary terms were stipulated for the payment of contingent compensation to star talent. A sign of the increasing complexity of participation arrangements came, however, when super agent Lew Wassermann of MCA secured a deal in 1950 with Universal for his client James Stewart for work on *Winchester '73* (1950) and *Harvey* (1950). According to the terms agreed, the sum of $200,000 was paid for Stewart's work on *Harvey* while for *Winchester '73* he waived a fee in favor of 50 percent of net profits. What made Stewart's contract significant was the complexity and extent of detailed terms set out to define "net profits." Across the ten pages of the contract's "Exhibit A," a series of deductions were scheduled to be met before Stewart's participation could be triggered. Distribution fees of 25 percent for the US and Alaska and 30 percent for all other territories were to be deducted, together with all "expenses incidental to distribution," including costs relating to advertising and print reproduction, taxes, checking costs, freight duties, any censorship charges, transportation costs, and trade association dues paid to the MPAA. Finally, the studio had to recoup all production costs and make a charge for overheads. After these deductions, the film could be counted as going into profit, although the net continued to be subject to deductions for any ongoing distribution expenses.[8]

Participation deals have therefore been a well established practice in the symbolic commerce of Hollywood stardom but the expanding rewards paid to stars have contributed to the financial excesses of conglomerate Hollywood. With the inflation of star salaries in the 1990s, a common model of star participation emerged of a fixed fee of $20 million as an advance against 20 percent or more of first-dollar gross. In cases where a film pulled together several high-profile participants, the division of percentages had a critical impact on the possibility of a studio seeing reasonable profits from even hit titles. To land the services of Carrey for *How the Grinch Stole Christmas*, Universal awarded the star 17 percent of the gross, while director Ron Howard and producing partner Brian Grazer shared 13 percent. In recognition of the film's literary source, a further 4 percent was offered to the Dr. Seuss estate, and so in total, 34 percent of first-dollar gross was committed to the main participants on the film. Estimates placed the production budget at around $123 million and expenditure on prints and advertising at approximately $40 million to $45 million (Busch, 2000: 4). As the film grossed $260 million in the domestic market and $85 million internationally, *The Grinch* gifted a substantial portion of Universal's income to the multiple gross participants.

Similarly, on *Men in Black II* (2002), Sony relinquished a sizeable share of receipts to the key talent. For *Men in Black*, Tommy Lee Jones reportedly received a fee of $7 million plus 5 percent of the gross, which it was speculated saw him land around $28 million, while Will Smith received $5 million and no participation in the gross. By the time the sequel came round, however, Smith had enjoyed hits which confirmed him as a major box-office draw, and so equaled Jones in commanding $20 million against 10 percent of the gross. With director Barry Sonnenfeld claiming $10 million plus 10 percent, and producer Steven Spielberg accepting a nominal fee in return for 20 percent of the gross, exactly half of the gross was committed to the principal talent. Disney chairman Joe Roth was quoted as saying "that kind of deal is just bad for the business," while John Calley, chairman of Sony, the studio behind the series, voiced his regret that "The problem you face is that when you give the talent what they want, there is nothing left for the studio" (both cited in Brown, 1998).

In the case of *Men in Black II*, Sony's dealings with the main talent fell into the sequel trap: successful franchises encourage further installments but lock studios into rehiring the same lead talent, giving stars considerable leverage in negotiations over compensation. It was exactly this trap which the former Carolco producers Mario Kassar and Andrew Vajna confronted on *Terminator 3: Rise of the Machines* when hiring Arnold Schwarzenegger to reprise the role he'd made famous in the previous two installments of the film series. In his account of the Schwarzenegger deal, Edward J. Epstein (2010: 61–7) explains how, using funding raised from the German film finance firm Intermedia, Kassar and Vajna were able to acquire the sequel rights to the series for $14 million. Production funding was accrued by selling distribution rights to three studios: Warner Bros. paid $52 million for North America, Toho-Towa picked up the Japanese rights for $20 million, and Sony Pictures Entertainment got the rest of the world for $77 million. However, these backers only provided funds on condition Schwarzenegger appeared in the film. Although Schwarzenegger had stood at the forefront of the A-plus list in the early 1990s, before *Terminator 3* his two most recent releases, *End of Days* (1999) and *The 6th Day* (2000), had performed relatively poorly at the domestic box office, grossing $67 million and $35 million respectively, although both showed Schwarzenegger could still pull in respectable audiences overseas (with international grosses of $212 million and $61 million respectively). By the time *Terminator 3* was in principal photography, *Collateral Damage* (2002) was also on release, grossing only $40 million domestically and $38 million internationally. Schwarzenegger's star power was therefore certainly waning, but nonetheless, if they were to get their film made, Kassar and Vajna were in a weak bargaining position.

In these circumstances, Schwarzenegger's lawyer, Jacob Bloom, was able to press for lucrative terms on his client's behalf. To secure certain tax advantages for the star, Schwarzenegger was not paid directly but rather his services were loaned out from his own company, Oak Productions. In the letter of agreement between T-3 Productions ("the Producer"), Intermedia Film Equities Ltd. ("Intermedia"), Oak Productions, Inc. (the "Lender") and Schwarzenegger (the "Artist"), T-3 Productions consented to pay Oak fixed compensation in the form of a $29.25 million fee ($3 million paid upfront and the remainder in weekly installments over the period of principal photography) plus "overages" payments of $1.6 million for each week the production ran over schedule.[9] This sum represented an advance against contingent compensation of 20 percent of adjusted gross receipts, with payment deferred to the later of either the film reaching "Cash Breakeven" or

> the point at which (a) the total domestic box office ... gross receipts as reported in *Daily Variety*'s weekly box office chart and as confirmed by the domestic distributor from the theatrical release of the Picture exceeds $155,000,000; or (b) the total worldwide theatrical box office receipts as reported by the distributors in each territory from the theatrical release exceeds $380,000,000.

According to the terms of the contract, adjusted gross was defined as total distributor receipts across all media and from all territories less standard "off-the-top" deductions: collection costs (capped at $250,000), checking costs (capped at $250,000), trade association dues (capped at $100,000), residuals and taxes. Cash breakeven was arrived at after recouping from the adjusted gross an amount equal to the aggregate of the full cost of production, distribution expenses, interest and financing costs, a producer fee of $5 million paid to Kassar and Vanja, and an overhead charge paid to

Intermedia equal to ten percent of the bonded budget. Epstein reports the deal also included a perks package of $1.5 million to cover the luxuries of private jets, a gym trailer, deluxe suite accommodation while on location, limousines, and bodyguards (p. 62).

Whereas in the vertically integrated system participations were limited to a share of the theatrical box office, in the post-studio system revenues from video and television sales were also added to the "pot" from which participants could be paid. When the video market was still in its infancy, the Hollywood majors reached agreement with the talent guilds that revenues from the wholesale price of video units be split, with 80 percent retained by their home entertainment divisions and the remaining 20 percent reported as a "royalty" added to the pot. Introduced during the earliest years of the video market, justifications for the split were twofold: the studios argued they needed to retain a hefty cut to subsidize the nascent business and also to cover the costs of manufacturing, packaging, warehousing, distributing and marketing video units. While there is some credence to the latter argument, the former defense has become unjustified for since the maturation of the videocassette market in the mid 1980s and DVD boom of the late 1990s revenues from video sales and rentals have massively outstripped the box office. Regardless, the practice persisted, so that a star awarded, say, 20 percent of the gross, actually receives 4 percent (i.e. 20 percent of 20 percent) of total revenues. Studios have defended the royalty arrangement, arguing that even with films which are successful at the box office, they remain in debt until the majority of video revenues are paid, and so are deserving of the 80 percent share (Snyder, 2005: 1).

Aware of the value generated by video sales, the Hollywood majors have therefore dug their heels in and refused to concede ground on the royalty issue. As a partner at one leading talent agency commented "It's the one thing that they don't want to give in on . . . Even though it's only .001% of all actors who participate, they know it can mean 10s and 20s of millions of dollars" (quoted in Brodesser and Nary, 2004). Consequently participation in video revenues has become one of the most hotly contested matters in negotiations between stars and studios, with the capacity to demand special terms on video income becoming a major definer of star power. On *Terminator 3*, one of the key signs of Schwarzenegger's importance and value to the whole project was how Bloom could leverage exceptional terms so that 35 percent of video revenues were reported as a royalty, thereby granting the star 7 percent of video income (i.e. 20 percent of 35 percent) (Epstein, 2010: 92). With DVDs selling at a wholesale price of $15, this arrangement entitled Schwarzenegger to $1.05 from every unit sold.

Re-modeling Star Compensation

Since the dissolution of the vertically integrated system, the studios have lost direct control over stars. In conditions of dependent independence, stars and their representatives have been able to leverage deals granting massive fees and shares in revenues, leading to the view that in the post-studio system the studios have ceded power to the stars. With star fees inflating production costs, the studios have long looked to how they may curb the excesses of talent compensation, but by the first decade of the twenty-first century, developments in the film market were placing additional strains on the economics of talent. Theatrical admissions had flattened and after the huge windfall which followed the launch of DVD, from 2004 onwards consumer spending on home entertainment began to fall. By the end of the decade, Hollywood was also facing the challenges of producing and selling high-cost entertainment in a period of international economic crisis. With rising production costs and expenditure on prints and advertising, talent compensation therefore became one of the few variables which producers could play with (Fleming, 2008: 1).

In the context of these developments, the majors therefore embarked on measures aimed at reining in the cost of stars and winning back a measure of control. The major studios began refusing to green-light films giving away more than 25 percent of first-dollar gross to all participants. All the majors instituted the policy but agents regarded Disney, Fox, Paramount and Universal as the most hardline when applying the cap (Dunkley and Brodesser, 2002: 1). Even so, the rule could still be bent in the case of top talent: Universal was already capping total participations when they made an exception for Carrey, Howard and Grazer on *The Grinch*. However, Fox reportedly abandoned *Used Guys* when Carrey and Ben Stiller refused to reduce their gross deals (Fleming, 2008: 49). In a second development, producers began to replace first-dollar gross deals with "cash-breakeven" models (Horn, 2006: C1). In these arrangements, stars discount or waive their fee and defer their percentages till after a film has recouped its costs. For producers, the model has the benefits of removing hefty upfront fixed payments to talent, thereby lowering production costs and the threshold at which a film reaches profit, and guaranteeing costs are covered before any payout to participants. Talent can also gain advantages if by agreeing to waive their fee and defer participations they can negotiate for higher percentages after breakeven, including DVD revenues, which still remained a rich revenue stream even in the declining home entertainment market (Fleming, 2009: 7). These agreements represented "hybrid deal[s] . . . combin[ing] aspects of a net points deal and a gross point deal" (Snyder, 2009).

Again, Carrey presented a defining figure for innovation in star compensation. When he signed in August 2007 to the Warner Bros. comedy *Yes Man* (2008), four years had passed since his last hit, *Bruce Almighty* (2003) (see Figure 5.5). Since the highs of the 1990s, Carrey's box-office power had diminished. For *Yes Man*, he reportedly waived his usual $25 million fee, thereby reducing the production budget by around one third to $50 million, and in return received 33 percent of all revenues after the film recouped its costs and one-third of 100 percent of DVD revenues (Fleming, 2008: 1). As the star stood to get nothing upfront and no first-dollar gross, in *L.A. Weekly* Nikki Finke described it as "the *worst* talent deal ever" (original emphasis, 2007: 37). Cash-break arrangements were common in cases where star names were hired for low-budget independent productions but Carrey's deal related to a major studio release. While many in the industry viewed the deal with skepticism, shortly after *Yes Man* completed its theatrical run in the domestic market, where it grossed $98 million, Carrey's co-manager Eric Gold was quick to assert the star stood to make an estimated $35 million from the deal, maybe $5 million more than he might have done had he not waived his fee (Schuker, 2009: A20).

Other productions implemented cash-break arrangements in order to hire and compensate leading talent while controlling production costs. For *Indiana Jones and the Kingdom of the Crystal Skull*, Paramount faced the sequel trap by reuniting star Harrison Ford, director Steven Spielberg and executive producer George Lucas, the original team behind the trio of hits in the 1980s. For the new installment, Ford, Spielberg and Lucas, together with writer David Koepp, split 87.5 cents of every dollar but only after the film recouped its production costs and a 12.5 percent distribution fee by grossing $400m worldwide (Fleming, 2008: 1). On *Body of Lies* (2008), stars Leonardo DiCaprio and Russell Crowe, director Ridley Scott, and producer Donald DeLine split 40 percent of receipts but only after Warner Bros. recouped its costs on the film (p. 49). Crowe and Scott struck a similar deal for *Robin Hood* (2010) as did Nicolas Cage on *The Sorcerer's Apprentice* (2010) (Schuker, 2009: A20). By 2008, Disney had cut back on the number of films which the studio made and were refusing first-dollar gross deals, offering cash-breakeven arrangements instead (Thompson, 2008: 5). As production for the second two installments of the *Pirates of the Caribbean* series progressed consecutively, the studio carried a heavy outlay of around $525 million to make the films, and so insisted participants deferred their compensation until the films recouped costs. Nina Jacobson, president of Disney's Buena Vista Motion Pictures Group, remarked "You can find yourself under a traditional first-dollar gross deal, writing huge checks while you are bleeding. It just doesn't seem fair. It feels great to be writing checks in success. But it kills you to be writing checks in failure" (cited in Horn, 2006: C10). Star and director Clint Eastwood was already familiar with the cash-break model having reputedly employed such arrangements for several years on his films, which explains his record of stringently controlling budgets. With *Gran Torino* (2008), on which he directed and starred, Eastwood was reported to have enjoyed his largest ever payday, taking 30 percent of the gross after Warner Bros. recouped costs (Masters, 2009a).

Controlling the Stars?

The cash-break model protects against the risks of hiring high-priced talent and has been regarded as a sign of the studios winning back some control over stars. On the back of his client's success with the *Yes Man* deal, Eric Gold argued,

> The days . . . where the star gets whatever he [sic] wants and gets paid through the roof – those days are over, for everybody . . . You can be the hottest thing in Hollywood, but if the economics don't match it, it doesn't mean anything . . . The studios are pushing back and they have to play the margins. (quoted in Schuker, 2009: A20)

Gold was overstating the case, however, for in certain situations studios have limited leverage to insist stars leave behind their prized first-dollar deals. After *The Da Vinci Code* (2006) grossed $758 million at the worldwide box office alone, Sony were in a weak bargaining position to decline gross participations to the principal talent – star Tom Hanks, director Ron Howard and producer Brian Grazer – for the follow-on feature *Angels and Demons* (2009). With production about to start on *State of Play*, Universal were landed in the position of hurriedly having to find a replacement lead after Brad Pitt dropped out, and so when drafting Russell Crowe in at the last minute, the studio had no other choice but to agree to the star's demand for first-dollar gross (Fleming, 2008: 49).

Probably the biggest obstacle to the studios achieving a power shift in their favor may ironically be their very own accounting practices. Persuading the most prized talent to take cash-break deals demands transparent and fair book-keeping by the studios (p. 49; Moore, 2009). Yet lingering doubts remain over the honesty of studio accounting: "Since even the mafia envies the ability of studios to cook their books, movies never go into profit. Ever" (Snyder, 2009). Home entertainment offers rich rewards to participants but the availability of precise sales data remains limited. Even top agents and managers can never be sure how films featuring their clients have performed on video. To prevent stars and directors from making larger claims on video revenues, it is in the interests of the studios to restrict access to video data. Stephen Einhorn, president of New Line Home Entertainment, admitted "As a matter of policy, we just don't give out numbers" (cited in Horn, 2005: A35). Leading video market analyst Tom Adams notes "It's been traditional for studios to brag about box-office performance . . . But it's also been traditional to keep the home video data very tightly held" (p. A35). Further problems arise from television licensing deals over the difficulties of disaggregating the fee paid for a single title when conventionally films are sold in blocks. If the studios are to wrestle back the financial power ceded to stars, confidence will need to be instilled with an overhaul of Hollywood's accounting practices. Whether the major studios will be prepared to do so is another matter.

Regardless of whether it is the studios or the talent who hold the balance of power, the economics of stardom in Hollywood follow a logic peculiar to the industry. For Charles Bloye, an executive at Carlton Film Distributors, "A producer who complains about the cost of talent is like a sailor griping about the sea – it's just the environment" (quoted in Ulmer, 1998: 71). That environment is not characterized by the chaos of sheer unpredictability but yet there are no certainties. Can stars stabilize demand? Do they provide insurance? Evidence suggest not. David Schiff of the United Talent Agency observed stars "give studios a sense of security . . . Sometimes it's a false sense of security" (quoted in Natale, 1994: 4 and 41). Star compensation not only makes big demands on the budget and profits of a film, but hiring stars can indirectly escalate costs, for "once costly stars climb aboard a project, studios tend to ratchet up the scale with stunts and effects. They wind up trying to turn every movie into a tentpole" (Thompson, 2008: 5). In which case, why employ stars? Despite the misgivings and doubts attached to the value of stars, industry judgment holds out belief that stars maybe just what is needed to create a success. As one anonymous studio executive observed, "no star is worth the money you pay him – except in the right movie" (quoted in Natale, 1994: 4).

Notes

1   Analysis of data from Quigley (2009: 8) and the US Census Bureau (n.d.a and n.d.b).
2   Analysis of data from MPAA (2008: 3; 2009: 2 and 2010: 3) and Adams Media Research figures in EMA (2008: 8 and 2009: 19).
3   Box-office reporting is an inexact science and even the most likely figures can at best be considered systematically calculated guesstimates.
4   Analysis of data from MPAA (1998; 2000: 11; 2009: 11; and 2010: 13).
5   Author's analysis of data from D'Alessandro (2000; 2001; 2002; 2003; 2004; 2005 and 2006), Klady (1995b, 1996; 1997; 1998 and 1999), Ludemann and Hazelton (1991), MPAA (2011: 3), Quigley (2009: 8) and *Variety* (1992; 1993; 1994; 2007; 2008; 2009 and 2010).
6   Pokorny defines these categories in relative rather than absolute terms. "High-budget films" stand for "those films exceeding the average production costs of all films produced by the majors in that year by 50 per cent or more, medium-budget films are those whose production costs fell between 75 per cent and 150 per cent of average production costs, and low-budget films were those costing less than 75 per cent of average production costs" (2005: 294).
7   From contract summary dated 10 June 1936 in the Paramount production files at the Margaret Herrick Library.
8   Summary of details from Exhibit A of the Stewart contract dated 14 February 1950.
9   Letter of agreement, 10 December 2001, at http://cache.gawkerassets.com/ assets/images/7/2010/04/t3_contract-1.jpg.

6

"The Will Smith Business"

Will Smith is a product of the post-studio star system. Following his transition from television to film in the 1990s, Smith joined the Hollywood A-list. Although by the first decade of the twenty-first century star-led films no longer featured at the forefront of Hollywood hits, Smith stood out as the only star to regularly appear in films amongst the top rankings of the annual box office. Smith's film fame was achieved through cross-media stardom, transferring the popularity he accomplished in music and television to launch his big-screen career. As a freelancer, Smith has worked for all the Hollywood majors and through his independent production company he has extended his creative and business activities while building up an enduring working relationship with a single studio (Columbia). Smith is therefore representative of the dependent independence which characterizes the post-studio system. Commercial success at the domestic box office has been matched by his international popularity, and aware of the importance of overseas territories, Smith and his company have intentionally carved out an international strategy to promote the Smith brand. Smith is therefore in every way typical of the post-studio system. And yet as a commercially successful black star in a market where white stardom is usually the only indicator of value, Smith's promotion to the A-list pantheon is remarkable. From his early career in rap music, Smith frequently attracted criticisms that his success came from a denial of racial difference, portraying a form of black masculinity which could easily be marketed and consumed in mainstream media markets: for historian of hip hop Nelson George, Smith is "Tom Hanks with a tan" (1998: 111). Like Hanks, Smith

Hollywood Stardom, First Edition. Paul McDonald.
© 2013 Paul McDonald. Published 2013 by John Wiley & Sons, Ltd.

cultivated an image of easy-going affability which could be accommodated into the popular market. Smith was the exception who proved the rule, becoming *the* black star amongst the white elite of Hollywood stardom.

This chapter therefore takes Smith to illustrate the symbolic commerce of post-studio stardom. It situates Smith within the main trends which have characterized that system while also observing how his success has come from a careful management of racial identity across music, television and film. When positioned within these dynamics, Smith therefore provides a case for understanding the star as image, creative agent, capital and entrepreneur.

Cross-media Stardom

Smith's film stardom was founded on the pre-sold fame he enjoyed from his careers in music and television. In 1985, Smith teamed with fellow Philadelphian, DJ and musician Jeff Townes, to form the hip hop duo DJ Jazzy Jeff and the Fresh Prince. With their first single "Girls Ain't Nothin' but Trouble" (1987) Smith and Townes broke into *Billboard* magazine's Hot 100 and subsequently achieved hits with "Nightmare on My Street," "Parents Just Don't Understand" (both 1988) and "Summertime" (1991). After winning two Grammys, in 1992 Smith and Townes were honored at the National Association for the Advancement of Colored People's (NAACP) Image Awards as Outstanding Rap Artists.

Smith's musical stardom was achieved within the larger context of the mainstreaming and cultural assimilation of hip hop and rap. Emanating from the South Bronx during the 1970s, and tied to urban African-American youth culture, hip hop emerged as a locationally and racially defined sound. Although ostensibly an underground or "ghetto" culture, as tracks from the Sugarhill Gang, Grandmaster Flash and the Furious Five, and Run DMC found listeners in national and international markets, the audience for hip hop widened (Greenberg, 1999). By 1990 there could be no doubts that hip hop had been absorbed into the spectrum of pop music as MC Hammer's "U Can't Touch This" and Vanilla Ice's "Ice Ice Baby" both made it into the top five of the Hot 100 to become paradigms of "pop rap." Smith and Townes carved out careers through this musical transition. With their light-hearted and comedic tracks, the duo took their music in a more marketable direction than the militant stance of Public Enemy or "gangsta rap" of NWA (Niggaz with Attitude). Smith and Townes's second album

He's the DJ, I'm the Rapper (1988) went triple platinum and made it to fourth position on the US charts. As Matt Diehl notes, "even the [album's] title seemed intentionally instructional, designed for an audience unused to hip hop vocab" (1999: 123). George's verdict on Smith was that he "has won by applying that essential hip hop rule – keeping it real. His version of real just has more to do with the mall than the 'hood'" (1998: 111). Conscious of criticism from hip hop purists, Smith frequently defended his music: "Rap . . . is a music based on being the best through arguing, insulting and battling verbally with each other. It's about competition. But I don't think it has to be angry. In fact, when it first started, rap was about having fun" (quoted in Buchalter, 1992: 16). For Adam Krims, the humor and sense of aimless fun which permeated the recordings and videos of Townes and Smith placed the duo in the tradition of "party rap," "designed for moving a crowd, making them dance, or perhaps creating or continuing a 'groove' and a mood" (2000: 55). Townes and Smith followed in a well established tradition, and Krims argues the focus on fun and entertainment in the party genre derived from the very origins of rap. For devotees of "hardcore" realism and authenticity, however, Smith and Townes were trivial commercialized froth. Not only was their music affable and welcoming but, coming from Philadelphia, the duo were not even from the New York, which in the imagination of artists and the record-buying public still "held something of a monopoly on 'representing'" hip hop culture (p. 123).

Smith's musical stardom was not only built on an accessible sound. The mainstreaming of hip hop coincided with the rise of the cable channel Music Television (MTV). After MTV launched in the US during 1981, regional versions were rolled out in Europe (1987–), Australia (1987–), Asia (1991–) and Brazil (1990–), aimed at addressing a global youth culture. In its earliest years, as the channel's playlist was heavily focused on rock, MTV largely became a showcase for white acts. Despite criticism from artists and music executives about its exclusory music policy, MTV stuck to the rock format, and only after the video for Michael Jackson's "Billie Jean" (1983) made it onto the playlist did more black artists begin to appear (Banks, 1996: 39–41). A clear sign of the channel's changing programming came with the launch of the hip hop show *Yo! MTV Raps* (1988–95) with a pilot episode featuring DJ Jazzy Jeff and the Fresh Prince.

Apart from the exposure which MTV provided, the music video form also granted a platform on which Smith was able to create the performed identity as "the Fresh Prince." With their hit singles, the duo adopted a narrative form in which Smith's raps told tales of the antics which befell the hapless Prince. With "Girls Ain't Nothin' but Trouble," the Prince gets into unfortunate situations with a series of women he meets, while in "Nightmare on My Street" his dreams are haunted by the Freddie Kruger character from the Elm Street series of film horrors (1984/1985/1987/1988/1989/1991/1994/2003/2010). "Parents Just Don't Understand" played out generational divisions as Mom buys Prince an embarrassing wardrobe of clothes for school and he then gets busted for driving her Porsche. "I Think I Can Beat Mike Tyson" (1989) had the Prince pick a fight with the heavy-weight boxing champion, only to enter the ring, receive one punch, and run away. The videos adopted a linear narrative form in which Smith acted, and as the Prince made repeat appearances across tracks, so he became a continuous character. Rapped in the first person, the tracks created an autobiographic link between performer and protagonist as the Prince became Smith's alter ego. Smith claims to have taken the sobriquet after "A couple of teachers at school started calling me 'Prince' because I was so charming. And in 1985, 'fresh' was the new slang so I said 'Fresh Prince'" (Sevin, 1991). Whether this is true of not, qualities of charm and wit were always evident in Smith's rap persona. Unlike the rapid editing which increasingly came to characterize the MTV aesthetic, Smith and Townes's videos had a more static style with little cutting and preserving spatial continuity by using studio sets. This had two notable effects. It created a dramatic performance space for Smith to act out the situations which befell the Prince, and this overtly artificial space contrasted with the urban realist backdrop familiar in many hip hop videos, so that the Prince was seen to belong to the studio, not "the streets."

   With the figure of the Fresh Prince, Smith created a distinct identity which was then carried over to television sitcom. Combining artistic and media brand extensions, this cross-media transfer achieved the transition from Will Smith rapper to Will Smith comedy actor. Benny Medina, an executive with Warner Bros. Records, approached Smith about an idea for a new TV sitcom. With the backing of Quincy Jones as executive producer, the show received the approval of Brandon Tartikoff, then chief of NBC Entertainment (Buchalter, 1992: 17; Esterly, 1992: 17). After recklessly spending his music earnings, Smith was facing bankruptcy, and so needed the opportunity (Dillow, 1993: 13): "In '87–'88 I was rich," he admitted, "in '89 I was broke" (quoted in Poulson-Bryant, 1995: 47). NBC debuted *The Fresh Prince of Bel-Air* in September 1990 and ran the series for six seasons. Medina had based the concept for the show on his own experience as a black teenager from the LA district of Watts, who in his case was raised by

Table 6.1   Nielsen annual ratings for *The Fresh Prince of Bel-Air.*

Season		Ranking[1]	Rating[2]	Share[3]
6	18 Sep. 1995 – 22 May 1996	55 (equal)	9.6	15
5	20 Sep. 1994 – 17 Apr. 1995	49 (equal)	10.4	16
4	21 Sep. 1993 – 18 Apr. 1994	24 (equal)	13.5	21
3	21 Sep. 1992 – 18 Apr. 1993	14 (equal)	14.6	23
2	16 Sep. 1991 – 12 Apr. 1992	18	14.5	23
1	17 Sep. 1990 – 14 Apr. 1991	39	13.1	21

Sources: Quigley (1992: 23A; 1993: 23A; 1994: 23A; 1995: 23A; 1996: 17A; and 1997: 20A)
[1] Position amongst top primetime programs in the season.
[2] Percentage of all possible viewers.
[3] Percentage of television sets in use turned on to the show.

a Jewish family in Beverly Hills (Esterly 1992: 17; Rohter, 1990). With its core premise, the series shared a lot in common with earlier sitcoms such as *The Beverly Hillbillies* (1962–71), *The Jeffersons* (1975–85) and *Diff'rent Strokes* (1978–86), but with Smith on board, the concept was adapted to connect with Smith's own background and music stardom. Andy Borowitz, one half of the husband-and-wife producing-writing team on the series, openly acknowledged "This is a vehicle to bring the hip-hop sensibility and Will Smith to television" (quoted in Rohter, 1990). A modest success in its first season, the series rose in popularity during the second and third seasons when ratings data estimated nearly one quarter of the total television audience were watching (Table 6.1).

While preserving the Fresh Prince image, the series made no direct connection between Smith's music persona and his television character. Instead, connections between Smith's two careers were left implicit rather than explicit. Although "Fresh Prince" was included in the series title, Smith played the character "Will Smith," a teenager from West Philadelphia who goes to live with his wealthy aunt and uncle, the Banks, at their mansion in Bel-Air. For the series' opening title sequence, the music, visual and performance style was uncannily reminiscent of Smith's music videos, and Townes periodically made appearances in episodes playing the character "Jazz." As the first series worked to establish Smith's character, frequently situations were created requiring "Will" to rap or dance, and music was noticeably used as a mechanism to map and define class and generational identities or tensions amongst members of the Banks family and other characters. In a moment of heightened self-referentiality, in one episode the punchline to a piece of dialog had James Avery as the paternal-istic uncle Philip Banks tells his nephew "sometimes, parents just don't understand." On his role in the series, Smith remarked "I'm basically playing myself" (quoted in Rohter, 1990), although arguably that "myself" was already an act anyway. Smith's sitcom character was never directly por-trayed as the Fresh Prince moved to television but the series made enough nods towards Smith's parallel career to acknowledge that in everything but name, "Will" was Smith's music persona transposed to the small screen. Rather than exporting a definite, distinct character, what the exchange between music and television created was an image built around good-natured qualities of charm, honesty and courtesy, producing a figure who is confident without being arrogant, quick witted but with a tendency to make stupid mistakes, and of whom it is repeatedly asserted that he comes from urban street culture and yet never appears to be of that culture.

Mr. Smith Goes to Hollywood

Smith's television career had hardly begun when he commenced a parallel career in film. Recording for the first season of *Fresh Prince* had only just finished when production began on *Where the Day Takes You* (1992), a serious drama about the harsh realities confronting a group of homeless youths in Los Angeles in which Smith played a small supporting role as the wheelchair-bound Manny. With his concurrent careers, it would be easy to presume the move to film marked one more step extending the Will Smith brand but with his initial film roles Smith did not simply reproduce the Fresh Prince persona. With his music, Smith claimed to "write lyrics my mother can listen to" (quoted in Buchalter, 1992: 17), but as Manny, several of Smith's lines amounted to him spouting a string of profanities. *Where the Day Takes You* did not give Smith an immediate entry to Hollywood: produced by Cinetel Films and distributed by New Line Cinema, the film belonged to the independent sector, receiving a limited release and grossing less than $400,000. *Made in America* (1993), Smith's second film, posi-tioned him closer to the Hollywood mainstream. Produced by Le Studio Canal+, Regency Enterprises, Alcor Films, Stonebridge Entertainment and Kalola Productions, the film was given a wide release by Warner Bros., grossing $105 million worldwide. Smith played Tea Cake Walters, friend and admirer of Zora Mathews, played by Nia Long. As a comedy, the film placed Smith on more familiar ground. Although Tea Cake lacked the cocky confidence of Smith's music and television persona, Smith's manner of performance shared the same laidback affability and fluid physicality which characterized the Fresh Prince persona. Smith did not take a lead role, yet the film appeared to be trading off the growing capital of his name, for while opening credits gave top billing to Whoopi Goldberg and Ted Danson as Zora's parents, Smith was billed third, straight after the title, even though he had very little actual screen time in the film, far less than Long.

Smith's third film played on the Smith/Prince brand while marking creative departures from his music and television identity. Produced by Metro-Goldwyn-Meyer (MGM), *Six Degrees of Separation* (1993) adapted John Guare's hit Broadway play for the screen. On stage, the play had garnered a range of prestige credits, with nominations for a Tony Award for Best Play and Pulitzer Prize for Drama, and winning the award for Best Play from the New York Drama Critics' Circle. The film version again represented a departure from Smith's established music and television identity. In the drama, art dealer Flan Kittredge (Donald Sutherland) and his wife Ouisa (Stockard Channing) allow a young man Paul into their expensive New York apartment after he claims to have been stabbed in a mugging and to know their children at university. Based on the real life exploits of hustler David Hampton, Paul is a con artist who employs similar deceptions to ingratiate his way into, and then steal from, the homes of wealthy New Yorkers (Werner, 1993). In Paul's case he even claims to be the son of Sidney Poitier. An easy ability to charm was therefore an essential attribute for anyone to convincingly play Paul, and the role allowed Smith to apply qualities which he'd already conveyed as part of his mediated identity. At the same time, the role also presented challenges. Paul's Ivy League charade could not be credibly conveyed by the familiar manners of the Fresh Prince, and Smith prepared for the role by taking acting lessons, hiring a dialog coach, and adapting both his speech and walking patterns (Gordon, 1994). Smith therefore immersed himself in the task of representing Paul by recognizing the need to adapt and transform what he performed. But this only went so far. As chasing girls was a major component of Smith's music and television persona, then Paul's homosexuality contradicted the existing Smith brand, and when Paul is seen to kiss his male lover, then possibly to preserve the brand, Smith reportedly refused to touch lips with his co-actor.

Six Degrees of Separation placed Smith's stardom within a confluence of commercial and artistic value. Rather than his ability to portray Paul, Smith acknowledged he was hired because his name could leverage production financing (p. 56). MGM's co-chairman, Alan Ladd Jr., believed the film had an assured appeal for older moviegoers but acknowledged that the casting of Smith was self-consciously aimed at tapping into the youth market (Honeycutt, 1992: 5). Still, despite Smith's presence, the film did very little business, grossing only $6.4 million in North America. Given the nature of the material, this result was maybe unsurprising, but commercial concerns had not motivated Smith to take the role anyway. "The biggest considera-tion for me," he said, "was: If I pull this role off, I'm a legitimate actor. [Hollywood] really doesn't respect TV actors; film is the medium to succeed in. I want to be considered by Spike Lee and Martin Scorsese. I want people to know there is something beyond what I do on *Fresh Prince*" (quoted in Morrison, 1993: 4). Playing Paul therefore represented a negotiation of artistic legitimization and cultural credibility, for the role not only placed Smith in an adaptation of an award-winning Broadway play but also pro-vided an opportunity to demonstrate some actorly versatility.

Village Hollywood provided the context for the production of Smith's film stardom. Doing films for Warner Bros. and then MGM linked Smith with the modern studio system. When he made his first three films, Smith was a client of International Creative Management, but in May 1993 he changed agents, leaving ICM for Creative Artists Agency who represented him in all areas: film, television and music. Speaking on behalf the agency, Anna Perez commented "Smith is looking to CAA to take his career to the next plateau" (quoted in Moerk, 1993). A team was formed around Smith, headed by Ron Meyer, with Doug Robinson handling film and Lee Gabler focusing on television. Ken Stovitz and David Lonner were tasked with seeking out film projects and other vehicles for Smith. CAA continued representing Smith as his star value increased over the decade, and the services of PMK were retained for PR matters. Meanwhile, Medina, his fellow series creator Jeff Pollack, and James Lassiter (an old school friend of Smith's from Philadelphia) acted on his behalf as personal managers.

To this point Smith had not taken a lead role in film or appeared in a major commercial success. With agency dealings kept in secret behind closed doors, it is impossible to prove if this is the case, but the shift to CAA may have been instrumental to determining Smith's film stardom. After signing with CAA, his first film was the buddy action movie *Bad Boys* (1995). Financed and distributed by Sony's Columbia Pictures, the film teamed Smith with fellow television actor Martin Lawrence – best known for his central role in the comedy series *Martin* (1992–7) – as the two cops Mike Lowery and Marcus Burnett. Casting two black actors at the center of a major studio release was certainly uncommon. Initially the film was developed at Paramount and later at Disney by the producing duo of Jerry Bruckheimer and Don Simpson (both CAA clients) as a vehicle for the white comedians Dana Carvey and Jon Lovitz. When the project faltered in development, Mark Canton, chairman of Columbia Pictures, moved to bring the film to the studio. Columbia was already interested in making a film with Smith and so Canton and his deputy Barry Josephson took credit for the decision to cast him alongside Lawrence (C. Fleming, 1998: 198–9). Smith was acutely aware of how the film broke the mold of popular Hollywood fare: "The significance of *Bad Boys* to me was that two black stars were in a film that was treated like a big film [by Columbia]. Outside of Eddie Murphy and Whoopi Goldberg, you don't see this level of attention given to too many films [with black actors]" (quoted in Welkos, 1995). *Vibe*, Quincy Jones's magazine of African-American music and entertainment, celebrated *Bad Boys* for bringing together two major black comedians: "Two for the price of one. Call it *Beverly Hills Cop²* meets *Miami Twice*" (Poulson-Bryant, 1995: 47).

Filmed between the fourth and fifth seasons of *The Fresh Prince*, *Bad Boys* has a significant place in Smith's stardom for several reasons. It was the first film for which he achieved star billing, albeit shared with Lawrence. Secondly, *Bad Boys* became the first step in the close working relationship which developed between Smith, Columbia and the studio's parent company Sony. On his next film, *Independence Day* (1996), Smith worked for Fox, but then returned to Columbia for *Men in Black*. Shortly before *Men in Black* was released, in June 1997 Smith signed a multi-year contract with Sony's Columbia Records division to become a solo artist, dropping the Fresh Prince moniker to record under his own name (Sandler, 1997). Finally, *Bad Boys* was Smith's first outright hit as a film actor: Columbia opened the film in North America across 2,132 screens and it went on to gross $65.8 million domestically and a further $75.6 million internationally. *Independence Day* and *Men in Black* topped the global box office in the years of their release, and although Smith's next two films *Enemy of the State* (1998) and *Wild Wild West* (1999) could not equal those mammoth hits, they still managed respectable ticket sales. The period from *Bad Boys* to *Wild Wild West* was therefore central to marking out Smith's commercial status, as the five films collectively grossed over $2 billion worldwide.

Within the racial parameters of Hollywood stardom, Smith's commercial value is outstanding. Before Sidney Poitier in the late 1960s, no black actors appeared on the Quigley poll of top money-making stars, and over a decade would pass until Eddie Murphy in the 1980s acquired the status of a major box-office draw (Table 6.2). Smith appeared on the poll for first time in 1997 and over the next 12 years he would make another seven appearances, topping the poll for 2008 on the strength of *Hancock* (2008) (see Table 1.1). Although never equaling the commercial heights of Smith, Denzel Washington was the only other black actor to appear on the poll in this period.

This begs the question, why did Smith succeed at the box office when other black actors – Lawrence for example – did not? Smith's image made no explicit statement about race but yet his screen work did not ignore matters of racial identity entirely. On *Fresh Prince*, a lot of the comedy certainly in the early series came from not only generational differences but also how Will's urban origins were posed as a form of cultural authenticity that exposed the white-identified bourgeois airs and graces of the Banks family. Racial tensions also intermittently emerged as an undercurrent in several of Smith's films. For example in *Bad Boys*, a shop owner, nervy at having two black guys in his store, pulls a gun on Lawrence/Burnett and Smith/Lowery when they legitimately try to pay for goods, dismissing their claim to be cops. No explicit reference to race is made in the scene but the situation is immediately comprehensible. Set in the South during the post-Civil War reconstruction, *Wild Wild West* was littered with opportunities for Smith to make comic play on slavery. It would be too easy therefore to conclude Smith's success depended on ignoring or emptying out racial difference. At the same time, Smith certainly downplayed that difference. On his music, Smith responded to criticisms from hip hop purists by claiming "We make rap music universal . . . It's more than the black experience" (quoted in Reeves, 1999: 221). Speaking in the year of *Bad Boys*, Smith claimed his cross-media transition was possible because he always played a "regular guy": "I think because my character on television and my character in my records was just a regular guy, that makes the cross [to films] less difficult" (quoted in Welkos, 1995). For Smith the shift was nothing special: "You know, when I look at a spectacular cross, it's like Robin Williams going from *Mork and Mindy* to the character he played in *Awakenings*. That's a cross. I don't look at what I've done as that big. I'm just a regular guy. Bruce Willis is a regular guy. You see Bruce Willis doing anything because he's a regular guy" (quoted in Welkos, 1995).

Despite these claims, it is difficult to see Smith as simply playing the regular guy. Even in the earliest years of his film career, the characters of the legless Manny, lovelorn Tea Cake, charismatic Paul, and gun-toting

Table 6.2   African-American actors on the Quigley poll, 1932–2009.

		Ranking
2009	Denzel Washington	10
2008	Will Smith	1
2007	Will Smith	2
	Denzel Washington	5
2006	Will Smith	(tie) 3
	Denzel Washington	(tie) 3
2005	Will Smith	7
2004	Denzel Washington	6
2002	Denzel Washington	8
2001	Denzel Washington	6
	Will Smith	7
2000	Eddie Murphy	4
	Martin Lawrence	7
1999	Will Smith	7
1998	Eddie Murphy	8
1997	Will Smith	4
1993	Whoopi Goldberg	9
1992	Whoopi Goldberg	6
1989	Eddie Murphy	7
1988	Eddie Murphy	2
1986	Eddie Murphy	2
	Whoopi Goldberg	8
1985	Eddie Murphy	2
1984	Prince	8
1983	Eddie Murphy	2
1982	Richard Pryor	5
1969	Sidney Poitier	6
1968	Sidney Poitier	1
1967	Sidney Poitier	7

Source: compiled from Quigley (2010)

playboy Lowery were anything but regular or commonplace. As his career progressed, the world-saving heroics of Captain Steven Hiller in *Independence Day*, alien-hunting exploits of J in *Men in Black* (chosen for the clandestine unit because he is one of the "best, of the best, of the best"), conspiracy-busting adventures of Robert Clayton Dean in *Enemy of the State*, daring do of Captain James West in *Wild Wild West*, mystical insights of a golf caddy in *The Legend of Bagger Vance* (2000), or the world-champion confidence of Cassius Clay in *Ali* (2001) showed Smith playing exceptional guys. In many ways, these roles involved a departure from his music and television origins, and understandably so, for as a fundamentally youthful figure the Fresh Prince could only ever have a limited shelf life. As he entered his film career, Smith did not therefore reproduce that persona, yet a core Smith brand was preserved as elements of the comedic charm which characterized the Prince were still to be found in the characters of Lowery, Hiller, J, Dean and West. Rather than commonplace regularity, the actual constant running through Smith's work was the sense of charm he enacted. Across music, television and film, Smith cultivated a core set of qualities that formed his branded personality. In film, regardless of the individual character, Smith always conveyed qualities of amiability, pleasantness and politeness. When he stepped away from portraying those values, as in *Seven Pounds* (2008), the result was commercial failure. Smith did not therefore mask his racial identity but first and foremost always worked at presenting himself as a charming guy who just happens to be black.

Sindiependence

Smith's stardom is positioned within the dependent independence which characterizes the post-studio star system. His international exposure has been conditional upon films made by the Hollywood majors, and although not tied to any studio, Smith has preserved close working relations with Columbia. At the same time, he has exercised producing power through the entertainment and artist management company Overbrook Entertainment.

Formed by Smith and Lassiter, Overbrook was named after the Philadelphia high school they both attended. Smith credits Lassiter's place in his career as "the brains behind the brand" (quoted in Richardson, 2007). Overbrook was established in November 1997 when Smith and Lassiter landed a four-year first-look deal with Universal brokered by attorney Ken Hertz of Hansen, Jacobsen, Teller & Hoberman. Universal gained first-look on Smith's film and television projects for four years, and although his solo music was handled by Sony, the new deal also gave Interscope Records, half-owned by the Universal Music Group, distribution rights for recordings from Overbrook (Cox, 1997a; Galloway, 1997). Universal were rumored to be providing Overbrook with $5 million per year to cover development costs, overheads, fees and expenses (*The Hollywood Reporter*, 1997). As an independent, Overbrook has relied on key intermediaries to represent the company in negotiations with studios and television networks. Jason Sloane of Sloane, Offer, Weber & Dern handled legal affairs, while at CAA Richard Lovett (the agency's president) and Ken Stovitz looked after Overbrook's dealings, before the latter left the agency in May 2007 to join Overbrook as co-partner alongside Smith and Lassiter (Fleming, 2007a).

On the back of the Universal deal, Smith's name was rapidly linked to a raft of film projects for the studio, including the alien mystery *K-Pax*, superhero movie *The Mark*, space drama *Star City*, romantic drama *Love II Love You*, a remake of *Play Misty for Me* (1971), a second remake of *Cat People* (1942 and 1982), and romantic comedy *Anything for You* (Chetwynd, 1998; Fleming, 2000b; Kit, 1999b; Lyons and Petrikin, 1999; and Petrikin, 1998b and 1999). In the case of the latter, singer Whitney Houston was due to star alongside Smith, and it was also rumored she would appear in a remake of the *cinéma du look* feature *Diva* (1981) produced by Overbrook and Brownhouse Productions (Houston's company) (Lyons and McNary, 2000). Outside of the arrangement with Universal, Smith and Overbrook were also linked to projects with Warner Bros., including a further remake of *A Star is Born* (1937/1954/1976) and the thrillers *Smuggler's Moon* and *The Lineup* (Fleming, 1998; Hindes 1999b and Kit, 2000).

Despite all this activity, Overbrook's time at Universal never bore fruit. Smith and Lassiter acknowledged their own inexperience of movie production was largely responsible for this failure. "We were learning how to produce movies," said Smith. "Unfortunately, our learning time was on Universal's dime" (quoted in Richardson, 2007). These difficulties were added to when within a year of the deal being struck, Universal made large-scale changes in its senior management (see Chapter 5), and, as Lassiter reflected, "the new regime really didn't embrace us" (Siegel, 2008b: 17). When the initial four-year term expired, therefore, in January 2002 Overbrook signed a three-year first-look deal with Columbia. "Will Smith and James Lassiter have helped create some of this studio's most entertaining and profitable motion pictures," commented Columbia's Chairwoman Amy Pascal. "We wanted to expand that relationship and make Overbrook a part of our development team. We don't want to just make films starring Will Smith. We want to be in the Will Smith business and with this deal, we are committing to an artist and a producer who share our commercial and creative taste" (quoted in Harris, 2002). Overbrook reciprocated, issuing a statement saying "Home is a place where you feel completely comfortable, and you get unconditional support, and Columbia Pictures has been that place to us for many years" (quoted in Harris, 2002). After signing the initial Columbia deal, Smith and Overbrook embarked on a flurry of development activity, buying spec scripts and optioning books. Overbrook became a valuable unit for Columbia, producing a run of hits starring Smith, including *Hitch* (2005), *The Pursuit of Happyness* (2006), and *Hancock*. Profiting from this success, Columbia was keen to renew the alliance, and in December 2008 signed with Overbrook for a further five years (Siegel, 2008a).

The relationship between Smith/Overbrook and Columbia/Sony demonstrates the complexities of dependent independence in the interactions between stars, sindies and the majors of conglomerate Hollywood. Just looking at the period from Overbrook's first Columbia deal in 2001 to the point of renewal in 2008, these interactions can be summarized in five ways:

1. Films featuring the star which were developed and made by the sindie under a first-look deal with the aligned studio. With *Hitch*, *The Pursuit of Happyness* and *Hancock*, Overbrook capitalized on its star principal and established a winning streak for Columbia, although the somber drama *Seven Pounds* only achieved a relatively modest box office.
2. Films featuring the star and made for the aligned studio but without the involvement of the sindie. With *Men in Black II* (2002) and *Bad Boys II* (2003), Columbia exploited the sequel potential of Smith's past hits. Both films were made by independent production outfits other than Overbrook. Steven Spielberg's Amblin Entertainment and MacDonald Parkes Productions, the company of producers Laurie MacDonald and Walter F. Parkes, had been behind the original *Men in Black* and re-teamed for the follow-up. After Simpson's death in 1996, Bruckheimer continued working through a production company under his own name, but in recognition of his former partner's role in creating the original concept behind the cop buddy movie series, *Bad Boys II* was produced through Don Simpson/Jerry Bruckheimer Films.
3. Films featuring the star, made by the sindie, but for a major other than the aligned studio. While maintaining his relationship with Columbia, Smith interspersed work for the studio with the Overbrook productions *I, Robot* (2004) for Fox and *I Am Legend* (2007) Warner Bros.
4. Films made by the sindie but not featuring the star and released by a distributor other than the aligned studio. Warner Bros. had courted Smith and Overbrook during the period at Universal, and these advances

continued once Overbook moved to Columbia. For Warner, Overbook made *Showtime* (2002) starring Robert De Niro and Eddie Murphy, and music video director Chris Robinson was hired for *ATL* (2006). Subsequently, Fox Searchlight handled releasing for the Overbrook drama *The Secret Life of Bees* (2008).

5. Films not featuring the star but made by the sindie and released by the aligned studio. Sony and Columbia handled distribution for *Saving Face* (2004), a low-budget comedy-drama about a Chinese-American woman and her mother, while the studio's subsidiary Screen Gems looked after the North American release of *Lakeview Terrace* (2008), a racially conscious thriller with Samuel L. Jackson in the lead.

These interactions reflect different shades of dependent independence. No conditions of exclusivity lock star, sindie and studio together, yet the three parties work closely through a range of variable collaborative arrangements that differ by degree on a case-by-case basis.

Through Overbrook, Smith's producing and managerial influence extended beyond film to other media. Smith's own stardom was built across media and very early on he regarded Overbrook as a multiple media outfit:

> What we found with my career is that one aspect of the entertainment industry built upon another . . . It started with music, then television and then the film world crumbled shortly thereafter. What we're trying to do is create a company that has the synergy to take a music star, for example, and parlay that into success in film and television. (quoted in Schneider and Adalian, 2000: 24)

Overbrook's music division was formed in February 1999 to release the soundtrack album for *Wild Wild West*, distributed by Interscope through the Universal deal, and released on 15 June 1999 to precede the film's opening in early July (Cox and Petrikin, 1999). Given Smith's background, it was inevitable that Overbrook would expand into television production, although ventures in this direction produced few results. A new television division was formed in September 1998 with the hiring of David Tochterman, former Senior Vice President of Creative Affairs at television producer and distributor Carsey-Werner (Hontz, 1998). Although Overbrook was committed to offering the studio first-look on the films it developed, Smith's company was at liberty to pursue television projects elsewhere, and by 2000 Overbrook had a wide array of dramas and animated or comedy series in development through co-production deals with Regency TV, Touchstone Television and NBC Studios (Schneider and Adalian, 2000). These partnerships were largely unproductive, however, and apart from the comedy pilot *Loose Cannon* (2000) for Warner's WB Network, Overbrook's television output was limited to the comedy series *All of Us*. Smith and his wife, actor-producer-director-writer Jada Pinkett Smith, were joint creators and executive producers for series, and Overbrook presented the series as loosely based on the Smiths' own family life, describing the series as

> inspired by the domestic adventures of entertainment superstars Will Smith and Jada Pinkett-Smith . . . reflect[ing] a new generation's enlightened attitude toward the extended family dynamic with humor, sensitivity and heart. This humorous and heartwarming comedy is a fresh, timely look at many young parents' new, compassionate attitude toward how divorced parents raise their children together. (Overbrook, 2009)

From 2003 to 2006, *All of Us* ran for three seasons on the United Paramount Network, and following the merger of UPN with The WB, the resulting CW Network ran a final season. Overbrook's attempts at diversifying to become a multi-platform media enterprise were therefore limited, and the company predominantly remained a film production outfit, building a solid reputation as one of the leading sindies in conglomerate Hollywood.

Overbrook is only part of Smith's business affairs and he has used his stardom and wealth in other ways to promote African-American enterprise. With his wife, Smith invested in the ethnic personal and beauty-care products manufacturer Carol's Daughter in an arrangement brokered by Steve Stoute, Chief Creative Officer of the New York based advertising and brand consultancy Translation. Linking the Smiths with Carol's Daughter was just part of a wider strategy pursued by Stoute, who had become a leading exponent of entertainment marketing by matching African-American stars from entertainment and sports with campaigns for Fortune 500 companies. Marrying corporate interests with urban culture, Stoute said his aim was to assist executives in understanding what he described as the "tanning of America" by sharing the experiences and values shared by a generation of African-American, Latin-American and white consumers for whom rap and hip hop had become a core cultural reference point (Lowry, 2007). In July 2005, Smith also invested in The Momentum Experience, a theatrical film distribution company set up by producers Nia Hill and D'Angela Steed together with actor Duane Martin. It was the company's objective to enable audiences to theatrically release independent films from African-American filmmakers which otherwise went straight-to-DVD. Bypassing conventional channels of theatrical exhibition, Momentum had the aim of tapping into the live urban theatre movement familiar to African-American audiences, showing films with a supporting program of live comedy in non-traditional venues such as playhouses and concert theatres located in key urban markets. As Hill explained, the "distribution model was born out of a shared desire by everyone involved to control the African-American cinematic image from start to finish" (McClintock, 2005: 4 and 30). Romantic comedy *The Seat Filler* (2004) was screened at venues in the top 20 urban markets during summer 2005 but subsequently Momentum fell dormant.

Smith and the Global Film Market

Independence Day and *Men in Black* were released during the prime season in the annual box-office calendar, and following the commercial success of the films, Smith earned the label "Mr. Summer" (Parks, 1999). As *Men in Black* was released in early July 1997 over the equivalent five-day weekend as when *Independence Day* opened the year before, Smith himself jokingly referred to this high point in the summer season as "Big Willie Weekend" (Thompson, 1997). With *Wild Wild West, Men in Black II* and *Hancock* all released over the corresponding weekends in future years, so the label stuck. Positioned close to 4 July, Smith's visibility therefore became linked into the calendar of national holidays in the US.

While Smith occasionally did films for other studios, Overbrook's deal with Columbia made the star a key asset for the studio. After *Ali*, he appeared for Columbia in a run of five films which each grossed over US$270 million at the global box office (see Table 6.3). *Men in Black II* (US$441.8 million worldwide) and *Hancock* (US$624.3 million worldwide) in particular stood out as major hits. In the years they are released, Smith's films consistently ranked amongst the top 10 grossing titles at the domestic box office: *Men in Black II* ranked eighth, while *Bad Boys II* and *Hitch* were both 10th in their respective years, and *Hancock* fourth. Apart from outings for the *Spider-man* franchise and the James Bond series, the latter which Sony adopted in 2006, in the first decade of the twenty-first century Columbia's annual performance at the domestic box came to rest on Smith's summer movies.

Table 6.3 Will Smith and the studios: domestic and international box-office grosses by studio, 1995–2008.[1]

	Columbia		Disney		DreamWorks		Twentieth Century Fox		Warner Bros.	
	Dom.	Int.	Dom.	Int.	Dom.	Int.	Dom.	Int.	Dom.	Int.
Seven Pounds (2008)	70.0	98.2								
Hancock (2008)	227.9	396.4								
I Am Legend (2007)									256.4	329.0
The Pursuit of Happyness (2006)	163.6	143.5								
Hitch (2005)	179.5	188.6								
I, Robot (2004)							144.8	202.4		
Bad Boys II (2003)	138.6	134.7								
Men in Black II (2002)	190.4	251.4								
Ali (2001)	58.2	29.5								
The Legend of Bagger Vance (2000)					30.9	8.5				
Wild Wild West (1999)									113.8	108.3
Enemy of the State (1998)			111.5	139.1						
Men in Black (1997)	250.7	338.7								
Independence Day (1996)							306.2	511.2		
Bad Boys (1995)	65.8	75.6								
Per studio										
Total films	9		1		1		2		2	
Total gross domestic b.o.	1,344.7		111.5		30.9		451.0		370.2	
Total gross overseas b.o.		1,656.6		139.1		8.5		713.6		437.3
Total gross b.o.	3,001.3		150.6		39.4		1,164.6		807.5	
Average per film	333.5		150.6		39.4		582.3		403.7	

Source: compiled using data from www.boxofficemojo.com.
[1]Figures are for films in which Smith took star billing and so does not include his supporting appearances in *Where the Day Takes You* (1992), *Made in America* (1993), or *Six Degrees of Separation* (1993), and cameo in *Jersey Girl* (2004). It also does not include the animated feature *Shark Tale* (2004) for which he contributed voice work. Table covers Smith's films up to *Seven Pounds*, the last film made under Overbrook's original first-look deal with Columbia.

Smith's popularity in North America was matched at the international box office. With few exceptions, Smith's films achieved higher grosses overseas than in the domestic market (Table 6.3). Across the international box office, in the years they were released, *Men in Black II* ranked sixth, *Hitch* ninth and *Hancock* fifth, while *I, Robot* (ninth) and *I Am Legend* (15th) delivered overseas hits for Fox and Warner Bros.[1] As discussed in the previous chapter, the global box office for Hollywood films is largely made of up of just a few key territories, and Smith's international popularity came from capturing audiences in those countries. For example, by the end of 2008, *Hancock* was ranked amongst the annual top 10 films in nearly all the world's most valuable film markets (Table 6.4). In Germany, France, Italy, Spain and the UK/Ireland alone, *Hancock* attracted 16.5 million admissions, accounting for nearly 84 percent of the 19.7 million tickets sold for the film in the 27 territories of the European Union (EAO, 2010). While less valuable to Hollywood in terms of box-office dollars, *Hancock*'s performance in Brazil and Mexico ensured Smith reached audiences in the dominant markets of Latin America. As the film rolled out internationally between July to September 2008, so the presence of Mr. Summer was spread across global space, and to achieve this exposure, Smith's international visibility was managed through the international distribution networks of the majors. For the world's leading markets, Sony used its overseas offices to self-distribute *Hancock* (see Table 6.4), while in Russia the film was handled through the studio's co-venture with Disney, Buena Vista Sony Pictures Releasing, and the services of local distributors such as Alexandra, Falcon, Intercom or Forum were utilized in Central and Eastern European territories.

Smith's international success cannot be attributed to the marketing efforts of the major studios alone, for he has played an active role in global publicity drives for his films. To publicize the opening of *Hitch* in the UK, Smith attended three premieres across England in a single day, a feat which placed him in the *Guinness Book of Records* (Blackstock, 2005). Smith's involvement in publicizing his films was part of a conscious strategy to self-promote his stardom around the world: when visiting countries to publicize his films, he reportedly worked to learn just enough of the native language to deliver a short speech (Siegel, 2008b: 17). Smith and his other Overbrook executives have openly declared their international ambition. "It's been said," Smith remarked, "'Why sell something to 10 people when you can sell it to 10 million people?'... You have to have a global perspective" (quoted in Holson, 2006). "We only believe in hitting home runs in

Table 6.4 Will Smith circles the world: *Hancock* in key international markets.

	Distributor	Release date	Admissions (ranking amongst annual top films)
North America	Sony	2 July 2008	31,747,392 (4)
Key international territories			
Europe			
UK and Ireland	Sony	2 July 2008	4,775,691 (6)
Germany	Sony	3 July 2008	3,846,331 (5)
France	Sony	9 July 2008	3,077,695 (9)
Spain	Sony	18 June 2008	2,845,842 (2)
Italy	Sony	12 Sept. 2008	1,930,596 (7)
Russian Federation/CIS	Buena Pictures Sony	10 July 2008	3,878,481 (7)
Asia-Pacific[1]			
Japan	Sony	30 Aug. 2008	2,553,542 (15)
Australia	Sony	3 July 2008	1,841,771 (9)
Latin America			
Mexico	n/a	4 July 2008	3,812,602 (9)
Brazil	n/a	11 July 2008	2,700,000 (5)

Sources: EAO (2009 and 2010), Screen Australia (2010)
[1] *Hancock* also attracted significant audiences in China and Hong Kong. Admissions figures were unavailable for these territories, however in China the film was released by the China Film Group and grossed US$14.8m, making it the twelfth most successful film that year at the national box office, while in Hong Kong it grossed US$3.05m to end the year ranked tenth.

every country of the world," Stovitz admitted: "There's a map of the world in my office that literally covers the entire wall. That's my market. If there's a universally relatable human emotion in a project, then we want to deliver it to the entire world" (quoted in Netzer, 2008). Hollywood's global presence and appeal is widespread but in certain parts of the world still remains minimal. Conscious of these limitations, Overbrook adopted a strategy of targeting specific territories to boost Smith's visibility. Lassiter has acknowledged that "For *I, Robot* it was Russia, in South Africa it was *Ali*" (quoted in Holson, 2006). On another occasion, he elaborated, "It is a lot of work, but to Will's credit, he is willing to start at zero for each territory." Lassiter explains, "In Russia, he is not 'Will Smith.' He is some guy showing his movie. After going back time and time again, people finally begin to say, 'Hey, you're the guy from *I, Robot*'" (quoted in Siegel, 2008b: 17).

By the latter decades of the twentieth century, economic growth in India and China saw Hollywood hungrily eyeing both countries for the enormous untapped potential they represented. Huge mass populations were counterbalanced by the relatively low penetration of Hollywood films at the box office. Sony used Smith's stardom as part of its promotional efforts in India. In February 2006, Smith made his first visit to the country when he was flown out to launch Pix, Sony Entertainment Television's English-language movie cable channel. This occasion linked Hollywood stardom to a new international market opportunity, as Pix became the fourth Hollywood movie channel to start up in India, screening films from the Sony Pictures library (including titles from Columbia and MGM) and targeting the country's growing urban middle-class (Mathur, 2006; Pearson, 2006). During the trip, Smith also worked at increasing his personal visibility in the territory, making a guest appearance on the television talent show *Indian Idol* (2004–) and presenting at the Filmfare Awards, India's oldest and most esteemed film honors. India, however, has represented a hard market for Hollywood to crack as the popularity of indigenous "Bollywood" or Hindi-language films have left a mere 5–10 percent of the annual box office to Hollywood imports. To strengthen their presence in the territory, Hollywood studios have therefore worked at forming collaborative arrangements with Indian partners. Overbrook followed this trend when in August 2006 a deal was signed with Indian media and entertainment company UTV to co-produce a live-action film for US$10m and an animated feature for US$20m. UTV agreed to provide funding to a certain level beyond which Overbook paid, with Sony having a first-look agreement on both films and UTV distributing in India (Bharatan Iyer, 2006; Frater, 2008). By December 2008, Overbrook was eyeing further international opportunities, partnering with D Media to form Red Pearl Pictures, a new distribution company for releasing western films in the Middle East. *Hancock* grossed around US$3m in Arabic-speaking countries and it was the aim of the venture to increase access to Hollywood entertainment in the region, particularly in Abu Dhabi, Dubai, Egypt, Qatar, and Saudi Arabia (Jaafar and Fleming, 2008).

China presented different challenges, with the national industry and market under the state control of the China Film Group Corporation. After China joined the World Trade Organization in 2002, protectionist measures were introduced, with imports capped at 20 films per year and a blackout instituted on the screening of imported films during the main holiday periods in order to maximize audiences for domestically produced features.

These barriers directly confronted Smith and Overbrook: when in December 2007 the Chinese authorities imposed an unofficial three-month ban on US imports over disputes concerning intellectual property issues and the US supply of weapons to Taiwan, the action locked *I Am Legend* out of the market (Frater, 2007). However, the film received a premiere in Hong Kong, at which Smith attended and took the opportunity to meet with Han Sanping, head of China Film, to plead the case for the film. Although unsuccessful on that occasion, shortly afterwards *The Pursuit of Happyness* (titled *Happiness Knocks at the Door* in China) became the film which ended the blackout when authorities approved a release in January 2008 (Landreth, 2007). During his Hong Kong trip, Smith also met with local actor-director-producer Stephen Chow to discuss plans for collaboration on a remake of the child action movie *The Karate Kid* (1984) (Scott, 2007). The resulting production, *The Karate Kid* (2010), is interesting from many angles. Not only does the narrative tell a tale of harmonious relations formed across geographic and cultural differences but production of the film also demonstrated the strategic workings of Smith and Overbrook's international ambitions. Although Chow ultimately did not work on the film, engaging a Chinese partner could qualify the film as a Chinese co-production rather than an import. When Overbrook and Columbia therefore secured China Film as a co-production partner, the film could circumvent China's trade barriers, and signing martial arts veteran Jackie Chan to play a supporting role in the film built more bridges (Siegel, 2009).

Smith is representative of many trends defining the post-studio system in conglomerate Hollywood: the dependent independence of stars, the creative and business extensions of the star brand, and the importance of addressing the star brand to international markets. What is maybe most interesting about Smith is how he illustrates star agency in the system. Smith is not simply an effect or product of the system but a smart and knowing manipulator of the system. His active involvement in Overbrook's international strategy demonstrates a highly self-conscious understanding of how to maximize his brand. These efforts are not limited to Smith alone. On *The Karate Kid*, his son Jaden took the lead role, and so the film helped broaden exposure for the wider Smith family. Even though the father took no role in the narrative, the film still offered a platform for raising awareness of the Will Smith brand, for during the end credits of the film, the star makes appearances alongside his son in a series of production stills. Smith therefore takes an active hand in his own brand construction. A large part of that work has involved his shrewd negotiation of racial difference, enacting a mediated identity which does not shun race but yet packages this in a manner which can be easily marketed across different media and territorial markets.

Note

1   International ranking for *I Am Legend* is based on the total gross for 2007 only. In a departure from Smith's status of "Mr. Summer," the film was released across a number of territories in December 2007, and by the end of the year the film had grossed $116 million at the international box office. However the film continued its international roll-out through the first four months of 2008, in the course of which adding another $213 million to its cumulative international gross.

PART THREE
Star Performance

7

Spectacular Acts

Stars are performed brands. Whatever other factors contribute to the production of stardom, film stars are only stars because they perform in films.

So far this study has explored the broad contextual conditions of industrial structures, company operations, market trends and contractual arrangements for how these shape the symbolic commerce of stardom. Any analysis of film stardom must include, however, consideration of how stardom is produced on-screen. Script, cinematography, lighting and editing are active in the construction of the star performance. Agents, managers, producers, writers, directors and the technical crew all play their parts in bringing the starring act to the screen. But these inputs exist beyond the star. The star specifically contributes to the star performance through acting, the mode of performance specifically concerned with the representation of dramatic character through the media of the voice and body. It is the concern of this chapter to examine the dynamics at work in the symbolic construction of the star performance. It looks at the star performance as an effect of both narrative and spectacle produced through elements of film form and enacted by the star's voice and body. Looking at performance, the chapter therefore explores how the star brand is enacted on-screen.

To anchor this discussion, the chapter focuses on a single star in a specific film. According to the Quigley poll, from 1990 to 2009 Tom Cruise was the period's most enduring money-maker (see Table 1.1). In the period Cruise maintained a record of box-office hits rivaled only by Tom Hanks (see Figure 5.1). In the year it was released, *Mission: Impossible 2* (2000) finished

Hollywood Stardom, First Edition. Paul McDonald.
© 2013 Paul McDonald. Published 2013 by John Wiley & Sons, Ltd.

second in the annual box-office rankings for North America and scored the highest gross of any film in the international market: *M:I-2* took $125.4 million domestically and $331 million internationally. Produced by Cruise's sindie Cruise/Wagner Productions for Hollywood major Paramount, *M:I-2* became Cruise's second most commercially successful film in terms of worldwide gross (surpassed by *War of the Worlds* (2005) with $591.7 million worldwide). Exhibitors voted Cruise the top money-maker for 2000 and when James Ulmer compiled his Ulmer Scale that year, Cruise was ranked third after Julia Roberts and Hanks, with a bankability rating of 98 percent.[1] In Ulmer's estimation, Cruise was "worth every penny. He has never had a bad performance. And he promotes his films" (2000: 15).

With *M:I-2*, Cruise appeared in an action drama, a genre he'd already built a strong association with. Cruise first played Ethan Hunt – agent with the secretive Impossible Missions Force (IMF) – in *Mission: Impossible* (1996), and returned four years later to reprise the role for this second installment of the series. *M:I-2* constructs a tale around the endeavors of Hunt and his IMF team to foil a plot which threatens to not only hold a major drugs manufacturer to ransom but also unleash a deadly virus which could kill millions. At the research laboratory of Biocyte Pharmaceuticals in Sydney, molecular biologist Dr. Vladimir Nekhorvich (played by Radé Sherbedgia) has cultivated the super-virus "Chimera" and antidote "Bellerophon." Anyone infected with Chimera dies a horrible death in a matter of hours but at the start of the film Nekhorvich injects himself with Chimera and urgently leaves with a consignment of Bellerophon to take a flight to the US and seek the assistance of his old friend "Dimitri." On the plane it is revealed Dimitri is actually Cruise/Hunt. But all is not as it seems. Nekhorvich has been duped for "Hunt" is actually rogue former IMF agent Sean Ambrose (played by Dougray Scott) who kills the scientist to steal the Bellerophon. Ambrose deceived Nekhorvich by wearing a rubber mask exactly reproducing Cruise/Hunt's face and an electronic chip to replicate his voice. Ambrose and his gang of accomplices escape, taking Nekhorvich's case carrying the Bellerophon. Before his death Nekhorvich sent a video recording of his planned movements to IMF headquarters, and so the real Hunt is recalled from vacation to track Ambrose. To assist him, Hunt must link up with Ambrose's former lover, British professional thief Nyah Nordoff-Hall (played by Thandie Newton). There then unfolds a narrative in which Nordoff-Hall goes undercover by re-acquainting herself with Ambrose but when he discovers the deception, her life is threatened. Along the way, Hunt learns Nekhorvich developed Bellerophon for the scientific purpose of creating as an antivirus to combat all strains of influenza but in order to develop the cure it was necessary to cultivate the lethal Chimera. Biocyte's CEO sponsored the research to exploit the commercial value of Bellerophon and so Ambrose has stolen the drug to extort a heavy ransom from Biocyte and he intends to use the funds to buy share options in the company. When he killed Nekhorvich, however, Ambrose was unaware the scientist was carrying the virus in his own blood. Ambrose therefore finds himself with a cure but no virus and so must obtain Chimera before he can leverage the deal with Biocyte. After Nordoff-Hall injects herself with the last sample of Chimera to avoid Ambrose killing her, she has only hours to live and the film builds to a climax in which Hunt kills Ambrose, destroys the evil plot, retrieves the Bellerophon, and saves Nordoff-Hall.[2]

Coming after two decades in which action cinema had played a large part in defining commercial popularity, *M:I-2* appeared on the cusp of change in the film market before fantasy and comic book franchises went on to define popularity over the next decade. Working with this example, the chapter therefore analyzes star performance in a film which not only characterized popular Hollywood in the period but also marked a commercial high point in Cruise's career. Furthermore, as *M:I-2* includes a number of self-conscious references to Cruise's branded image, then the film itself reflects on stardom and the workings of the star act.

Star Attraction

Writing on early cinema, Tom Gunning describes the tendency for many films to revel in the "ability to *show* something" (1986: 57) as forming what he calls the "cinema of attractions." In these cases, film created exhibitionist spectacle, contrasting with the voyeuristic tendency of narrative film to tell stories. Once narrative production came to dominate, Gunning suggests this exhibitionist tendency went "underground, both into certain avant-garde practices and as a component of narrative films, more evident in some genres (e.g. the musical) than in others" (p. 57). However, this view maybe unnecessarily limiting, for as a display constructed to be looked at, any film remains to some extent a form of show or spectacle. Like theater or opera, film is a "performing art," a type of show staged for public exhibition. Narrative film stages stories, combining the voyeuristic representation of symbolically constructed diegetic worlds with the exhibitionist presentation of spectacular show.

As figures in film narrative, actors are situated within these dual aspects. Actors represent characters in the narrative but by appearing in a medium of public presentation they are also spectacle. Stardom arises from the hierarchical distinctions between actors formed by the differential distribution of wages, the creative decision-making powers granted to actors, or the uses of actor names in marketing media. But the hierarchy of actors is also produced on-screen. By appearing in a performance medium, all film actors are spectacle. Stars, however, are distinguished from this general ensemble – that is, the general spectacle of actors – for they are *spectacular* figures. Compared to their fellow performers, stars are presented in ways to appear more fabulous, compelling, marvelous, extravagant, incredible, dazzling, stunning and exciting.

This spectacularization of the star is a symbolic effect with a commercial purpose. While it may be debatable whether the presence of stars can or cannot actually sell films (see Chapter 5), regardless of outcome, if stars are to have any value they must at least be visible. Film is a medium of visibility – it shows something – but intensifying the visibility of the actor is fundamental to the work of the star performance so that the star becomes an attraction within an attraction. It is by spectacularizing star performance that the star is shown off as a film's key performing asset. While the spectacularization of the actor is constant throughout star performance, it reaches particular highpoints where moments are staged precisely to display the star attraction. Most obvious of these moments is the star entrance. Before the film is viewed, before the film is consumed, anticipation of a star's performance is built through advance marketing media. It may very well be this hype which draws the consumer to the film. When the film therefore plays, the star's entrance is a moment of great significance and importance, for it fulfils anticipation by finally revealing the star. This game of anticipation/fulfillment, however, can only partly explain the significance of the star entrance. Conceivably, many viewers may never have encountered the marketing for a film they watch, or may have no recollection of it by the time they come to see a film, particularly if viewed for the first time in a secondary release windows such as DVD or free-to-air television. Consequently the star entrance stages the more general function of announcing the lead performing attraction. The star entrance serves both the presentational and representational aspects of narrative film with the spectacular purpose of announcing "here is the star" and the narrative purpose of announcing "here is the person who (very likely) will play the central character."

Figure 7.1   Extravagant star entrance: *Mission: Impossible 2*. Producers Tom Cruise and Paula Wagner; director John Woo; distributed by Paramount Pictures.

Due to its importance and significance, the star entrance is a highly orchestrated moment. In *M:I-2*, Cruise initially appears on the flight with Sherbedgia/Nekhorvich, but as will soon transpire, this is actually Ambrose masquerading as Hunt. Cruise as Hunt therefore actually enters the film in the next scene following the hijacking of the flight. An accelerated helicopter shot sweeps over the barren landscape of Dead Horse Point State Park, Utah, to pick out Cruise/Hunt precariously rock climbing at a dizzy height on a narrow ridge without ropes or protection (Figure 7.1). Cruise/Hunt is a man alone, risking his life in an inhospitable wilderness. Initially it is not entirely clear who the figure is for the camera is too far away, but as the camera nears the climbing figure, so Cruise's face becomes visible. Given the hazards of the situation it would be reasonable to presume this is a stunt double or the creation of computer-generated effects, although publicity around the film worked hard to assure Cruise was actually climbing the rock protected by ropes removed in post-production.[3] Both character and star are shown to be in danger, and as critic Manohla Dargis (2000) noted, the actuality of Cruise performing the stunt creates a spectacle of the star running counter to the digitally generated show commonly seen in action cinema of the period.

> Much has been made in the entertainment press . . . that Cruise performed many of his own stunts . . . And it's no wonder – the climbing scene is spectacular, both in its panoramic beauty and . . . the audience's shivery thrill of recognition that it's the star himself . . . In the age of the digital, this sort of

flamboyant stuntwork might seem anachronistic . . . But Cruise's physical
daring is necessary precisely because digital effects have become so persuasive. In the age of virtual reproduction, the star body has become the test
bed of authenticity, the last stand of the real.

Through music, the scene also makes one of what will become many self-
reflexive plays on Cruise's on-screen identity, for the soundtrack carries the
song "Souca Na Na," a reworking by Zap Mama of the frequently covered
standard "Iko Iko," the song playing over Cruise's entrance during the
opening credits of *Rain Man* (1988). Here music adds to the spectacularization of the star with an inter-textual reference that has no other purpose
than to foreground a common star presence between two films, forming
an in-joke for any viewers appreciative of the allusion.

As if the climb were not dangerous enough already, Cruise/Hunt leaps
from one crag to another but in doing so misses his footing, sliding over
the edge and only saving himself from certain death by grabbing a hold
with his very fingertips (Figure 7.2). When he has recovered his control,
Cruise/Hunt completes the climb, but no sooner has he reached the summit
than he is delivered a message from his IMF controller. Potentially this
could have been transferred very easily by hand, but this is the IMF and
they don't do things that way. Instead, the delivery involves a helicopter, a
missile and a pair of customized sunglasses through which play a pre-
recorded briefing informing Cruise/Hunt of his mission to retrieve Chimera
and link up with Newton/Nordoff-Hall (Figure 7.3). The moment creates
a further reflexive gesture towards Cruise's on-screen identity, for by the
time of *M:I-2* the sight of Cruise wearing black sunglasses had become a

Figure 7.2 Cruise/Hunt hangs on: *Mission: Impossible 2*. Producers Tom Cruise
and Paula Wagner; director John Woo; distributed by Paramount Pictures.

Figure 7.3 Cruise/Hunt takes a message: *Mission: Impossible 2*. Producers Tom Cruise and Paula Wagner; director John Woo; distributed by Paramount Pictures.

Figure 7.4 Cruise and shades: *Risky Business*. Producers Jon Avnet and Steve Tisch; director Paul Brickman; distributed by Warner Home Video.

common image familiar from the star's earlier performances in *Days of Thunder* (1990), *Rain Man* and *Top Gun* (1986) (where he became a product placement model for Ray-Ban shades), and receding back to the moment when he first appears in *Risky Business* (1982) (Figure 7.4). Following in the tradition of the *Mission: Impossible* television series, once the briefing has played out, Cruise/Hunt is warned the message will self destruct in five seconds, and he tosses away the glasses just as they explode

Figure 7.5   Cruise/Hunt accepts his mission: *Mission: Impossible 2*. Producers Tom Cruise and Paula Wagner; director John Woo; distributed by Paramount Pictures.

(Figure 7.5). With the flashy camerawork, amazing scenery, death defying antics, highly contrived situations, explosive pyrotechnics, and self-reflexive quotations, Cruise enters the film in a moment where spectacle mounts on spectacle. This scene could be regarded as "excess" for it is highly elaborate and apart from Hunt receiving the briefing it has absolutely no narrative consequence. However the purpose of the scene has little to do with telling the story and more to do with creating show, for which it is not at all excessive but entirely essential, for it serves the key purpose of introducing and establishing Cruise as the film's spectacular attraction.

With the "false" appearance on the plane followed by the real appearance on the rock, Cruise's arrival in *M:I-2* forms a double entrance, a convention common to many of the star's films. Frequently Cruise first appears in moments where he is somehow initially obscured or disguised, so that his entrance stages a revelation within a revelation. For *Minority Report* (2002), when Cruise first appears he is seen from behind until a cut reverses the angle through 180 degrees to show him face-on walking towards the camera. With *Interview with the Vampire* (1994), it takes seven minutes before Cruise enters, and when he does, only his hand and then his back are seen before his face is fully revealed. Likewise, in *Collateral* (2004), with 13 minutes already passed a hand is first seen before the full body of the star is shown.

Mission: Impossible presents another case of the double entrance. Cruise appears in the very opening shot of the film but his presence is obscured for Hunt is wearing a disguise in order to trick information from an interrogatee, thereby deferring the star's entrance for a couple of minutes until the moment where he reveals himself by removing the latex mask he is wearing. That gesture demonstrates a more standard convention of the star entrance, in which the showing of the face – usually framed in medium shot or close-up – becomes the absolute confirmation of the star's presence. "Several different bodies," Richard Maltby notes, "may be used to construct a single performance: voices are dubbed, stunt artists are used for danger-ous action sequences, and sometimes hand models and body doubles provide body parts to substitute for the actors" (2003: 371). Notably, when substituting stars with stunt men and women, or body doubles for nude or sex scenes, the face is obscured so as not to give the game away and break the illusion. With so many other bodies capable of dissembling, it is the face which ultimately authenticates the star's presence. Consequently, a great deal of the spectacularizing of the star is actually condensed into the showing of the face. Revealing the body, or parts of the body, is just not enough to confirm the presence of the star, and so it is only with the show of the face that the star ultimately becomes visible. Roland Barthes described Greta Garbo as "an admirable face-object" (1957: 56) and the same could be said of stars in general, for their status as both actor and asset is quintessentially tied into the objectification of the face. In many ways, the star entrance is a moment predicated on the revelation or spec-tacularization of the face as the core physical, symbolic and commercial feature of star performance.

Many of Cruise's entrances are extravagant, becoming "over the top" moments. *M:I-2* presents a particularly extravagant star entrance and similar spectacular moments are created for Cruise's entrances in *Days of Thunder*, *Jerry Maguire* (1996) and *War of the Worlds*. To the sound of heavy drum beats, Cruise first appears in *Days of Thunder* riding a motorbike on an empty racetrack but is initially obscured for he is held at a distance in extreme long shot and it is not until he nears the camera and his face becomes visible that he is clearly identified. On *Jerry Maguire*, at first only Cruise's voice is heard narrating over a montage of sports men and women, until two minutes into the film he becomes visible as he springs into shot from behind a bank of television monitors, putting his face on show. Cruise/Maguire is attending a convention as the eponymous sports agent where he plays the room by swiftly moving between delegates and fast talking promises to everyone he meets. Great energy is brought to the moment, for the scene is constructed as a rapid series of short shots which are spatially and temporally discontinuous but are given coherence by the central presence (i.e. the face) of the star. Overall, the speed of the cuts and the jumps in time and space give Cruise/Maguire a "whirlwind" entrance. Maguire dominates the narrative situation as Cruise dominates the screen. With *War of the Worlds* an extreme aerial long shot swoops over a freight yard, and as it hones in on a crane lifting containers, Cruise as Ray Ferrier is revealed seated in the cabin. Cruise/Ferrier has been in the shot from the very beginning but the camera works to find and isolate him in the enormity of the space, with the search ending once his face becomes visible.

In contrast to these ostentatious moments, Cruise's arrival in other films is comparatively subdued and understated, yet still shots are organized to stress the importance and significance of the star entrance. In *A Few Good Men* (1992), following a soldier's death at the US Naval Base at Guantanamo Bay, a captain assures his fellow officers that the ensuing investigation will be in safe hands as "division will assign the right man for the job." This immediately cues a cut to a new scene where Cruise as military attorney Lt. Daniel Kaffee is found on a playing field practicing his batting skills. When compared to the extravagance of *M:I-2* or *Days of Thunder*, Cruise's entrance in *A Few Good Men* appears restrained, but the moment is still constructed as special and the star is distinguished from the general spectacle. Although the shot is constructed entirely for Cruise's moment of appearance, for a fleeting instant he doesn't emerge until walking into shot from frame left. Another actor appears in the background but use of a shallow depth of field places him out of focus while Cruise is crisply captured in the foreground (Figure 7.6). In *Far and Away* (1992) and *Vanilla*

Figure 7.6 Subdued star entrance: *A Few Good Men*. Producers David Brown, Rob Reiner and Andrew Scheinman; director Rob Reiner; distributed by Columbia TriStar Home Entertainment.

Sky (2001), Cruise is simply revealed by the camera tilting upwards or making a short mobile sweep across a room, while in *The Firm* (1993) Cruise is distinguished from the melee of a basketball game by isolating him in a medium shot as he utters an expletive. Although less "showy" than Cruise's hyperbolic entrances, these moments nevertheless still work to show off the star.

As a moment entirely orientated toward displaying the actor, the entrance marks the most obvious instance of spectacularizing the star. Yet the entrance is just part of the overall dynamic running throughout star performance which continually seeks to exhibit the key performing attraction.

The Performance of the Medium

In the star performance, the combination of story and show, of narrative and spectacle, is achieved at two levels. Together the technological and formal elements of photographic framing, camera movement, lighting, editing and sound recording mediate the presentation and representation of the actor to form the primary *performance of the film medium*. At a secondary level, the *performance of the actor* sees the body and voice used as media to represent but also present the character. This dual performance – of medium and actor – applies to all performers in film but contributes to the production of stardom by how elements of film form and the actions of the voice and body are used to hierarchically emphasize and thereby spectacularize the presence of particular performers.

Early in *M:I-2* Cruise/Hunt arrives in Seville to intercept Newton/ Nordoff-Hall. The two first catch sight of one another inside a hall where a group of flamenco dancers are performing. Through the prism of the film medium, the scene creates four tiers in a hierarchy of performers. Scattered around the hall are many anonymous extras shot collectively in groups to set the scene by fleshing-out the diegesis, populating the space and creating a sense of location and atmosphere. Secondly, the dancers also contribute to setting the scene but are given greater emphasis as medium-long and medium shots are used to identify and isolate parts of a dancer's body – the hands, feet, face. This more intimate framing brings the film viewer closer to the dancers than the extras and an internal audience is also formed within the scene as the extras fix their looks onto the dancers. This emphasis on the dancers is enhanced by lighting which is used to illuminate the

Figure 7.7   Cruise/Hunt looks: *Mission: Impossible 2*. Producers Tom Cruise and Paula Wagner; director John Woo; distributed by Paramount Pictures.

low platform they perform on with their audience kept in semi-darkness, while the camera moves inwards to the dancing group and a single shot captures dancing feet in slow motion.

Distinguished from these anonymous groupings are Cruise/Hunt and Newton/Nordoff-Hall. Both are introduced to the scene with medium-shots separating them from the larger space while at the same time camera movements track their passage as they walk amongst the people gathered in the hall. In this respect, both receive equal treatment by the medium, but a final hierarchical distinction is formed when the two catch sight of one another. Cruise/Hunt stops as his attention is caught by something out of frame, and to emphasize the moment the camera moves towards him, thereby tightening the framing from a medium head-and-shoulders shot to something nearing a close-up on the face (Figure 7.7). By this movement and reframing, camerawork is used to communicate the character is about to experience or do something important. A cut to the next shot reveals Newton/Nordoff-Hall as the object of that look. Unlike the isolated figure of Cruise/Hunt, Newton/Nordoff-Hall is positioned amongst a group of extras. Although she emerges from that group and is thereby distinguished from them, the framing keeps her in medium-shot and as her head is dipped, she does not return the look (Figure 7.8). Through the performance of the medium, Newton/Nordoff-Hall is therefore distinguished from the general ensemble as someone of narrative significance but her status is exceed by that of Cruise who is given greater emphasis through framing, camera movement and an organization of shots which position him as the

Figure 7.8   Newton/Nordoff-Hall is looked at: *Mission: Impossible 2*. Producers Tom Cruise and Paula Wagner; director John Woo; distributed by Paramount Pictures.

figure with greatest narrative knowledge. Here, with these few shots, the performance of the medium affirms the hierarchical distinction between supporting actor and star.

Using the medium to construct this look achieves a number of effects. Through his possession and control of knowledge, Cruise/Hunt is marked out as the protagonist, the core centre of narrative action and incident. By knowing, Hunt can now act: he has located the woman and so can progress with his mission. In terms of narrative structure, the hierarchy of performers can therefore be explained by how elements of film form create a "hierarchy of discourses" (MacCabe, 1974) or "hierarchy of knowledge" (Branigan, 1992: 72–6): Hunt is followed, isolated and emphasized for only he and the viewer share knowledge about the mission and the plan to recruit Nordoff-Hall, while she quite "innocently" thinks she is merely there to steal an expensive necklace, and the dancers and guests are oblivious to all these goings on. But the significance of the moment comes from more than just placing Cruise/Hunt in the plotting of the chain of cause and effect. When Cruise/Hunt looks, he doesn't just know, he responds and feels. Cruise/Hunt is more than just a protagonist, an agent of action; he is the central affective and emotional focus for this narrative moment. "Focalization," argues Edward Branigan, "involves a character . . . actually *experiencing* something through seeing or hearing it. Focalization . . . extends to . . . complex experiencing of objects: thinking, remembering, interpreting, wondering, fearing, believing, desiring, understanding, feeling guilt" (original emphasis, p. 101). When Cruise looks, he gives a fixed intense stare which conveys how Hunt feels about seeing Newton/Nordoff-Hall. It is a look which not only marks recognition of her importance to his mission but also signals the first glimmers of desire. This is actually an effect of acting rather than the medium, for although framing and editing create a point of view exchange, it is only the use of the body – specifically the face – which can communicate the quality and manner of how Cruise/ Hunt looks. Still the medium contributes to the moment for the use of close-up not only makes Cruise's facial details practically visible and read-able but also intensifies his already intense look by isolating him in frame to mark him as both the central *knowing* and *feeling* consciousness of the film. This combination of effects makes Cruise/Hunt a figure of identifica-tion. Through the organization of shots, the viewer adopts Hunt's perspec-tive, sharing his *viewpoint*, i.e. where he looks, but also his *point of view*, i.e. how he responds to, interprets and feels about what he sees (Maltby, 2003: 347). Identification is therefore formed by "alignment" between char-acter and viewer (Smith, 1995: 83).

This scene offers just one example of how the performance of the medium contributes to the production of stardom on-screen through ensemble differentiation, for the formal elements of film are used to con-struct distinctions between the hierarchy of performers. Here the perform-ance of the medium creates the narratological effects of focalization, point of view and identificatory alignment to position the star actor as the centre of the story, while at the same time framing him as the focal point of the screen spectacle. In the narrative Hunt looks and knows but at the same time Cruise is also made a figure to be looked at. All performers in the scene contribute to the production of the narrative and are also placed on display, but the performance of the medium structurally orders different tiers of performers towards enhancing and intensifying the narrative and spectacular significance of the star.

The Performance of the Actor

While elements of film form mediate the presence of the actor and thereby contribute to the construction of character, it is in the uses of the voice and body to portray character that the performance of the actor is to be found. All film acting brings together a figure who is represented (the character) and the figure who does the representing (the actor). Narrative film aims to create plausible and believable on-screen worlds and so the standard measure of success in film acting is the degree to which the actor forms a credible representational link with the character. Hypothetically this would result in pure and total representation, with the actor transparently disappearing into character, yet for an audience knowingly watching a display of artifice played out on a screen, there is always the lingering knowledge that this is all "just an act." Consequently, no matter how credibly a character is played, the actor always remains visible, and so "the audience experiences the presence of the performer as well as – in the same body as – the presence of the character" (Maltby, 2003: 380). Regardless of whether audience members judge Cruise does or does not make a believable IMF agent, at every moment he will always be experienced as both Hunt and Cruise. Combining the representation of character with the presentation of the actor, this splitting or doubling of the actor's body relates to the dual aspects of the film medium: Hunt is a figure of the narrative while Cruise is a figure of spectacle. It is precisely this co-existence of character and actor in the same body which ensures the star act is simultaneously both story and show.

This duality relates to all actors in the narrative but the division becomes most acutely evident with the star. Many, possibly the majority, of actors who appear in *M:I-2* will be unfamiliar to audiences. For example, when Scott/Ambrose executes the plan to hijack the plane carrying Nekhorvich, the co-pilot passes out and collapses over his controls after inhaling the gas which the villainous plotters pipe through the emergency oxygen system. The co-pilot character is unnamed and the actor is unlikely to be a familiar face to most viewers.[4] Still there is the doubling of the body for there remains residual awareness that this is not a pilot but rather an actor playing a pilot. In Cruise's case, however, the division between actor and character becomes more pronounced for in a career that had already seen him play 16 leading roles, Cruise came to *M:I-2* as an entirely familiar figure, so that at each and every moment in the film he appears as both Ethan Hunt and "Tom Cruise." In *M:I-2*, Cruise doesn't just appear as Hunt but also as the guy who played, amongst other roles, Maverick in *Top Gun*, Brian Flanagan in *Cocktail* (1988), Charlie Babbit in *Rain Man*, Ron Kovic in *Born on the Fourth of July* (1989) and of course Ethan Hunt in *Mission: Impossible*. Knowledge of the actor's body differentiates the star from other actors in the on-screen hierarchy of performers. Whoever plays the pilot remains an anonymous body but Cruise is a recognizable, known and named body. Moreover, the status of Cruise as a known figure is essential to this whole early sequence, for Scott/Ambrose's deception can only fool because it presumes that not only the character Nekhorvich but also the audience are already familiar with, and so are able to recognize, a specific voice and body. Recognition leads Nekhorvich to trust Dimitri (i.e. Hunt) while it can also be reasonably presumed that foreknowledge of Cruise's roles in other films may encourage audience members to believe he will feature in the film as a force for good and upholder of the law. The killing of Nekhorvich by someone who looks and sounds exactly like Cruise therefore creates a shock and is a further part of the film's self-conscious play upon Cruise's mediated identity.

It is precisely because actor and character are one and the same body that it is with acting that belief in what has been described as the charismatic theory of stardom (see Chapter 1) holds greatest influence. As the voice and body are physically part of the individual performer, then star acting appears as a charismatic statement of individual expression, for any significance or meaning generated in acting appears innate and to simply issue from the actor. To break from the seductive appeal of the charismatic theory it is therefore necessary to recognize the star act, like all instances of branding, as a work of symbolic and commercial production. This requires finding the terms to break apart the apparent naturalness of the actor and character relationship to open it up for analysis. Going beyond the simple actor/character dyad, Stephen Heath (1981: 178–82) poses a model in which "agent," "character," "person," "image" are all components in constructing the "figure" in film. While useful, Heath's own account of his model is not only rather obscurantist and oblique but also his application of the terms is open to misunderstanding and confusion. It is therefore necessary to clarify the model and in so doing to revise the terms. "Agent" defines the function, or what can be described as the *role*, performed by a person contributing to the progression of the narrative. *Character* meanwhile defines the qualities or traits distinguishing a person as an individual. If role defines what the figure *does*, character describes who s/he *is*. "Person," for Heath, is the "individual . . . who actualizes – is the support for, plays, represents – agent and character" (p. 180), which in the case of narrative film may be more straightforwardly understood as the *actor*.

In *M:I-2*, Cruise/Hunt performs an obvious role: stop Ambrose's plot and save the girl. Not only does the narrative play out a clear and unambiguous structure of hero and antagonist but self-reflexively draws attention to the archetypicality of Cruise's role by referring to Greek mythology and the legendry hero Bellerophon who slay the monster Chimera. Robert

Towne's script brings this mythological content to the fore: in the very opening scene, as Sherbedgia/Nekhorvich is seen working in the lab at Biocyte, his voice-over narrates "every search for a hero must begin with something that every hero requires – a villain. Therefore, in the search for our hero, Bellerophon, we created a monster, Chimera." As the film then unfolds, structurally Cruise emerges as the hero/Bellerophon/cure while Ambrose is the monster/Chimera/virus. Part of Cruise's acting is therefore concerned with performing the actions necessary to achieve the functions of his role.

At the same time, Hunt is also portrayed as a particular type of person. Richard Dyer (1998: 106–17) sees a number of elements contributing to the construction of character in film. Familiarity with a film's story, characters, promotional materials, genre, star and criticism may all shape audience preconceptions of a character prior to viewing a film. Both the names of the character and the star can define certain traits: the surname "Hunt" holds resonances of tenacious and lethal pursuit, and when Thomas Cruise Mapother IV shortened his surname to "Cruise" he acquired a title signifying cool and controlled movement. Facial features, physical build, and costume all produce a set of outward appearances that give meaning to the figure. Hunt works for a quasi-governmental organization and yet Cruise's shoulder length hair and preference for tight fitting T-shirts and leather jackets artfully suggest he is no institutionalized drone. Objects can become indices of character if they appear to hint at certain traits. When Cruise/Hunt engages Newton/Nordoff-Hall in a car dual in the hills outside Seville, his choice to drive an open top Porsche attaches connotations of speed, power and freedom to the character. For Dyer, elements of *mise-en-scène* displayed in "lighting, color, framing, composition, placing of actors . . . can be used to express the personality or state of mind of characters" (p. 117). Globe-trotting between Utah, Seville and Sydney, Hunt traverses a cosmopolitan *mise-en-scène*. He moves from the desolation of the desert, to the warm seductive ambience of a Spanish night to the stark technological fortress of the Biocyte HQ, but with each context he can function in and command whatever environment he meets. Clearly Hunt is a man who does bestride the world.

Knowledge about and impressions of character are formed through what a character says and what others say about the character. Hunt speaks of himself, and is spoken of, as a man who thrives on embracing danger. When the IMF controller Swanbeck, played by Anthony Hopkins, explains the mission to Hunt and the role of Nordoff-Hall in that mission, Cruise/Hunt immediately rejects the idea; he claims it will be very difficult to get her to do it, to which Hopkins/Swanbeck responds "Well, this is not Mission Difficult, Mr. Hunt, it's Mission Impossible. Difficult should be a walk in the park for you." Despite initial reservations, Newton/Nordoff-Hall agrees to accept the mission, but to avoid Ambrose becoming suspicious when she suddenly turns up in his life again, she recommends creating a situation where she'll land in "serious trouble" requiring help from outside. In reply, Cruise/Hunt coolly says of himself "Serious trouble, Nyah, is something that I can always arrange."

Where Heath's categories become most confusing is in his account of "image," for he seeks to apply the term to both the literal photographic image shown on-screen but also in a manner similar to how Dyer conceptualizes "star image," i.e. as an inter-textual bundle of meanings, exceeding the particular role, which are derived from pre-existing performances and other media texts. To avoid this confusion, a distinction must be drawn then between the technology and aesthetics of what earlier was described as the performance of the *medium*, with the star's trans-media identity (following the arguments outlined in Chapter 2) regarded as the *brand*. As few performers in film carry strong recognition, then the brand is a component restricted to only stars and other well known actors. Finally, Heath binds his categories together in what he calls the "figure," the "circulation between agent, character, person and image, none of which is able simply and uniquely to contain, to *settle* that circulation" (original emphasis 1981: 182). What *figure* therefore describes is the flow of meanings and effects between the other categories.

Adapting Heath's model provides the foundations for a complex and dynamic model of star performance. Audiences are presented with the figure which, according to the revised terms outlined above, is the combined outcome of role, character, actor and medium. These components apply to all instances of acting in film but in the case of the star the branded identity of the performer is added to that mix. This model provides a framework and terms for understanding star acting as a dynamic process in which the figure materializes through the constant interaction between multiple elements of action and meaning. The star brand becomes an element in the formation of the figure but as the brand is formed across films, so it exceeds any specific instance of an enacted figure. On-screen the brand is produced, that is to say performed, by the star playing a succession of figures across films. As a multiple-media construct, that brand is equally the product of the star's appearances in other media (Figure 7.9).

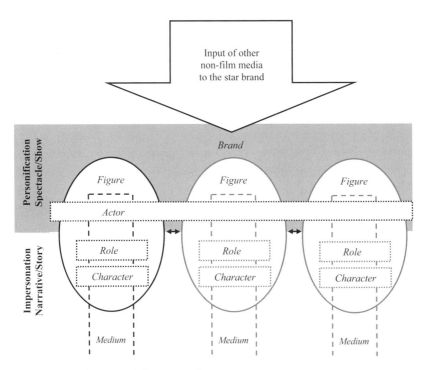

Figure 7.9   Elements of the star performance.

Missing from Heath's model is an account of how these various elements are held in combination. To see this model at work, it is therefore necessary to appreciate how the voice and body materialize and cohere each of the components to make the figure a distinct and identifiable person represented and presented in the star act. As already discussed the performance of the *medium* records and presents the voice and body of the star, particularly the face. Bodily form is given to the figure through the corporeality of the *actor*. Previously it was noted Cruise brings to *M:I-2* a known and named body and voice. Regardless of the character he plays, Cruise's dark hair, short to medium height, athletic build and enduring boyish looks present a familiar bodily shape and set of features which maintain strong physical recognizability. For *M:I-2*, Cruise is costumed in tight-fitting outfits which show off this body, for example during the rock-climbing entrance and later with the break-in at the Biocyte laboratories and the climatic fight with Scott/Ambrose. Vocally, in his performances Cruise generally speaks with a clear but low pitch, holding an even volume and steady rhythm to suggest calm authoritative control. It is precisely this vocal register which the false Hunt (played of course by Cruise) reproduces as part of the act to deceive Nekhorvich in the plane.

Through the media of the voice and body, the star performs the narrative actions of the *role*. At the micro-analytic level of physical gesture, the narrative chain of cause and effect can only be preserved because Cruise's right hand alone performs certain key actions: e.g., retrieving the sunglasses which the IMF use to send his mission brief; taking from Newton/Nordoff-Hall a memory card carrying a video revealing Ambrose's ransom plot; pressing play to run a sound recording of the Biocyte CEO's voice to unlock a door into the company's laboratories; and pulling the trigger of his pistol three times to finally kill Ambrose. Equally, the voice and body represent the distinctive traits of *character*. In contrast to the general state of control which Cruise's voice conveys, frequently the roles he plays give him brief moments where the volume and pace of the voice is racked up to convey explosive anger. Both registers are in play during the scene in *M:I-2* when Cruise/Hunt must tell Newton/Nordoff-Hall about her part in the mission and the need to renew her relationship with Scott/Ambrose. Hunt is confronted with a conflict between love and duty: professionally he must instruct her about the mission but emotionally he not only fears for the dangers she will be put in but is also deeply uncomfortable with how the woman he is falling for will be morally compromised by engaging in a false but intimate relationship with the villain. Newton/Nordoff-Hall is clearly angered by the demands placed on her but Cruise/Hunt contains his feelings and retains his professional cool. He speaks in a composed manner until the point where he feels compelled to ask her "Would it make you feel any better if I didn't want you to do this?" and she retorts "Yeah, much," at which point Cruise's voice breaks control and snaps back "Then feel better!" Here through the uses of the voice, Cruise is able to convey Hunt as someone who is both a cold professional and a passionately protective lover. Using the body and voice to perform the purposes of the role and traits of character can be explained in narratological terms as the enactment of "functions" and "indices," with "the former correspond[ing] to a functionality of doing, and the latter to a functionality of being" (Barthes, 1966: 93). Although the plot driven narrative of the action film places heavy emphasis on the functional agency of the voice and body – for the hero must say and do things of consequence – still the enactment of character indices are equally necessary to convey the type of person who can achieve those actions. Hunt kills the hero and foils the plot but he is also a composed man of noble principle but with a fiery heart.

Branded Performance

After medium, agent, character and actor, it is necessary to consider the place of the star brand in the performance of the figure. Dyer sees the link between star and role in terms of how successfully a "fit" is achieved between the star's identity and the role/character construction (1998: 126–31). In the case of *M:I-2*, the cool self-confident assurance of Hunt effectively matches the self-assured independence which Cruise had already portrayed in a string of roles from *Risky Business* to *Top Gun*, *The Color of Money* (1986), *Rain Man*, *Days of Thunder*, *A Few Good Men*, *The Firm* and *Jerry Maguire*. "Cruise established his onscreen persona" by performing "the cocky loner who plays by his own rules, confronts a crisis, then is triumphantly transformed" (Kaufman, Malley, Rammairone and Weinstein, 1998: 52).

Although the term "fit" may suggest the brand is a pre-existing entity which is more or less successfully matched with the character, it is important to recognize the star brand as an identity produced (at least in part) through acting. If there is a fit between Hunt and the Cruise, the link is produced only in performance as the brand is enacted through the voice and body. Reflecting on the actor/character relationship, Barry King (1985: 30) describes "impersonation" as instances of performance where an actor transforms the voice and body to represent character differences, which contrast with "personification" where vocal and bodily continuities are maintained so that the actor may seem to be simply playing him or herself. As all acting brings together the actor with the character or role, then no act can ever entirely be attributed to the role/character or the actor. Rather, impersonation and personification describe degrees of balance between the elements which make up the enacted figure. With personification, preserving regularities in the uses of the voice and body make the actor a recognizable figure regardless of the particularities of the role or character, whereas impersonation sees the voice and body used to enact the functions of role and indices of character specific to the particular narrative circumstances.

Star acting is forever situated in the co-existence of these two opposing performance principles, with personification foregrounding the actor over

the role/character to create continuity and similarity, against the privileging
of role/character over actor in impersonation to produce discontinuity and
difference. Emphasizing the presence of the actor, personification is necessary to spectacularizing the star brand as a visible, familiar and known
figure. With personification, King says "the actor is limited to parts consonant with his or her personality" (p. 30). As stars are highly mediated
identities, however, any viewer's perception of a star's personality is the
product of multiple and serial media representations, and so the star personality is already a deeply performed identity. If a star is judged to be
playing him- or herself on-screen, it is precisely because s/he is repeating
meanings and effects seen in other film performances, magazine articles,
television interviews, etc. Criticisms of star acting often arise because the
actor is seen to always be the same in each role, but this is exactly what is
demanded by the symbolic commerce of Hollywood. Producers pay stars
inflated compensation packages precisely to be a very visible and familiar
asset. Even so, as each film sees the star responding to particular narrative
circumstances, s/he never creates absolute sameness in each role. In *M:I-2*,
Cruise's manner of moving and speaking shares commonalities with not
only his portrayal of Hunt in *Mission: Impossible* but also his acting in *Top
Gun*, *Days of Thunder*, *A Few Good Men* and *The Firm*. At the same time,
Cruise had never previously played a role which required him to use his
body and voice to enact the exact circumstances of *M:I-2*. Consequently,
personification and impersonation do not represent mutually exclusive
performance principles but rather dual components of the star performance. In *M:I-2*, Cruise is Cruise but also Hunt. Star acting tailors personification to the needs of impersonation while achieving personification
through repeated instances of impersonation.

This integration of representation with presentation is configured
through the smallest details of star acting. James Naremore (1988: 4) suggests stars can be "known for an ideolect [sic], a set of performing traits
that is systematically highlighted in films and sometimes copied by impres-
sionists." Ideolectic features exceed the mere somatic substance of the star
body, for they are acted similarities and differences, physically performed
distinctions made in the actions of moving and speaking. At the most
obvious level, the star ideolect is evident in the overt madcap physical play
of a performer such as Jim Carrey, or the vocal multiplication of identities
within a single performance which at one point characterized the performances of Robin Williams. Other distinctions, however, are not produced by
the body overall but by small isolated actions. One example of this is

Cruise's famous distinctive smile, a feature shown off numerous times within and between films. As Cruise established his stardom in the mid 1980s, he repeatedly played a particular manifestation of swaggering masculinity, and key to manifesting that attitude was the smile, a broad grin beamed across an array of pearly white teeth. As Dargis (2000) describes it

> During the 80s the smile would become Cruise's signature, his trademark . . . it became synonymous with sex and box-office appeal. It defined Cruise's burgeoning star persona as pleasant, extroverted, open, friendly, neither overly macho nor aggressive, and, crucially, as someone to whom all things came naturally. It was the easy-does-it, no-problem grin, a smile without fangs or irony . . . a mouth crammed with big white American teeth . . . turning a simple human reflex into an epic of conquest and seduction . . . throughout most of the 80s the essential Cruise remained the guy who grinned from an F-14 cockpit and laughed his way around a pool table.

The smile not only featured in *Top Gun* (Figure 7.10) but was also on show with subsequent roles in *The Color of Money* and *Cocktail* (Figures 7.11 and 7.12). "The smile kept glowing until 1988 and *Cocktail*," Dargis observes, "when all of a sudden it seemed wrong, a sign of Cruise's superficiality and the yuppie-scum arrogance he signaled. For six years he turned down the high beam. For better and for worse, critically and commercially, he starred in movies that proved just how serious he could be." Even so, in *Rain Man*, where the brash overconfidence of the Cruise brand was subdued, still the smile briefly broke through (Figure 7.13). Probably the ultimate confirmation of the smile as a hypersemiotized sign of Cruise's presence came as the grin became a thing of self-parody. This was evident with Cruise's cameo in the action packed spoof film-within-a-film pre-credits sequence of *Austin Powers in Goldmember* (2002), which culminates in Cruise smiling direct to camera (Figure 7.14). Here the joke works through many levels of star meaning, as Cruise plays the action star Cruise imitating comic star Mike Myers in his most famous role as the oversexed British spy Powers.[5]

In *M:I-2* the smile contributes to enacting the furtherance of the film's narrative circumstances. When Ambrose masquerades as Hunt to intercept Nekhorvich on the plane, a complex chain of performance relationships is created as Cruise must play Ambrose who is pretending to be Hunt as enacted by Cruise. Although only fleeting, the glimpse of the familiar smile is just part of this act designed to fool the scientist but also the audience. Later during the car duel, flashes of the Cruise smile represent Hunt as a man for whom life-threatening danger is mere play (Figure 7.15). At

Figure 7.10   Cruise smiles: *Top Gun*. Producers Jerry Bruckheimer and Don Simpson; director Tony Scott; distributed by Paramount Pictures.

Figure 7.11   Cruise smiles: *The Color of Money*. Producers Irving Axelrad and Barbara De Fina; director Martin Scorsese; distributed by Touchstone Home Video.

another level, the smile also becomes the cause for further self-reflexive play on the Cruise brand. When confronting Cruise/Hunt during the shoot-out in the Biocyte labs, Scott/Ambrose says "You know, that was the hardest part of having to portray you – grinning like an idiot every 15 minutes." As the film builds towards its climax, Hunt uses prosthetic masks to substitute himself for Ambrose's lieutenant, Stamp (played by Richard Roxburgh), and then apparently delivers "himself" to Ambrose. Unaware

Figure 7.12 Cruise smiles: *Cocktail*. Producers Robert W. Cort and Ted Field; director Roger Donadson; distributed by Touchstone Home Video.

Figure 7.13 Cruise smiles: *Rain Man*. Producer Mark Johnson; director Barry Levinson; distributed by MGM Home Entertainment.

of the switch, Scott/Ambrose plans to kill "Hunt" but before doing so addresses his victim with "How about giving us a big smile?" In the one film, a single physical feature of the Cruise idiolect therefore serves both impersonatory and personificatory purposes, for the distinctive smile enacts specific narrative functions (i.e. fooling Nekhorvich) and character

Figure 7.14　Cruise smiles: *Austin Powers in Goldmember*. Producers John Lyons, Eric McLeod, Demi Moore, Mike Myers, Jennifer Todd and Suzanne Todd; director Jay Roach; distributed by New Line Home Entertainment/Entertainment in Video.

Figure 7.15　Cruise/Hunt laughs at danger: *Mission: Impossible 2*. Producers Tom Cruise and Paula Wagner; director John Woo; distributed by Paramount Pictures.

traits (i.e. displaying Hunt's casual disregard for danger), while also specularizing the star brand by forming connections between films and drawing attention to Cruise as Cruise.

It is precisely through the co-presence of personification and impersonation that the star performance enacts the star brand and negotiates the balance of familiarity and uniqueness fundamental to the film commodity. By foregrounding the presence of a star, personification vertically differentiates a film from films without stars. At the same time, by forming vocal and physical continuities, personification not only links the films of a specific star but also horizontally differentiate those films from the films of other stars. And yet if viewers are to pay for future performances by a star, then some sense of uniqueness has to be achieved, and so the voice and body must be used to also create impersonatory differences between roles played by the one star. This contrast in turn reflects the dual aspects of narrative and spectacle which characterizes narrative film, for impersonation is focused on representing a figure in the story world while personification promotes the presentation and show of the actor. The fascinations of the star act arise precisely because these principles are not held in opposition but rather merged through the voice and body of the single performer. Furthermore, by means of personification and impersonation, the voice and body of the star manage the balance between familiarity and uniqueness fundamental to the film commodity. "Stardom, like the movies themselves," Dargis notes, "depends on standardisation and differentiation." Star acting provides producers and distributors with a means for signaling product differentiation through the performer and performance. Overall, star performance combines a series of contrasting symbolic and commercial principles:

Narrative	Spectacle
Story	Show
Representation	Presentation
Impersonation	Personification
Role/character over actor	Actor over role/character
Actor-as-representer	Actor-as-asset
Star-as-role/character	Star-as-star
Difference	Continuity
Differentiation	Standardisation
Uniqueness	Familiarity
	Vertical differentiation between films with and without stars
Horizontal differentiation between films featuring the same star	Horizontal differentiation between films featuring different stars

It is in the combination of these principles that the significance and attractions but also the commercial value of the star performance is produced.

Turning to matters of genre and marketing further illuminates understanding of the star act as branded performance. Connecting the star brand to genre brings together two systems of expectation. "The repetitive and cumulative nature of genre films," Rick Altman explains,

> makes them . . . quite *predictable*. Not only can the substance and the ending of most genre films be predicted by the end of the first reel, but the repeated formulaic use of familiar stars usually makes them predictable on the basis of the title and credits alone . . . [Star names] designate more than just actors and actresses – they guarantee a certain style, a particular atmosphere and a well-known set of attitudes. (original emphasis, 1999: 25)

Both genre and stardom work as systems for product differentiation as they equally identify what a film will and will not offer. Genre, as Steve Neale notes, "is ubiquitous, a phenomenon common to all instances of discourse: there is a generic aspect to all texts" (2000: 2). Film stardom is therefore continually produced within and through generic forms. Genres are "multi-dimensional" (p. 2) for they are categories formed from several elements, of which stars may be one. Genres are in part defined by the stars appearing in them, while star brands are in turn defined by genre. Stars therefore contribute to genre formation, while genres are active in the formation of the star brand.

As Neale notes, however, "most films are multiply generic," and the same can be said of star brands. A star's career may traverse several genres although through a succession of roles s/he may become closely associated with a particular genre, granting of course that the genre itself is probably not generically pure. Before *M:I-2*, Cruise had assembled a career which had seen him take lead roles in comedies of teenage experience (*Losin' It* (1983) and *Risky Business*), fantasy (*Legend* (1985)), a biopic (*Born on the Fourth of July*), period drama (*Far and Away*), legal thrillers (*A Few Good Men* and *The Firm*), horror (*Interview With the Vampire*), and psychological drama (*Eyes Wide Shut* (1999)). Starting with *Top Gun* in 1986, however, Cruise commenced an association with action that would continue through *Days of Thunder* and then *Mission: Impossible*. Grossing nearly $354 million worldwide, *Top Gun* became a defining statement in Cruise's commercial and symbolic status. When the producing and directing team from *Top Gun* overtly repeated that film's basic formula of maverick outsider character, speed machines, competition and a girl for *Days of Thunder*, maybe unsurprisingly the latter was referred to as "Top Gun 2" (C. Fleming, 1998: 143) or "Top Car." *Days of Thunder* was an attempt to create continuity with limited variation, although after a disappointing worldwide gross of only $157.9 million, the film represents just one example of how even the most sure-fire package of recurrent elements cannot guarantee success in the film market. But six years later, as *Mission: Impossible* grossed $457.9 million worldwide, the combination of Cruise and action was proved to still make a big impact in the market. By the time of *M:I-2*, therefore, Cruise had assembled a career which was generically diverse but his stardom was founded on commercial success in action. It was an association which would continue as action was combined with other generic credentials for the sci-fi action thrillers *Minority Report* and *War of the Worlds*, period action drama *The Last Samurai* (2003), action comedy *Knight and Day* (2010) and further run-outs for the Ethan Hunt character in *Mission: Impossible 3* (2006) and *Mission Impossible: Ghost Protocol* (2011).

As these examples indicate, Cruise's action films are always multiply generic. *M:I-2* provided all the stunts, fights, gun-play and explosions demanded of an action movie at the very start of the twenty-first century, but these features were also combined with elements of romance. Cruise/ Hunt saves the world from the deadly effects of Chimera and the wicked exploitation of Bellerophon but his motivations for so doing are entirely explained through his wish to save the woman he loves. *M:I-2* very obviously belongs to Cruise's action oeuvre, but with its romantic current, it is a film which equally belongs to an alternative lineage of the star's films extending back through *Eyes Wide Shut*, *Jerry Maguire*, *Far and Away* and *Cocktail* to *All the Right Moves* (1983). The star brand is therefore a multiply generic construct produced between and within films. A star may traverse multiple genres but becomes best known for only one or two, and with any film combining elements from various genres, the star brand provides a means for binding together inflections from different generic tendencies. In the case of *M:I-2*, the Cruise brand centrally unites the film's mix of action with some romance.

Altman argues genre is potentially an ineffective way of differentiating films in the market: "Like generic supermarket products, genre films can be made and distributed by any producer . . . How much more rewarding is a strategy of avoiding generic identification, instead stressing the *particular plus* that the studio brings to the genre" (emphasis added, 1999: 115). "By definition," Altman argues, "genres can never be fully controlled by a single studio, whereas individual studios have exclusive access to contract actors" (p. 115). Emphasizing the "particular plus" of the enacted star brand through marketing therefore differentiates between generic products. Film marketing aims to raise public awareness and thereby influence purchasing decisions, and it is in this intertwining of communication with selling where the symbolic commerce of the star brand plays a crucial role. Any star performance is a marketing device, for casting the star imports the star brand into a film as a way of signaling similarities and differences to position the film as a particular offering in media markets. Chapter 1 discussed how marketing media propagate the star name but those same media also provide the means for circulating and dispersing the star body. Name and body are disseminated across the promotional media of theatrical trailers, television or radio spot advertisements, and websites, but also feature in the publicity channels of press kits, junkets, press screenings and gala premieres.[6]

As a vehicle for product differentiation, the star performance must become a highly visible statement in the market. Not only is the brilliance of the star attraction achieved on-screen but also through the spectacular circulation of that performance. By organizing and coordinating the visibility of the star performance, marketing and distribution strategies show the brand, or to adopt a term which emphasizes the performativity of that visibility, they *stage* the brand. Film marketing and distribution stage the brand by creating a platform in the market for showing off the star attraction. Producing a series of micro-messages about a film, marketing media form highly compressed clusters of impressions conceptualizing what a film promises to deliver. Promotions for many films involve creating a number of poster designs but with *M:I-2* a single layout was created which prominently featured Cruise's name accompanied by an image of his face and upper torso in an action pose set against a fiery background. Here the star communicated the film, for the poster entirely conceptualized the movie through Cruise. Compressing the narrative concept into a single image of the star was a convention already well established in promotions for Cruise's films. More specifically the design for *M:I-2* followed the practice of using Cruise's face alone (and in many cases only the right profile) seen with the posters for *Jerry Maguire*, *Mission: Impossible*, *The Firm*, *Days of Thunder*, *Born on the Fourth of July* and *Risky Business*. In these cases, the star was the message and the message was Cruise.

Distribution patterns position the star performance in the market, inviting consideration of how the visibility of the star brand is staged across the organization of time and space. *M:I-2* started its theatrical run in North America. By releasing the film on Wednesday 24 May 2000, Paramount expanded the first weekend so that by the end of five days the studio could boast the film had opened with a staggering $78.8 million gross.

Furthermore, as Memorial Day followed on Monday 29 May, the film also benefitted from the holiday audience to finish the weekend with a gross of nearly $91.8 million. Memorial Day is traditionally taken as the start point of Hollywood's summer, and *M:I-2* was Paramount's major event movie offering for the season, although DreamWorks appeared to have prematurely kicked off the summer three weeks earlier by opening the Roman epic *Gladiator* starring Russell Crowe and Disney followed two weeks after with its animated family feature *Dinosaur*. Understanding how distribution uses the star brand as a positioning statement also requires seeing how the star performance is situated relative to other films on release at the same time. *M:I-2* was followed through June and July by the other leading event movies from the majors, as Disney released its live action car theft drama *Gone in 60 Seconds* starring Nicolas Cage, Warner Bros. opened the maritime adventure *The Perfect Storm* with George Clooney in the lead, Mel Gibson fought the American War of Independence for Sony's *The Patriot*, Disney's Miramax subsidiary brought out the horror spoof *Scary Movie*, Fox commenced a new sci-fi franchise with *X-Men*, DreamWorks paired Harrison Ford with Michelle Pfeiffer for the supernatural gothic thriller *What Lies Beneath*, and Universal created a comedy showcase for Eddie Murphy to play eight different roles in *Nutty Professor II: The Klumps*. Star and genre therefore combined in *M:I-2* to provide Paramount with the means to differentiate the studio's key tentpole movie of the summer season in this congested marketplace.

For the North American theatrical release, Paramount opened *M:I-2* wide across 3,653 screens in Canada and the United States. Over the next six weeks up to the release in Japan, the film was then rolled out in all of Hollywood's major international markets. By the end of its run, *M:I-2* had earned over 60 percent of its worldwide box office in international territories, with over 77 percent of that share coming from the film's performance in just 12 countries (Table 7.1). Worldwide releasing and the compressed temporality of the international release schedule therefore meant that for a few weeks at least, Cruise's performance achieved near global ubiquity. Subsequently, as that performance was passed through the secondary release windows of pay-TV and home video, it extended its commercial afterlife. *M:I-2* has long ago disappeared from cinema screens and may now only occasionally get a television airing, but with the "long tail" economics of online retail, over a decade later Cruise's performance is still available.[7]

As actor and asset, stars are performed and performing brands, symbolic commercial identities enacted on screens both large and small. Combining

212   Spectacular Acts

Table 7.1   Global performance of the star act: main markets for
Mission: Impossible 2.

	Distributor	Release date	Gross ($) (ranking amongst annual top films)
North America	Paramount	24 May 2000	215.4 (2)
Key International Territories			
Europe			
Germany	UIP	6 July 2000	25.0 (2)
UK and Ireland	UIP	7 July 2000	26.4 (5)
Spain	UIP	7 July 2000	12.5 (3)
Italy	UIP	7 July 2000	11.5 (4)
France	UIP	26 July 2000	21.8 (5)
Asia-Pacific			
Australia	UIP	1 June 2000	13.2 (2)
South Korea	n/a	17 June 2000	13.9
Taiwan	n/a	17 June 2000	11.3
Japan	UIP	8 July 2000	94.1 (1)
Latin America			
Argentina	UIP	16 June 2000	7.1
Brazil	n/a	22 June 2000	9.0
Mexico	UIP	30 June 2000	10.4

Sources: EAO (2001), www.boxofficemojo.com and www.imdb.com.

narrative with spectacle, the star act is produced through the performances
of the medium and the actor. Operating as signs of continuity and difference, star acts are part of the currency of conglomerate Hollywood, positioning films in the market. With an industry now tuned to simultaneously
pushing its premium titles across globally extended markets, and then
continuing to exploit them through a series of aftermarkets, the star performance becomes a show distinguished as much by its omnipresence as
by its permanence.

Notes

1   It is not clear when Ulmer's survey was taken that year but it is likely the rankings were prepared before *M:I-2* had completed its run internationally and so
the outcome didn't reflect the commercial impact of the film.

2   Robert Towne's script for the film also constructs a narrative which is a thinly veiled copy of the Alfred Hitchcock thriller *Notorious* (1946) in which a European woman, whose reputation is tarnished by criminal association, is required by an American agent to go undercover and spy on a former lover, but when her cover is blown she is poisoned and must be saved by the agent.

3   Many stars claim to do their own stunts but before covering a film, insurance companies usually insist stars are prevented from endangering themselves (Epstein, 2010: 94–8). Cruise's work on *M:I-2* may therefore have been an exception to common industry practice. On the "Impossible Shots" featurette included with the DVD edition of the film, stunt coordinator Brian Smrz, expert climber Ron Kauk, director John Woo, and stunt double Keith Campbell all sing the praises for Cruise's decision to do his own stunt work on the climbing scene, thereby adding to the hype around the spectacularization of the star performance.

4   He is television actor Daniel Roberts.

5   As Naremore notes, the existence of a star's idiolect is often confirmed by acts of impersonation. Shortly after *M:I-2* was released, at the 2000 MTV Movies Awards Ben Stiller appeared with Cruise in a specially created comedy skit built around the premise of a long-serving stunt double who obsessively mimics the star. When playing the double, Stiller's imitation of the Cruise smile provided a crucial point of connection between him and his parodic reference. The skit even included shots of Stiller and Cruise side-by-side pulling the same famous grin. Cruise has made no secret of his allegiance to Scientology but in January 2008 a rare candid insight into his beliefs became available when one of the organization's internal videos from 2004 was leaked documenting the ceremony celebrating conferment of the International Association of Scientologists' Freedom Medal of Valor on Cruise. This included an interview showing the star talking about his commitment to "KSW" (Keeping Scientology Working), countering "SPs" (Suppressive Persons) and claiming "we are the authorities on getting people off drugs, we are the authorities on the mind, we are the authorities on improving conditions . . . we can rehabilitate criminals, way to happiness, we can bring peace, errrr, and unite cultures." For most of the clip Cruise spoke with an earnest tone to communicate his commitment, but in the moments where he broke into laughter, the flash of his smile was enough to bring the world of Hollywood film crashing into the scene. Over the internet the recording spread rapidly through viral video and the clip became an object of humour with many professional and amateur comedians creating numerous parodies of the scene. In one of the most effective of these, comic actor Miles Fisher lampooned the scene for *Superhero Movie* (2008), delivering a rambling speech in which he claimed he "can eat planets" and punctuating the scene with a series of mad, explosive laughs while mimicking the Cruise grin.

6 In film marketing, promotion describes forms of paid advertising, while publicity represents any activity intended to attract media coverage but without buying advertising space or time.

7 Chris Anderson advanced the concept of the "long tail" to explain how online retailing can supply an inventory extending beyond mass demand items to minority interest goods, forming a "mass of niches" (2007: 5). Six months after its North American theatrical opening, *M:I-2* was released in the US on home video formats on 7 November 2000. At that point it was a mass-market title but, as time passed, demand inevitably declined. Even so, years later, the film and Cruise's performance remain available amongst the thousands of titles for sale through e-tailers such as Amazon.com.

8

Prestige Stardom and the Awards System

While the A-list sit atop the economic hierarchy of actors, as a cultural industry, film is subject to other measures of value beyond the purely financial. In Hollywood, where the A-list are prized for their potential box-office impact, there is an alternative hierarchy of high-profile perform-ers who are respected, celebrated and esteemed for their artistic achieve-ments. With some actors, economic and artistic hierarchies intersect, but as in many other cases they don't, so artistic prestige functions as an alternative measure or index of star status related to, yet independent of, commercial value.

A-list status is produced by economic valorization demonstrated through the actor's record of appearing in commercially successful films. Chapter 1 offered alternative configurations of the star with actorly and prestige star-doms, the products of artistic valorization over commercial credentials achieved whenever performers accrue a sustained record of performances which attract illustrious reviews and other critical commentary. As sug-gested in the earlier chapter, prestige stars are effectively a subset of actorly stars: they are the "A-list" of artistically valorized performers, distinguished by their acquisition and accumulation of cultural honors. Demarcating "the Best" from the rest, awards offer a direct and tangible expression of actorly prestige. Awards represent a form of currency in film culture, the value of which is not defined, at least ostensibly, by the commercial terms of the money economy but rather by the effects they achieve in what James F. English (2005) refers to as the "economy of prestige." Film awards have

Hollywood Stardom, First Edition. Paul McDonald.
© 2013 Paul McDonald. Published 2013 by John Wiley & Sons, Ltd.

symbolic rather than economic value: they are tokens of esteem, and as such can be understood as representing a form of what Pierre Bourdieu describes as "symbolic capital" (1984: 230).

This chapter therefore explores prestige stardom as a form of star status which co-exists with, but does not mirror, the economic standing of the A-list. As this argument involves making a departure from the more familiar understanding of stars as signs of commercial value, so the chapter will first set out some conceptual ground with a discussion of the "anti-economic" logic which Bourdieu suggests permeates cultural production. This logic is intrinsic to the configuration of prestige stardom as will be illustrated through a study of Daniel Day-Lewis. Numerous film awards ceremonies are held each year, the most famous of which – and of greatest importance to Hollywood – are the annual awards of the Academy of Motion Picture Arts and Sciences (AMPAS), or the "Oscars" as they are familiarly known. In a third section, the chapter therefore examines the factors at work in producing the symbolic value of the Oscars, before considering how the awards function to legitimize certain forms of acting performance. Although the conferment of the awards is based on artistic rather than commercial achievements, still the Oscars produce effects in the film market, and so the final part of the chapter is concerned with how the Academy Awards position the performances of lead actors between both the prestige economy and the money economy.

Cultural Production and Symbolic Capital

Understanding the artistic valorization of prestige stardom and the currency of awards is helped by exploring Bourdieu's work on what he refers to as the "field of cultural production." Bourdieu's sociology broadly applies the concept of "fields" to describe specific arenas of interaction, with the field of cultural production representing the arts. By using the term field, an explicitly spatial metaphor is adopted to conceptualize how cultural practitioners and their works occupy structured relations in which they are hierarchically positioned according to the distribution of different forms of capital. Conventionally, under capitalism the terms "economy" and "capital" are applied to describe mercantile exchange, but for Bourdieu this restricted definition of economy blocks consideration of a broader "economy of exchanges" which extends beyond commercial relationships (1983b: 242). He therefore expands the concept of capital beyond monetary or financial resources to describe others types of asset which can be accumulated and used to obtain advantage. Of these, symbolic capital, or what is "commonly called prestige, reputation, fame" (1984: 230), has value in the field of cultural production because it serves to hierarchically differentiate between artistic practitioners.

A defining feature of the field of cultural production is how it operates by a logic which inverts conventional economic reasoning. Symbolic capital, in the form of artistic prestige, is prized and obtains value precisely for how it appears to disavow economic (in the financial sense) capital. In Bourdieu's terms, cultural production forms an "anti-economy" or "upside-down economic world" (1983a: 40), where the value of symbolic capital is realized by the "'refusal' of the 'commercial'" (1977: 75). Consequently exchanges of symbolic capital assume the character of "A commerce in things which are not commercial" (1996: 148). Due to the dominant perception of financial transactions as the only definition of economy, "other forms of exchange [are rendered] as non-economic, and therefore *disinterested*" (original emphasis, 1983b: 242). In the inverted economics of cultural production, practitioners may therefore acquire symbolic capital precisely by creating works or undertaking actions which reject the market to become statements of economic disinterest. Although not economic in the mercantile sense, the circulation of symbolic capital in this context still follows an economic logic. As John B. Thompson (1992: 15) notes,

> Within fields that are not economic in the narrow sense, practices may not be governed by a strictly economic logic (e.g. may not be orientated towards financial gain); and yet they may none the less concur with a logic that is economic in a broader sense, in so far as they are orientated towards the augmentation of some kind of "capital" (e.g. cultural or symbolic) or the maximization of some kind of "profit" (e.g. honor or prestige).

Cultural practitioners may therefore "accumulate" and "invest" symbolic capital in search of symbolic "profits."

Distributions of economic and symbolic capital hierarchically organize the positions which are objectively available to practitioners in the field. Foundational to the structuring of the cultural field is the opposition which Bourdieu poses between "heteronomy"/"autonomy," poles on a continuum which demarcates the degrees to which forms or acts of cultural production may be judged to be directed either towards or against market forces. Heteronomous production embraces the market and so, according to the anti-economic logic of the cultural field, is rich in economic capital but consequently poor in symbolic capital, with the reverse defining autonomous production. These opposing principles bifurcate the field between a sub-field of "large-scale production," in which producers produce for the market, and the autonomous sub-field of "restricted production" governed by economic disinterest where "producers produce for other producers" (Bourdieu, 1983a: 39).

Although cultural production has long sustained charismatic belief in the talents of painters, authors and composers as individual creators, it is commonly acknowledged that the creation of artworks "rests on an extensive division of labor" (Becker, 1982: 13). For Bourdieu, however, cultural production involves more than just the collective making of the work. He describes the work of art as "an object which exists as such only by virtue of the (collective) belief which knows and acknowledges it as a work of art" (1983a: 35). For works to become art, they must be recognized as such, and so the field brings together not only all those engaged in the collective material production of the art work but also agents, intermediaries and institutions involved with the symbolic production of belief in the work (p. 37). Recognition is key to "consecrating" or legitimizing certain objects or acts as art, shaping the differential distribution of symbolic capital as some works are recognized and respected as art while others aren't. Bourdieu therefore sees the field of cultural production as bisected by a secondary axis marking high and low degrees of consecration. Whatever value attaches to that capital of consecration depends on who does the consecrating. Bourdieu distinguishes the "charismatic consecration" conferred by cultural producers on the works on their competitors, against the "bourgeois" or "institutionalized" consecration endowed by official and authoritative arts organizations, and the "popular" consecration which results from the choices made by the consuming public (pp. 50–1). Across the axes of heteronomy/autonomy and high/low consecration, what the field therefore represents is a "space of positions" which is expressed through the "position-takings" of those practitioners who are active in the field (p. 30) (Figure 8.1). Although a very powerful hierarchical structure, practitioners do not occupy fixed positions, and the field is a dynamic space in which those involved negotiate and struggle over their artistic legitimacy through the acquisition and investment of symbolic and economic capital. Over time, a cultural practitioner will create a "trajectory," "the series of positions successively occupied by the same writer in the successive states of the literary field, it being understood that it is only in the structure of a

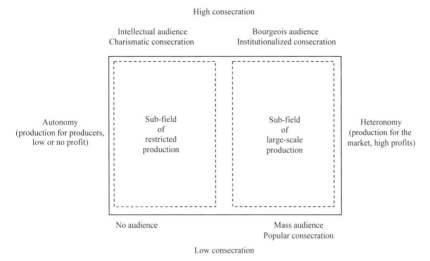

Figure 8.1   Bourdieu's field of cultural production. Source: based on Bourdieu (1983a: 49 and commentary 50–1).

field that the meaning of their successive positions can be defined" (Bourdieu, 1986: 189).

Middle-brow Hollywood and the Prestige Star

What Bourdieu offers is a broad model for understanding the hierarchical principles at work in cultural production. His own application was however limited by the historical examples he considered, with the French literary field of the late nineteenth century a predominant example (Bourdieu, 1983a and 1996). To emphasize the anti-economic logic of the field, Bourdieu dwelled mainly on the autonomous sub-field of restricted production, with the result that he had little to say about large-scale, "heteronomous" commercial cultural production (Hesmondhalgh, 2006: 217). Moreover, his historical focus did not address the emergence, growth and consolidation during the twentieth century of the mass media industries of recorded music, film, radio and television (p. 219). Bourdieu's work cannot therefore be simply and directly transposed to the study of film. Instead, what it offers is a set of concepts to work with, principally his identification of the anti-economic logic which powerfully determines artistic status in cultural production, the hierarchical organization of the field through the distribution of symbolic and economic capital, and the importance of the production of belief to the recognition and consecration of cultural practitioners and their works. Adapting Bourdieu ideas for studying the symbolic commerce of Hollywood stardom, it is therefore necessary to apply these concepts to two questions: where is Hollywood film positioned in the field; and how does the differential distribution of economic and symbolic capital configure the hierarchical status of stars?

As a high-cost enterprise directed at large and frequently mass audiences, feature film production, and Hollywood film-making specifically, is positioned towards the heteronomous pole of large-scale production. But in a field which grants greatest legitimacy to anti-commercial activity, Hollywood film has consequently long faced critical dismissal if not derision. Tatiana Heise and Andrew Tudor (2007) use Bourdieu's field theory for a comparative study of how film art movements emerged in Britain and Brazil during the 1920s and '30s. Mapping the range of film activity in these periods, for both contexts "general Hollywood product" is placed at the extremity of the heteronomous pole and as lacking in critical consecration. This position certainly accords with enduring perceptions of Hollywood film as purely popular commercial entertainment. Yet this perception rests on a single monolithic conception of Hollywood production which ignores the diversity of output from the major studios. Has there ever been such a thing as "general" Hollywood product? Historically, Hollywood has remained a resolutely narrative cinema, and yet within the bounds of narrative has produced a remarkable variety of film types (Bordwell, 2006: 10–11). If considering just the period 1990–2009 which this study focuses upon, while the major Hollywood studios turned out event movies aimed at the largest possible audience, they also targeted more narrowly defined tastes with genre films and movies for kids. Universal's *Schizopolis* (1996), Columbia's *The People vs. Larry Flynt* (1996), Fox's *The Crucible* (1996), Paramount's *Orange County* (2002) or Warner Bros.' *Eyes Wide Shut* (1999) and *The Good German* (2006) offer just a few examples of the majors also producing and releasing so-called "specialised" films.[1] Moreover, with the emergence of the Indiewood subsidiary divisions in the early 1990s (see Chapter 4), the studios created a third tier of production and distribution situated between the large-scale production of the majors and the restricted production of the genuinely independent sector. For example, after its acquisition by Disney, former independent producer-distributor Miramax made and released the controversial *kids* (1995) and biographical drama *Basquiat* (1996), while Sony Pictures Classics produced the ensemble drama *The Company* (2003) and comedy crime thriller *Sleuth* (2007), and Universal's Focus Features subsidiary produced the homage to 1950s film melodrama *Far from Heaven* (2002).

Rather than creating a generalized type of product catering for a homogenized mass audience, Hollywood can best be understood as proffering a limited diversity of film content variously addressing a restricted variety of audience tastes. Hollywood may be situated in the sub-field of large-scale production but rather than bundle the whole of Hollywood output together as a single commercial mass, it is necessary to recognize the studios produce films which occupy multiple positions scattered between popular and more "bourgeois" tastes. While avoiding the elitism or the formal reflexivity and experimentation which characterizes avant-garde "high" culture, Hollywood otherwise produces across a spectrum which accommodates "middle-brow" and "popular" tastes (Bourdieu, 1989: 16; Gans, 1999: 75–93). Hollywood creates plot-driven spectacles of action, thrills and sensation aimed at the popular market, along with more "serious," "thoughtful" and "moving" fare. It is the latter which defines middle-brow Hollywood. For Bourdieu, middle-brow culture combines "two normally exclusive characteristics, immediate accessibility and the outward signs of cultural legitimacy" (1989: p. 323). As the middle-brow "give[s] the impression of bringing legitimate culture within the reach of all" (p. 323), so one expression of the middle-brow imagination in film can be seen in screen adaptations of classic drama and literature

Applying Bourdieu's model to Hollywood not only provides a framework for thinking about the positioning of films but also of stars in the field. Film actors are differentially positioned in the field by how they come to accumulate and represent economic and symbolic capital in human form. A-list names are positioned towards the heteronomous pole of the field, for their status is defined by the actor's record of commercial success as measured by box-office grosses or sales of home entertainment units. In contrast, the prestige star is a figure rich in symbolic capital but, at least when compared to the market value of the A-list, relatively poor in economic capital. As leading figures in Hollywood production, prestige stars can never completely claim artistic autonomy and still belong to the sub-field of large-scale production, but rather than the box office, it is the accumulation of award nominations and wins, or of positive critical notices from the culturally legitimated press, which defines their status. It has already been established that based on the performance of their films in the market and the compensation packages they were able to demand, in the years 1990–2009 the A-list was populated by the likes of Jim Carrey, Tom Cruise, Mel Gibson, Tom Hanks, Julia Roberts and Arnold Schwarzenegger. In contrast, taking just Academy Award nominations and wins as a one measure of status, then Jeff Bridges, Cate Blanchett, George Clooney, Judi Dench, Morgan Freeman, Philip Seymour Hoffman, Diane Keaton, Julianne Moore, Jack Nicholson, Sean Penn, Kevin Spacey, Meryl Streep, Denzel Washington and Kate Winslet provided the period with a line-up of prestige stars.

Prestige stardom is a product of middle-brow Hollywood. Prestige stars are distinguished from the leading names of the most commercially popular forms of cinema but as figures in film they can only claim a certain level of cultural legitimacy. Bourdieu argues film as a medium has not achieved the standing of "the fully consecrated arts . . . theatre, painting, sculpture, literature and classical music" (1990: 96). Set within this strata of legitimacy, prestige stars fail to attain the same cultural status as the leading practitioners of those arts – the acclaimed authors, fine artists, composers and sculptors, or the actors of the legitimized dramatic stage. Prestige stars may not belong to the most legitimized forms of art but still gain kudos from association with consecrated culture. For example, multi-Oscar-winners Seymour Hoffman and Streep added to their prestige cache by jointly appearing in the 2008 screen adaptation of the stage play *Doubt: A Parable*, winner of the 2005 Pulitzer Prize for Drama and the Tony Award for Best Play. Hollywood has steered clear of trying to adapt for the big screen the philosophic writings and high-brow novels of Irish writer Iris Murdoch, but this did not prevent Miramax and its co-production partners from hiring Dench and Winslet to share the portrayal of her in *Iris* (2001), a film which viewed Murdoch's life in terms of an enduring romance and noble battle against Alzheimer' disease. Dench's long career includes film and television adaptations of Anton Chekhov, Terence Rattigan, George Eliot, Oscar Wilde, Jane Austen and William Shakespeare, and with the film *Shakespeare in Love* (1998) she appeared in a much-lauded fictionalized comedy-drama which was honored with five Oscars. As Dench shows, unlike the financial index of star status, where the value of women expires by the time they are in their 30s (see Chapter 1), the prestige economy may embrace age as a measure of artistic durability.

Prestige status depends on the disavowal of the commercial market. At one level, this is achieved by taking up a position in the overall system of production by not appearing in films or genres directed at the popular market. As already suggested, this need not mean working outside Hollywood for the major studios themselves create diverse streams of production. What it does mean though is not working on films directed at the mainstream. Making this choice will very likely be accompanied by a further act of economic disavowal, for the star must accept lower financial rewards than his or her A-list peers. At a secondary level, economic disavowal is enacted through performance. Whatever positions stars occupy in the field are always materialized in performance. As the previous chapter discussed, the representation of character is always enacted through the media of the voice and body. For Bourdieu (1983b), capital can be "objectified" (i.e. expressed in material objects) or "embodied" (i.e. as the inhabited properties of the body). In Hollywood, the star performance is an enactment of objectified and embodied capital, for the performance is part of the material content of films and is inhabited through the voice and body. The previous chapter considered how star performance rests on the tension between representation and presentation, or impersonation and personification. In the economic dynamics of the cultural field, this tension is active in positioning the star performance as an instance of objectified and embodied capital. For the value of the A-list star to be realized, the actor must be a recognizable, visible and marketable identity, and so in performance the presentational aspect of personification must exceed the representation of character. In contrast, prestige stars acquire their reputations for how their performances are led by the impersonatory work of character portrayal, rejecting commercial appeals in favor of economically disinterested artistic goals. If personification enacts the heteronomous principle of performing for the market, impersonation rejects the stable, repetitious identity on which A-list status depends to enact the autonomous principle of investing in the purely artistic objective of character representation.

As discussed in the last chapter, however, any performance is balanced between personification and impersonation, and so the prestige star cannot and does not completely disappear into the role. Whether playing Queen Victoria, Queen Elizabeth I, Lady Bracknell or M in the James Bond series, Dench is always Dench, and even after her carefully crafted vocal transformations, Streep always remained Streep. Indeed, overt signs of transformation – changing the shape of the body, adopting a particular voice or accent, or moving in a different way – may actually become part of the spectacle of the prestige performance, as the display of transformation becomes a show of actorly craft. This investment in actorly transformation on-screen may be complemented off-screen by the prestige star using interviews to make declarations of personal commitment to the demands of his or her art, or otherwise refusing interviews altogether, for these are inevitably linked into the processes of film promotion and publicity. While an actor's choice of roles or manipulations of the voice and body can become gestures against the market, ultimately it is left to the critics to consecrate and recognize the artistic legitimacy of performance. The production of prestige stardom is therefore not confined to the production of performance alone but involves the production of belief in the merits of a performance. Accordingly, prestige stardom can survive, and may even thrive on, the poor financial returns of a film if this can then be accompanied by the riches of positive critical recognition. With their judgments and reviews, critics and other film commentators frame the meaning of – and thereby contribute to the positioning of – the actor's voice and body in the field.

Daniel Day-Lewis and Anti-Star Stardom

In a career which has spanned three decades, Daniel Day-Lewis has taken a succession of lead roles and received widespread star media coverage, becoming the subject of magazine articles, newspaper interviews and a few biographies. His fame positions him on a hierarchy which grants him more power, influence and profile than the vast majority of film actors working in Hollywood. He is a marketable figure: on posters his name appears above the film title and trailers emphasize his presence in films. Although a figure in the symbolic commerce of Hollywood, Day-Lewis's status is formed around his overt rejection of the market. Unlike his A-list peers, Day-Lewis's status is the outcome of his self-conscious production of artistic autonomy and the recognition and acceptance of that stance by the legitimizing institution of critics. Day-Lewis has never appeared in a "hit," if that term in measured in purely in commercial terms, but yet he has banked a wealth of symbolic capital with award nominations and wins. Biography does not determine positioning in the field of cultural production but in Day-Lewis's case it worth noting he has acquired a certain amount of symbolic capital by familial association alone. Grandson of British film producer Sir Michael Balcon, who in the 1920s founded Gainsborough Pictures and later headed Ealing Studios, and son of Poet Laureate Cecil Day-Lewis and actress Jill Balcon, even before entering films Day-Lewis had gained the capital of artistic lineage. These associations were added to with his 1995 marriage to Rebecca Miller, daughter of Pulitzer Prize winning American playwright Arthur Miller. Day-Lewis's fame is based on embracing artistic autonomy but this does not mean he has not acquired a branded identity. Rather Day-Lewis's rejection of the market has seen him precisely find a place in the market by cultivating what amounts to a prestige brand.

Day-Lewis articulates the anti-commercial logic of prestige stardom, acquiring the symbolic capital of award-winning distinction by enacting a series of gestures of economic disinterest which reject the pull of the market. His career has seen him repeatedly appear in middle-brow product. As Bourdieu noted, accessible adaptations of well-known literary works are a standard category of middle-brow production. Before he started working in productions from the Hollywood studios, Day-Lewis had appeared in adaptations of "quality" literature, taking a supporting role in the 1985 film version of E. M. Forster's 1908 study of upper-class English Edwardian society *A Room with a View* and starring as the surgeon and intellectual Tomas in the 1988 adaptation of Milan Kundera's 1984 philosophic novel *The Unbearable Lightness of Being* set against the backdrop of the Prague Spring. This literary vein continued once Day-Lewis entered Hollywood, where he built up a record of appearing in film versions of well-known works of literature. He took the lead in Twentieth Century Fox's 1992 adaptation of James Fenimore Cooper's lengthy 1826 novel of the French and Indian War, *The Last of the Mohicans*, and played the male lead in Columbia's 1993 production *The Age of Innocence*, a screen version of Edith Wharton's 1920 novel of 1870s upper-class New York society. Day-Lewis starred in Fox's 1996 production of his own father-in-law's renown drama *The Crucible*, an allegory for McCarthyism, the reputation of which was confirmed by winning the Tony Award for Best Play when first staged in 1953. Along with these literary adaptations, Day-Lewis has also appeared in films inspired by literary works. On Miramax's production *Gangs of New York* (2002), Day-Lewis took a supporting but stand-out role in a film based on Herbert Asbury's 1928 non-fiction historical study *The Gangs of New York*, and played the lead role in *There Will Be Blood* (2007) based on Upton Sinclair's 1927 novel *Oil!*. By this cross-fertilization of media, Day-Lewis has assumed associations with fully consecrated cultural forms to become a "literary" film star.

In his choice of films and performance practice, Day-Lewis has enacted the principle of artistic autonomy by a series of refusals or negations of the commercial marketplace. A-list stardom depends on establishing a strongly personified on-screen identity but Day-Lewis's fame has been achieved without the fixing of a stable image. In the UK and Irish production *My Left Foot* (1989), Day-Lewis portrayed the true-life story of Christy Brown, an Irish born writer and artist who suffers from cerebral palsy. Brown added to Day-Lewis's record of eclectic roles, which already included the gay racist gang member Johnny in *My Beautiful Laundrette* (1985), upperclass suitor Cecil in *A Room with a View*, and the Czech doctor Tomas in *The Unbearable Lightness of Being*. When *My Beautiful Laundrette* and *A Room with a View* opened simultaneously in the US, star film critic Roger Ebert wrote in the *Chicago Sun-Times* "Seeing these two performances side by side is an affirmation of the miracle of acting . . . That one man could play these two opposites is astonishing" (quoted in Lewis, 2007: 37). Jim Sheridan, director and writer of *My Left Foot*, has remarked "A big star is someone who projects a particular image from one film to the next, like John Wayne and Clint Eastwood. Daniel disappears so completely into a role, how can he project an image?" (quoted in Barra, 1996: 90).

Alongside his refusal of image, Day-Lewis has also demonstrated artistic autonomy by his much reported dedication to actorly craft. With dramatic film-making, the principle artistic aim of naturalist acting is the believable representation of character. Acting is legitimized as "good" if it can be judged to involve some gesture towards closing the gap between actor and character so that the performer becomes fully integrated into the diegetic on-screen world. In Day-Lewis's case, he has cultivated an image of himself as an actor who "disappears" into character to engross himself in the dramas he enacts. Stories abound of the obsessive lengths he has taken to immerse himself into the roles he plays. As the disabled Brown in *My Left Foot*, Day-Lewis prepared by reportedly learning to paint with his foot (p. 91). On *The Last of the Mohicans* he spent time familiarizing himself with the life of a frontiersman, learning how to navigate the land without a compass and to hunt and trap using eighteenth-century tools (Loewenstein, 1997: 94). For *In the Name of the Father* (1993) he played an Irishman wrongly convicted on terrorist charges and his preparations included losing a lot of weight, and before shooting a scene where a confession is beaten out of him, he stayed awake for three nights and let himself be interrogated by real policemen (Corliss, 1994: 68). When filming *The Age of Innocence* in New York, he stayed at a Victorian hotel, registered under the name of his character Newland Archer, and walked the streets in period clothing (p. 68). As *The Boxer* (1997) Day-Lewis trained with former world featherweight champion Barry McGuigan (Loewenstein, 1997: 94) and to play Bill "The Butcher" Cutting in *Gangs of New York*, he spent months perfecting knife-throwing and reading literature of the time to perfect the vernacular (Lyall, 2003: 1). For *The Unbearable Lightness of Being* he learnt Czech and on *The Ballad of Jack and Rose* (2005), written and directed by his wife, the couple lived apart so he could understand the isolation of a dying man perplexed about his family (Lewis, 2007: 38). Day-Lewis has explained his motivation for acting is "the gravitational pull of another life that fires one's curiosity" (quoted in Loewenstein, 1997: 94). Michael Mann, who directed Day-Lewis in *The Last of the Mohicans*, has said "He doesn't perform or act but mutates" (quoted in Abramowitz, 2008: E13). Description of Day-Lewis as "a chameleonic star" (Corliss, 1994: 66) therefore encapsulates the essential paradox of a Hollywood performer whose star identity is based on the refusal of a fixed image. It is not that Day-Lewis does not have a brand but rather that his brand is formed around projecting the refusal of a personified performed identity and thereby rejecting the market.

A-list stardom depends on the visibility of the performer – visibility on-screen and visibility through media reporting of his or her life off-screen. As a film performer, Day-Lewis is highly visible, yet by his refusal of a personified on-screen identity and the stories of actorly dedication, he has cultivated an image of invisibility. Even so, while this dedication to the representation of character is directed at the disappearance of the actor, as tales of Day-Lewis's fanatical working processes have been widely covered in media reporting, so they've become visible and therefore part of a publicly circulated actorly image. In an article for *Vogue* titled "Disappearing Act," it was noted that "While the typical movie star plays versions of himself, myths grew up around the rigor with which Day-Lewis got ready for roles, checked his ego at the door, and vanished inside" (Kerr, 2001: 298). By this mythology, Day-Lewis has paradoxically achieved invisibility in the midst of visibility as his refusal of image and show of artistic dedication has cultivated invisibility through the highly visible channel of cinema, and media reporting has made that invisibility a matter of public knowledge.

This invisibility is not confined to performance alone. Day-Lewis has geographically distanced himself from the Hollywood milieu, setting up home in County Wicklow, Ireland. Possibly the greatest act of invisibility which any film actor can perform is to no longer appear in films. Between *The Boxer* in 1997 and *Gangs of New York* in 2002, Day-Lewis took several years out from his film career, and even once he returned to film, he only irregularly worked, making films every two to three years. "As long as he keeps acting," observed the *Vogue* article, "his performances will be intense."

But they may be fewer and farther in between, like the show put on by a desert plant that blooms unpredictably, and only when it's ready" (pp. 341–2). Day-Lewis's actorly image has seen him accumulate a high degree of symbolic capital but he has also made gestures aimed at rejecting the hierarchical status of the prestigious artist by aligning himself with artisanal activities. While starring in *The Crucible*, he joined with carpenters to build the set (Loewenstein, 1997: 90) and during his career hiatus after *The Boxer* he was also rumored to have served as apprentice to a Florentine cobbler (Dahl, 2008: 88). Day-Lewis has been described as an actor who "prefers the reclusive lifestyle of a male Garbo" (Holden, 1994: 25), alluding to the famous isolation of the legendary MGM star of 1920s and '30s. In the opinion of Paul Thomas Anderson, who directed Day-Lewis on *There Will Be Blood*, the star's low degree of public exposure aids and complements his immersion into character: "One of the advantages that Daniel has . . . is you don't see him everywhere, so you don't really know who he is or suffer through having to see him every day in the newspaper. So he already has that advantage to be somebody else" (quoted in Dahl, 2008: 84).

This refusal of a stable, marketable identity has been accompanied by a rejection of straightforwardly commercial production. Before *The Last of the Mohicans*, Day-Lewis worked outside of Hollywood, but from that film onwards he played roles, albeit irregularly, for five of the major studios or their subsidiaries while starring in films for independent outfits such as IFC Films and The Weinstein Company. Although Day-Lewis's stardom was channeled through Hollywood, his choice of film projects did not however position him with the commercial mainstream. With the exception of the costly production *Gangs of New York*, he worked on medium-budget features. These films were never hits, generally falling in the mid-to-low strata amongst the annual rankings of the top-grossing films in North America (Table 8.1). Domestic box office is just one revenue stream for Hollywood films, and distributors only receive a portion of the gross, but even so comparing the North American gross to the production budget, the films which Day-Lewis has starred in have, in commercial terms, been at best modest successes and otherwise failures. However, those films have seen Day-Lewis acquire and bank a wealth of symbolic accolades with numerous awards and nominations.

Day-Lewis's anti-star gestures – his refusal of image, actorly obsessiveness and overt invisibility – are therefore echoed by his position in the film market. In the limited economic terms of financial success, Day-Lewis is

Table 8.1 Daniel Day-Lewis: the grosses and the glory, 1992–2009.

	North American distributor	Budget ($m)	North American gross ($m)	Rank[1]	Honors
Nine (2009)	The Weinstein Company	80.0	19.7	120[2]	1 award, 5 nominations[3]
There Will Be Blood (2007)	Paramount Vantage/Miramax	25.0	40.2	73[4]	25 awards, 2 nominations
The Ballad of Jack and Rose (2005)	IFC Films	1.5	0.7	n/a	1 award
Gangs of New York (2002)	Miramax	97.0	77.8	33[5]	17 awards, 4 nominations
The Boxer (1997)	Universal	n/a	6.0	161[6]	1 nomination
The Crucible (1996)	Twentieth Century Fox	25.0	7.3	143[7]	
In the Name of the Father (1993)	Universal	13.0	25.1	54[8]	1 award, 5 nominations
The Age of Innocence (1993)	Columbia	30.0	32.3	51	2 nominations
The Last of the Mohicans (1992)	Twentieth Century Fox	40.0	75.5	20	2 awards, 1 nomination

Sources: compiled from data at www.boxofficemojo.com, www.imdb.com and analysis of D'Alessandro (2003: 26), Klady (1995b: 17; 1997: 22 and 1999: 34) and Variety (1993: 22; 1994: 14; 2009: 10 and 2010: 12).

[1] According to Variety's end-of-year reporting of the top-grossing films in North America.
[2] Released in mid-December 2009 and continued into 2010. Ranked here according to position as if run were completed in 2009.
[3] Three of these award/nominations were for the ensemble cast.
[4] Released in the last days of 2007 and so ranked according to main year of release 2008.
[5] Released late December 2002 and continued into 2003. Ranked here according to position as if run were completed in 2002.
[6] Released on the final day of 1997 and so ranked according to main year of release 1998.
[7] Released in November 1996 and continued into 1997. Ranked here according to position as if run were completed in 1996.
[8] Released on the last day of 1993 and so ranked according to main year of release 1994.

not a star because he lacks the commercial clout of the A-list, but in the anti-economic economy of cultural production, he carries value as a prestige sign of objectified and embodied symbolic capital. Day-Lewis's fame may not be configured around a personified image but yet he remains a marketable attraction: films are promoted through his name and reputation as an actor of distinction. Although that fame is largely configured around his show of economic disinterest and rejection of the conventional appearances of stardom, it is his anti-stardom which is the very basis for Day-Lewis's stardom.

The Symbolic Authority of the Oscars

Cultural awards represent tangible emblematic resources or assets which can be accumulated and invested in order to achieve the "profits" of artistic status, esteem and reputation. In film culture, the economy of prestige is sustained by an annual international system of awards: festival awards, industry award, critics awards, and audience awards. All bestow a certain degree of distinction on recipients but as each category is decided by different classes of voter, so the source of the award determines the degree of consecration attached. Audience awards are decided by the personal likings of "lay" voters and hold little symbolic value because their conferment is underpinned by the heteronomous interests of the consumer market. In contrast, industry, festival and critics awards carry greater weight for not only are they bestowed according to what are seen to be the more informed judgments of professional practitioners and intermediaries from the field of cultural production itself, but they are predicated on the autonomous principle of celebrating artistic merit. The latter categories of awards therefore incline towards what in Bourdieu's terms is the charismatic consecration of producers by fellow cultural professionals.

Individual awards form hierarchical distinctions between cultural practitioners but there is also a pecking order of annual award schemes. Amongst film awards the Oscars, bestowed by the Academy of Motion Picture Arts and Sciences (AMPAS), hold the greatest authority. This meritorious system is based on the autonomous principle of celebrating the artistry rather than the commerce of film, with awards "given annually to honor outstanding achievements in theatrically released feature-length motion pictures" (AMPAS, 2009: 1). As Steve Pond observes, "the importance and significance of the Academy Awards is tied to the perception that they genuinely are awarded for merit" (2005: 14). Emanuel Levy (2001b: 338) pinpoints the cultural significance of the Academy Awards when he describes the Oscars "as an institutionalized yardstick of artistic quality." As Levy notes, "Through the Oscar, the Academy functions as peers, critics, and tastemakers. No other award so well combines critical and popular judgment" (p. 44). Oscar prestige is therefore a middle-brow creation, honoring art in popular culture by conferring artistic validity on products which to varying degrees are commercially orientated.

Awards provide tangible markers of artistic prestige yet whatever value is attached to them is entirely arbitrary: why should a 13½-inch statue of a gold knight holding a sword and standing on a reel of film, the iconic figure of the Oscars, be so imbued with significance by the film community? Whatever value the Oscars have is the outcome of the production of belief in their authority. The value of Academy Awards depends on collective belief in their value and recognition that the works or acts they celebrate are things of value. This belief is sustained by a combination of factors. First, the authority of the Oscars is supported by the commercial and cultural dominance of Hollywood film in the world's leading film markets. The Academy's membership is predominantly drawn from the US professional film community, and although the Oscars are open to embracing a wide diversity of films from across the world, for over 80 years now the voting of the Academy has overwhelmingly focused on celebrating English-language – and in most cases American-produced – films which frequently come from the Hollywood majors. While apparently set apart from the film market, the hegemonic status of the Oscars in the international system of film awards mirrors the economic dominance of Hollywood in international territories, but through the symbolic terms of the prestige economy.

Second, belief in the value of the Oscars is sustained by belief in the Academy as an authoritative organ for the industry. When the Academy was formed in 1927, it had two purposes: to create an industry-wide body to mediate in labor disputes and to guard against perceptions of the moral turpitude of the movies by "establish[ing] the industry in the public mind as a respectable, legitimate institution, and its people as reputable individuals" (1929 Academy annual report cited in Shale, 1993: 2). On the former point, the Academy received criticism that it acted as "a company union for the producers" (Frank Gillmore, President of the stage performers union Actors' Equity Association, cited in Clark, 1995: 53), and with the formation of the Screen Actors Guild (SAG) in 1933, the Academy was defeated in this purpose. However, the inauguration of the Oscars in 1929 provided an instrument for legitimizing the industry. Subsequently, while moral criticisms of the movies may have receded, the Oscars continue to serve a legitimizing function: the awards create a circle of belief in their own value, for by celebrating the art of cinema, they reciprocally confirm cinema as an art. This authority is also affirmed by maintaining a closed membership system "limited to those who have achieved distinction in the arts and sciences of motion pictures" (AMPAS, 2011). By restricting its members to distinguished figures working in the film professions, the Academy positions itself as an informed and influential arbitrator in recognizing art in film.

Third, there is the placing of the Oscars in the annual calendar of American film awards. Since the 6th Academy Awards were held on 16 March 1934, the pattern has been to host the awards ceremony on a date in either March or February each year.[2] This sees the ceremony occur two to three months after the conclusion of the year for which achievements are honored. In the intervening period, other leading rounds in the awards calendar have already taken place, including the National Board of Review Awards, Los Angeles Film Critics Association Awards and SAG Awards (Table 8.2). Since 1944, the Hollywood Foreign Press Association (HFPA) has awarded the "Golden Globes." It is the mission of the HFPA to "recognize outstanding achievements by conferring annual Awards of Merit, (Golden Globe® Awards), serving as a constant incentive within the entertainment industry, both domestic and foreign, and to focus wide public attention upon the best in motion pictures and television" (HFPA, 2011). Held in January each year, the Golden Globes precede the Oscars and by honoring more or less the same categories of achievement in the same award year as the Academy, the Golden Globes could be regarded in many respects as a direct competitor for the Oscars. Yet any excitement or anticipation generated is repeatedly over-shadowed as commentators only discuss the Globes for how they may provide a forecast of forthcoming Oscar nominations and winners. Sitting at the tail end of the awards season, potentially the Academy Awards could lose their importance, yet the perception has endured that other events in the film awards calendar are mere precursors to the Oscars.

Finally, the symbolic value of the Oscars is produced through the process by which the awards are actually decided and conferred. To recognize and celebrate solitary winners, the Oscars must enact a ritual of exclusion, conducted under the authority of professional peers. This progresses

Table 8.2 Annual cycle of film-acting awards in the US.[1]

Month[2]	Award	Voters and awarding body	Started
December	National Board of Review Awards	Professional members of the National Board of Review of Motion Pictures	1929
December	New York Film Critics Circle Awards	Professional members of the New York Film Critics Circle	1936
December	Critics' Choice Awards	Professional members of the Broadcast Film Critics Association	1995
January	People's Choice Awards	Sponsored by Proctor & Gamble and voted for by members of the public	1975
January	National Society of Film Critics Awards	Professional members of the National Society of Film Critics	1966
January	Los Angeles Film Critics Association Awards	Professional members of the Los Angeles Film Critics Association	1975
January	Golden Globes	Professional members of the Hollywood Foreign Press Association	1944
January	SAG Awards	Professional members of the Screen Actors Guild	1995
February	Independent Spirit Awards	Previous Spirit Awards nominees and paying members of Film Independent	1984
March	Golden Raspberry Awards (the "Razzies")	Paying public members of the Golden Raspberry Award Foundation	1981
March	Academy Awards (the "Oscars")	Professional members of the Academy of Motion Picture Arts and Sciences	1929
June	MTV Movie Awards (the "Golden Popcorn")	Members of the public	1992

[1] To identify award rounds with relevance to Hollywood stardom, the table is limited to only those awards which confer honors in acting categories, and so does not include other important events in the film calendar such as the American Film Institute Awards, Directors Guild of America Awards or Writers Guild of America Awards.

[2] As many awards ceremonies have moved between months, this chronology is inexact. Recorded here are the most regular months award ceremonies were held in the period 2000 to 2010 and the chronology is organized to follow the order in which ceremonies are held for the films of the previous year. Exceptions here are the National Board of Review Awards and New York Film Critics Circle Awards which are presented in December, and the Critics' Choice Awards which are announced in December but presented the following month. Falling in the last month of the calendar year which they are celebrating, these become the first rounds in the annual awards cycle.

through the phases of eligibility and submission, two rounds of voting, and then the awards ceremony. To be considered, achievements by individuals must be attached to particular films, and to be eligible for submission any film must fulfill certain criteria.

> All eligible motion pictures . . . must be:
> a. feature length (defined as over 40 minutes),
> b. publicly exhibited [using professional standard equipment],
> c. for paid admission in a commercial motion picture theater in Los Angeles County,
> d. for a qualifying run of at least seven consecutive days,
> e. advertised and exploited during their Los Angeles County qualifying run in a manner considered normal and customary to the industry, and
> f. within the Awards year deadlines.(AMPAS, 2009: 5–6)

Voting for the awards is conducted by secret ballot restricted to active and life Academy members who are organized under 15 branches defined by craft specializations, e.g. art directors, cinematographers, editors and visual effects, with the Actors Branch retaining the largest membership (1,183 in 2011), inevitably including previous nominees and award-winners.

Voting is a two stage process of preferential balloting.[3] Initially, candidates are selected through the nomination ballot. Taking all the films which meet the aforementioned criteria, the Academy compiles an annual "Reminder List of Eligible Releases" which is circulated to members in late December, together with forms to register votes for nominations in 25 categories. Members can only vote for nominees in the category or categories represented by the branch to which they belong, which in the case of the Acting Branch means members vote for nominees in four categories: Actress in a Leading Role, Actor in a Leading Role, Actress in a Supporting Role, and Actor in a Supporting Role. Forms are returned unsigned in late January to the accountancy firm PricewaterhouseCoopers (PwC) and just over a week later nominees in all categories are announced at an early morning (5.30am Pacific Time) press conference held at the Academy's Samuel Goldwyn Theater in Beverly Hills. There then follows the Final Ballot, where voting is opened up to the entire Academy membership to cast their votes on nominees in all categories, and the poll closes a few days before the awards ceremony takes place.

As Bourdieu noted, the value of symbolic capital depends on recognition. In purely practical terms, the voting process serves the purpose of elimination, but its larger cultural function comes from how the voting stages the recognition, and therefore the legitimization, of certain works and practitioners as worthy exemplars of artistic merit. With the voting completed, the ceremony therefore becomes the ultimate act of recognition, as legitimacy is affirmed and confirmed in an act of widespread collective witnessing. This is achieved at two levels: the witnessing inside the closed world of the award venue by the Academy and other privileged invited guests; and the global mediated event of the televised "Oscarcast," which allows the general public to observe the outcomes of the Academy's decisions. This dual audience for the ceremony exactly articulates the middle-brow status of the Oscars, for the awards are at once a statement of elite selection and of popular approval and fascination.

By taking these factors together, it becomes possible to see how the symbolic value of the Oscars is not the outcome of the individual accomplishments of award nominees or winners. Rather, the Oscars become symbolic capital as belief in their value is produced collectively through Hollywood's global dominance, the awards system and the institutionalized force of the Academy as a forum for the recognition and consecration of artistic achievements in film.

Oscar Prestige and Legitimized Acting

Acknowledging differences in the nature of achievements made by nominees, the Academy's branches are entitled to formulate their own special rules. In the case of the acting categories, rules are in place to regulate the distinction between "leading" and "supporting" status as there is no hard and fast distinction between these categories. Current regulations permit a "performance by an actor or actress in any role shall be eligible for nomination either for the leading role or supporting role categories," with the caveat that "determination as to whether a role is a leading or supporting role shall be made individually by members of the branch at the time of balloting." (AMPAS, 2009: 11). Tabulation of nominations in leading and supporting categories is conducted simultaneously and if a single performance receives nominations under both categories, in the system of preferential voting it will be entered on the ballot only in the category where it first receives the number of votes to be nominated. If a single performance receives enough votes to be nominated in both categories, or if a performer

attracts enough votes to be nominated in the same category for two different performances, then in either situation the performance or performer
will only be nominated once as determined by the preferential tabulation
process (p. 11). This does not prevent, however, a performer from achieving
nominations for separate performances under the leading and supporting
categories. Historically, dual nominations for performers in the lead and
supporting categories have been rare, although the incidence has increased
since the early 1980s. Most recently, in 2002 Julianne Moore was nominated
for the lead in *Far from Heaven* and her supporting performance in *The
Hours*, and two years later Jamie Foxx received a supporting nomination
for his role in *Collateral* while winning the award for Actor in a Leading
Role with *Ray*. In the lead-up to the 80th awards in 2007, Cate Blanchett
picked up nominations for the lead in *Elizabeth: The Golden Age* and her
supporting performance in *I'm Not There* although ultimately missed the
opportunity to take home a statue.

According to the criteria outlined earlier, in any year hundreds of films
fulfill the bureaucratic requirements to be eligible for submission. Yet one
factor severely limits the possibilities for the majority of films to be considered. Tradition weighs on the Oscar ritual in the form of historically
embedded taste. Future beliefs about whether a particular performance
or film is worthy of nomination or an award is always at least partly produced through a history of trends in what the Academy has previously
believed to be achievements of merit. Something of those trends can be
identified by considering the 160 performances which represented all the
nominees and winners in the Best Actor and Actress categories from the
years 1994 to 2009. In his analysis of winning roles over the first seven
decades of the Academy Awards, Emanuel Levy identified the Academy's
preference for rewarding performances based on the lives of real-life figures,
with a stronger incidence of this trend amongst men than women (2001b:
194–95). This trend has persisted: in the period 1994–2009, 21% of nominations and 50% of winners in the Leading Actress category, and 31%
nominations and 31% winners in the Leading Actor category, were for
performances based on biographical figures. Within this trend, the Academy
has shown preferences for nominating and honoring performances representing certain categories of true life figures (**winners in bold**):

English royalty: **Helen Mirren *The Queen*** (2006), Cate Blanchett *Elizabeth*
(1998) and *Elizabeth: The Golden Age* (2007), Judi Dench *Mrs. Brown*
(1997) and Nigel Hawthorne *The Madness of King George* (1994).

Popular entertainers, particularly singers: **Marion Cotillard** *La Vie en Rose* (2007), Joaquin Phoenix and **Reese Witherspoon** *Walk the Line* (2005) and **Jamie Foxx** *Ray* (2004). If extended to encompass figures moving in the general world of entertainment, then this category also includes Leonardo DiCaprio *The Aviator* (2004) and Ian McKellen *Gods and Monsters* (1998).

Figures from the fully consecrated arts: i.e. literature (**Nicole Kidman** *The Hours* (2002), Judi Dench *Iris*, **Philip Seymour Hoffman** *Capote* (2005), Johnny Depp *Finding Neverland* (2004), Geoffrey Rush *Quills* (2000), Javier Bardem *Before Night Falls* (2000), and Miranda Richardson *Tom & Viv* (1994)), concert music (Emily Watson *Hilary and Jackie* (1998) and **Geoffrey Rush** *Shine* (1996)), and painting (Ed Harris *Pollock* (2000) and Salma Hayek *Frida* (2002)). If this category is defined broadly speaking by figures noted for their "intellectual" achievements, then Russell Crowe *A Beautiful Mind* (2001) also fits here.

The latter ensemble also shades into a uniquely female category: Kidman as Virginia Woolf, Dench as Iris Murdoch and Watson as Jacqueline du Pré could equally be grouped with Angelina Jolie *Changeling* (2008), **Charlize Theron** *Monster* (2003), and **Hilary Swank** *Boys Don't Cry* (1999) as "the tragic woman."

In contrast, a body of male nominees and winners have represented real-life national leaders (Morgan Freeman *Invictus* (2009), Frank Langella *Frost/Nixon* (2008), **Forest Whitaker** *The Last King of Scotland* (2006) and Anthony Hopkins *Nixon* (1995)), or otherwise figures whose lives are touched by actual political circumstance (**Sean Penn** *Milk* (2008), David Strathairn *Good Night, and Good Luck* (2005), Don Cheadle *Hotel Rwanda* (2004) and Woody Harrelson *The People vs. Larry Flynt* (1996)).

With the figure of the boxer (Will Smith *Ali* (2001) and Denzel Washington *The Hurricane* (1999)), the ring has become a fertile dramatic arena.

Alongside royalty, artists and politicians, the Academy also likes to see the lives of extraordinary ordinary people acted out, with wins for **Julia Roberts** *Erin Brockovich* (2000) and **Sandra Bullock** *The Blind Side* (2009) showing the Academy's fondness for stories of strong mothers holding the family together while confronting social injustices.

Several of these categories also expand to fictional characters. Julie Christie *Away from Her* (2006), Imelda Staunton *Vera Drake* (2004) and Julianne Moore *Far from Heaven* (2002) and *The End of the Affair* (1999) all performed the tragic woman. **Hilary Swank** *Million Dollar Baby* (2004) gave a rare female inflection on the boxer, and although Mickey Rourke as *The Wrestler* (2008) belonged to a different sport, the film followed many conventions of the boxing movie. Fascination with music both popular and classical has also accommodated **Jeff Bridges** *Crazy Heart* (2009) and Richard Dreyfuss *Mr. Holland's Opus* (1995).

By selectively legitimizing the acting of certain character types, the Oscars equally de-legitimize a far wider array of other types of performances and performers. Whole genres fail to be recognized by the Academy. As already noted in Chapter 5, in the 1990s action film stood at the forefront of the box office, and in the following decade fantasy and comic book adaptations took over, yet nowhere did lead performances in these films feature amongst the Academy's preferences. This systematic exclusion can be understood according to the logic of the cultural field, for although the value of the Oscars remains within the context of large-scale production – and so the achievements they celebrate are never entirely liberated from the trappings of commerciality – as expressions of the middle-brow disposition the Academy Awards set themselves apart from the most popular terrain of the market. The Academy does not like horror, while dual wins for **Helen Hunt** and **Jack Nicholson** in *As Good As It Gets* (1997), together with nominations for Meryl Streep *The Devil Wears Prada* (2006) and Diane Keaton *Something's Gotta Give* (2003), are rare cases of the Academy consecrating comedy acting. Generally the Academy has not rewarded performances in out-and-out comedies but at most has made concessions to dramas with comic tones, as seen with the nominations granted to Judi Dench (*Mrs. Henderson Presents* (2005)), Bill Murray (*Lost in Translation* (2003)), Jack Nicholson (*About Schmidt* (2002)), and Dustin Hoffman (*Wag the Dog* (1997)). This sample also confirms the Academy's preference for recognizing English-language performances. Between 1994 and 2009, only 3 percent of total nominations and 6 percent of all winners were in a language other than English: i.e. **Marion Cotillard** *La Vie en Rose*, Catalina Sandino Moreno *Maria Full of Grace* (2004), Fernanda Montenegro *Central Station* (1998), **Roberto Benigni** *La vita e bella* (1997) and Massimo Troisi *Il Postino* (1994).

There is no set template for the "Oscar performance" and occasions continually arise where sure-fire predictions are proved empty. Even so, enduring patterns in the Academy's preferences suggest that it is possible to find parameters circumscribing Oscar contending material. Tradition powerfully defines what the Academy is prepared to recognize but is even more powerful in determining the types of performance which will not be legitimized.

Prestige vs. Profit?

The Academy Awards are founded on economic disinterest, rewarding artistic merit rather than financial profits. Oscar winners do not even receive any financial compensation for their achievements. Oscar prestige is therefore overtly disconnected from market considerations, but not entirely so. Only in the rarest of cases does the Academy consecrate popular hits but the symbolic capital of nominations and awards is still deployed in the market with the aim of milking financial returns. Bourdieu argued that

> it has to be posited simultaneously that economic capital is at the root of all the other types of capital and that these transformed, disguised forms of economic capital . . . produce their most specific effects only to the extent that they conceal . . . the fact that economic capital is at their root, in other words . . . at the root of their effects. (1983b: 252)

Symbolic capital is therefore a transformed or "disguised" form of economic capital: in cultural production, its value may arise from disavowing the market, but nevertheless it can still achieve economic ends. This invites the question – does Oscar prestige "cash in on kudos" (Groves, 2001: 10)?

In the years 1994–2009, 126 of the 152 films which represented the 160 nominees continued their release over the period of the nominations and awards, indicating distributors strategically staged the release of those films which they strongly suspected to have potential for generating ticket sales through the Oscar buzz (Figures 8.2 and 8.3).[4] By the end of their North American runs nearly, 67 percent of the films featuring nominated performances in the actor and actress categories had grossed less than £50 million and only 18 percent grossed over £100 million. Generally, Oscar prestige was not therefore linked into the hit driven market, although a few performances appeared in movies ranked amongst *Variety*'s end of year top tens. These had either completed their runs (*Silence of the Lambs*, *Gladiator* and *Erin Brockovich*) several months before the awards season or had already attracted over 90 percent of their North American gross by the time of the nominations were announced (*The Blind Side*) (Figures 8.4 and 8.5).

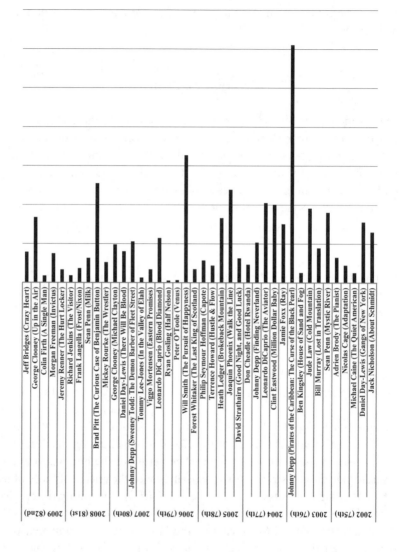

Jeff Bridges (Crazy Heart)
George Clooney (Up in the Air)
Colin Firth (A Single Man)
Morgan Freeman (Invictus)
Jeremy Renner (The Hurt Locker)
Richard Jenkins (The Visitor)
Frank Langella (Frost/Nixon)
Sean Penn (Milk)
Brad Pitt (The Curious Case of Benjamin Button)
Mickey Rourke (The Wrestler)
George Clooney (Michael Clayton)
Daniel Day-Lewis (There Will Be Blood)
Johnny Depp (Sweeney Todd: The Demon Barber of Fleet Street)
Tommy Lee-Jones (In the Valley of Elah)
Viggo Mortensen (Eastern Promises)
Leonardo DiCaprio (Blood Diamond)
Ryan Gosling (Half Nelson)
Peter O'Toole (Venus)
Will Smith (The Pursuit of Happyness)
Forest Whitaker (The Last King of Scotland)
Philip Seymour Hoffman (Capote)
Terrence Howard (Hustle & Flow)
Heath Ledger (Brokeback Mountain)
Joaquin Phoenix (Walk the Line)
David Strathairn (Good Night, and Good Luck)
Don Cheadle (Hotel Rwanda)
Johnny Depp (Finding Neverland)
Leonardo DiCaprio (The Aviator)
Clint Eastwood (Million Dollar Baby)
Jamie Foxx (Ray)
Johnny Depp (Pirates of the Caribbean: The Curse of the Black Pearl)
Ben Kingsley (House of Sand and Fog)
Jude Law (Cold Mountain)
Bill Murray (Lost in Translation)
Sean Penn (Mystic River)
Adrien Brody (The Pianist)
Nicolas Cage (Adaptation)
Michael Caine (The Quiet American)
Daniel Day-Lewis (Gangs of New York)
Jack Nicholson (About Schmidt)

2009 (82nd)
2008 (81st)
2007 (80th)
2006 (79th)
2005 (78th)
2004 (77th)
2003 (76th)
2002 (75th)

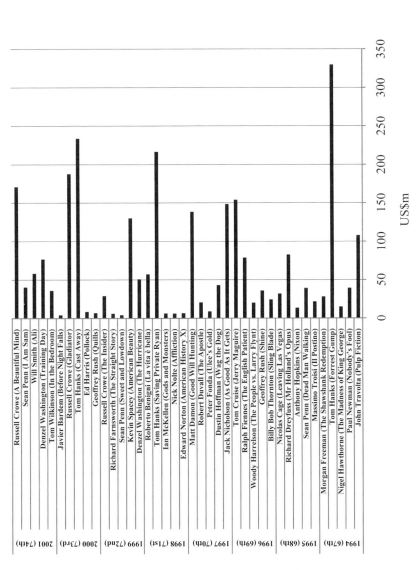

Figure 8.2 Best Actor nominees and winners: gross box office, 1994–2009. Sources: compiled using data from www.boxofficemojo.com and www.the-numbers.com.

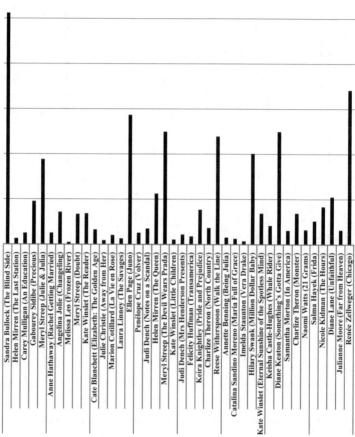

Sandra Bullock (The Blind Side)
Helen Mirren (The Last Station)
Carey Mulligan (An Education)
Gabourey Sidibe (Precious)
Meryl Streep (Julie & Julia)
Anne Hathaway (Rachel Getting Married)
Angelina Jolie (Changeling)
Melissa Leo (Frozen River)
Meryl Streep (Doubt)
Kate Winslet (The Reader)
Cate Blanchett (Elizabeth: The Golden Age)
Julie Christie (Away from Her)
Marion Cotillard (La Vie en Rose)
Laura Linney (The Savages)
Ellen Page (Juno)
Penélope Cruz (Volver)
Judi Dench (Notes on a Scandal)
Helen Mirren (The Queen)
Meryl Streep (The Devil Wears Prada)
Kate Winslet (Little Children)
Judi Dench (Mrs Henderson Presents)
Felicity Huffman (Transamerica)
Keira Knightley (Pride and Prejudice)
Charlize Theron (North Country)
Reese Witherspoon (Walk the Line)
Annette Benning (Being Julia)
Catalina Sandino Moreno (Maria Full of Grace)
Imelda Staunton (Vera Drake)
Hilary Swank (Million Dollar Baby)
Kate Winslet (Eternal Sunshine of the Spotless Mind)
Diane Keaton (Something's Gotta Give)
Keisha Castle-Hughes (Whale Rider)
Samantha Morton (In America)
Charlize Theron (Monster)
Naomi Watts (21 Grams)
Salma Hayek (Frida)
Nicole Kidman (The Hours)
Diane Lane (Unfaithful)
Julianne Moore (Far from Heaven)
Renée Zellweger (Chicago)

2002 (75th)   2003 (76th)   2004 (77th)   2005 (78th)   2006 (79th)   2007 (80th)   2008 (81st)   2009 (82nd)

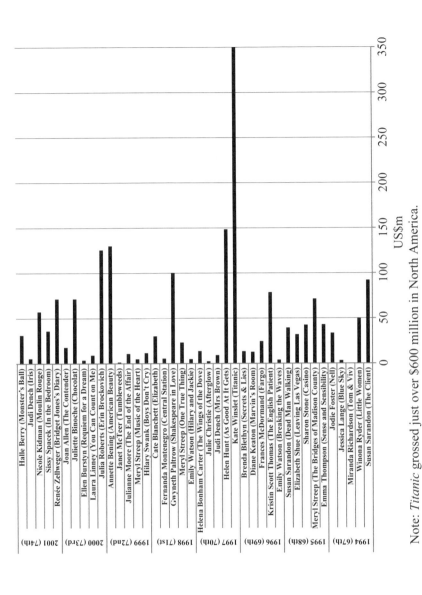

Figure 8.3 Best Actress nominees and winners: gross box office, 1994–2009. Sources: compiled using data from www.boxofficemojo.com and www.the-numbers.com.

Note: *Titanic* grossed just over $600 million in North America.

	Jeff Bridges (Crazy Heart)
	George Clooney (Up in the Air)
	Colin Firth (A Single Man)
	Morgan Freeman (Invictus)
	Jeremy Renner (The Hurt Locker)
	Richard Jenkins (The Visitor)
	Frank Langella (Frost/Nixon)
	Sean Penn (Milk)
	Brad Pitt (The Curious Case of Benjamin Button)
	Mickey Rourke (The Wrestler)
	George Clooney (Michael Clayton)
	Daniel Day-Lewis (There Will Be Blood)
	Johnny Depp (Sweeney Todd: The Demon Barber of Fleet Street)
	Tommy Lee-Jones (In the Valley of Elah)
	Viggo Mortensen (Eastern Promises)
	Leonardo DiCaprio (Blood Diamond)
	Ryan Gosling (Half Nelson)
	Peter O'Toole (Venus)
	Will Smith (The Pursuit of Happyness)
	Forest Whitaker (The Last King of Scotland)
	Philip Seymour Hoffman (Capote)
	Terrence Howard (Hustle & Flow)
	Heath Ledger (Brokeback Mountain)
	Joaquin Phoenix (Walk the Line)
	David Strathairn (Good Night, and Good Luck)
	Don Cheadle (Hotel Rwanda)
	Johnny Depp (Finding Neverland)
	Leonardo DiCaprio (The Aviator)
	Clint Eastwood (Million Dollar Baby)
	Jamie Foxx (Ray)
	Johnny Depp (Pirates of the Caribbean: The Curse of the Black Pearl)
	Ben Kingsley (House of Sand and Fog)
	Jude Law (Cold Mountain)
	Bill Murray (Lost in Translation)
	Sean Penn (Mystic River)
	Adrien Brody (The Pianist)
	Nicolas Cage (Adaptation)
	Michael Caine (The Quiet American)
	Daniel Day-Lewis (Gangs of New York)
	Jack Nicholson (About Schmidt)

2009 (82nd)
2008 (81st)
2007 (80th)
2006 (79th)
2005 (78th)
2004 (77th)
2003 (76th)
2002 (75th)

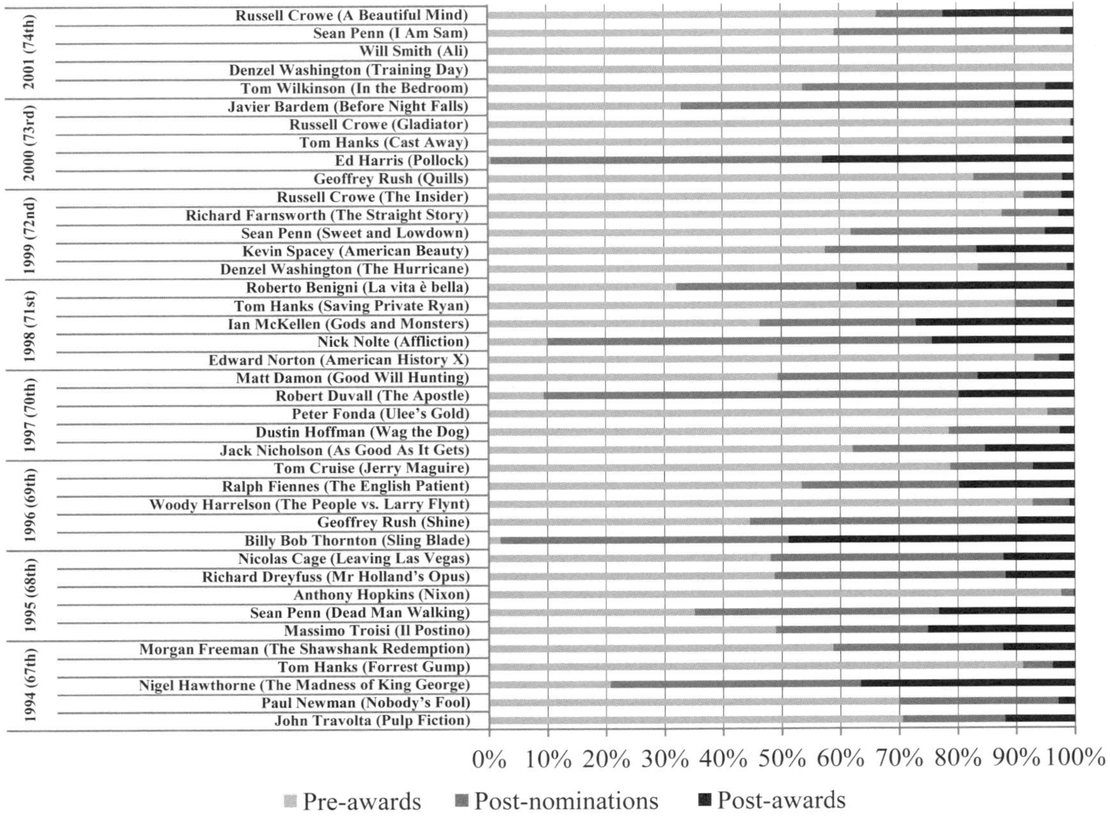

Russell Crowe (A Beautiful Mind)
Sean Penn (I Am Sam)
Will Smith (Ali)
Denzel Washington (Training Day)
Tom Wilkinson (In the Bedroom)
Javier Bardem (Before Night Falls)
Russell Crowe (Gladiator)
Tom Hanks (Cast Away)
Ed Harris (Pollock)
Geoffrey Rush (Quills)
Russell Crowe (The Insider)
Richard Farnsworth (The Straight Story)
Sean Penn (Sweet and Lowdown)
Kevin Spacey (American Beauty)
Denzel Washington (The Hurricane)
Roberto Benigni (La vita è bella)
Tom Hanks (Saving Private Ryan)
Ian McKellen (Gods and Monsters)
Nick Nolte (Affliction)
Edward Norton (American History X)
Matt Damon (Good Will Hunting)
Robert Duvall (The Apostle)
Peter Fonda (Ulee's Gold)
Dustin Hoffman (Wag the Dog)
Jack Nicholson (As Good As It Gets)
Tom Cruise (Jerry Maguire)
Ralph Fiennes (The English Patient)
Woody Harrelson (The People vs. Larry Flynt)
Geoffrey Rush (Shine)
Billy Bob Thornton (Sling Blade)
Nicolas Cage (Leaving Las Vegas)
Richard Dreyfuss (Mr Holland's Opus)
Anthony Hopkins (Nixon)
Sean Penn (Dead Man Walking)
Massimo Troisi (Il Postino)
Morgan Freeman (The Shawshank Redemption)
Tom Hanks (Forrest Gump)
Nigel Hawthorne (The Madness of King George)
Paul Newman (Nobody's Fool)
John Travolta (Pulp Fiction)

2001 (74th)
2000 (73rd)
1999 (72nd)
1998 (71st)
1997 (70th)
1996 (69th)
1995 (68th)
1994 (67th)

0% 10% 20% 30% 40% 50% 60% 70% 80% 90% 100%

■ Pre-awards   ■ Post-nominations   ■ Post-awards

Figure 8.4 Best Actor nominees and winners: box office (%) by award phase, 1994–2009. Sources: compiled using data from www.boxofficemojo.com and www.the-numbers.com.

	2009 (82nd)	2008 (81st)	2007 (80th)	2006 (79th)	2005 (78th)	2004 (77th)	2003 (76th)	2002 (75th)
Sandra Bullock (The Blind Side)								
Helen Mirren (The Last Station)								
Carey Mulligan (An Education)								
Gabourey Sidibe (Precious)								
Meryl Streep (Julie & Julia)								
Anne Hathaway (Rachel Getting Married)								
Angelina Jolie (Changeling)								
Melissa Leo (Frozen River)								
Meryl Streep (Doubt)								
Kate Winslet (The Reader)								
Cate Blanchett (Elizabeth: The Golden Age)								
Julie Christie (Away from Her)								
Marion Cotillard (La Vie en Rose)								
Laura Linney (The Savages)								
Ellen Page (Juno)								
Penélope Cruz (Volver)								
Judi Dench (Notes on a Scandal)								
Helen Mirren (The Queen)								
Meryl Streep (The Devil Wears Prada)								
Kate Winslet (Little Children)								
Judi Dench (Mrs Henderson Presents)								
Felicity Huffman (Transamerica)								
Keira Knightley (Pride and Prejudice)								
Charlize Theron (North Country)								
Reese Witherspoon (Walk the Line)								
Annette Bening (Being Julia)								
Catalina Sandino Moreno (Maria Full of Grace)								
Imelda Staunton (Vera Drake)								
Hilary Swank (Million Dollar Baby)								
Kate Winslet (Eternal Sunshine of the Spotless Mind)								
Keisha Castle-Hughes (Whale Rider)								
Diane Keaton (Something's Gotta Give)								
Samantha Morton (In America)								
Charlize Theron (Monster)								
Naomi Watts (21 Grams)								
Salma Hayek (Frida)								
Nicole Kidman (The Hours)								
Diane Lane (Unfaithful)								
Julianne Moore (Far from Heaven)								
Renée Zellweger (Chicago)								

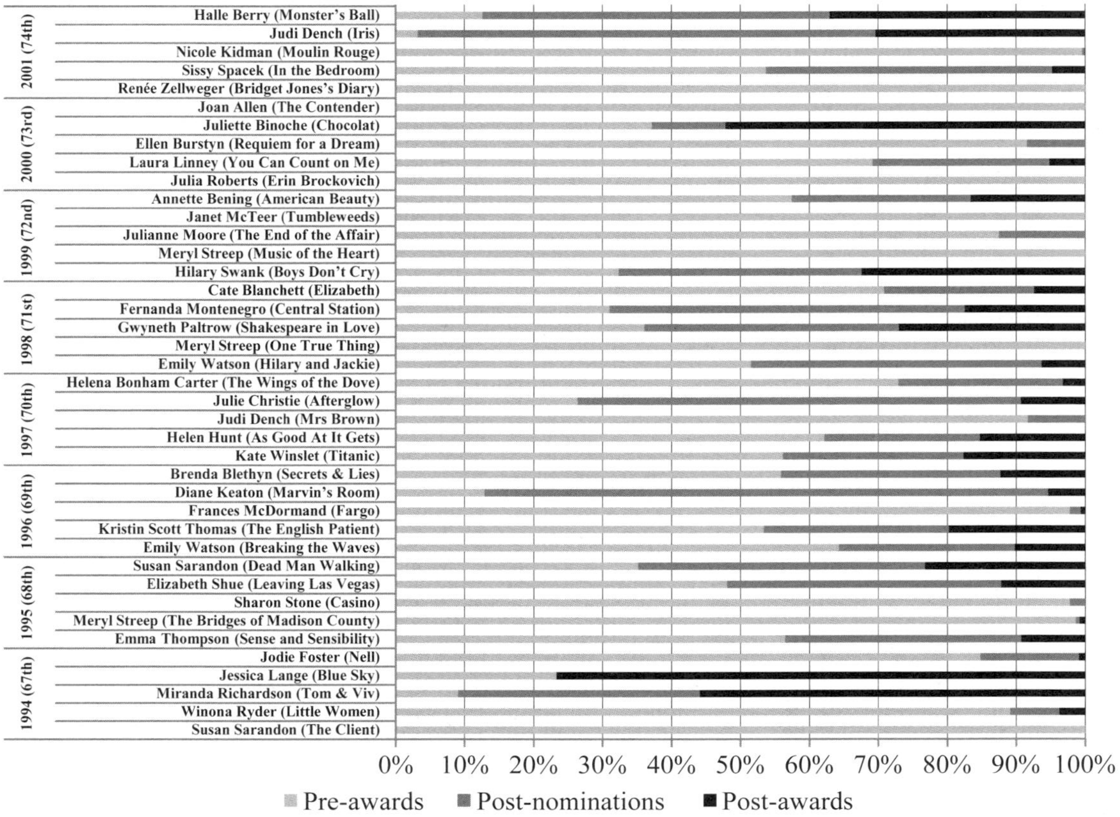

Figure 8.5 Best Actress nominees and winners: box office (%) by award phase, 1994–2009. Sources: compiled using data from www.boxofficemojo.com and www.the-numbers.com.

These were films whose commercial standing was not made by the Oscars. Where the financial effects of the Oscars could be detected was amongst the nominees belonging to the mid and lower tiers of the box office market. Here there was a group of films which attracted the majority of their audiences through the exposure arising from Academy recognition. *Blue Sky* (1994), *Dead Man Walking* (1995), *La vita è bella, Shakespeare in Love, Boys Don't Cry* (1999), *Monster's Ball* (2001), *The Pianist* (2002), *Monster, Million Dollar Baby, The Last King of Scotland, There Will Be Blood, The Reader* (2008) and *Crazy Heart* featured 41 percent of all winners in the Lead Actor and Actress categories between 1994 to 2009, and all attracted over 60 percent their tickets sales in the period after the nominations were announced. Of these, Jessica Lange in *Blue Sky*, Charlize Theron in *Monster* and Forest Whitaker in *The Last King of Scotland* were the only nominees for these films, and so that whatever economic effects the Oscars had on box office can only be attributed to the buzz created around those individual performances. With the others, the Oscar effect was more dispersed, as award-winning performances featured in films which received multiple nominations in the main award categories. For example, Hilary Swank's award-winning performance in *Million Dollar Baby* featured in a film which not only collected awards for Best Picture, directing and Supporting Actor, but also nominations for Lead Actor, editing and writing. Likewise, Adrien Brody's award for the lead in *The Pianist* was accompanied by wins for Roman Polanski and Ronald Harwood in the directing and adapted screenplay categories, with the film also picking up four other nominations.

As these cases show, consecration of the award-winning performance can be surrounded by, and no doubt aided by, a wider base of prestige credentials which collect around a single film. Equally, the prestige package can benefit from the accumulated honors which a single performer's prior record of awards and nominations brings to a film. This was certainly the case of Daniel Day-Lewis's nomination and eventual award for his performance as oil businessman Daniel Plainview in *There Will Be Blood*. Day-Lewis won his first Oscar for *My Left Foot* and subsequently gained nominations in the Lead Actor category with *In the Name of the Father* and *Gangs of New York*. A co-production from Miramax and Paramount's Vantage specialty subsidiary, *There Will Be Blood* opened on 26 December 2007 in the US on just two screens. As a tale of greed, treachery and murder set in Southern California at the start of the twentieth century, which can be read as a critique of capitalism, the film was unlikely to tap into the mainstream popular market and was certainly not the kind of fare likely to receive much interest in the Christmas holiday period. The timing and scale of release was strategic, however. By opening in December, the film not only fulfilled the eligibility criteria to be submitted for consideration in voting for the 80th Academy Awards at the start of the following year but was also beginning its run just as the nomination forms were issued. Over the next four weeks, the release expanded from two to 51 to 129 screens, following the pattern of platform releasing, a familiar strategy for specialized distribution whereby a film opens on a few screens in metropolitan centers with the aim of attracting positive critical notices to generate the "buzz" and "word of mouth" to support the widening of the release for an extended run over several months (Figure 8.6). Day-Lewis's prestige stardom brought to the film his symbolic capital, which included not only his award and two nominations from the Academy but also four Golden Globe nominations. Before the Oscars he'd already collected numerous awards for his performance as Plainview, including a Golden Globe and awards from the New York Film Critics Circle, the National Society of Film Critics, the Los Angeles Film Critics Association, and the Screen Actors Guild.

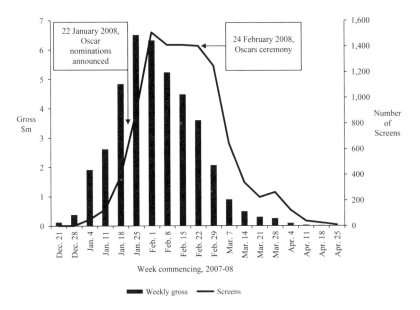

Figure 8.6   *There Will Be Blood*: box office and release pattern. Source: compiled from data at www.boxofficemojo.com.

By the time the Oscar nominations were announced on the morning of Tuesday 22 January 2008, the film was playing on 389 screens in North America and had grossed nearly $9 million. It picked up nominations in eight categories (a standard only equaled that year by *No Country for Old Men*) including Best Picture and Achievement in Directing. In the lead actor category, Day-Lewis was pitched into competition against George Clooney for *Michael Clayton*, Johnny Depp in *Sweeney Todd: The Demon Barber of Fleet Street*, Tommy Lee Jones for *In the Valley of Elah* and Viggo Mortensen in *Eastern Promises*. In the same award year, *Spider-man 3*, *Shrek the Third*, *Transformers*, *Pirates of the Caribbean: At World's End* and *Harry Potter and the Order of the Phoenix* had topped the annual box-office rankings in North America. *Transformers* and *Pirates* picked up three nominations in the technical categories but otherwise these films were entirely ignored in the Academy's "artistic" categories. Depp was an Oscar contender for his lead role in *Sweeney Todd*, which grossed nearly $153 million across all territories, but while audiences worldwide were prepared to spend nearly $1 billion on tickets to see him star in *Pirates*, the Academy was unprepared to smile on that performance.[5]

With multiple nominations behind it, *There Will Be Blood* continued its run. On the weekend following the nominations the scale of release expanded to 885 screens and a week later nearly doubled to 1,507, giving the film wide but still comparatively restricted coverage when measured against the 4,100-plus screens which all the hits of 2007 had opened on. Leading up to the awards ceremony on Sunday 24 February 2008, the scale of release continued at a similar level, and during the few weeks between the nominations and the ceremony, the film grossed nearly $26 million. On the night, Day-Lewis picked up the statue and Robert Elswit won for the film's cinematography. By the following weekend, *There Will Be Blood* was still playing on 1,248 screens before the release was scaled back. Although the main excitement of the awards was over, following the ceremony the award winning afterglow was enough to carry the film through to 1 May 2008 when it concluded its run, grossing a further $5 million for an overall North American total of just over $40 million. Over the five months of the full run, 65 percent of the gross was therefore accumulated in the five weeks between the nomination announcement and the awards ceremony. To take advantage of the international hype created by the Oscars, in that same small window the film was also rolled out in all of Hollywood's major overseas markets except Japan. Compared to the hits of 2007, *There Will Be Blood* was small fry: if the entire North American run had been completed that year, the $40 million gross would have ranked the film just 61st amongst the year's film grosses. Based on an average 2007 ticket price in the US of $6.88 (MPAA, 2008: 4), *There Will Be Blood* played to an estimated 5.8 million cinemagoers in North America, compared to the nearly 49 million who saw *Spider-man 3.*[6] Whatever commercial success *There Will Be Blood* did enjoy was almost entirely built on the symbolic capital of Oscar nominations and awards. *There Will Be Blood* profited – both symbolically and commercially – from Day-Lewis's prestige stardom and cache of award credentials, while also reciprocally serving as a platform to further enhance and strengthen his status.

On the evening of 27 February 2011, Melissa Leo took to the stage at the Kodak Theatre to accept the Academy Award for Best Supporting Actress for her performance in *The Fighter* (2010). Closing her acceptance speech, she concluded on a rousing note with "thank you Academy because it's 'bout selling motion pictures and respecting the work." Probably unintentionally, because such matters are to be disavowed on the big occasion, Leo drew attention to the dual aspect of the Oscars. As a meritorious system, the Oscars are all about "respecting the work" but at the same time the awards are a commercial system for "selling motion pictures." According to the anti-economic logic of the field of cultural production, the symbolic and cultural authority of the Oscars can only be achieved by denying or disguising the commercial currents of the awards system, and yet the awards are fully integrated into the symbolic commerce of Hollywood. Paralleling the meritorious ritual of eligibility, submission, voting and ceremonial witnessing, there is the commercial ritual by which the whole buzz created around the nominations and awards becomes the engine for promoting and publicizing films in the market.

Prestige stardom is a product of the consecrating and legitimizing effects of the awards system. Unlike the commercial obviousness of the A-list performance, the acting of the prestige star appears as a gesture against the market, and the symbolic value of the Oscar-nominated performance is founded on a show of economic disinterest. Instead, through the eclectic roles s/he takes, through the refusal of a commercially valuable personified image, through the actorly craft of vocal and physical transformation, the prestige star exemplifies the autonomous principle of artistic interest. Although in every way belonging to the symbolic commerce of Hollywood stardom, the prestige star appears to stand for art against commerce, a figure of artistic principle rejecting the market whose eminence is yet entirely dependent on the market.

Notes

1   By the 1990s, the phrase "specialised film" was widely used by distributors and exhibitors as something of a catch-all term for any type of film which departed from the features characterizing mainstream production. Although widely applied, the term remained rather nebulous, and possibly the only direct attempt to define what might be included under the heading came from the UK Film Council. While including archive classic re-releases alongside foreign-language films and documentaries, the UKFC's definition also encompassed certain narrative characteristics.

> Whereas mainstream films might be regarded as falling within popular and recognisable genres . . . Specialised films are often less easy to define and thus more difficult to categorise in this way . . . With mainstream films, the subject matter is generally immediately obvious, appealing and easy to communicate to audiences. Specialised films often deal with more complex and challenging subject matters that are less easy to communicate . . . Within the mainstream . . . the film's narrative and cinematic style are generally quite straightforward, uncomplex, conventional and with high production values. Specialised films are often characterised as having a more innovative or unconventional storytelling style or aesthetic and may deviate from the straightforward narrative structure found in mainstream cinema. Overall, the film is more dependent on story, character development and a challenging subject matter than on high production values, effects and star names.
>
> (UKFC, n.d.)

2   Apart from an interval in the late 1950s to early 1980s when events were often held in April.
3   According to the preferential system of balloting, each Academy member holds a single vote and casts that vote, depending on the category, against a choice of five individual achievements or films in order of preference. Achievements or films which receive the majority of first choice votes are thereby nominated and any which receive no votes are eliminated. Achievements or films gaining the fewest votes are also eliminated with the votes of those members who made those selections their first choice then becoming redistributed according to the second choice of those members, with the process repeated until five nominees are eventually selected (AMPAS, n.d.). While complicated and potentially confusing, the benefit of the system is that the vote of every Academy member is eventually cast against one of the nominees.
4   The difference between the total number of films and the total nominees arises because *Dead Man Walking, Leaving Las Vegas* (1995), *The English Patient*

(1996), *As Good As It Gets, American Beauty* (1999), *In the Bedroom* (2001), *Million Dollar Baby* and *Walk the Line* all picked up dual nominations in the Lead Actor and Actress categories.

5 Although in voting for the 76th Academy Awards he was nominated for his performance as Captain Jack Sparrow in *Pirates of the Caribbean: The Curse of the Black Pearl* (2003).

6 According to Box Office Mojo, in North America *There Will Be Blood* grossed $40,222,514 and *Spider-man 3* $336,530,303.

9

Starring Julia Roberts

Amongst female leading performers working in Hollywood from 1990 to 2009, Julia Roberts was indisputably the period's most valuable female screen asset (see Table 1.1). Roberts's on-screen brand was formed around successive enactments of feisty sweetness, playing characters who are kind, amiable, friendly, considerate, pleasant and delightful, while equally determined, strong-willed, brave, energetic and (politely) aggressive. Reflecting on nearly two decades of the star's career, Ben Brantley of *The New York Times* observed "Her range onscreen runs from feisty but vulnerable ('Pretty Woman,' 'Erin Brockovich') to vulnerable but feisty ('Sleeping with the Enemy,' 'Closer'). Her strength, as far as her public is concerned, *is in her sameness*, which magnifies everyday human traits to a level of radioactive intensity, and a feral beauty that is too unusual to be called pretty" (emphasis added, 2006: E6). Her performed identity was perceived to be at once exotic and yet commonplace. Brantley called her "a down-home Garbo . . . an Everywoman who looks like nobody else" (p. E6). After directing Roberts in *Flatliners* (1990) and *Dying Young* (1991), Joel Schumacher said "She reminds me of no one else, and yet you feel you know her right away" (quoted in Schneller, 1991: 160).

Hollywood stardom is a dynamic system: star status is never permanent but always contingent on the mutability and vicissitudes of the film market. Like the life-cycle of products, the trajectory of star brands follows a common pattern, with an initial phase as the performer is introduced to the market but has no immediate commercial impact, then experiences sales growth, matures as sales stabilize, and then encounters declining sales before eventual withdrawal from the market. Over this trajectory, the commercial value of the star brand may survive short-term dips as s/he appears in two or three films which perform poorly in the market, but the romantic drama of stardom still allows for the possibility of a "comeback" as the performer returns to popular acceptance and public recognition with a new hit. Yet this cannot stop the inevitable waning of star power and even the biggest names eventually fall.

Roberts's life-cycle commenced the introductory stage with a walk-on part in the straight-to-video feature *Firehouse* (1987) and continued through supporting roles in *Blood Red* (produced in 1986 but released theatrically in 1989), *Satisfaction* (aka *Girls of Summer*) (1988) and TV-movie *Baja Oklahoma* (1988) until *Mystic Pizza* (1988) and *Steel Magnolias* (1989) established her as a potential leading name. Big box-office returns for *Pretty Woman* (1990) and *Sleeping with the Enemy* (1991) inaugurated the growth stage although this was cut short when Roberts took nearly two years out from acting. *People* magazine ran a story in February 1993 headed "Whatever Happened to Julia Roberts?" and *Variety* listed her in their "Lost and Found" column (Spada, 2004: 172). On her return with *The Pelican Brief* (1993), Roberts showed she could still bring in hits, although there followed a fallow period of three to four years as she appeared in films which either failed in the market or otherwise were un-commercial propositions. Roberts's stardom survived this hiatus and the run of films from *My Best Friend's Wedding* (1997) to *Erin Brockovich* (2000) marked the maturity phase in which her box-office performance reached some stability. Furthermore, with *Erin Brockovich* Roberts won a Best Actress Oscar, and this phase was also the critical highpoint of her career after which her star equity went into decline.

This chapter is concerned with the life-cycle of the Roberts brand and how that trajectory was enacted through performance. After initially examining how the growth phase consolidated Roberts's performative brand, the main body of the chapter concentrates on the mature phase, looking at the enactment and staging of the Roberts brand with an analysis of how *Runaway Bride* presented a combination of star performance and genre to position the film in the market. Also in this phase, Roberts's Oscar-winning performance in *Erin Brockovich* added a quota of prestige to the popular brand, and a third section examines the production of belief in Oscar prestige which followed the film's release. Finally, the chapter concludes by tracing the decline of the Roberts brand and how this was managed through performance.

Defining the Brand

As part of ensemble female casts in *Mystic Pizza* and *Steel Magnolias*, Roberts was already performing her brand of feisty sweetness when she landed the role of Vivian Ward in *Pretty Woman*. Originally scripted as a dark drama to be produced by the independent company Vestron, producer Steve Reuther sold the project to Disney and the Hollywood major transformed the film into a light romantic comedy (Dutka, 1991: 23). Roberts was not the headline star, for she received second billing opposite Richard Gere, but the massive critical attention attracted by her performance, plus the huge commercial success of the film, made *Pretty Woman* foundational to Roberts's stardom.

As Ward, Roberts played a street hooker working Hollywood Boulevard until she is picked up by a powerful Wall Street corporate raider, Edward Lewis (Gere), who pays her $3,000 to accompany him for six days. Lewis is ruthless in business and emotionally cold but something about Ward warms his heart and by the time their business arrangement concludes, the separation makes both parties realize what they miss and the narrative concludes in a climatic romantic (re)-union. *Pretty Woman* was not the first incarnation of Roberts's feisty sweetness but as the film became Roberts's earliest – and ultimately most successful – commercial hit, it consolidated a set of meanings that would go on to define her brand. Strutting down the Boulevard, Roberts performs all the self-assurance Ward needs to get by in her profession. At the same time she is soft and vulnerable: when Gere/Lewis takes her back to his hotel, she is visibly intimated by the overbearing opulence of the Regency Beverly Wilshire. She laughs at re-runs of *I Love Lucy* on television, adores old black-and-white movies, and cries at a performance of *La Traviata*. Ward comes from "the streets" and changes in costuming across the narrative chart a rags-to-riches story from cheap trashy attire to couture gowns. Physically and vocally, Roberts embodies this transition as brusque, sharp stabbing actions and speech give way to soft, flowing movements and tones. When confronted with the outcome of this transformation, her friend and former sex-worker colleague Kit De Luca (Laura San Giacomo) exclaims "Cinder-fuckin'-rella." This is a spontaneous response to hearing about her friend's good fortunes but it also describes the character of Ward, her narrative trajectory, and the mix of spirited lovability which Roberts enacts, for as Ward, Robert's performs Cinderella with attitude. By the end of the film, Ward's make-over is complete and she'll never return to the streets. However, it is questionable whether she made any change at all or simply uncovered qualities that were hidden and merely needed unlocking. As Tamar Jeffers McDonald (2010: 30) notes, Hollywood's retellings of the Cinderella story

> constantly juggle the emphasis on the external transformation, trying to give it the focus of something new and exciting (often visually) while also suggesting simultaneously that the change is actually a return to an authentic self previously forgotten or unachieved (often narratively) ... Cinderellas ... are shown, through their metamorphoses, "to be what they really are."

Observing the external transformation of Roberts/Ward, San Giacomo/De Luca comments "Sure don't fit in down on the Boulevard looking like you do," but immediately adds "not that you ever did." Ward was therefore always a pretty woman in waiting. She has not changed to become sweet but rather freed herself from the "act" of being streetwise.

Grossing $178.4 million at the domestic box office and $285 million international, *Pretty Woman* was a major hit, ending 1990 ranked second amongst the top-grossing films in North America (Ludemann and Hazelton, 1991: 12). That year she also appeared as part of the ensemble cast for *Flatliners*, which did moderately well at the box office, but it was *Pretty Woman* which convinced exhibitors to rank her on the Quigley poll for the first time in 1990. *Pretty Woman* elevated Roberts into the star hierarchy. For *Mystic Pizza* Roberts was paid $50,000 and followed this with $90,000 for *Steel Magnolias*. She did not have the box-office clout to demand more than $300,000 for *Pretty Woman* and $550,000 for *Flatliners*, but with a hit behind her, the price for her acting services rapidly increased to $1 million for *Sleeping with the Enemy*, $3 million on *Dying Young* and $8 million for *Hook* (1991) (Dutka, 1991). Although *Pretty Woman* became the career-defining film for Roberts, it was not until *Sleeping with the Enemy* that she received star billing. After the film grossed $101.6 million domestically and $73.4 million international, there was clear evidence Roberts's name and presence could carry a hit. Joe Roth, Chairman of Twentieth Century Fox, the studio responsible for producing and releasing the film, said of Roberts:

> When you have Julia's name on the marquee you have the biggest female star in the world, one of less than 10 people in the world who can "open" a picture simply because she's in it ... And she's arguably the only actress on the list.

That's what's so exciting about this phenomenon. At least at this moment, there's someone who broke the taboo about gender. Julia is up there with Costner, Gibson, Schwarzenegger. She can carry a picture regardless of genre, domestic or abroad. (quoted in Dutka, 1991: 8)

In the space of less than two years, Roberts had therefore become *the* female A-lister.

Pretty Woman strongly associated Roberts with romantic comedy although as her career progressed she worked across a broad range of genres. Even so, despite the diversity of the characters she played or genres she featured in, whether cheating death as a medical student in the moralistic horror *Flatliners*, surviving an abusive marriage in the thriller *Sleeping with the Enemy*, caring for a terminally ill partner in the tragic love story *Dying Young*, playing Tinkerbell in a retelling of the Peter Pan tale for the fantasy adventure *Hook*, or cracking an assassination conspiracy as a legal student in the thriller *The Pelican Brief*, in one way or another Roberts enacted her brand of feisty sweetness. By the end of this run, with four films grossing over $100 million at the domestic box office, which in the 1990s remained a key index of commercial success, Roberts was confirmed as a major box-office attraction. *Pretty Woman* also provided a context to display what became a distinct physical marker of the Roberts brand. As Vincent Canby (1990: H17) wrote in *The New York Times* "Julia Roberts smiles (and smiles and smiles), transforming *Pretty Woman* into one of the most successful and endearing Cinderella movies ever made about a whore." Roberts's smile became a signature feature, stretching across her uncommonly wide mouth to reveal an immaculate set of upper dentures. The smile became a stand-out idiolectic feature, functioning as a condensed statement of her star visibility: "Julia Roberts's smile is a little too wide, her lips a little too full, her laugh a little too loud. But then, movie stars become movie stars by exaggerating their traits, not underplaying them, n'est-ce pas?" (Carr, 1997).

Roles as a cut-throat journalist in the screwball adventure-comedy *I Love Trouble* (1994) and as a betrayed wife in the light-hearted family drama *Something to Talk About* (1995) preserved the Roberts brand but commenced a downturn in her commercial value. As her status in the money economy declined, Roberts took roles which marked departures from her A-list status and had the appearance of self-consciously mapping a career trajectory aimed at banking the symbolic capital of artistic consecration. Before she joined the A-list, with her performance in *Steel Magnolias*

Roberts was nominated for the Actress in a Supporting Role Oscar, and a second nomination came in the Best Actress category for her performance in *Pretty Woman*. Although she didn't win on either occasion, she did pick up awards for the same performances in the equivalent categories at the Golden Globes. As noted in the previous chapter, the Academy rarely consecrates comedy in any form, and so the nomination for *Pretty Woman* was something of a rarity for it did not represent surefire Oscar material. While *Pretty Woman* would forever continue to define the Roberts brand, her lead or supporting roles in *Dying Young, Mary Reilly* (1996) – a period drama based on a literary classic – the historical-political drama *Michael Collins* (1996), and the melodrama *Stepmom* (1998), all had the appearance of gestures aimed at building her credibility as a legitimate actor by showcasing the star in "serious" dramas. Furthermore, by taking supporting or cameo roles in films from esteemed directors, the Roberts brand acquired prestige by association. With *The Player* (1992), *Prêt-à-Porter* (1994) and *Everyone Says I Love You* (1996), Roberts did films for the multi-Oscar-nominated director Robert Altman and two times Academy-Award-winner Woody Allen. It is unlikely anyone would have expected these serious dramas and auteurist showcases to deliver the same box-office riches as the romcoms and thrillers, and indeed they didn't, but these creative choices contributed towards assembling a profile for Roberts as a bankable star who could and would make sojourns to work outside the commercial mainstream. Roberts therefore performed a brand which not only reconciled sweet lovability with feisty spiritedness but also carried those meanings across dual career trajectories mixing the laughs or thrills of light popular entertainment with the gravitas of serious dramatic product.

As discussed in Chapter 5, A-list status may not necessitate delivering a hit with every film but does demand actors attract big box office at regular intervals. Roberts therefore returned from her "wilderness years" (Macaulay, 2003: 14) with the romantic comedy *My Best Friend's Wedding* (1997). Although her role departed from established genre convention, for she played a woman who desires but does not get her man – "a pretty woman who doesn't win" (Travers, 1997: 47) – the film still showcased a now familiar star-genre package. With a worldwide gross of $299.3 million, the film demonstrated Roberts could still headline major hits. At the start of 1998 Roberts returned to the rankings in the Quigley poll and appeared in 12th position on *The Hollywood Reporter*'s rankings of star power (Burman, 1998). When Warner Bros. polled distributors and exhibitors in foreign territories during early 1998, industry opinion confirmed Roberts as the highest-grossing actress of the previous decade. Warner's Senior Vice-President of International Theatrical Distribution, Veronika Kwan-Rubinek, remarked "She's still the one . . . If Julia Roberts is attached to a project, people will want to finance it" (quoted in Grove, 1998). Roberts's brand could be dispersed across several genres but *My Best Friend's Wedding* confirmed the value of the brand was most successfully exploitable in romantic comedy. In a particular type of vehicle, i.e. the romantic comedy, Roberts showed she could pull in massive audiences across Hollywood's major territories (see Figure 5.6): as one international distribution executive remarked, "It's all about her smile . . . When she smiles, her movies make money . . . [Audiences] buy tickets to see her, but only in certain types of roles" (quoted in Grove, 1998).

Enacting and Staging the Brand

Romantic comedy defined Roberts's commercial value, and revisiting the genre, she scored consecutive romcom hits in 1999 with *Notting Hill* and *Runaway Bride*. The latter most obviously milked the Roberts brand, for it carried strong links with *Pretty Woman*, re-uniting Roberts with Gere and the earlier film's director Garry Marshall. Roberts played Maggie Carpenter, a women living and working in the small town of Hale who repeatedly jilts fiancés at the altar. New York journalist Ike Graham (Gere) has a cynical view of women and when he hears about Maggie he writes a scathing piece in his daily column describing her as a "man-eater," but when Carpenter complains about factual inaccuracies in the story, he loses his job. Graham is commissioned to do a freelance piece and so in search of the facts that will see him vindicated, he travels to Hale where Maggie is soon to go up the aisle with her fourth fiancé.

With its familiar combination of star and genre, and the re-grouping of key creative talent, *Runaway Bride* appears at first sight to be in every way a neatly packaged construct entirely conceived as a vehicle to replay the star's greatest commercial success. When released, one critic described the film as "more package than picture" (Ansen, 1999). But *Runaway Bride* was not originally conceived as a showcase for the Roberts brand; rather it became one. Paramount Pictures first took up the basic concept in 1989 but the film crawled through development over the next ten years, in which time the script went through numerous rewrites with Geena Davis, Demi Moore, Sandra Bullock and Téa Leoni all reported at various stages to be due to star (Dunkley and Galloway, 1998: 13; Fleming, 1996; and *The Toronto Star*, 1992). Roberts's agent, Elaine Goldsmith-Thomas, forwarded the script to her star client who showed some interest but rather like Carpenter she was reluctant to commit. Only after Gere came on board did Roberts sign up to the film in July 1998 and the following month Marshall was confirmed as director (Hindes, 1998; Hindes and Petrikin 1998). Roberts took an up-front fee of $17 million and Gere $12 million, with both participating in the back-end gross. Paramount struck an agreement with Disney's Touchstone Pictures to co-finance the movie, with Paramount handling domestic releasing and Disney signed for international distribution (Carver and Dawtry, 1998; Goldstein, 1999).

Since the film was not planned as a Roberts vehicle, rather than an inevitable or "natural" uniting of star with genre hit, *Runaway Bride* invites consideration of how performance produces a fit between the narrative's central role/character and the star brand. For this task, the model of actor, role, character and brand outlined in Chapter 7 provides a useful analytic framework towards exploring how the dynamics of personification and impersonation create continuity and discontinuity between Roberts's portrayal of Carpenter and her performances in other films. Following generic convention, *Runaway Bride* combines an "adversarial relationship turning to love," "break-up and make-up" and "wedding that goes wrong but it's just as well" common to romantic comedy (Jeffers McDonald 2007: 118–19). As a light-hearted romance about a woman who is first bound into a relationship with the wrong man until she meets the right man with whom she falls in love, Carpenter's story shares a common narrative arc with *Notting Hill*. Carpenter is therefore a specific role but with a narrative structure found elsewhere in romantic comedy and more specifically Roberts's own films.

This role structure intersects with the portrayal of Carpenter as a particular character type. To a large degree, both the role and the character are creations of the script by Sarah Parriott and Josann McGibbon. At the New York bar Graham frequents, Carpenter's most recently jilted fiancé and the bar's owner both read aloud Graham's column in which she is likened in the script to the archetype of the "man-eater," represented by various mythic figures: Erinys, "the devouring death goddess" of ancient Greece, Indian goddess Kali known to "devour her boyfriend Shiva's entrails," and in Indonesia "the bloody-jawed man-eater" Ragma (Parriott and McGibbon, n.d.: 8). Having set up this definition, much of the remaining film is then concerned precisely with contradicting this account of Carpenter. Moving from the bar to the town of Hale, Carpenter's close friend Peggy Flemming (Joan Cusack) and acquaintance Mrs. Pressman (Jane Morris) visit her in the family hardware store where she works, anxious about the impact of the story. Here the script describes Carpenter in terms designed to immediately contradict Graham's diatribe. "We follow MAGGIE down the back stairs inside The Hale Hardware Store, the prettiest, most welcoming shop of its kind anywhere in small town USA. Somehow the place has taken on the spirit of the owner's daughter; both shop and shop-girl radiate brightness, charm, and possibility" (p. 10). These character qualities are aurally and visually represented through the double performances of medium and actor. Even before Hale is seen, the soundtrack establishes a counterpoint through non-diegetic music, shifting from the piano jazz of the bar to the plaintiff strings and harmonica playing as a bird's-eye-view crane shot looks down Main Street, Hale. Visually, the bar is dark and enclosed, while Hale is open and bathed in sunshine. Compared to the bar, the store is bright and airy. Lighting is used to give the impression of sunlight pouring through the windows of the store importing an aura of warmth. The place is well stocked with functional, utilitarian goods that all connote earthy practicality, qualities echoed by the dressing of Roberts/Carpenter in denim dungarees. Carpenter's small-town world is clearly distinguished from the big city in which Graham works: it encapsulates who she is.

Music, location, the set, lighting and costume all contribute towards representing Carpenter's wholesomely honest appeal. But this figure cannot be created by the script and the medium alone. Through the voice and body, it is the actor who, in Stephen Heath's (1981: 180) terms, must "actualize" character qualities. Roberts enacts Carpenter into existence for only the performance of the actor can provide the ultimate proof of what the script describes. After an opening-credits sequence in which Roberts/Carpenter is seen galloping on horseback away from her most recent abandoned wedding, the hardware store provides Roberts/Carpenter with her first dialog scene. Although very brief, it is a scene in which impersonation and personification co-exist in the enactment of a figure who is both role/character and star. Roberts enacts the necessary functions of the role and defining indices of character but at every moment remains visible as Roberts. Entering down a flight of stairs, Roberts walks with a light, loose step. As she provides a customer with a very specific vintage bath tap he is looking for, she conveys her playful familiarity with him, telling him in a light cheerful tone while shaking her head "Mr. Paxton, I think you are out of the doghouse with Mrs. Paxton." When she looks at him, she directs

Figure 9.1   Roberts/Carpenter smiles: *Runaway Bride*. Producers Roberts W. Cort, Ted Field, Scott Kroopf and Tom Rosenberg; director Garry Marshall; distributed by Touchstone Home Video.

the Roberts smile his way and as he leaves gives him a friendly pat on the arm. Roberts is recognizable as Roberts but at the same time with just a few words and actions her voice and body succinctly perform the impersonatory work of conveying Carpenter's open and honest affability. A sense of lively energy is actualized when the camera follows her as she crosses the shop floor and quickly responds to another customer's query about air conditioning before he even has time to fully articulate his question.

Other actors have appeared in the scene but only Roberts/Carpenter is framed in isolation with a medium-shot held to capture the star face. Roberts/Carpenter's immediate response to the visit by Cusack/Flemming and Morris/Pressman is to flash them the star's signature smile (Figure 9.1). This single micro-gesture encapsulates the much broader co-mingling of impersonation with personification which defines the whole star performance. On the one hand, the smile is entirely justified by the character's narrative circumstances: as Carpenter is bright and charming, she outwardly displays welcoming signs to her friends. At the same time, it signals the unique presence of Roberts, and the smile appears many other times in the film: when the new fiancé Bob is describing plans for the couple to go trekking on Annapurna for their honeymoon; on each of the old video recordings of her aborted weddings; when Gere/Graham tells her how he proposed to his ex-wife; when she tries on a wedding dress for her marriage to Bob; at the annual Hale luau; as she speaks on the phone to Gere/Graham, walks down the aisle for her abandoned wedding to him, and of

Figure 9.2   Carpenter is Julia Roberts: *Runaway Bride*. Producers Roberts W. Cort, Ted Field, Scott Kroopf and Tom Rosenberg; director Garry Marshall; distributed by Touchstone Home Video.

course when she finally and inevitably does marry him. There is even a moment where the film makes a self-reflexive joke on the smile: when Roberts/Carpenter apologizes to Cusack/Flemming for unintentionally flirting with her husband, her friend only promises to forgive her if she performs the "duck-billed platypus," a piece of play from their childhood days which sees Roberts/Carpenter pulling her face into what appears to be a caricature of the famous star smile (Figure 9.2). As Roberts/Carpenter breaks down in laughter, so the real smile returns. On each occasion the smile is revealed, it is always fully motivated by the plot. At the same time, however, it becomes a show of the star idiolect with moments held in contemplation of the star as "face-object." In these moments the dual aspects of the star performance as narrative and spectacle are combined, for the smile belongs to Carpenter and Roberts, representing the character's unerring good cheer at the same time as presenting the star presence. A mutual fit of brand and character is therefore achieved, for with the smallest of vocal and physical actions, Roberts enacts a quality of sweetness which is particular to Carpenter at the same time as reproducing qualities found in the star's other film roles. The resulting figure is an impersonation of Carpenter and a personification of the Roberts brand.

Paramount's releasing of *Runaway Bride* staged the Roberts brand as a crucial component of the studio's strategy for the 1999 North American summer season. Released domestically across 3,158 screens on 30 July, *Runaway Bride* opened to a three-day gross of over $35 million, contributing to setting what at the time was a new record for that point in the year as total sales from all films that weekend reached an estimated $155 million (Hindes, 1999c). Roberts provided Paramount with a brand vehicle to vertically and horizontally differentiate its product in the market that season. *Runaway Bride* topped the box office for that weekend, with the nearest competition ($29.2 million weekend gross) coming from low-budget camcorder horror *The Blair Witch Project* distributed by Artisan, which had just expanded to a wide release in its third week. Warner Bros.' shark horror *Deep Blue Sea* was the only other major new release that weekend, grossing a little over half ($19.1 million) what the Roberts vehicle took. "Two awesome sets of teeth did battle this weekend in America," wrote critic Sean Macaulay (1999) in *The Times*: "Both are genetic marvels, in box-office terms at least, built to demolish anything in their path. One belonged to an 8,000lb killer shark in Renny Harlin's *Deep Blue Sea*, the other to Julia Roberts . . . The shark didn't stand a chance."

Any star brand is a positioning statement, and beyond the initial weekend, opening a romantic comedy fronted by the leading A-list female star differentiated Paramount's main offering in the whole summer event movie season. With *The Mummy*, Universal re-versioned the studio's horror heritage and started the summer early before deploying the Roberts brand in *Notting Hill* and releasing the teen gross-out comedy *American Pie* and Hollywood-on-Hollywood comedy *Bowfinger*. Disney's Buena Vista distribution arm followed its customary pattern of addressing different audience segments with major family-orientated animation (*Tarzan*) and live action drama (*The Sixth Sense*) titles. Fox used *Star Wars: Episode 1 – The Phantom Menace* to re-launch its lucrative sci-fi series while Sony opted for comedy with *Big Daddy* and DreamWorks remade *The Haunting*. Warner traversed genres with *Deep Blue Sea* and the action/adventure/sci-fi/comedy *Wild Wild West*, while Time Warner's New Line Cinema subsidiary released the character-based comedy *Austin Powers: The Spy Who Shagged Me*. In a summer featuring Eddie Murphy in *Bowfinger*, Adam Sandler in *Big Daddy*, Bruce Willis in *The Sixth Sense*, Will Smith in *Wild Wild West*, Mike Myers's return as Austin Powers, and John Travolta in Paramount's other major offering of the summer, *The General's Daughter*, the Roberts brand marked a particular "flavor" of star, horizontally differentiating offerings from Paramount and Universal amongst a tranche of star-driven movies.

Conflicting with this logic of differentiation, however, was the appearance in quick succession of two romcoms starring Roberts. Universal originally scheduled *Notting Hill* for release on 11 June but when it was announced *Runaway Bride* would open just seven weeks later, press reports rumored Paramount were trying to intimidate Universal into letting the studio partner on the film, on the understanding that if Universal conceded, *Runaway Bride* would then be moved back to Thanksgiving (Fleming, 1999). Both studios denied the rumors but still *Notting Hill* moved forward to 28 May, Memorial Day weekend. Although *Notting Hill* was still showing across 708 screens on the weekend *Runaway Bride* opened, over the previous nine weeks it had already accumulated over 95 percent of what eventually became its total North American gross. Temporal separation therefore enabled both films to benefit from the Roberts brand without cannibalizing their respective audiences. Furthermore, Rob Friedman, Vice Chairman of Paramount's Motion Picture Group, suggested the two films captured slightly different audiences, with *Notting Hill* doing well with sophisticated urban audiences while *Runaway Bride* additionally crossed over to Middle America. Friedman described Roberts as a movie star "in the classic sense . . . Everyone can relate to her on some level . . . Women are not threatened by her . . . And men are attracted to her at the same time as they admire her strength" (quoted in Natale, 1999). Surveys conducted by the market research firm CinemaScore of the Friday opening-night audiences for *Runaway Bride* in Santa Monica, Tampa, Florida, and Coral Springs, Florida, showed the gender mix for the audience to be skewed 67/37% female/male, with women positively grading the film A- and men B+. The film attracted a broad age demographic, spread 18–24yrs 24%, 25–34yrs 23% and 53% aged 35 or older. Amongst the factors drawing the audience to the film, 71% of the sample identified Roberts and 61% Gere (CinemaScore, 1999). *Notting Hill* eventually grossed $116 million domestic and $247.8 million international, while *Runaway Bride* grossed $135.5 million in North America and $157.2 million overseas, becoming in the space of a decade the sixth and seventh films featuring Roberts to gross over $100 million in the domestic market (Natale, 1999). *Notting Hill* and *Runaway Bride* were respectively ranked 12th and ninth amongst the highest-grossing titles for 1999 in North America (D'Alessandro, 2000: 20), and when the Quigley poll ran for 1999, exhibitors unsurprisingly voted Roberts the top money-maker (Table 1.1).

In this mature phase of the star life-cycle, Roberts was at her commercial peak (see Figure 5.4), but while audiences gave *Runaway Bride* the popular vote, responses amongst critics ran cool to dismissive. "Forget the 'Bride,' The Audience Should Run" was the review title in *The Washington Post*

(Howe, 1999). "[Gere] and Mr Marshall's reunion with Ms. Roberts," wrote Janet Maslin (1999) in *The New York Times*,

> guarantees a comedy that's easy on the eyes and dependable in the laugh department. But "Runaway Bride" also, like Maggie, shows signs of strain. Chemistry-wise, it can't bode well for a romantic comedy to feature two stars who apparently posed for the poster art on separate days . . . the film is like a ride through a car wash: forward motion, familiar phases in the same old order and a sense of being carried along steadily on a well-used track. It works without exactly showing signs of life.

With the film framed as a re-run of *Pretty Woman*, Roberts's place in the film was an inevitable talking point for reviews. In one of the few positive appraisals, *Variety*'s Todd McCarthy (1999) wrote "Roberts has a perfect role as Maggie, an open, loveable, slightly neurotic but capable girl-next-door – she even knows what's wrong with her man's car when it breaks down – and she's perfect in it. Her face and feelings are accessible without being obvious, she can be goofy, sporty or amorous with ease, and she's radiant almost regardless of circumstances." For Kenneth Turan (1999) in the *Los Angeles Times*, however, rather than achieve a fit between star and character, the performed amiability of the Roberts brand rendered the possibility of the character rejecting partners at the altar entirely implausible:

> Roberts . . . is in full movie-star mode, lithe, smiling and game for all kinds of physical humor, including pratfalls and the making of comically ridiculous faces. This is all great fun, but Maggie is such a terrific person it doesn't really fit with the film's need to paint her, at least in part, as someone who has thoughtlessly ruined any number of lives.

Meanwhile, Hal Hinson (1999) in the *New Times LA* judged Carpenter to be a reprehensible and entirely unlikeable character, which the Roberts brand had the effect of endorsing, for "the star's signature smile and gamine charm seem premeditated and manipulative" giving the impression that she "likes this little game of breaking men's hearts and, seemingly, has no intention of changing her ways." As a fully visible component of the film, the Roberts brand became the prism through which critical opinion was defined and divided.

Producing Oscar Prestige

With Roberts's performance in *Runaway Bride*, commercial success was met with critical contempt, exemplifying the anti-commercial logic which shapes artistic valorization in the field of cultural production. *Erin Brockovich*, Roberts's next film, however provided one of the rare instances where a performance breaks from that logic, for major commercial success was accompanied by critical respect. Playing the eponymous heroine, Roberts became the first woman to be paid a $20 million salary to appear in a film. With a domestic gross of $125.6 million and international box office totaling $130.7 million, *Erin Brockovich* didn't quite achieve the commercial heights of Roberts's previous two films but was still indisputably a hit, becoming Roberts's eighth film overall – and third in a row – to gross over $100 million in the domestic market and ending 2000 ranked 10th amongst the highest-grossing films that year in North America (D'Alessandro, 2001: 20). After her previous Oscar nominations, Roberts eventually reached the pinnacle of artistic legitimization in Hollywood as her performance was recognized and consecrated by the Academy.

Based on real events, *Erin Brockovich* tells a David-and-Goliath story in which Roberts plays a single mother who takes clerical work at a small local law firm to support her three children. In the course of her duties she uncovers papers detailing the long-term contamination of the drinking water supply for the small community of Hinkley, and links the pollution to the nearby facility of Pacific Gas & Electricity. After an extended battle, Brockovich, her boss Ed Masry (Albert Finney) and the people of Hinkley emerge victorious, winning the biggest settlement payout for a direct action lawsuit in US history. The role and character created continuities and discontinuities with Roberts's previous performances. Although there were no assassinations, the basic investigative narrative bore similarities with *The Pelican Brief*. Many scenes provided opportunities for Roberts to play her feisty side, for example when she must confront Finney/Masry to argue herself into a job, or shouting at noisy bikers in her neighborhood when they stop her kids from sleeping, and challenging the patronizing treatment she receives from the experienced legal team of another firm who partner on the PG&E case. At the same time, Erin is shown to be sweet, caring and vulnerable: she works hard to support her kids, feels guilty when her work leads her to neglect them, and she ultimately succeeds in her legal battle because what she lacks in formal legal education she more than makes up

Figure 9.3 Roberts/Brockovich understands: *Erin Brockovich*. Producers Danny De Vito, Michael Shamberg and Stacey Sher; director Steven Soderbergh; distributed by Columbia TriStar Home Video.

for with the grassroots sympathy and compassion she brings to understanding the plight of PG&E's victims (Figure 9.3). Roberts enacts these character qualities while at the same time creating a figure who outwardly eschews the performed softness and glamorous saintly halo evident in past roles. Roberts/Brockovich repeatedly swears and her trashy dress sense attracts disapproving looks from her colleagues. In the corpus of Roberts's films, Brockovich's wardrobe is closest to the attire worn as Ward in *Pretty Woman* when she is still working Hollywood Boulevard, only this time she doesn't get to be prettified (or at least not very much). Her dizzying high heels not only distance her from the professional protocols of the legal world but also result in Roberts adopting a stomping walk that contributes to signifying Brockovich's gritty determination (Figure 9.4). While maintaining the core meanings of the Robert's brand, in this performance physical actions and costume equally achieve the impersonatory effect of creating marked differences between Roberts's performances.

Ostensibly, the Oscars are about *recognizing* artistic value: works and performances are created which the Academy then honors. But as the previous chapter discussed, the annual ritual of nominations and awards don't just find artistic worth but rather play a key part in *producing* belief in the value of certain works and acts. Consequently Roberts's performance as

Figure 9.4   Trashy woman: *Erin Brockovich*. Producers Danny De Vito, Michael Shamberg and Stacey Sher; director Steven Soderbergh; distributed by Columbia TriStar Home Video.

Brockovich provides a case for examining the confluence of factors and processes involved in producing the symbolic capital of Oscar prestige. The production of belief in the Oscar-winning performance involves a multitude of inputs and micro-actions from distributors, Academy members, publicists, industry commentators and movie reviewers. Even before the film was made, *Erin Brockovich* had credentials which already fulfilled certain of the unwritten requirements for Oscar contention. Combining an enjoyable story and a serious message, *Erin Brockovich* spoke to a middlebrow sensibility for it was entertainment but with a conscience. Drawing on actual events, Roberts's performance immediately addressed the Academy's taste for nominating performances representing real-life figures: only the year before Hilary Swank had landed the award for Actress in a Leading Role with her performance as the tragic Brandon Teena/Teena Brandon in *Boys Don't Cry*. More specifically, *Erin Brockovich* echoed other tales based on true-life material portraying spirited woman fighting large corporations as enacted by Sally Field in *Norma Rae* (1979) and Meryl Streep in *Silkwood* (1983), performances which received an Oscar win for Field and a nomination for Streep. Director Steven Soderbergh brought his own quota of artistic cachet to *Erin Brockovich*. Although he'd never won an Oscar, Soderbergh was nominated for the screenplay of his directorial feature debut *sex, lies and videotape* (1989) and that film picked up the Palme d'Or at the Festival de Cannes and three Golden Globe nominations.

Released across 2,948 screens in North America on 17 March 2000, *Erin Brockovich* comfortably qualified for eligibility in the award year. With the nomination process for the Academy Awards still four months away, in early September 2000, *Variety's* Richard Natale (2000: 36) was already predicting Roberts would feature amongst the nominees. From 1 December 2000, Universal re-released the film in Los Angeles and New York with the aim, as the studio's Chairwoman Stacey Snider stated, "to remind Academy voters" (quoted in Goodridge, 2000b). By that point a critical consensus was emerging in the trade and quality press that Roberts was a certainty for a nomination. Rick Lyman in *The New York Times* wrote "For best actress, Ms. Roberts is widely considered to have a lock on a nomination" (2000: E3). It was the opinion of Todd Longwell in *The Hollywood Reporter* that "The race for Best Actress is . . . cut and dried. It is between Julia Roberts . . . and . . . Julia Roberts" (2001: S4). For Peter Rainer, *New York Magazine's* film critic and chairman of the National Society of Film Critics, there was "a thin field, she's extremely well-liked in Hollywood and the performance is sort of the completed Julia Roberts" (quoted in Longwell, 2001: S4). *Screen International's* Mike Goodridge wrote:

> there can be nothing more certain that Roberts . . . will snag a best actress Academy Award nomination for Erin Brockovich . . .
>
> Why such certainty? Even though the film was released in March, her hugely charismatic, screen-chewing turn as the real-life crusader Brockovich was so intrepid, convincing and unlike anything else that the romantic comedy queen has done that critics roared with approbation . . .
>
> Is hers the best performance of the year by an actress in a leading role? Probably not, but then again it was the best performance of the year by a giant movie star in a much-liked hit film. (2000a: 17)

Daily Variety listed the film and Roberts amongst "The Contenders": "Like 'Norma Rae' . . . 'Brockovich' benefits primarily from a front-and-center leading lady, an eager, principled woman who risks her future and changes a system without compromising her beliefs" (Speier, 2000). Owen Gleiberman of *Entertainment Weekly* described Roberts's performance as "a really magical piece of star acting in which the movie is unthinkable without her larger-than-life sexual wattage. Here is a case where star quality and fine acting are inseparable" (quoted in Galloway, 2001: S11). It was the opinion of the *Los Angeles Times*'s Kenneth Turan that "The hardest thing to do these days is a traditional studio movie that delivers on its premise. That's what Erin Brockovich does, and so does Julia Roberts. It is refreshing to see a performance that has a good chance of winning the Oscar that is actually worth it" (quoted in Galloway, p. S16). Roberts was not without competition, however. Laura Linney in *You Can Count on Me* and Ellen Burstyn in *Requiem for a Dream* were also considered by many leading critics as strong contenders (e.g. Turan, 2001b). Although released very early in the award year, there was widespread anticipation *Erin Brockovich* and Roberts would repeat the feat of *Silence of the Lambs* (1991) which had similarly opened in the first quarter of the calendar year but still saw Jodie Foster win the Best Actress award.

When the nomination ballot forms were mailed on Tuesday 9 January 2001, voting members of the Academy were presented with a Reminder List of Eligible Releases containing 242 features. Nomination forms were returned by 2 February 2001 and 11 days later the nominees were announced. *Erin Brockovich* was nominated in five categories, including Best Picture, Best Director and a Best Actress nomination for Roberts. She was joined by fellow nominees Linney, Burstyn, Joan Allen in *The Contenders* and Juliette Binoche for *Chocolat*. Although Roberts was the only lead female nominee playing a character based on an actual biographical person, real-life figures dominated the Best Actor category: Javier Bardem played persecuted Cuban writer Reinaldo Arenas in *Before Night Falls*, Geoffrey Rush was the Marquis de Sade in *Quills*, and Ed Harris in *Pollock* appeared opposite Marcia Gay Harden, who also picked up a nomination in the Actress in a Supporting Role category (Levy, 2001a).

A day after the nominations were announced, commentators were already marking Roberts as favorite (Welkos and King, 2001: F18; Bone and Alberge, 2001). Screenings of the nominated pictures commenced from 17 February at the Academy's Samuel Goldwyn Theater. Just before the final ballots forms were mailed to Academy members on 28 February 2001, *The Hollywood Reporter* (2001) polled its website readers on the question "who should win the Oscar for best actress?" From 9,701 responses, Burstyn and Roberts emerged equal first on 41 percent each with Linney a long way behind on 7 percent. Even so, the weight of critical opinion was behind Roberts. On the likely winner for Best Actress, Sean Macaulay (2001) in *The Times* commented: "You can bet the house on this one. Julia Roberts, no question, down the line, 100 per cent. Roberts's full-on megawatt performance in Erin Brockovich felt like a cert the day it opened. Single mom, moms with cancer, kids with cancer, a big bad faceless corporation, a fight for justice – and all of it true." When the final ballot closed on 20 March, Terry Press, head of marketing at DreamWorks, envisaged that "If Julia Roberts doesn't win, it's going to be the biggest upset of the night" (quoted in Lyman, 2001: 5). As a whole year had passed since the original release, *Erin Brockovich* had nothing to gain commercially from the awards ritual. Since August 2000 the film had been out on video formats and was due to debut on the Starz pay-cable channel from Saturday 17 February 2001 (Natale, 2001a). The film's producers Michael Shamberg and Stacy Sher said "the film is pretty much played out theatrically both domestically and overseas" but the nominations "are less about commerce and more about the thrill of being recognized for good work" (quoted in Gray, 2001). By the time Roberts picked up the statue at the Oscars ceremony at the Shrine Auditorium on 25 March, for the same performance she'd already collected awards from the Los Angeles Film Critics Association, National Board of Review, Hollywood Foreign Press Association and Screen Actors Guild.

Erin Brockovich selectively drew on the meanings of the Roberts brand for effects that combined commercial value with artistic consecration. Box-office success further affirmed her A-list status while at the same time the scope of the brand was extended as the production of belief in Oscar cachet cultivated recognition and acceptance of Roberts as an actor deserving respect. By gaining Oscar winning prestige, Roberts's performance as Erin Brockovich represented a form of embodied and enacted symbolic capital. For a performer whose fame was founded on light, popular entertainment, it could be presumed that her award-winning status may have secured a new standing for Roberts in the field of cultural production. Yet one performance alone could not, however, grant complete artistic legitimacy and reinvent Roberts as a prestige star, and so with a string of hits behind her, Roberts's status and position in the field continued to be defined by how well she fared according to the heteronomous principle of the commercial popular market.

Falling Star

After *Erin Brockovich*, Roberts's star equity waned and she never delivered another film grossing over $100 million in the domestic market. How can this decline be explained? In one respect it is just part of the "natural" life-cycle: stars rise but will inevitably fall. Secondly, Roberts's receding stardom coincided with the decade in which the value of Hollywood's star films at the box office generally diminished (see Chapter 5). As fantasy and comic-book franchises came to define popularity, few star-driven films scored well at the box office and only Will Smith (see Chapter 6) could claim a regular record of delivering hits. Third, as Hollywood stardom has historically been almost entirely driven by white male star brands, Roberts's stardom was something of an anomaly anyway, and so in a market where female stardom has always been secondary and marginal, her fame constantly existed on precarious ground. Finally, there was the factor of age. As discussed in Chapter 1, Hollywood's rare band of female leads reach a glass ceiling during their early 30s. When *Erin Brockovich* was released, Roberts was 32 years old. The film made her an Oscar-winner and her last three films had collectively grossed $929.6 million worldwide. She may have been at the peak of the "mature" phase in the star life-cycle but her physical maturity could only mean that, according to the commercial and symbolic logics of Hollywood stardom, her time at the top would end sooner rather than later. Roberts's career in the first decade of the twentieth century provides an example for looking at how the decline of the star brand is managed and moreover how that decline is mediated through performance.

Roberts's star value did not disappear overnight. *Erin Brockovich* was just about to be released when Roberts signed up to star opposite Brad Pitt in *The Mexican* (2001) and to work again with Soderbergh by joining an ensemble of star and leading names for *Ocean's Eleven* (2001). Initially *The Mexican* had been conceived "as an $8-million to $10-million independent film with breakout potential" (Natale, 2001b: F1 and 10) but when Pitt and Roberts joined, the budget was rumored to have leapt to $35 million (Christy, 2001). DreamWorks opened the film across 2,951 screens in North America and the investment in production and distribution indicates the studio anticipated the film would be a star-driven hit. It eventually grossed $147.8 million worldwide, ending the year 38th amongst the highest-grossing films in North America (D'Alessandro, 2002: 39), which although reasonable, was a lot less than might be expected from a brace of big star names.

A major problem with *The Mexican* came from its attempt to blend genres, styles and tones. Director Gore Verbinski described it as "a romantic comedy . . . but with a little bit of Sam Peckinpah" (quoted in Turan, 2001a: F1). Critics applied multiple hybrid terms to define the film: "Hard-tocategorize pic, which will have buffs thinking Peckinpah or [Quentin] Tarantino lite" (McCarthy, 2001: 39); a "picaresque caper" that is a "would-be-Peckinpah, wannabe-Tarantino, could-be-Gilliam story" (Schwarzbaum, 2001: 52–3); a "romantic action dramedy," "modern fairy tale," "screwball romp" and "gender comedy" (Simon, 2001); "a screwball road film" (Holden 2001); "a shaggy-dog tale, part romantic comedy, part offbeat action à la *Pulp Fiction*, part homage to Sam Peckinpah" (Natale, 2001a: F1); and "a romantic comedy trying to shake hands with a Western" (Taylor, 2001). For Barbara Ellen writing in *The Times*, (2001: 14),

> What emerges is an uneasy mix of romance, comedy and violence. Screenwriter J. H. Wyman clearly couldn't decide whether to go with *Raising Arizona*-style Coen Brothers or to have blood splattering into the dust, so rather unwisely he tries for both. One minute it's all high maintenance slapstick, ramshackle car chases and cutesy dialogue . . . The next, the tone changes to deadly serious, and there are graphic depictions of bullets drilling into skulls.

Similar negative judgments attached to Roberts's performance. "Roberts overacts in the early bickering scenes," wrote Emanuel Levy in *Screen International*, "but improves after her character is kidnapped. Playing a variant of her typical tough-but-vulnerable role, she gives a fluent if not terribly commanding performance as a woman who can tell what is wrong with everyone else's relationships, but cannot really understand what is wrong with hers" (2001c). In the eyes of *Variety*'s Todd McCarthy "Roberts submerges the glamour-puss stuff as much as humanly possible for her to give a spirited reading of a mentally limited but lively working-class woman" (2001: 44). Stanley Kauffmann in *The New Republic* gave a caustic assessment:

> If Roberts's appeal survives this picture, then heaven really smiles on her. Not only is the story clumsy and incredible, but – what is truly surprising – her role is terrible. In fact, she has no role: she just has a lot of scenes and antics and talk. The writer and the director were so strained to keep her part interesting that they sent her to the toilet three times. While we watch. It's disgraceful. It's not the impropriety that bothers . . . but the desperation to zing things up. All that's missing – and it may come – is a headline in the picture's ads: "Julia Roberts Pees". (2001)

Jim Tharp, DreamWorks's Head of Distribution, defended Roberts against her critics: "It was a different sort of role for her, different than some (critics) expected . . . That's what turned them off and resulted in some negative reviews, though of course some were very positive, as well" (quoted in DiOrio, 2001: 46). However this argument could not protect the film or the performance as an uneasy mixing of genres, styles and tones created a context that conflicted with and confused the Roberts brand.

Throughout her career Roberts had always interspersed starring leads with supporting and more minor roles. As the decade progressed she continued in this manner with supporting leads in *America's Sweethearts* (2001) and *Charlie Wilson's War* (2007), together with membership of the ensemble casts for *Ocean's Eleven, Full Frontal* (2002), *Closer* (2004) and *Ocean's Twelve* (2004), and minor roles in *Confessions of a Dangerous Mind* (2002) and *Grand Champion* (2002). As the instances of these subsidiary roles increased, however, Roberts's exposure as a starring name became intermittent. On *The Mexican* she was second billed after Pitt and so three years passed between her last genuine starring lead in *Erin Brockovich* and her next in *Mona Lisa Smile* (2003). Roberts signed to the film in October 2001 as part of a multiyear deal she agreed with Revolution Studios, a production outfit established by Joe Roth (Lyons, 2000). *America's Sweethearts* was the first outcome of that arrangement and *Mona Lisa Smile* was co-produced between Revolution and Roberts's own sindie company, Red Om (Kit, 2001). Roberts played a teacher working in 1953 at the conservative Wellesley College where she becomes an inspirational figure to a group of young women. While the character's influence is primarily pedagogic, the role cast Roberts as a maternal figure: not only does she steer her students to learn "progressive" life lessons but as those roles were played by a new breed of up-and-coming young female performers – Kirsten Dunst, Julia Stiles and Maggie Gyllenhaal – Roberts assumed the status of matriarchal-star.[1] However, critics of her performance judged there to be a clash between the construction of character and the legacy of Roberts's performed brand:

> busybody Katherine appears more than simply angry with the mid-century
> sexism that her charges have . . . internalised – she seems utterly unplugged
> from reality in 1953, as if that cross-country train had rudely sped her into
> some pre-second wave time warp; Roberts's totally contemporary perform-
> ance, leaning heavily on nose-flaring incredulity, only intensifies the feeling
> of disconnect . . . As Katherine's burdens mount in the form of disapproving

administrators, milquetoast beaux, and [her student] Betty's poisoned ink-spilling, Roberts holds steady with her Haunted Fawn Gaze™ (see *Sleeping with the Enemy, Mary Reilly*) until [director] Newell clears the set for her Protracted Snit Fit™ (see *Notting Hill, Erin Brockovich*). (Winter, 2003)

Scarcely modifying her standard screen persona to play an early-'50s proto-feminist, [Roberts] amplifies the artificiality of a period story falsely informed by contemporary values rather than those of the time . . .
. . . The central role might have been more convincing with a flintier actress to lend some weight. Roberts gives the character her regular mix of high spirits and vulnerability, which never fully gels with the idealistic, savvy woman; even Katherine's passion for art is undersold. Every time the actress erupts into her mile-wide smile and rippling laugh, she undermines any integrity in the performance with self-aware movie-star charisma. (Rooney, 2003: 48 and 53)

After watching [Roberts's] one-woman crusade to save young female minds from men and marriage, you might think that *Mona Lisa Smile* should have been called The Prime of Miss Erin Brockovich. (Landesman, 2004)

Grossing $141.3 million worldwide, the film did respectable business and given its subject matter could never have been expected to be a massive hit. However, critical responses indicated the Roberts brand was not only diminishing in commercial value but also losing symbolic credibility.

When *Mona Lisa Smile* was released in December 2003, Roberts was 36 and the role tempered her on-screen brand to acknowledge and accom-modate her maturity. A further strategy employed in managing the aging of the Roberts brand came from attempts to substitute cash for kudos, counterbalancing the decline in economic capital with gestures aimed at increasing the symbolic capital of prestige credentials. Stepping outside the commercial mainstream where her stardom had been founded, Roberts flirted with Indiewood cred on *Full Frontal*, a low-budget production from Soderbergh for Miramax, and later with the indie production *Fireflies in the Garden* (2008). Roberts also built associations with the fully legitimized arts, specifically the serious dramatic theater. She appeared in *Closer*, a screen adaptation of Patrick Marber's highly celebrated stage drama and nominee for the 1999 Tony Award for Best Play, before making her stage debut in the 2006 limited-run revival of "Three Days of Rain" at the Bernard B. Jacobs Theater, New York. When originally produced, the play received critical acclaim and writer Richard Greenberg was a finalist for the

1998 Pulitzer Prize. Roberts appeared taking the dual roles of Nan and her character's mother Lina. Appearing on stage not only represented an act of creative brand extension by transposing Roberts's fame between performance media but also associated the star with the fully legitimized Broadway theater. As Ed Siegel of *The Boston Globe* observed,

> A gorgeous smile and perky demeanor can get you far in Hollywood. They can get you onto the podium at the Oscars, where you can make a fool of yourself in your acceptance speech.
>
> But even with the 2001 Academy Award for "Erin Brockovich," Roberts must have decided it was time for *really* serious actress cred and turned to theatrical properties. (original emphasis, 2006: E1)

Roberts's stardom ensured the production played to sell-out audiences but critics did not view her performance positively. "Roberts, a cinematic ball of fire, wanders around the stage in the first act as if she's looking for the Prozac," wrote Siegel: "Even though she gets to flash that smile and show a little life on-stage" by the second act as Lina "Roberts remains problematic . . . You think she'd be able to handle a Southern accent, but her voice wanders all over the 48 contiguous states, sometimes within the same sentence" (p. E9). In his review for *The New York Times*, Ben Brantley confessed to being a "Juliaholic" but judged Roberts's performance wooden and unconvincing:

> she makes her entrance in the first act and freezes with the unyielding stiffness of an industrial lamppost, as if to move too much might invite falling.
>
> Sometimes she plants one hand on a hip, then varies the pose by doing the same on the other side. Her voice is strangled, abrupt and often hard to hear. She has the tenseness of a woman who might break into pieces at any moment. (2006: E6)

"And yet, and yet," he claimed,

> I found myself fascinated by the way her facial structure (ah, those cheekbones!) seems to change according to how the light hits her. In repose, her face seems impossibly, hauntingly eloquent . . . And on the few occasions she smiles, it's with a sunniness that could dispel even 40 days and 40 nights of

rain. None of this . . . in any way illuminates her characters or Mr. Greenberg's play. (p. E6)

Both Siegel and Brantley were reviewing the quality of Roberts's performance but their evaluations implicitly suggest the main problem with the performance came from the uneasy clash between the impersonatory play of character representation and the personified show of Hollywood stardom. Roberts could not be accepted or recognized as a legitimate stage actor for she brought too much of Hollywood to the stage.

On *The Mexican*, Roberts had been billed second to Pitt and as her stardom declined her fame seemed ever more dependent on acting opposite major male stars. With *Ocean's Eleven* and *Ocean's Twelve*, she appeared in two major hits but in a supporting role to an entire ensemble of male leads. By the time of *Charlie Wilson's War* (2007), Roberts appeared to have accepted the age disparity in Hollywood stardom, as the 40-year-old took a supporting role in an on-screen couple with the 51-year-old Tom Hanks. Her stardom turned in upon itself to the extent that in *Ocean's Twelve*, narrative circumstances demand that her character Tess solves a tricky situation by pretending to be the star Julia Roberts. Garry Marshall returned to familiar generic territory in 2010 with the ensemble romcom *Valentine's Day*, but while romance is blossoming everywhere across the film's parallel narrative strands, Roberts is consigned to singly mothering her son. Roberts plays a minor role which only takes up around six minutes of screen time but even so it was rumored she was paid $3 million against 3 percent of the gross (Brodesser-Akner, 2010). In *Pretty Woman*, probably the most famous sections of the film (and landmarks in Roberts's stardom) are the two sequences where she goes shopping amongst the expensive boutiques of Rodeo Drive. Dressed in her trashy hooker clothes, she is initially snubbed by supercilious shop assistants, but after the spending power of Gere/Lewis gives her a classy make-over, she confronts the assistants who formerly rejected her by telling them they made a "Big mistake. Big. Huge." Looking sweet but talking feisty, the moment encapsulates the character and the Roberts brand. The moment is a turning point; it makes the film and the film made Roberts's stardom. When *Valentine's Day* therefore contrives a coda in which Roberts as Captain Kate Hazeltine rides up Rodeo Drive in a limousine and repeats the famous line, despite all the big money and rich rewards she was paid, the moment is the greatest admission that the Roberts brand now rested on former glories. Roberts illustrates how the star brand traverses a common life-cycle pattern enacted through performance but most revealing is what her example demonstrates of the gendered and ageist barriers which circumscribe Hollywood stardom.

Note

1 Only ten years separated Gyllenhaal and Roberts's actual ages.

10

Conclusion

This study had two aims: to outline a critical and conceptual perspective described as the symbolic commerce of stardom, and to apply this to the workings of Hollywood stardom in the years 1990 to 2009.

Star studies take the star image as a central working concept thereby escaping the mystificatory presumptions arising from the charismatic theory of stardom by recognizing stars only have presence in public culture as figures formed from collections of texts. Attention to the textual construction of star identities encourages analysis of stardom as a system of discourse based on the production and circulation of certain kinds of knowledge and meaning about figures performing in film. Both perspectives – star-as-image and stardom-as-discourse – are essential to any study of Hollywood stardom for stars are fundamentally figures of meaning. However, these perspectives also set a semiotic threshold limiting the work of analysis to only addressing questions of meaning and representation. Ultimately this leaves film scholarship with an incomplete and insufficient understanding of what a star is, for in Hollywood – and the same can be said of any industry organized for the production, distribution and exhibition of popular film – stars are both meaning and money. It is the aim when studying the symbolic commerce of stardom to therefore consistently appreciate the co-existence and integration of the symbolic/ cultural and economic/commercial aspects of stars. This is necessary for in stardom commercial actions are undertaken through symbolic means while the semiotic content of the star images are always situated in market conditions.

Hollywood Stardom, First Edition. Paul McDonald.
© 2013 Paul McDonald. Published 2013 by John Wiley & Sons, Ltd.

Adopting this perspective certainly does not necessitate rejecting the star image concept but it does demand taking that idea in other directions. Consequently, in order to emphasize the duality of the star – that is of the star as actor and asset – here the idea of the star brand has been advanced. The commerce of popular film does not sell stars but rather sells films through stars. Star brands create perceptions which position films in the market. One of the core characteristics of the film commodity is the need to communicate a place in the market by striking a balance between familiarity and uniqueness and star brands aid in this process by operating as signs of similarity and difference. The significance and signification of the star brand comes from how the circulation of the star name and body evoke meanings which create similarities and differences to position films within the market across axes of vertical and horizontal product differentiation. It is easy to see this positioning at work in the promotional play of marketing materials and how release patterns stage the temporal and spatial visibility of films, but film stars are fundamentally film actors, and so whatever effects they have in the market always return to matters of performance. In the symbolic commerce of stardom it is therefore always necessary to consider how the voice and body enact the dynamics of similarity and difference through the play between personification and impersonation.

Taking this perspective also involves a range of other considerations. Stars sit atop the hierarchy of acting talent in Hollywood. To appreciate how star status is produced requires attention to the widespread exposure of star names, how star-led films perform in the market, the astronomical levels of compensation paid to stars, and the applications of film form and the uses of the performer's voice and body in the creation on-screen of the star performance as a spectacular attraction. A-list stardom is measured by commercial success but film is a cultural industry and as such success is also measured by the "anti-commercial" logic of accumulating the symbolic capital of artistic consecration. In Hollywood this leads to the prestige star becoming an alternative configuration of stardom to the commercially defined A-list. It is also the case that the career trajectory of even A-list performers may oscillate between different sectors of the field of cultural production to accrue economic and symbolic profits by making creative choices to appear not only in popular offerings but also films with the potential for substituting kudos over cash. It is not something which has been explicitly addressed here but implicitly the preceding analysis has departed from the star image approach by holding onto the idea that stars retain agency in cultural production. With the study of star images and discourses, stars become only texts; there is nothing but discourse and this has the effect of removing any attention to stars as figures which actually do something within the film industry. Viewing stars as agents in cultural production does not mean neglecting the structural conditions influencing star status. Hollywood stardom is entirely dependent on high levels of investment in production and distribution and is filtered through the tight oligopoly of the major studios which hold economic and cultural dominance over the majority of the world's richest film markets. Stars are mass-mediated figures and so their status is equally contingent on broader cultural and social dynamics which define "popular" definitions of identity and which have their most obvious effects in how race, gender and age delimit the range of star images which are ever on offer at any point in Hollywood history.

Focusing on just two decades, this study has discussed a specific "cast" of actors who defined the star hierarchy in a particular period. Stardom is a work of production, forming a sub-system within Hollywood's larger system for the making, selling and showing of films. As Hollywood moved from the vertically integrated system of the 1930s and early 1940s to the post-studio system which emerged over the decades following the Second World War, the relationship of stars to studios fundamentally changed. Whereas in the vertically integrated system, the major studios retained exclusive control over the careers of the majority of stars through the term contract, in the new system stars became freelancers. In the vertically integrated system, stardom was almost entirely produced internally by the studios but the key characteristic of the post-studio system came from how the production of stardom moved outside the studios to be conducted through a network of external service providers. Stars in the vertically integrated system already hired agents, managers, attorneys and publicists to handle their affairs but in the post-studio system these roles and functions assumed new importance as key intermediaries between the freelance stars and both the studios who employed them and the other media channels which reported on their lives. Whereas the former system imposed tight controls over the making, deployment and ownership of stars, the post-studio system granted new freedoms. More stars, for example, moved into independent production by establishing their own companies. However this change did not remove the importance of just a few major studios. During the vertically integrated era, a small cluster of eight studios were at the center of Hollywood. As successive waves of conglomeration transferred their ownership, those studios changed hands but most survived to become components in large diversified media corporations. As these companies retained oligopolistic dominance over Hollywood's domestic and international markets, so a few major companies continued to be the only conduit through which films could reach the levels of exposure and visibility necessary to sustain stardom. Consequently, in the transition from vertically integrated stardom to post-studio stardom, stars moved from a system of limited independence to one of dependent independence.

In a market where consumer demand is always uncertain and capricious, Hollywood employs stars for one reason – from the persistent belief that stars can bring the economic benefits of helping to open movies and lead them to financial success. Aware of their potential value, stars (through their representatives) demand and can get high levels of compensation for their services. Consequently the economics of Hollywood stardom rests on a core paradox – stars are hired at considerable cost to protect against losses. While the industry looks to stars to bring in the box-office bounty, it is accepted stars cannot secure consistent financial success and at best may only ever deliver intermittent hits. Stardom therefore survives across the highs and lows. Doubts about the value of stars have been a constant feature of Hollywood history; however, those doubts intensified over the period studied here as changing patterns of mass popular taste saw many films featuring star names fail in the market while the box office was overwhelmed by movies built around serialized concepts without any star presence. At the same time, Hollywood witnessed massive inflation in the costs of hiring star labor as salaries ballooned and gross participation deals granted talent significant shares of revenues regardless of profit. In the period studied here, the foundational economic paradox of stardom was therefore strained even further as stars cost more but delivered less. In response, the studios instituted a new regime aimed at reining in costs and controlling the price of stars.

Although focused on a relatively short period of Hollywood history, this study is crossed by the dynamics which have characterized the post-studio system and the long enduring tensions which have shaped the symbolic commerce of stardom. When these matters are considered together, the Hollywood star emerges as creative agent, performing and performed brand, textually constructed identity, commercial asset, high-cost investment and prestige sign. For critical, analytical and historical studies of film stardom, the challenge is then to consistently hold onto these many facets to form a multi-dimensional conceptualization of the star and of stardom.

Appendix

Academy Award Nominees and Winners in the Actress and Actor in a Leading Role Categories, 1990–2009

Hollywood Stardom, First Edition. Paul McDonald.
© 2013 Paul McDonald. Published 2013 by John Wiley & Sons, Ltd.

Year	Actress in a Leading Role Nominee/Winner	Film	Actor in a Leading Role Nominee/Winner	Film
2009	**Sandra Bullock**	**The Blind Side**	**Jeff Bridges**	**Crazy Heart**
	Helen Mirren	The Last Station	George Clooney	Up in the Air
	Carey Mulligan	An Education	Colin Firth	A Single Man
	Gabourey Sidibe	Precious	Morgan Freeman	Invictus
	Meryl Streep	Julie and Julia	Jeremy Renner	The Hurt Locker
2008	Anne Hathaway	Rachel Getting Married	Richard Jenkins	The Visitor
	Angelina Jolie	Changeling	Frank Langella	Frost/Nixon
	Melissa Leo	Frozen River	**Sean Penn**	**Milk**
	Meryl Streep	Doubt	Brad Pitt	The Curious Case of Benjamin Button
	Kate Winslet	**The Reader**	Mickey Rourke	The Wrestler
2007	Cate Blanchett	Elizabeth: The Golden Age	George Clooney	Michael Clayton
	Julie Christie	Away from Her	**Daniel Day-Lewis**	**There Will Be Blood**
	Marion Cotillard	**La Vie en Rose**	Johnny Depp	Sweeney Todd: The Demon Barber of Fleet Street
	Laura Linney	The Savages	Tommy Lee-Jones	In the Valley of Elah
	Ellen Page	Juno	Viggo Mortensen	Eastern Promises
2006	Penélope Cruz	Volver	Leonardo DiCaprio	Blood Diamond
	Judi Dench	Notes on a Scandal	Ryan Gosling	Half Nelson
	Helen Mirren	**The Queen**	Peter O'Toole	Venus
	Meryl Streep	The Devil Wears Prada	Will Smith	The Pursuit of Happyness
	Kate Winslet	Little Children	**Forest Whitaker**	**The Last King of Scotland**

2005	Judi Dench	*Mrs Henderson Presents*	**Philip Seymour Hoffman**	*Capote*
	Felicity Huffman	*Transamerica*	Terrence Howard	*Hustle & Flow*
	Keira Knightley	*Pride and Prejudice*	Heath Ledger	*Brokeback Mountain*
	Charlize Theron	*North Country*	Joaquin Phoenix	*Walk the Line*
	Reese Witherspoon	***Walk the Line***	David Strathairn	*Good Night, and Good Luck*
2004	Annette Benning	*Being Julia*	Don Cheadle	*Hotel Rwanda*
	Catalina Sandino Moreno	*Maria Full of Grace*	Johnny Depp	*Finding Neverland*
	Imelda Staunton	*Vera Drake*	Leonardo DiCaprio	*The Aviator*
	Hilary Swank	***Million Dollar Baby***	Clint Eastwood	*Million Dollar Baby*
	Kate Winslet	*Eternal Sunshine of the Spotless Mind*	**Jamie Foxx**	***Ray***
2003	Keisha Castle-Hughes	*Whale Rider*	Johnny Depp	*Pirates of the Caribbean: The Curse of the Black Pearl*
	Diane Keaton	*Something's Gotta Give*	Ben Kingsley	*House of Sand and Fog*
	Samantha Morton	*In America*	Jude Law	*Cold Mountain*
	Charlize Theron	***Monster***	Bill Murray	*Lost in Translation*
	Naomi Watts	*21 Grams*	**Sean Penn**	***Mystic River***
2002	Salma Hayek	*Frida*	**Adrien Brody**	***The Pianist***
	Nicole Kidman	***The Hours***	Nicolas Cage	*Adaptation*
	Diane Lane	*Unfaithful*	Michael Caine	*The Quiet American*
	Julianne Moore	*Far from Heaven*	Daniel Day-Lewis	*Gangs of New York*
	Renée Zellweger	*Chicago*	Jack Nicholson	*About Schmidt*

(Continued)

	Actress in a Leading Role Nominee/**Winner**	Film		Actor in a Leading Role Nominee/**Winner**	Film
2001	**Halle Berry**	**Monster's Ball**		Russell Crowe	A Beautiful Mind
	Judi Dench	Iris		Sean Penn	I am Sam
	Nicole Kidman	Moulin Rouge		Will Smith	Ali
	Sissy Spacek	In the Bedroom		**Denzel Washington**	**Training Day**
	Renée Zellweger	Bridget Jones's Diary		Tom Wilkinson	In the Bedroom
2000	Joan Allen	The Contender		Javier Bardem	Before Night Falls
	Juliette Binoche	Chocolat		**Russell Crowe**	**Gladiator**
	Ellen Burstyn	Requiem for a Dream		Tom Hanks	Cast Away
	Laura Linney	You Can Count on Me		Ed Harris	Pollock
	Julia Roberts	**Erin Brockovich**		Geoffrey Rush	Quills
1999	Annette Bening	American Beauty		Russell Crowe	The Insider
	Janet McTeer	Tumbleweeds		Richard Farnsworth	The Straight Story
	Julianne Moore	The End of the Affair		Sean Penn	Sweet and Lowdown
	Meryl Streep	Music of the Heart		**Kevin Spacey**	**American Beauty**
	Hilary Swank	**Boys Don't Cry**		Denzel Washington	The Hurricane
1998	Cate Blanchett	Elizabeth		**Roberto Benigni**	**La Vita è bella**
	Fernanda Montenegro	Central Station		Tom Hanks	Saving Private Ryan
	Gwyneth Paltrow	**Shakespeare in Love**		Ian McKellen	Gods and Monsters
	Meryl Streep	One True Thing		Nick Nolte	Affliction
	Emily Watson	Hilary and Jackie		Edward Norton	American History X

Year				
1997	Helena Bonham Carter	The Wings of the Dove	Matt Damon	Good Will Hunting
	Julie Christie	Afterglow	Robert Duvall	The Apostle
	Judi Dench	Mrs. Brown	Peter Fonda	Ulee's Gold
	Helen Hunt	**As Good As It Gets**	**Jack Nicholson**	**As Good As It Gets**
	Kate Winslet	Titanic	Dustin Hoffman	Wag the Dog
1996	Brenda Blethyn	Secrets & Lies	Tom Cruise	Jerry Maguire
	Diane Keaton	Marvin's Room	Ralph Fiennes	The English Patient
	Frances McDormand	**Fargo**	Woody Harrelson	The People vs. Larry Flynt
	Kristin Scott Thomas	The English Patient	**Geoffrey Rush**	**Shine**
	Emily Watson	Breaking the Waves	Billy Bob Thornton	Sling Blade
1995	**Susan Sarandon**	**Dead Man Walking**	**Nicolas Cage**	**Leaving Las Vegas**
	Elizabeth Shue	Leaving Las Vegas	Richard Dreyfuss	Mr Holland's Opus
	Sharon Stone	Casino	Anthony Hopkins	Nixon
	Meryl Streep	The Bridges of Madison County	Sean Penn	Dead Man Walking
	Emma Thompson	Sense and Sensibility	Massimo Troisi	Il Postino
1994	Jodie Foster	Nell	Morgan Freeman	The Shawshank Redemption
	Jessica Lange	**Blue Sky**	**Tom Hanks**	**Forrest Gump**
	Miranda Richardson	Tom & Viv	Nigel Hawthorne	The Madness of King George
	Winona Ryder	Little Women	Paul Newman	Nobody's Fool
	Susan Sarandon	The Client	John Travolta	Pulp Fiction

(Continued)

Year	Actress in a Leading Role Nominee/Winner	Film	Actor in a Leading Role Nominee/Winner	Film
1993	Angela Bassett	What's Love Got to Do With It	Daniel Day-Lewis	In the Name of the Father
	Stockard Channing	Six Degrees of Separation	Laurence Fishburne	What's Love Got to Do With It
	Holly Hunter	***The Piano***	**Tom Hanks**	***Philadelphia***
	Emma Thompson	Remains of the Day	Anthony Hopkins	Remains of the Day
	Debra Winger	Shadowlands	Liam Neeson	Schindler's List
1992	Catherine Deneuve	Indochine	Robert Downey, Jr.	Chaplin
	Mary McDonnell	Passion Fish	Clint Eastwood	Unforgiven
	Michelle Pfeiffer	Love Field	**Al Pacino**	***Scent of a Woman***
	Susan Sarandon	Lorenzo's Oil	Stephen Rea	The Crying Game
	Emma Thompson	***Howards End***	Denzel Washington	Malcolm X
1991	Geena Davis	Thelma & Louise	Warren Beatty	Bugsy
	Laura Dern	Rambling Rose	Robert De Niro	Cape Fear
	Jodie Foster	***Silence of the Lambs***	**Anthony Hopkins**	***Silence of the Lambs***
	Bette Midler	For the Boys	Nick Nolte	The Prince of Tides
	Susan Sarandon	Thelma & Louise	Robin Williams	The Fisher King
1990	**Kathy Bates**	***Misery***	Kevin Costner	Dances With Wolves
	Anjelica Houston	The Grifters	Robert De Niro	Awakenings
	Julia Roberts	Pretty Woman	Gerald Depardieu	Cyrano de Bergerac
	Meryl Streep	Postcards from the Edge	Richard Harris	The Field
	Joanne Woodward	Mr and Mrs Bridge	**Jeremy Irons**	***Reversal of Fortune***

Source: AMPAS (2010)

References

Aaker, David A. (2002) *Building Strong Brands*. London: Simon & Schuster.

Aaker, Jennifer L. (1997) "Dimensions of Brand Personality," *Journal of Marketing Research*, 34(3), pp. 347–56.

Abramowitz, Rachel (2008) "It's No Act, He Mutates," *Los Angeles Times*, 25 February, pp. E13–4.

Abramowitz, Rachel (2010) "Can Julia Roberts Come Back on Her Own Terms?" *Los Angeles Times*, 12 January, http://latimesblogs.latimes.com/movies/2010/01/julia-roberts-tom-hanks-comeback.html.

AFI (n.d.) "AFI's 100 Years . . . 100 Stars," www.afi.com/100Years/stars/aspx.

AFI (1999) "America's Greatest Legends," www.afi.com/Docs/100Years/stars50.pdf.

Albert, Steven (1998) "Movie Stars and the Distribution of Financially Successful Films in the Motion Picture Industry," *Journal of Cultural Economics*, 22(4), pp. 249–70.

Altman, Rick (1999) *Film/Genre*. London: British Film Institute.

AMPAS (n.d.) "Preferential System of Balloting," *Internal publication*. Los Angeles, CA: Academy of Motion Picture Arts and Sciences

AMPAS (2009) *The Academy Awards: 82nd Annual Rules for Distinguished Achievements during 2009*. Beverly Hills, CA: Academy of Motion Picture Arts and Science.

AMPAS (2010) "The Official Academy Awards® Database," http://awardsdatabase.oscars.org/ampas_awards/BasicSearchInput.jsp.

AMPAS. (2011) "Academy Member Invitations," www.oscars.org/academy/members/invitations.html.

Andersen, Kurt (1998) "The Tom Hanks Phenomenon," *The New Yorker*, 7 December, pp. 104, 106, 115–24 and 127–8.

Anderson, Chris (2007) *The Long Tail: How Endless Choice is Creating Unlimited Demand*. London: Random House.

Anon. (1998) Press book *Saving Private Ryan*. DreamWorks LLC, Paramount Pictures Corporation and Amblin Entertainment, Inc.

Ansen, David (1999) "Box Office Heat," *Newsweek*, 9 August, p. 68.

Arnold, Gary (1990) "'Terminator 2' to Cost Roughly $80 Million," *The Washington Times*, 23 October, p. F4.

ATA (2010) "Actors' Agent Search," www.agentassociation.com/frontdoor/actors_agent_search.cfm.

Bakker, Gerben (2001) "Stars and Stories: How Films Became Branded Products," *Enterprise and Society*, 2(3), pp. 461–502.

Banks, Jack (1996) *Monopoly Television: MTV's Quest to Control the Music*. Boulder, CO: Westview.

Barra, Allen (1996) "Is This the Scariest Actor Alive?" *Los Angeles Magazine*, November, pp. 88–91.

Bart, Peter (2007) "Does Star Power Translate to B.O. Power," *Variety*, 22 October, pp. 6 and 51.

Barthes, Roland (1957) "The Face of Garbo," in (1986) *Mythologies*. London: Paladin.

Barthes, Roland (1966) "Introduction to the Structural Analysis of Narratives," in (1977) *Image, Music, Text*. London: Fontana, pp. 79–124.

Basinger, Jeanine (2009) *The Star Machine*. New York: Vintage.

Bates, James (1996) "Big Movie Stars Get Big Salaries, Big Executives Whine – Big Deal," *Los Angeles Times*, 8 March, pp. D1 and 4.

Becker, Christine (2008) *It's the Pictures That Got Small: Hollywood Film Stars on 1950s Television*. Middletown, CT: Wesleyan University Press.

Becker, Howard S. (1982) *Art Worlds*. Berkeley: University of California Press.

Bennett, Peter D. (1988) *Dictionary of Marketing Terms*. Chicago: American Marketing Association.

Bharatan Iyer, Shilpa (2006) "H'wood Dips into B'wood," *Daily Variety*, 22 August, pp. 4 and 14.

Bialik, Carl (2010) "Lights, Camera, Calculator! The New Celebrity Math," *The Wall Street Journal*, 27 February, http://online.wsj.com/article/SB10001424052748704479404575088143982459472.html.

Biederman, Donald E. (1999) "What Hath Ovitz Wrought? Agents v. Managers Revisited," *Vanderbilt Journal of Entertainment Law and Practice*, 5, pp. 5–19.

Blackstock, Colin (2005) "Best Supporting Actor Will Smith Breaks Record with Three Premieres in a Day," *The Guardian*, 23 February, p. 6.

Boland, Michaela (2008) "Icon Wraps Dendy Buy," *Variety*, 19 May, p. 12.

Bone, James and Dalya Alberge. (2001) "Billy Elliot Takes on Gladiator," *The Times*, 14 February, p. 3.

Bordwell, David (2006) *The Way Hollywood Tells It: Story and Style in Modern Movies*. Berkeley: University of California Press.

Bourdieu, Pierre (1977) "The Production of Belief: Contribution to an Economy of Symbolic Goods," in (1993) *The Field of Cultural Production*. Cambridge: Polity, pp. 74–111.

Bourdieu, Pierre (1983a) "The Field of Cultural Production, or: The Economic World Reversed," in (1993) *The Field of Cultural Production*. Cambridge: Polity, pp. 29–73.

Bourdieu, Pierre (1983b) "The Forms of Capital," in John G. Richardson (ed.) *Handbook of Theory and Research for the Sociology of Education*. New York: Greenwood, pp. 241–58.

Bourdieu, Pierre (1984) "Social Space and the Genesis of Classes," in (1992) *Language and Symbolic Power*. Cambridge: Polity, pp. 229–51.

Bourdieu, Pierre (1986) "Principles for a Sociology of Cultural Works," in (1993) *The Field of Cultural Production*. Cambridge: Polity, pp. 176–91.

Bourdieu, Pierre (1989) *Distinction: A Social Critique of the Judgment of Taste*. London: Routledge.

Bourdieu, Pierre (1990) *Photography: A Middle-brow Art*. Cambridge: Polity.

Bourdieu, Pierre (1996) *The Rules of Art: Genesis and Structure of the Literary Field*. Cambridge: Polity.

Bowser, Eileen (1990) *The Transformation of Cinema: 1907–1915*. Berkeley: University of California Press.

Branigan, Edward (1992) *Narrative Comprehension and Film*. London: Routledge.

Brantley, Ben (2006) "It's Her! It's Her! And, Oh Yeah, There's a Play," *The New York Times*, 20 April, pp. E1 and 6.

Brennan, Judy (1996) "Mr. Freeze Is Heating up Hollywood's Money Race," *Los Angeles Times*, 15 July, pp. F1 and 8.

Brennan, Judy and Lawrence Cohn (1993) "H'w'd Tussles with the Value of Starpower," *Daily Variety*, 16 March, pp. 1 and 29.

Bret, David (2011) *Elizabeth Taylor: The Lady, the Lover, the Legend, 1932–2011*. Edinburgh: Mainstream.

Brodesser, Claude and Dave McNary (2004) "It Takes Talent to Divvy Up DVD," *Variety*, 23 February, p. 10.

Brodesser-Akner, Claude (2009) "Obama Trumps Gump," *Advertising Age*, 4 February, http://adage.com/article/madisonvine-news/obama-tops-tom-hanks-atop-survey-influential-celebs/134328.

Brodesser-Akner, Claude (2010) "For Valentine's Day, Julia Roberts Was Paid $500,000 a Minute . . . All Six of Them," *New York*, 11 February, http://nymag.com/daily/entertainment/2010/02/julia_roberts_valentines_day.html.

Brodie, John and Anita M. Busch (1996) "Star Prices Breaking the Bank," *Daily Variety*, 8 March, pp. 7 and 22.

Brown, Corie (1998) "Hollywood's New Math," *Newsweek*, 19 January, p. 65.

Buchalter, Gail (1992) "Then I Heard My Father's Voice," *Parade*, 2 February, pp. 16–17.

Bulbeck, Pip (2008) "Icon Acquires Dendy, Grows Down Under," *The Hollywood Reporter*, 25 February, pp. 10 and 36.

Burman, John (1998) "Star Power '98," *The Hollywood Reporter*, 24 February, pp. 19–26.

Busch, Anita M. (1996a) "Bat-cast firms George, Arnold," *Daily Variety*, 13 March, pp. 1 and 36.

Busch, Anita M. (1996b) "Spielberg, Hanks near Deal at Par," *Daily Variety*, 29 July, pp. 1 and 21.

Busch, Anita M. (2000) "34% of 'Grinch' 1st-dollar Gross to Participants," *The Hollywood Reporter*, 5 December, pp. 4 and 75.

Busch, Anita M. and Michael Fleming (1995) "Canton's Cash and Carrey," *Daily Variety*, 19 June, pp. 1 and 35.

Busch, Anita M. and Beth Laski (1995) "Carrey Caught in $20 Mil 'Liar'," *Daily Variety*, 7 August, pp. 1 and 40.

B|W|R (n.d.) Intro, www.bwr-pr.com.

Canby, Vincent (1990) "One Look and I Knew It Was You," *The New York Times*, 30 December, pp. H17 and 25.

Carr, Jay (1997) "The Evolution of Julia Roberts; Warm, Wary, Savvy – and Mischievous," *The Daily News of Los Angeles*, 19 June, www.lexisnexis.com/uk/nexis/results/docview/docview.do?docLinkInd=true&risb=21_T1363925877 5&format=GNBFI&sort=BOOLEAN&startDocNo=101&resultsUrlKey=29_ T13639258779&cisb=22_T13639258778&treeMax=true&treeWidth=0&csi= 157105&docNo=101.

Carver, Benedict (1998) "Icon Invades U.K." *Daily Variety*, 13 November, pp. 1 and 35.

Carver, Benedict and Adam Dawtry (1998) "BV Int'l Takes 'Bride' O'seas," *Daily Variety*, 29 October, pp. 1 and 16.

Caves, Richard (2000) *Creative Industries: Contracts between Art and Commerce*. Cambridge, MA: Harvard University Press.

Chetwynd, Josh (1998) "Smith Lands on 'K-Pax' Alien Mystery for Uni," *The Hollywood Reporter*, 20 April, pp. 1 and 19.

Christy, George (2001) "The Great Life," *The Hollywood Reporter*, 2 March, p. 100.

CinemaScore. (1999) "Runaway Bride," *The Hollywood Reporter*, 3 August, p. 98.

Clark, Danae (1995) *Negotiating Hollywood: The Cultural Politics of Actors' Labor*. Minneapolis: University of Minnesota Press.

Cones, John W. (1992) *Film Finance and Distribution: A Dictionary of Terms*. Los Angeles: Silman-James.

Corliss, Richard (1994) "Dashing Daniel," *Time*, 21 March, pp. 66–9.

Cox, Dan (1995) "Carrey's $ 20 mil 'Cable' Bill," *Daily Variety*, 14 June, pp. 1 and 43.

Cox, Dan (1997a) "Smith Talks Shingle at U," *Daily Variety*, 12 November, pp. 1 and 19.

Cox, Dan (1997b) "Stars Push Pic Perks," *Daily Variety*, 27 June, pp. 1 and 50.

Cox, Dan and Chris Petrikin (1999) "Overbrook is Ready," *Daily Variety*, 12 February, p. 6.

Curtis, Tony and Barry Paris (1993) *Tony Curtis: The Autobiography*. New York: William Morrow & Co.

Csaba, Fabian Faurholt and Anders Bengtsson (2006) "Rethinking Identity in Brand Management," in Jonathan E. Schroeder and Miriam Salzer-Mörling (eds.) *Brand Culture*. Abingdon: Routledge, pp. 118–35.

Dahl, Sophie (2008) "Free Radical," *Men's Vogue*, February, pp. 83–9.

D'Alessandro, Anthony (2000) "The Top 250 of 1999," *Variety*, 10 January, pp. 20–1.

D'Alessandro, Anthony (2001) "Top 250 of 2000," *Variety*, 8 January, pp. 20–1.

D'Alessandro, Anthony (2002) "Top Grossing Pics of 2001," *Variety*, 7 January, pp. 38–9.

D'Alessandro, Anthony (2003) "Top 250 of 2002," *Variety*, 6 January, pp. 26–7.

D'Alessandro, Anthony (2004) "The Top 250 of 2003," *Variety*, 12 January, pp. 14–15.

D'Alessandro, Anthony (2005) "Domestic Top 250 of 2004," *Variety*, 10 January, pp. 14–15.

D'Alessandro, Anthony (2006) "Domestic Top 250 of 2005," *Variety*, 9 January, pp. 52–3.

Dargis, Manohla (2000) "Ghost in the Machine," *Sight and Sound*, July, www.bfi.org.uk/sightandsound/feature/46.

Davies, Gary and Rosa Chun (2003) "The Use of Metaphor in the Exploration of the Brand Concept," *Journal of Marketing Management*, 19(1/2), 45–71.

Davis, L. J. (1989) "Hollywood's Secret Agent," *Daily Telegraph (Weekend)*, 25 November, p. 11.

Dawes, Amy. (1996) "Hollywood's Pay Daze," *L. B. Press-Telegram*, 19 July, p. 24.

Dawtry, Adam. (1996) "Icon's Majestic Buy," *Daily Variety*, 20 November, p. 51.

deCordova, Richard (1990) *Picture Personalities: The Emergence of the Star System in America*. Urbana: University of Illinois.

Delamoir, Jeanette and Tanya Nittins (2006) "Celebrity Names/Brand Names: Nicole Kidman, Chanel No. 5 and Commodification," in Bernadette Walker-Gibbs and Bruce Allen Knight (eds) *Re-visioning Research and Knowledge for the 21st Century*. Teneriffe: Post Pressed, pp. 29–48.

De Vany, Arthur and W. David Walls (1999) "Uncertainty in the Movie Industry: Does Star Power Reduce the Terror of the Box Office?" *Journal of Cultural Economics*, 23(4), pp. 285–318.

Diehl, Matt (1999) "Pop Rap," in Alan Light (ed.) *The Vibe History of Hip Hop*. New York: Three Rivers Press, pp. 121–33.

Dillow, Gordon (1993) "Will Smith Settles Down and Gets Real," *TV Guide*, 23 January, pp. 11–14.

DiOrio, Carl (2001) "'Mex' Numero Uno," *Daily Variety*, 5 March, pp. 1 and 46.

Dobuzinskis, Alex (2009) "Hollywood Rethinks Use of A-list Actors," Reuters, 13 November www.reuters.com/article/2009/11/13/us-alist-idUSTRE5AC5AI20091113.

Douglas, Kirk (1988) *The Ragman's Son: An Autobiography*. New York: Simon & Schuster.

Douglas, Kirk (2007) *Let's Face It: 90 Years of Living, Loving and Learning*. Hoboken, NJ: John Wiley & Sons.

Dunkley, Cathy (1995) "Gibson's Icon Braving Sales,"*The Hollywood Reporter*, 5 September, pp. 3 and 106.

Dunkley, Cathy and Claude Brodesser (2002) "H'w'd at War with Piece-niks," *Variety*, 25 November, pp. 1 and 56.

Dunkley, Cathy and Stephen Galloway (1998) "DiCillo, Leoni Films Wash Up on Lakeshore," *The Hollywood Reporter*, 21 May, pp. 9 and 13.

Dutka, Elaine (1990) "Hollywood's Pink Ghetto," *The Record*, 20 December, p. C21.

Dutka, Elaine (1991) "The Power of Julia," *Los Angeles Times (Calendar)*, 9 June, pp. 8–9 and 23–6.

Dyer, Richard (1987) *Heavenly Bodies: Film Stars and Society*. Basingstoke: Macmillan.

Dyer, Richard (1998) *Stars*. London: British Film Institute.

EAO (2001) *Focus 2001: World Film Market Trends*. Strasbourg: European Audiovisual Observatory.

EAO (2009) *Focus 2009: World Film Market Trends*. Strasbourg: European Audiovisual Observatory.

EAO (2010) "Hancock," *LUMIERE: Data Base on Admissions of Films Released in Europe*, http://lumiere.obs.coe.int/web/film_info/?id=30031.

Eliot, Marc (2004) *Cary Grant: A Biography*. New York: Harmony.

Ellen, Barbara (2001) "Big Guns Shoot Blanks," *The Times (Times 2)*, 26 April, pp. 13–14.

Eller, Claudia (1994) "Stallone Cuts $20 Million Movie Deal," *The Oregonian*, 21 December, p. E8.

EMA (2008) *2008 Annual Report on the Home Entertainment Industry*. Encino, CA: Entertainment Merchants Association.

EMA (2009) *2009 Annual Report on the Home Entertainment Industry*. Encino, CA: Entertainment Merchants Association.

English, James F. (2005) *The Economy of Prestige: Prizes, Awards, and the Circulation of Cultural Value*. Cambridge, MA: Harvard University Press.

Epstein, Edward Jay (2006) *The Big Picture: Money and Power in Hollywood*. New York: Random House.

Epstein, Edward Jay (2010) *The Hollywood Economist: The Hidden Financial Reality behind the Movies*. New York: Melville House.

Esterly, Glenn (1992) "Prince of a Guy," *TV Guide*, 15 February, pp. 16–19.

Farr, John. (2008) "James Stewart: On the Actor's Centennial, His Ten Best Films," *The Huffington Post*, 14 May www.huffingtonpost.com/john-farr/james-stewart-on-the-acto_b_101633.html.

Feeney, Mark. (2004) "Hail to the Streep," *Boston Sunday Globe*, 25 July, pp. N11 and 14.

Finke, Nikki (2007) "The Worst Talent Deal Ever?" *L.A. Weekly*, 24 August, pp. 37–8.

Fleming, Charles (1998) *High Concept: Don Simpson and the Hollywood Culture of Excess*. London: Bloomsbury.

Fleming, Michael (1995a) "'Cable' Rate Sky High," *Daily Variety*, 9 June, pp. 1 and 51.

Fleming, Michael (1995b) "Icon Snaps Up Kings Road Pix," *Daily Variety*, 20 October, pp. 1 and 28.

Fleming, Michael (1995c) "Sly Sees 'Daylight'," *Daily Variety*, 3 April, pp. 1 and 19.

Fleming, Michael (1996) "Bullock May Walk Down the Aisle in 'Runaway Bride'," *Variety*, 26 February, p. 4.

Fleming, Michael (1998) "Smith Eyes Reborn 'Star'," *Daily Variety*, 19 November, pp. 1 and 18.

Fleming, Michael (1999) "Roberts Romances This Summer," *Daily Variety*, 2 March, p. 51.

Fleming, Michael (2000a) "Top Salaries Not Suffering," *Daily Variety*, 31 October, p. 23.

Fleming, Michael (2000b) "'Play Misty' Remake on Tap," *Daily Variety*, 14 December, p. 31.

Fleming, Michael (2005) "'Apocalypto' Now for Mel," *Daily Variety*, 22 July, pp. 1 and 39.

Fleming, Michael (2007a) "CAA Agent Heading Over to Overbrook," *Daily Variety*, 8 May, pp. 1 and 14.

Fleming, Michael (2007b) "Shaking the Money Tree," *Variety*, 21 May, pp. 1 and 67.

Fleming, Michael. (2008) "Grossed Out," *Variety*, 16 June, pp. 1 and 49.

Fleming, Michael. (2009) "Ryan's Hope: A Pact Overhaul," *Variety*, 23 November, pp. 5 and 7.

Fleming, Michael and Josef Adalian (2005) "Plan C for Plan B?" *Daily Variety*, 4 January, p. 51.

Fleming, Michael and Dana Harris (2002) "Brads Mad for WB Pact," *Daily Variety*, 3 June, pp. 1 and 22.

Foreman, Liza (2005) "Par Goes to Plan B with 3-year Deal," *The Hollywood Reporter*, 23 June, pp. 1 and 34.

Foucault, Michel (1969) "What Is an Author?" in Donald F. Bouchard (ed.) (1977) *Language, Counter-memory, Practice: Selected Essays and Interviews by Michel Foucault*. Ithaca, NY: Cornell University Press, pp. 113–38.

Fox, Chloe (2009) "Tom Hanks Interview: On the New Dan Brown Movie *Angels & Demons*," *The Daily Telegraph*, 4 May, www.telegraph.co.uk/culture/film/starsandstories/5257472/Tom-Hanks-interview-on-the-new-Dan-Brown-movie-Angels-and-Demons.html.

Frater, Patrick (2007) "China Nixes Hollywood Pix," *Daily Variety*, 6 December, pp. 1 and 34.

Frater, Patrick (2008) "Arms Wide Open," *Variety (VPlus – Showmen of the Year)*, 15 December, p. 12.

Freer, Ian (2009) "In Conversation with Tom Hanks," *Empire*, June, pp. 179–84.

Frook, John (1991) "Superstars: Studios Weary of High Price Tags," *The Daily Breeze*, 21 April, p. D5.

Galloway, Stephen (1996a) "Gibson's Icon Reels in Majestic Films, Library," *The Hollywood Reporter*, 19 November, pp. 8 and 161.

Galloway, Stephen (1996b) "WB, Par both Clicking on Icon," *The Hollywood Reporter*, 8 February, pp. 1 and 21.

Galloway, Stephen. (1997) "Smith Looking First to Uni for Film, TV, Music," *The Hollywood Reporter*, 12 November, pp. 1 and 22.

Galloway, Stephen (2001) "Critical Mass," *The Hollywood Reporter (Oscar Watch: Critics Picks Special Issue)*, 12 January, pp. S6–16.

Galloway, Stephen (2004) "A Lasting Partnership," *The Hollywood Reporter*, 15 November, pp. 16 and 40.

Galloway, Stephen (2008) "Meryl's Choice," *The Hollywood Reporter*, 14 April, pp. I1 and 4.

Gans, Herbert J. (1999) *Popular Culture and High Culture* rev. edn.New York: Basic.

Gardner, Chris and Gregg Kilday (2002) "Fox Inks Gibson's Icon to 2-year Deal," *The Hollywood Reporter*, 15 March, pp. 1 and 33.

Gardner, David (2007) *The Tom Hanks Enigma*. London: John Blake.

George, Nelson (1998) *Hip Hop America*. New York: Penguin.

Gold, Richard (1990) "Name's the Game in Film Hype," *Daily Variety*, 28 June, p. 40.

Goldberg, Victor P. (1997) "The Net Profits Puzzle," *Columbia Law Review*, 97(2), pp. 524–40.

Goldman, William (1984) *Adventures in the Screen Trade: A Personal View of Hollywood and Screenwriting*. London: Futura.

Goldstein, Patrick (1999) "'Bride's' Long, Long Path to the Altar," *Los Angeles Times*, 3 August, pp. F1 and 4–5.

Gomery, Douglas (1992) *Shared Pleasures: A History of Movie Presentation in the United States*. Madison: University of Wisconsin Press.

Goodridge, Mike (2000a) "Best Actress, Best Supporting Actress," *Screen International*, 15 December, pp. 17–18.

Goodridge, Mike (2000b) "Universal Re-releases Erin Brockovich," *Screen International*, 1 December, p. 29.

Goodridge, Mike (2003) "The Grande Dame of the Cutting Edge," *Screen International*, 21 February, p. 16.

Goodwin, Christopher (2008) "Hollywood Signals Death of the Star System," *The Week*, 13 May, www.theweek.co.uk/27059/hollywood-signals-death-star-system.

Gordon, Geoff (1994) "Six Degrees of Trepidation," *The Advocate*, February, pp. 56–7.

Granger, Stewart (1981) *Sparks Fly Upwards*. New York: G. P. Putnam's & Sons.

Gray, Timothy M. (2001) "Oscar Pits 'Gladiator,' 'Tiger'," *Variety*, 19 February, p. 20.

Green, Abel (1959) "Names That Rode High in 1958," *Variety*, 7 January, pp. 1 and 56.

Greenberg, Steve (1999) "Sugar Hill Records," in Alan Light (ed.) *The Vibe History of Hip Hop*. New York: Three Rivers Press, pp. 23–33.

Grove, Christopher (1998) "Global Bankability," *Daily Variety (Showest Honors)*, 10 March, p. A13.

Groves, Don (2001) "'Traffic' Bumps Best; Bullock Bright," *Variety*, 2 April, pp. 10 and 45.

Guback, Thomas (1982) "Foreword," in Janet Wasko, *Movies and Money: Financing the American Film Industry*. Norwood, NJ: Ablex, pp. xi–xv.

Gunning, Tom (1986) "The Cinema of Attractions: Early Film, Its Spectator and the Avant-garde," in Thomas Elsaesser with Adam Barker (eds.) (1990) *Early Cinema: Space, Frame, Narrative*. London: British Film Institute, pp. 56–62.

Hall, Sheldon and Steve Neale (2010) *Epics, Spectacles and Blockbusters: A Hollywood History*. Detroit, MI: Wayne State University Press.

Hanby, Terry (1999) "Brands – Dead or Alive?" *Journal of the Marketing Research Society*, 41(1), pp. 7–18.

Harmetz, Aljean (1988) "Big Hollywood Salaries a Magnet for the Stars (and the Public)," *New York Times*, 25 July, p. C13.

Harmetz, Aljean (1989) "On Feeling Underpaid at $1 Million," *New York Times*, 27 November, pp. C13 and 17.

Harris, Dana (2002) "Bubbling Overbrook," *Daily Variety*, 31 January, p. 5.

Harris Interactive (1999) "Harrison Ford Nation's Favorite Movie Star for Second Year in a Row," 24 November. New York: Harris Interactive.

Harris Interactive (2000) "Harrison Ford the Most Popular Movie Star for Third Year in a Row," 6 December. New York: Harris Interactive.

Harris Interactive (2001) "Julia Roberts Most Popular Movie Star," 19 December. New York: Harris Interactive.

Harris Interactive (2002) "Tom Hanks is America's Favorite Movie Star," 23 December. New York: Harris Interactive.

Harris Interactive (2007) "Denzel Washington: America's Favorite Movie Star," 16 January. Rochester, NY: Harris Interactive.

Harris Interactive (2008) "Denzel Washington Remains America's Favorite Movie Star," 15 January. Rochester, NY: Harris Interactive.

Harris Interactive (2009) "Denzel Washington is America's Favorite Movie Star," 29 January. Rochester, NY: Harris Interactive.

Harris Interactive (2010) "Clint Eastwood is America's Favorite Movie Star," 16 January. New York: Harris Interactive.

Hayes, Dade (2006) "Golden Boy Shines Behind the Scenes," *Daily Variety (V Plus)*, 15 December, pp. 14 and 29.

Heath, Chris (2005) "The Hard-ass," *GQ*, March, pp. 238–44, 253, 302 and 305–6.

Heath, Stephen (1981) *Questions of Cinema*. London: Macmillan.

Heise, Tatiana and Andrew Tudor (2007) "Constructing (Film) Art: Bourdieu's Field Model in a Comparative Context," *Cultural Sociology*, 1(2), pp. 165–87.

Hesmondhalgh, David (2006) "Bourdieu, the Media and Cultural Production," *Media, Culture and Society*, 28(2), pp. 211–31.

Hettrick, Scott (1995) "Medavoy: Film Costs Face an 'Apocalyptic Future'," *The Hollywood Reporter*, 16 June, pp. 4 and 81.

HFPA (2011) "About the HFPA," www.goldenglobes.org/about.

Higashi, Sumiko (2004) "In Focus: Film History, or a Baedeker Guide to the Historical Turn," *Cinema Journal*, 44(1), pp. 94–100.

Hindes, Andrew (1995) "H'wood Finally Opening Vault to Female Stars," *Daily Variety*, 5 December, pp. 7 and 28.

Hindes, Andrew (1998) "'Bride' Reunites 'Pretty' Pair," *Variety*, 29 June, p. 9.

Hindes, Andrew (1999a) "Icon Shifts Shingle to Par," *Daily Variety*, 15 January, pp. 1 and 106.

Hindes, Andrew (1999b) "'Moon' Beams on Smith," *Daily Variety*, 1 July, pp. 1 and 16.

Hindes, Andrew (1999c) "'Runaway' Weekend a Record," *Daily Variety*, 2 August, pp. 1 and 21.

Hindes, Andrew and Chris Petrikin (1998) "'Bride' Woos Marshall for 'Pretty' Reunion," *Daily Variety*, 10 July, p. 5.

Hinson, Hal (1999) "There Goes the Bride," *New Times LA*," 29 July, p. 30.

Hirshenson, Janet and Jane Jenkins (2006) *A Star is Found: Our Adventures Casting Some of Hollywood's Biggest Movies*. Orlando: Harcourt.

Hoffman, Bill (2000) "The Sweet Mel of Success! $25 Mil is Tops in H'wood," *The New York Post*, 7 February, p. 9.

Holden, Anthony (1994) *Behind the Oscar: The Secret History of the Academy Awards*. New York: Plume.

Holden, Stephen (2001) "Sounds Like Tony Soprano but Just a Tad Weepier," *The New York Times*, 2 March, p. E14.

Hollywood Reporter, The (1997) "Uni Makes a Production Out of Will Smith Offer," 17 November, p. 8.

Hollywood Reporter, The (1999) "Roberts Awaiting a $20 Million Payday," 2 March, p. 96.

Hollywood Reporter, The (2001) "Sound Off!" 28 February, p. 6.

Holson, Laura M. (2006) "The Fresh Princes of Mumbai," *The New York Times*, 21 August, pp. C1 and 4.

Honeycutt, Kirk (1992) "Fresh Prince in '6 Degrees' Pic," *The Hollywood Reporter*, 9 November, pp. 5 and 15.

Honeycutt, Kirk (1998) "Gibson's Icon to Bow Output Firm in Britain," *The Hollywood Reporter*, 13 November, pp. 1 and 55.

Honeycutt, Kirk (1999) "Big Night of 100 Stars is AFI Sequel of the Century," *The Hollywood Reporter*, 13 January, pp. 4 and 64.

Hontz, Jenny (1998) "Ex-CW exec Tochterman to Overbrook," *Daily Variety*, 16 September, pp. 5 and 44.

Horn, John (2005) "DVD Sales Figures Turn Every Film into a Mystery," *Los Angeles Times*, 17 April, pp. A1 and 34–5.

Horn, John (2006) "Hollywood Studios Rewriting Pay System for Their Talent," *Los Angeles Times*, 13 January, pp. C1 and 10.

Hoskins, Colin and Rolf Mirus (1988) "Reasons for the US Dominance of the International Trade in Television Programmes," *Media, Culture and Society*, 10(4), pp. 499–515.

Howe, Desson (1999) "Forget the 'Bride,' the Audience Should Run," *The Washington Post*, 30 July, p. N45.

ICANN (1999) "Uniform Domain Name Dispute Resolution Policy," www.icann.org/en/udrp/udrp-policy-24oct99.htm.

Jaafar, Ali and Michael Fleming (2008) "Smith Targets the Mideast," *Daily Variety*, 4 December, pp. 1 and 17.

Jackson Turner, Frederick (1893) "The Significance of the Frontier," in (1996) *The Frontier in American History*. New York: Dover, pp. 1–38.

Jeffers McDonald, Tamar (2007) *Romantic Comedy: Boy Meets Girl Meets Genre*. London: Wallflower.

Jeffers McDonald, Tamar (2010) *Hollywood Catwalk: Exploring Costume and Transformation in American Film*. London: I. B. Tauris.

Johnson, Ted (1996a) "Can $20 Mil Fill the Bill?" *Variety*, 9 December, pp. 1 and 118.

Johnson, Ted (1996b) "Gibson Confirms Icon Pacts at Warner, Par," *Daily Variety*, 8 February, p. 7.

Kapferer, Jean-Noël (2008) *The New Strategic Brand Management: Creating and Sustaining Brand Equity Long Term* 4th edn. London: Kogan Page.

Kauffmann, Stanley (2001) "A Strain and a Relief," *The New Republic*, 26 March, p. 26.

Kaufman, Jason, David Malley, Nerina Rammairone and Alisa Weinstein (1998) "The $20 Million Club," *US*, August, pp. 51–8.

Kemper, Tom (2010) *Hidden Talent: The Emergence of Hollywood Agents*. Berkeley: University of California Press.

Kerr, Sarah (2001) "Disappearing Act," *Vogue*, December, pp. 298–301 and 341–2.

King, Barry (1985) "Articulating Stardom," *Screen*, 26(5), pp. 27–50.

King, Barry (1986) "Stardom as an Occupation," in Paul Kerr (ed.) *The Hollywood Film Industry*. London: Routledge and Kegan Paul, pp. 154–84.

King, Barry (1987) "The Star and the Commodity: Notes Towards a Performance Theory of Stardom," *Cultural Studies*, 1(2), pp. 145–61.

King, Geoff (2009) *Indiewood, USA: Where Hollywood Meets Independent Cinema*. London: I. B. Tauris.

Kit, Zorianna (1999a) "Gibson, Davey Drag Icon Films to Paramount," *The Hollywood Reporter*, 15 January, pp. 1 and 61.

Kit, Zorianna (1999b) "Uni Falls for Overbrook's 'Love'," *The Hollywood Reporter*, 25 January, p. 43.

Kit, Zorianna (2000) "WB Identifies 'Lineup' Project," *The Hollywood Reporter*, 24 August, pp. 3 and 25.

Kit, Zorianna (2001) "Roberts Smiles for 'Mona Lisa' at Revolution," *The Hollywood Reporter*, 24 October, pp. 1 and 19.

Klady, Leonard (1995a) "$10 Mil Gets Moore to 'Strip'," *Variety*, 20 February, p. 22.

Klady, Leonard (1995b) "The Lowdown on '94's Record Box Office Heights," *Variety*, 30 January, p. 17.

Klady, Leonard (1996) "B.O. Performance of Films in 1995," *Variety*, 8 January, pp. 38–40.

Klady, Leonard (1997) "B.O. Performance Hits High in '96," *Variety*, 13 January, pp. 19 and 22.

Klady, Leonard (1998) "Top 250 of 1997," *Variety*, 26 January, pp. 17–18.

Klady, Leonard (1999) "The Top 250 of 1998," *Variety*, 11 January, pp. 33–4.

Klady, Leonard (2010) "Roberts' Return," *Screen International*, August, pp. 46–7.

Krims, Adam (2000) *Rap Music and the Poetics of Identity*. Cambridge: Cambridge University Press.

Landesman, Cosmo (2004) "Smile That Lacks Charm," *The Sunday Times (Culture)*, 14 March, p. 14.

Landreth, Jonathan (2007) "'Happyness' is Warm Banbuster," *The Hollywood Reporter*, 21 December, www.hollywoodreporter.com/news/happyness-is-warm-banbuster-157670.

Laski, Beth (1995) "Meyer Makes Noise With $60 mil Stallone Pact," *Variety*, 14 August, pp. 5 and 12.

Leaming, Barbara (1989) *If This Was Happiness: A Biography of Rita Hayworth*. New York: Viking.

Lehu, Jean-Marc (2007) *Branded Entertainment: Product Placement and Brand Strategy in the Entertainment Business*. London: Kogan Page.

Levine, Michael (2003) *A Branded World: Adventures in Public Relations and the Creation of Superbrands*. Hoboken, NJ: John Wiley & Sons.

Levinson, Peter J. (2009) *Puttin' on the Ritz: Fred Astaire and the Fine Art of Panache*. New York: St. Martin's Press.

Levy, Emanuel (2001a) "Does Oscar Prefer Noble Themes to Good Films?" *Los Angeles Times*, 16 February, pp. F1 and 20–1.

Levy, Emanuel (2001b) *Oscar Fever: The History and Politics of the Academy Awards*. New York: Continuum.

Levy, Emanuel (2001c) "Two for the Road," *Screen International*, 2 March, p. 34.

Lewis, Judith (2007) "The Way He Lives Now," *L.A. Weekly*, 21 December, pp. 36–40.

Lipton, Jacqueline D. (2008). "Celebrity in Cyberspace: A Personality Rights Paradigm for Personal Domain Name Disputes," *Washington and Lee Law Review*, 65(4): pp. 1445–528.

Lloyd, Ian (2011) *Elizabeth Taylor: Last of the Hollywood Legends*. London: Andre Deutsch.

Loewenstein, Lael (1997) "A New Day Dawns," *Detour*, December/January, pp. 88–95.

Longwell, Todd (2001) "Shot in the Dark," *The Hollywood Reporter (Oscar Watch: Critics Picks Special Issue)*, 12 January, pp. S3–4.

Louis Harris & Associates (1993) "America's Favorite Stars," 16 August. New York: Louis Harris & Associates.

Louis Harris & Associates (1994) "Clint Eastwood Still America's Favorite Film Star," 31 October. New York: Louis Harris & Associates.

Louis Harris & Associates (1996) "Mel Gibson Tops the List of America's Favorite Movie Stars Followed by John Wayne (#2), Steven Segal (#3), Clint Eastwood (#4), Tom Cruise and Arnold Schwarzenegger (Equal #5)," 2 December. New York: Louis Harris & Associates.

Louis Harris & Associates (1997) "Clint Eastwood Tops This Year's List of America's Favorite Movie Stars," 10 December. New York: Louis Harris & Associates.

Louis Harris & Associates (1999) "Harrison Ford Moves Up to be America's Favorite Movie Star," 6 January. New York: Louis Harris & Associates.

Lowry, Tom (2007) "'A McKinsey of Pop Culture'?" *BusinessWeek*, 26 March, pp. 104–7.

Ludemann, Ralf and John Hazelton (1991) "Outsiders Outrun Track Favourites," *Screen International*, 11 January, pp. 10–12.

Luscombe, Belinda (2006) "7 Myths About Meryl," *Time*, 19 June, pp. 54–7.

Lyall, Sarah (2003) "The Daniel Day-Lewis Method: A Kind of Vanishing Act," *The New York Times (Arts and Leisure)*, 9 March, pp. 1 and 22.

Lyman, Rick (2000) "High-decibel Oscar Buzz," *The New York Times*, 20 December, pp. E1 and 3.

Lyman, Rick (2001) "Oscar, Master of Suspense," *The New York Times*, 21 March, pp. E1 and 5.

Lyons, Charles (2000) "Roth Signs First Star: Roberts," *Daily Variety*, 18 February, pp. 1 and 58.

Lyons, Charles and Dave McNary (2000) "Smith Set to Redo 'Diva' with Houston," *Daily Variety*, 2 February, p. 3.

Lyons, Charles and Chris Petrikin (1999) "Scribe Rodkey to Visit 'Star City' for Overbrook," *Daily Variety*, 24 August, p. 3.

Macaulay, Sean (1999) "Julia Finds What She's Looking For," *The Times (Times 2)*, 2 August, p. 45.

Macaulay, Sean (2001) "Each Way Bets and Dead Certs," *The Times (Times 2)*, 15 March, pp. 20–1.

Macaulay, Sean (2003) "The People's Princess," *The Times (Times 2)*, 13 March, p. 14–15.

MacKenzie, Drew (2004) "The $25 Million Club," *Chicago Sun-Times*, 23 March, p. 38.

MacCabe, Colin (1974) "Realism and the Cinema: Notes on Some Brechtian Theses," *Screen*, 15(2), pp. 7–27.

McCarthy, Todd (1999) "'Bride' Groomed for Success," *Variety*, 26 July, pp. 33 and 37.

McCarthy, Todd (2001) "DreamWorks Brings Out Big Guns for 'The Mexican'," *Variety*, 5 March, pp. 39 and 44.

McClintock, Pamela (2005) "Smith Building Pic Momentum," *Daily Variety*, 15 July, pp. 4 and 30.

McClintock, Pamela, Ali Jaafar, Nick Holdsworth, John Hopewell, Elsa Keslassy, Emilio Mayorga, Mark Schilling and Nick Vivarelli. (2010) "World Turns on Bigger B.O.," *Variety*, 18 January, pp. 4 and 11.

McCracken, Grant (1989) "Who is the Celebrity Endorser? Cultural Foundations of the Endorsement Process," *Journal of Consumer Research*, 16(3), pp. 310–21.

McDonald, Duff (2006) "The Celebrity Trust Index," *New York*, 26 February, http://nymag.com/nymag/columns/intelligencer/features/16143.

McDonald, Paul (2008) "The Star System: The Production of Hollywood Stardom in the Post-Studio Era," in Paul McDonald and Janet Wasko (eds.) *The Contemporary Hollywood Film Industry*. Malden, MA: Blackwell, pp. 167–81.

McDougal, Dennis (1998) *The Last Mogul: Lew Wassermann, MCA, and the Hidden History of Hollywood*. New York: Crown.

McNary, Dave (2000) "Sly, U Go Their Separate Ways," *Daily Variety*, 22 February, p. 5.

McNary, Dave (2005) "Par Goes for Grey Matter," *Daily Variety*, 3 January, pp. 1 and 27.

McNary, Dave (2009) "Icon's Brit Switch," *Daily Variety*, 2 November, p. 4.

McNary, Dave and Pamela McClintock (2005) "Brads Bond at Par," *Daily Variety*, 23 June, pp. 1 and 22.

Maltby, Richard (2003) *Hollywood Cinema*. 2nd edn. Malden, MA: Blackwell.

Mann, Denise (2008) *Hollywood Independents: The Postwar Talent Takeover*. Minneapolis: University of Minnesota Press.

Marketing Arm, The (2011a) "dbi," www.dbicelebrityindex.com/?page_id=1483.

Marketing Arm, The (2011b) "Star Alignment," http://themarketingarm.com/celebrity-talent.html.

Markham-Smith, Ian and Liz Hodgson (2001) *Nicolas Cage: The Man Behind Captain Corelli*. London: Blake.

Marshall, P. David (1997) *Celebrity and Power: Fame in Contemporary Culture*. Minneapolis: University of Minnesota Press.

Maslin, Janet (1999) "Pretty Woman is Back, But Now She's Cautious," *The New York Times*, 30 July, p. E25.

Masters, Kim (2009a) "Haggling with the Stars," *The Daily Beast*, 2 April, www.thedailybeast.com/articles/2009/04/02/haggling-with-the-stars.html.

Masters, Kim (2009b) "Sandra's $200 Million Year," *The Daily Beast*, 2 December, www.thedailybeast.com/blogs-and-stories/2009-12-02/how-sandy-got-her-groove-back.

Mathur, Arti (2006) "Smith to Unveil Sony's Film Web," *Daily Variety*, 15 February, p. 10.

Medved, Michael (1993) "Still Wishing on a Star," *The Sunday Times*, 8 August, pp. 24–5.

Mirror Group (2011) *Elizabeth Taylor: Hollywood Legend*. London: Trinity Mirror Media.

Moeran, Brian (2003) "Celebrities and the Name Economy," *Research in Economic Anthropology* 22, pp. 299–321.

Moerk, Christian (1993) "Smith Ankles ICM for CAA," *Daily Variety*, 18 May, p. 2.

Moore, Daniel S. (1996) "Icon-oclastic," *Daily Variety (NATO – Showest)*, 6 March, pp. N4 and 18.

Moore, Schuyler (2009) "It's Time for Everyone to Participate in a Simple Method of B.O. Accounting," *The Hollywood Reporter*, 14 October, p. 7.

Morin, Edgar (1961) *The Stars: An Account of the Star-System in Motion Pictures*. London: Evergreen Books.

Morrison, Mark (1993) "'I'm Extremely Confident in Who I Am,'" *USA Weekend*, 3 December, pp. 4–5.

Morton, Danelle (2000) *Meg Ryan*. New York: Time.

Mosby, John (1994) "Tom Hanks," *Satellite Times*, April, pp. 16–17.

Movie Weekly (1925a) "Enter This Contest Now! $1,000 in Prizes for a Name," 28 March, pp. 6 and 33.

Movie Weekly (1925b) "Joan Crawford Is the Winning Name," 19 September, pp. 16–17 and 47.

MPA (2005) *2004 International Theatrical Market*. Washington, DC: Motion Picture Association.

MPAA (1998) *1997 US Economic Review: Theatrical Data*. Washington, DC: Motion Picture Association of America www.mpaa.org./useconomicreview/1997/theatrical2.htm.

MPAA (1999) *1998 Economic Review*. Washington, DC: Motion Picture Association of America.

MPAA (2000) *1999 US Economic Review*. Washington, DC: Motion Picture Association of America.

MPAA (2008) *Theatrical Market Statistics 2007*. Washington, DC: Motion Picture Association of America.

MPAA (2009) *Theatrical Industry Market Statistics 2008*. Washington, DC: Motion Picture Association of America.

MPAA (2010) *Theatrical Market Statistics 2009*. Washington, DC: Motion Picture Association of America.

MPAA (2011) *Theatrical Market Statistics 2010*. Washington, DC: Motion Picture Association of America.

Mulier, Thomas (2007) "Nestlé Bets Americans Will Trade Lattes for Espressos," *The Globe and Mail*, 28 November, p. B18.

Murdoch, Blake (2001) "Icon Moves into Sydney with Big Distrib'n Plans," *The Hollywood Reporter*, 26 February, pp. 11 and 62.

Murray, Susan (2005) *Hitch Your Antenna to the Stars: Early Television and Broadcast Stardom*. New York: Routledge.

Naremore, James (1988) *Acting in the Cinema*. Berkeley: University of California Press.

Natale, Richard (1994) "It's All in the Stars," *Los Angeles Times (Calendar)*, 7 August, pp. 4 and 41–2.

Natale, Richard (1999) "Julia Roberts' Double Play," *Daily Variety (Focus)*, 8 September, p. A6.

Natale, Richard (2000) "No, It's Not Too Early to Start Talking Oscar," *Los Angeles Times*, 10 September, pp. F36, 48–9 and 50.

Natale, Richard (2001a) "Best Film Nod is Just the Ticket for Lucky Three," *Los Angeles Times*, 14 February, p. F4.

Natale, Richard (2001b) "Roberts and Pitt: 2 Big Stars for 1 Little Film," *Los Angeles Times*, 28 February, pp. F1 and 10.

Natale, Richard and Charles Fleming (1991) "Pic Packaging: H'wood's Near Myth," *Variety*, 7 October, pp. 1 and 217.

National Arbitration Forum (2002) "Kevin Spacey v. Alberta Hot Rods," Claim number FA0205000114437, www.adrforum.com/domains/decisions/114437.htm.

Neale, Steve (2000) *Genre and Hollywood*. London: Routledge.

Netzer, Jaime (2008) "Team Overbrook: Ken Stovitz," *Variety (VPlus – Showmen of the Year)*, 15 December, pp. 14 and 18.

Neumaier, Joe (2006) "29m Reese's Pieces," *Daily News*, 2 March, p. 14.

O'Donnell, Pierce and Dennis McDougal (1992) *Fatal Subtraction: The Inside Story of Buchwald v. Paramount*. New York: Doubleday.

Office of the Law Revision Council (2010) *Code of Laws of the United States of America: Title 15 – Commerce and Trade* 2006 edition http://uscode.house.gov/pdf/2009/2009usc15.pdf.

Olins, Wally (1989). *Corporate Identity: Making Business Strategy Visible Through Design*. London: Thames & Hudson.

Oppenheimer, Jerry and Jack Vitek (1986) *Idol: Rock Hudson – The True Story of an American Film Hero*. New York: Villard.

O'Sullivan, Charlotte (2001) "Over Hollywood's Hill," *The Observer (Review)*, 1 April, p. 9.

Overbrook (2009) "Television," www.overbrookent.com.

Papa, Joseph (2011) *Elizabeth Taylor: A Passion for Life – The Wit and Wisdom of a Legend*. New York: Harper Design.

Parks, Louis B. (1999) "Summertime: The Movies – Episode One," *The Houston Chronicle*, 12 August, p. 18.

Parriott, Sarah and Josann McGibbon (n.d.) "*Runaway Bride*." Unpublished script.

Parrish, James Robert (1972) *The Paramount Pretties*. New Rochelle, NY: Arlington House.

Parrish, James Robert (1997) *Whoopi Goldberg: Her Journey from Poverty to Megastardom*. Secaucus, NJ: Carol.

Pearson, Bryan (2006) "India: Growing Middle Class Increases Content Demand, Puts Greater Burden on Buyers," *Variety (VPlus)*, 3 April, p. A18.

Pepall, Lynne, Dan Richards and George Norman (2008) *Industrial Organization: Contemporary Theory and Empirical Applications* 4th edn. Malden, MA: Blackwell.

Perren, Alisa (2012) *Indie, Inc.: Miramax and the Transformation of Hollywood in the 1990s*. Austin: University of Texas Press.

Petrikin, Chris (1998a) "Best Femme Figures Wear Dollar Signs," *Variety*, 19 October, p. 6.

Petrikin, Chris (1998b) "Overbrook, U Orbit Space Tome," *Variety*, 26 October, p. 28.

Petrikin, Chris (1999) "'Cat' Scratch Again," *Daily Variety*, 30 March, p. 5.

Plaskin, Glenn (1990) "Reflections from the Edge," *Press-Telegram*, 16 September, pp. J1–3.

Pokorny Michael (2005) "Hollywood and the Risk Environment of Movie Production in the 1990s," in John Sedgwick and Michael Pokorny (eds.) *An Economic History of Film*. Abingdon: Routledge, pp. 277–311.

Pokorny Michael and John Sedgwick (2005) "Warner Bros. in the Inter-war Years: Strategic Responses to the Risk Environment of Filmmaking," in John Sedgwick and Michael Pokorny (eds.) *An Economic History of Film.* Abingdon: Routledge, pp. 151–85.

Pokorny Michael and John Sedgwick (2010) "Profitability Trends in Hollywood, 1929 to 1999: Somebody Must Know Something," *Economic History Review*, 63(1), pp. 56–84.

Pond, Steve (2005) *The Big Show: High Times and Dirty Dealings Backstage at the Academy Awards.* New York: Faber and Faber.

Poulson-Bryant, Scott (1995) "Flippin the Script," *Vibe*, May, pp. 44–8.

Premiere (1995) "The 100 Most Powerful People in Hollywood," May, pp. 115–31.

Premiere (1996) "The 1996 *Premiere* Power List: The 100 Most Powerful People in Hollywood," May, pp. 77–90.

Premiere (1997) "*Premiere*'s 1997 Power List: The 100 Most Powerful People in Hollywood," May, pp. 85–99.

Premiere (1998) "The Power List: The 100 Most Powerful People in Hollywood," May, pp. 65–81.

Premiere (2000) "The Power List: The 100 Most Powerful People in Hollywood," May, pp. 74–90 and 102.

Premiere (2003) "The Power List – The Class of '03: The 100 Most Powerful People in Movies," May, pp. 54–71.

Premiere (2004) "The Power List 2004 – The Dysfunction@l Family Album: The 100 Most Powerful People in Movies," June, pp. 56–78.

Premiere (2005) "Power Mania 05: Who's Your Daddy, Hollywood? The 50 People Who Can Make or Break the Movies We See," June, pp. 76–92.

Premiere (2006) "The Wild West Coast: The Power List 2006," June, pp. 62–76 and 106.

Quigley (1992) *International Television and Video Almanac* 37th edn., New York: Quigley Publishing.

Quigley (1993) *International Television and Video Almanac* 38th edn., New York: Quigley Publishing.

Quigley (1994) *International Television and Video Almanac* 39th edn., New York: Quigley Publishing.

Quigley (1995) *International Television and Video Almanac* 40th edn., New York: Quigley Publishing.

Quigley (1996) *International Television and Video Almanac* 41st edn., New York: Quigley Publishing.

Quigley (1997) *International Television and Video Almanac* 42nd edn., New York: Quigley Publishing.

Quigley (2009) *International Motion Picture Almanac* 80th edn., Groton, MA: Quigley Publishing Company.

Quigley (2010) "Top Ten Money Making Stars – of the Past 78 Years," www. quigleypublishing.com/MPalmanac/Top10/Top10_lists.html.

Quigley, Bill (2010) *Personal e-mail correspondence*, 5 August.

Ravid, S. Abraham (1999) "Information, Blockbusters, and Stars: A Study of the Film Industry," *Journal of Business*, 72(4), pp. 463–92.

Reeves, Marcus (1999) "Regional Scenes," in Alan Light (ed.) *The Vibe History of Hip Hop*, New York: Three Rivers Press, pp. 217–27.

Richardson, Nicole Marie (2007) "The Partners," *Black Enterprise*, March, p. 100.

Roach, Janet (1994) "What's Unusual about These Pictures?" *The New York Times (Arts and Leisure)*, 22 May, pp. 19–20.

Roberts, Randy and James S. Olson (1995) *John Wayne: American*. New York: Free Press.

Rogers, Henry C. (1980) *Walking the Tightrope: The Private Confessions of a Public Relations Man*. New York: William Morrow.

Rogers and Cowan (n.d.) "Talent," www.rogersandcowan.com/Default.aspx/Expertise/EntertainmentContent/Talent.

Rohter, Larry (1990) "'Fresh Prince of Bel Air' Puts Rap in Mainstream," *The New York Times*, 17 September www.nytimes.com/1990/09/17/arts/fresh-prince-of-bel-air-puts-rap-in-mainstream.html.

Rooney, David (2003) "Femme Pic Tries to Take '50s to School," *Variety*, 15 December, pp. 48 and 53.

Rose, Frank (1995) *The Agency: William Morris and the Hidden History of Show Business*. New York: HarperBusiness.

Rugaard, Jason (2010) "Death of the Movie Star – R.I.P (1920–2009)," *MovieMavericks*, 1 February, http://moviemavericks.com/2010/02/death-of-the-movie-star-r-i-p-1920-2009.

SAG (n.d.) *Screen Actors Guild Membership Rules and Regulations* www.sag.org/files/sag/documents/SAG_Membership_Rules_0.pdf.

Salomon, Julie (2002) *The Devil's Candy: The Anatomy of a Hollywood Fiasco*. Cambridge, MA: Da Capo.

Saltmarsh, Matthew (2009) "The Sweet Smell of Success," *The International Herald Tribune*, 20 February, p. 9.

Sandler, Adam (1997) "Smith, Col Records Pact," *Daily Variety*, 25 June, pp. 1 and 18.

Schickel, Richard (2009) "The Go-to Guy," *Film Comment*, March–April, pp. 28–34.

Schneider, Michael and Josef Adalian (2000) "Overbrook Turns on TV," *Daily Variety*, 11 December, pp. 1 and 24.

Schneller, Johanna (1991) "Bare Foot Girl with Cheek," *GQ*, February, pp. 158–65 and 214.

Schudson, Michael (1993) *Advertising, the Uneasy Persuasion: Its Dubious Impact on American Society*. London: Routledge.

Schuker, Lauren. A. E. (2009) "Hollywood Squeezes Stars' Pay in Slump," *The Wall Street Journal*, 2 April, pp. A1 and 20.

Schwarzbaum, Lisa (2001) "Guns N' Poses," *Entertainment Weekly*, 9 March, pp. 52–3.

Scott, Allen J. (2005) *On Hollywood: The Place, the Industry*. Princeton: Princeton University Press.

Scott, Mathew (2007) "US, Local Film Stars in Talks on Joint Projects," *South China Morning Post*, 8 December, p.1.

Screen Australia (2010) "Get the Picture: Top 50 Films in Australia in 2008," www.screenaustralia.gov.au/gtp/wctop08.html.

Sedgwick, John (2000) *Popular Filmgoing in 1930s Britain: A Choice of Pleasures*. Exeter: University of Exeter Press.

Sedgwick, John (2005) "Product Differentiation at the Movies: Hollywood, 1946 to 1965," in John Sedgwick and Michael Pokorny (eds.) *An Economic History of Film*. Abingdon: Routledge, pp. 186–217.

Sedgwick, John and Michael Pokorny (1999) "Comment: Movie Stars and the Distribution of Financially Successful Films in the Motion Picture Industry," *Journal of Cultural Economics*, 23(4), pp. 319–23.

Sedgwick, John and Michael Pokorny (2005) "The Characteristics of Film as a Commodity," in John Sedgwick and Michael Pokorny (eds.) *An Economic History of Film*. Abingdon: Routledge, pp. 6–23.

Segrave Kerry (2004) *Product Placement in Hollywood Films: A History*. Jefferson, NC: London.

Seno, Diana and Bryan A Lukas (2007) "The Equity Effect of Product Endorsements by Celebrities: A Conceptual Framework from a Co-branding Perspective," *European Journal of Marketing* 41(1/2), pp. 121–34.

Sevin, Francelia (1991) "A Talk with Will Smith," *Scholastic Update*, 6 September, p. 125.

Shackleton, Liz (1996) "Bruce Davey," *Screen International*, 1 March, p. 28.

Shale, Richard (1993) *The Academy Awards Index: The Complete Categorical and Chronological Record*. Westport, CT: Greenwood.

Sharkey, Betsy (2009) "Missing That Next-door Guy," *Los Angeles Times*, 31 May, p. D4.

Shipman, David (1994) *Judy Garland: The Secret Life of an American Legend*. New York: Hyperion.

Siegel, Ed. (2006) "Roberts Gets Lost in Lackluster 'Three Days'," *The Boston Globe*, 20 April, pp. E1 and 9.

Siegel, Tatiana (2008a) "Col Locking Down Smith," *Daily Variety*, 15 December, pp. 1 and 22.

Siegel, Tatiana (2008b) "Will Globe-trot for Grosses," *Variety (VPlus – Showmen of the Year)*, 15 December, pp. 2–3 and 17–18.

Siegel, Tatiana (2009) "Chan Set to Mentor 'Kid'," *Daily Variety*, 14 January, p. 4.

Simon, Brent (2001) "The Mexican," *Entertainment Today*, 2 March [retrieved from production file at Margaret Herrick Library, Los Angeles].

Slater, Robert (1997) *Ovitz*. New York: McGraw-Hill.

Smith, Murray (1995) *Engaging Characters: Fiction, Emotion, and the Cinema*. Oxford: Oxford University Press.

Snyder, Gabriel (2005) "H'wood Gets Grossed Out," *Variety*, 13 June, pp. 1 and 58.

Snyder, Gabriel (2009) "How Movie Stars Get Paid," *Gawker*, 2 April, http://gawker.com/5196154/how-movie-stars-get-paid.

Snyder, Gabriel and Claude Brodesser (2004) "The Second Coming of Icon," *Variety*, 8 March, p. 6.

Spada, James (2004) *Julia: Her Life*. New York: St. Martin's Press.

Speier, Michael (2000) "Erin Brockovich," *Daily Variety (67th Anniversary Issue – The Contenders)*, 15 December, p. 12.

Sprinkel, Katy (2011) *Elizabeth Taylor: The Life of a Hollywood Legend: 1932–2011*. Chicago: Triumph.

Staiger, Janet (1985) "The Hollywood Mode of Production to 1930," in David Bordwell, Janet Stagier and Kristen Thompson (eds.), *The Classical Hollywood Cinema: Film Style and Mode of Production to 1960*. London: Routledge, pp. 85–153.

Staiger, Janet (1990) "Announcing Wares, Winning Patrons, Voicing Ideals: Thinking about the History and Theory of Film Advertising," *Cinema Journal*, 29(3), pp. 3–31.

State of California (n.d.) "California Labor Code," www.leginfo.ca.gov/cgi-bin/displaycode?section=lab&group=01001-02000&file=1700-1700.4.

Stayton, Richard (1988) "A Mamet Metamorphosis?" in Leslie Kane (ed.) (2001) *David Mamet in Conversation*. Ann Arbor: University of Michigan Press, pp. 96–9.

Stine, Whitney (1985) *Stars and Star Handlers: The Business of Show*. Santa Monica, CA: Roundtable.

Taylor, Ella (2001) "Mob Rule," *LA Weekly*, 2 March, p. 33.

Thompson, Anne (1990) "Battling the Big Boys," *LA Weekly*, 4 May, p. 43.

Thompson, Anne (2008) "Stars' Paydays Due for Redo," *Variety*, 20 October, pp. 5 and 8.

Thompson, Bob (1997) "This Man in Black a Good Guy," *The Toronto Sun*, 25 June, p. 61.

Thompson, John B. (1992) "Editor's Introduction," in Pierre Bourdieu (1992) *Language and Symbolic Power*. Cambridge: Polity, pp. 1–31.

Thompson, John B. (1995) *The Media and Modernity: A Social Theory of the Media*. Cambridge: Polity.

Toronto Star, The (1992) "Ford and Davis in Major Movie," 17 August, p. B5.

Travers, Peter (1997) "She Will Survive," *US*, August, p. 47.

Turan, Kenneth (1999) "It Looked Good on Paper," *Los Angeles Times*, 30 July, pp. F1 and 14.

Turan, Kenneth (2001a) "Roberts and Pitt Take Dead Aim," *Los Angeles Times*, 2 March, pp. F1 and 22.

Turan, Kenneth (2001b) "Wide Open? Not Exactly," *Los Angeles Times (Calendar)*, 7 January, pp. 7 and 24–6.

Turner, Graeme (2004) *Understanding Celebrity*. London: Sage.

UKFC (n.d.) "Definition of Specialised Film – Full Version," London: UK Film Council, www.ukfilmcouncil.org.uk/media/pdf/r/2/Defining_Specialsied_Film_Update_20_04_08_.pdf.

Ulmer, James (1994) "U.S. Clout Astronomical in Global Galaxy of Stars," *The Hollywood Reporter*, 3 May, pp. 1, 29–35.

Ulmer, James (1998) "Fewer Stars Lay Claim to Fame," *Variety*, 23 February, pp. 1 and 71–2.

Ulmer, James (2000) *James Ulmer's Hollywood Hot List*. New York: St. Martin's Griffin.

Ulmer, James (2006) *James Ulmer's Hot List Actors vol. 6*. Los Angeles: The Ulmer Scale.

U.S. Census Bureau (n.d.a) "Population Estimates – 1990s: National Tables," www.census.gov/popest/data/historical/1990s/index.html.

U.S. Census Bureau (n.d.b) "Population Estimates – Vintage 2009: National Tables," www.census.gov/popest/data/historical/2000s/vintage_2009/index.html.

Variety (1956) "1955's Top Film Grossers," 25 January, pp. 1 and 15.

Variety (1957) "Top Film Grossers of 1956," 2 January, pp. 1 and 4.

Variety (1958a) "All-time B.O. Champs," 8 January, pp. 6 and 60.

Variety (1958b) "Top Film Grossers of 1957," 8 January, p. 30.

Variety (1984) "Big Rental Films of 1984," 16 January, pp. 16, 78 and 90.

Variety (1988) "Top Rental Films of '87," 20 January, pp. 19 and 100.

Variety (1989) "Big Rental Films of '88 in U.S.-Canada," 11 January, pp. 16, 22 and 24.

Variety (1990) "Big Rental Films of 1989 in U.S.-Canada," 24 January, pp. 24 and 188–9.

Variety (1992) "Top Rental Films for 1991," 6 January, pp. 82–4.

Variety (1993) "Top Rental Films for 1992," 11 January, pp. 22–4.

Variety (1994) "1993 Film Grosses," 24 January, pp. 14 and 21.

Variety (2007) "Domestic Top 250 of 2006," 8 January, pp. 20–1.

Variety (2008) "Domestic Top 250 of 2007," 7 January, pp. 14–15.

Variety (2009) "Domestic Top 250 of 2008," 12 January, pp. 10–11.

Variety (2010) "Domestic Top 250 of 2009," 11 January, pp. 12–13.

Verna, Anthony M. (2004) "www.whatsina.name," *Seton Hall Journal of Sports and Entertainment Law*, 14(1), pp. 153–73.

Vogel, Harold (2007) *Entertainment Industry Economics* 7th edn. Cambridge: Cambridge University Press.

Waldman, Alan (1995) "The Golden Few," *The Hollywood Reporter (Women in Entertainment Special Issue)*, 12 December, pp. S34–5.

Wasko, Janet (2003) *How Hollywood Works*. London: Sage.

Waterman, David (2005) *Hollywood's Road to Riches*. Cambridge, MA: Harvard University Press.

Weinstein, Mark (1998) "Profit-sharing Contracts in Hollywood: Evolution and Analysis," *Journal of Legal Studies*, 27(1), pp. 67–112.

Welkos, Robert W. (1995) "A Regular Guy Takes on the Aliens," *Los Angeles Times*, 10 December, http://articles.latimes.com/1995-12-10/entertainment/ca-12329_1_regular-guy.

Welkos, Robert W. and Susan King (2001) "'Gladiator', 'Tiger' Square Off With the Most Nods, Joining Three Other Films in the Fight for Best Picture," *Los Angeles Times*, 14 February, pp. F1 and 18.

WENN (2006) "Coffee Time for George Clooney," WENN Entertainment News Wire Service, 24 November, from Nexis UK www.lexisnexis.com/uk/nexis/results/docview/docview.do?docLinkInd=true&risb=21_T11996273691&format=GNBFI&sort=BOOLEAN&startDocNo=276&resultsUrlKey=29_T11996273699&cisb=22_T11996273698&treeMax=true&treeWidth=0&csi=300824&ndocNo=280.

Werner, Laurie (1993) "The Story Behind the Movie," *USA Weekend*, 3 December, p. 5.

Winter, Jessica (2003) "Different for Girls," *Village Voice*, 17 December, p. 66.

WIPO (n.d.) "Frequently Asked Questions: Internet Domain Names," www.wipo.int/amc/en/center/faq/domains.html.

WIPO (2000) "Julia Fiona Roberts v. Russell Boyd," WIPO Arbitration and Mediation Center, Administrative Panel Decision case no. D2000–0210, 29 May, www.wipo.int/amc/en/domains/decisions/html/2000/d2000-0210.html.

WIPO (2001) "Nicole Kidman v. John Zuccarini, d/b/a Cupcake Party," WIPO Arbitration and Mediation Center, Administrative Panel Decision case no. D2000–1415, 23 January, www.wipo.int/amc/en/domains/decisions/html/2000/d2000-1415.html.

WIPO (2006) "Tom Cruise v. Network Operations Center/Alberta Hot Rods," WIPO Arbitration and Mediation Center, Administrative Panel Decision case no. D2006–0560, 5 July, www.wipo.int/amc/en/domains/decisions/html/2006/d2006-0560.html.

Wood, Zoe (2010) "A-listers Square Up in Coffee Wars," *The Guardian*, 4 December, p. 55.

WPP (n.d.) "Who We Are," www.wpp.com/wpp/about/whoweare.

Wyatt, Justin (2000) "Independents, Packaging, and Inflationary Pressure in 1980s Hollywood," in Stephen Prince,*A New Pot of Gold: Hollywood under the Electronic Rainbow, 1980–1989*. Berkeley: University of California Press, pp. 142–59.

Zolotow, Maurice (1974) *Shooting Star: A Biography of John Wayne*. New York: Simon & Schuster.

Index

Page numbers in *italics* denote figures; those in **bold** denote tables.

Hollywood Stardom, First Edition. Paul McDonald.
© 2013 Paul McDonald. Published 2013 by John Wiley & Sons, Ltd.